Cybersecurity for Internet of Health Things

Editors

Mohiuddin Ahmed
School of Science, Edith Cowan University
Australia

Nazim Choudhury
Computer Science, University of Wisconsin
Green Bay, Wisconsin, USA

CRC Press
Taylor & Francis Group
Boca Raton London New York

CRC Press is an imprint of the
Taylor & Francis Group, an **informa** business
A SCIENCE PUBLISHERS BOOK

First edition published 2026
by CRC Press
2385 NW Executive Center Drive, Suite 320, Boca Raton FL 33431

and by CRC Press
4 Park Square, Milton Park, Abingdon, Oxon, OX14 4RN

Library of Congress Cataloging-in-Publication Data (applied for)

ISBN: 978-1-032-74903-7 (hbk)
ISBN: 978-1-032-77470-1 (pbk)
ISBN: 978-1-003-48326-7 (ebk)

DOI: 10.1201/9781003483267

Typeset in Palatino Linotype
by Prime Publishing Services

Dedicated to

"My well-wishers: Professor Barkat & his family"
– Mohiuddin Ahmed

"My loving family"
– Nazim Choudhury

Preface

Healthcare is one of the industries that has embraced and benefitted the most from improved internet connectivity and usage. Since the number of healthcare service seekers across the world is growing at a rapid pace, service providers rely on the internet-connected ecosystem, which is also known as the critical health infrastructure, Internet of Health Things (IoHT) or Internet of Medical Things (IoMT). The importance of IoHT was highlighted and realized well during the COVID-19 pandemic.

While these technologies provide tremendous benefits, they go hand in hand with malicious exploitation. Cybercrime costs are projected to hit 1 trillion USD per month by 2031, according to Cybersecurity Ventures. Healthcare is one of the most susceptible industries to cybercrime. There has been a massive surge in cyber-attacks, and newer variants of cyber threats are emerging.

This book addresses the challenges associated with modern healthcare, providing a bigger picture of the practices, cyber threat landscape, countermeasures, and their evolution, trends, and open research directions. It will serve as a valuable reference on the topic.

Acknowledgments

We are deeply grateful for the wonderful book editing experience and would like to express our sincerest appreciation to the publisher for their invaluable support. This journey has not only enhanced our editing skills but also strengthened our patience, communication, and perseverance. We extend our heartfelt thanks to all the contributors, reviewers, and the publishing team. Lastly, we owe a debt of gratitude to our family members, whose unwavering support and encouragement have been instrumental in completing this book.

Mohiuddin Ahmed
Nazim Choudhury

Contents

List of Contributors

Adnan Anwar
School of Information and Technology, Deakin University, Geelong, Australia

Alexander Pamenter
University of Wisconsin Green Bay, WI, 54311

Asif Alif
Islamic University, Kushtia, Bangladesh

Biplob Ray
School of Engineering and Technology, CQUniversity, Bundaberg, Australia

Fares Alharbi
Department of Computer Science, College of Computing and IT, Shaqra University, Shaqra, Saudi Arabia

Jesse Laeuchli
University of New South Wales (UNSW), Canberra, Australia

Kassim Kalinaki
Department of Computer Science, Islamic University in Uganda, Mbale, Uganda and Borderline Research Laboratory, Kampala, Uganda

Khondokar Fida Hasan
University of New South Wales (UNSW), Canberra, Australia

Khudeija Kassam
London South Bank University, London, UK

Kin Hei Look
School of Science, Edith Cowan University, Australia

Maheen Islam
Department of Computer Science and Engineering, East West University, Dhaka, Bangladesh

Mahmoud El-Khodr
School of Engineering and Technology, CQUniversity, Bundaberg, Australia

Md. Adnan Morshed
Department of Computer Science and Engineering, East West University, Dhaka, Bangladesh

Md. Hasanul Ferdaus
Department of Computer Science and Engineering, East West University, Dhaka, Bangladesh

Md. Mostofa Kamal Rasel
Department of Computer Science and Engineering, East West University, Dhaka, Bangladesh

Md. Sawkat Ali
Department of Computer Science and Engineering, East West University, Dhaka, Bangladesh

Michael Otradovec
University of Wisconsin
Green Bay, WI, 54311

Mohammad Habibur Rahman
BioRobotics Lab, Mechanical Engineering Department, University of Wisconsin Milwaukee, Wisconsin, USA

Mohammad Jabed Morshed Chowdhury
La Trobe University, Melbourne, Australia

Mohammad Manzurul Islam
Department of Computer Science and Engineering, East West University, Dhaka, Bangladesh

Mohammad Rifat Ahmmad Rashid
Department of Computer Science and Engineering, East West University, Dhaka, Bangladesh

Morshed Chowdhury
School of Information and Technology, Deakin University, Geelong, Australia

Mounika Baddula
School of Engineering and Technology, CQUniversity, Bundaberg, Australia

Muna Al-Hawawreh
School of Information and Technology, Deakin University, Geelong, Australia

Nazim Choudhury
University of Wisconsin
Green Bay, WI, 54311

Rajkumar Buyya
School of Computing and Information Systems, The University of Melbourne, Melbourne, Australia

Rashedul Amin Tuhin
Department of Computer Science and Engineering, East West University, Dhaka, Bangladesh

Sadia Nur Amin
Department of Computer Science and Engineering, East West University, Dhaka, Bangladesh

Saleh Masum
Department of Information and Communication Engineering, University of Rajshahi, Rajshahi, Bangladesh

Savitri Bevinakoppa
School of IT and Engineering, Melbourne Institute of Technology, Melbourne, Australia

Sofia Noor Rafa
Department of Computer Science and Engineering, East West University, Dhaka, Bangladesh

Taskeed Jabid
Department of Computer Science and Engineering, East West University, Dhaka, Bangladesh

Taylah Griffiths
School of Science, Edith Cowan University, Australia

Wai Kin Fung Ritz
School of Science, Edith Cowan University, Australia

Section I

Fundamental of Internet of Health Things

DOI: 10.1201/9781003483267-1

Chapter 1

Internet of Health Things (IoHT)

An Exploration of the Principles, Components, Architectures, Challenges, and Real-World Applications

Kassim Kalinaki

1. Introduction

The healthcare sector teeters on the brink of a technological upheaval propelled by the swift assimilation of Internet of Things (IoT) technologies within medical procedures and patient welfare [1]. The IoHT is a paradigm-shifting concept that promises to redefine how healthcare services are delivered, monitored, and managed. This cutting-edge approach harnesses the power of interconnected medical devices, sensors, and software applications to collect, transmit, and analyze vast health-related data, unlocking new frontiers in personalized and proactive care [2]. The transformative impact of the IoHT is already being felt across various domains within the healthcare ecosystem, reshaping patient experiences, operational efficiencies, and clinical decision-making processes [1–3].

Department of Computer Science, Islamic University in Uganda, Mbale, Uganda, Borderline Research Laboratory, Kampala, Uganda.
Email: kalinaki@ieee.org

DOI: 10.1201/9781003483267-2

Among the paramount utilities of IoHT technology lies in remote patient surveillance and telehealth. Wearable gadgets like fitness trackers and smartwatches have evolved into indispensable instruments for perpetual monitoring of vital signs, medication compliance, and general health status. This empowers healthcare practitioners to promptly track and address patient requirements in real-time, mitigating the necessity for hospital visits [4, 5]. Moreover, integrating IoHT solutions with telehealth platforms has revolutionized virtual consultations, transcending geographical barriers and increasing access to quality healthcare services, notably in remote or underserved locations [4]. Patients can now seamlessly share their health data with healthcare providers, facilitating more informed decision-making and personalized treatment plans. Beyond remote monitoring and telehealth, the IoHT drives transformative changes in predictive analytics and early disease detection [6]. Through harnessing the potency of big data and advanced analytics, healthcare institutions can unearth invaluable insights from the expansive volumes of data emanating from interconnected devices and electronic health records (EHRs). Predictive analytics algorithms possess the capability to discern patterns, trends, and risk factors, facilitating the early identification of potential health concerns and proactive interventions [3, 5, 7]. This proactive approach improves patient outcomes and reduces healthcare costs by preventing the escalation of chronic conditions and minimizing the need for intensive treatments. Another domain where the IoHT is making notable advancements is in asset tracking and supply chain management within healthcare facilities [2]. Radio-frequency identification (RFID) tags and real-time location systems (RTLS) can precisely track the location and movement of healthcare equipment, supplies, and individuals, ensuring efficient utilization and preventing misplacement or loss [8, 9]. Furthermore, medication management and adherence have long been significant obstacles in healthcare, often resulting into severe health outcomes and skyrocketing medical bills. IoHT solutions, such as smart pill bottles and medication dispensers, are revolutionizing patient care. These intelligent devices can monitor and track medication adherence, alerting patients to take their prescribed medicines at the appropriate times in what has been termed as personal healthcare of things [10–12]. Additionally, they can communicate with healthcare providers, enabling prompt intervention in non-compliance or adverse reactions, ultimately improving patient safety and treatment effectiveness. The IoHT also drives the development of smart hospitals, where connected devices and systems work harmoniously to enhance operational efficiency, patient safety, and overall healthcare delivery [13].

While the potential benefits of the IoHT in healthcare are extensive, it is imperative to confront the associated challenges and apprehensions. Foremost among these are data privacy and security, as IoHT devices gather and transmit sensitive personal health information [1, 2, 14]. Robust cybersecurity measures, encryption protocols, and stringent data governance policies must be implemented to safeguard patient privacy and ensure compliance with regulatory frameworks such as the Health Insurance Portability and Accountability Act (HIPAA) and the General Data Protection Regulation (GDPR). Moreover, interoperability and standardization play pivotal roles in ensuring seamless convergence and data exchange among diverse IoHT devices and healthcare systems [3]. Collaboration between healthcare providers, regulatory bodies, and technology companies is crucial to establishing sector-wide standards and protocols, fostering a seamless and interconnected healthcare ecosystem. Addressing these challenges will be essential to unlocking the full potential of the IoHT and ensuring its widespread adoption in the healthcare industry.

In conclusion, the IoHT stands as a transformative force in the healthcare industry, providing immense opportunities to improve patient care, enhance operational efficiencies, and unlock new frontiers in medical innovation. By leveraging the power of connected devices, real-time data analysis, and predictive analytics, the IoHT enables healthcare providers to offer personalized, proactive, and cost-effective care. As technology advances, the IoHT will undoubtedly play an increasingly pivotal role in shaping the future of healthcare, empowering healthcare professionals, and improving patient outcomes globally.

1.1 *Chapter Contributions*

Below are the main contributions of this chapter.

- Provision of an overview of IoHT, highlighting its potential to redefine patient care, diagnostics, and overall healthcare administration.
- A detailed discussion of the different foundational principles of IoHT that serve as the bedrock for its successful implementation.
- Presentation of the different components of IoHT, detailing how they contribute to a connected and efficient healthcare system.
- Presentation of the architecture of IoHT in healthcare systems.
- A discussion of the different challenges and considerations of IoHT in healthcare.
- Presentation of real-world applications of IoHT to enhance the overall patient outcomes.

1.2 Chapter Organization

After the introduction in the section, the remainder of this chapter is structured as follows: Section 2 details the different foundational principles of IoHT. Section 3 elaborates on the different components of IoHT in healthcare. Section 4 presents the architecture of IoHT in healthcare. Section 5 discusses the challenges and considerations of IoHT in healthcare. The different real-world cases are depicted in Section 6, and the conclusion in Section 7.

2. Foundational Principles of IoHT

At its core, the IoHT aims to optimize healthcare delivery by enabling seamless integration, data-driven decision-making, and efficient communication among various stakeholders within the healthcare ecosystem. As discussed in this section, this revolutionary approach is underpinned by several foundational principles that serve as the bedrock for its successful implementation and widespread adoption.

2.1 Interconnectivity and Interoperability

The IoHT thrives on the principle of interconnectivity, where diverse devices, systems, and platforms seamlessly communicate and exchange data [15]. Interoperability is a fundamental requirement that ensures these disparate components can interact and collaborate effectively. Standardized protocols, open data formats, and well-defined interfaces facilitate the seamless integration of medical devices, wearables, sensors, and healthcare information systems [16]. This interconnected ecosystem fosters collaboration among healthcare providers, patients, and other stakeholders, enabling coordinated care and improved outcomes [2].

2.2 Data Analytics and Intelligent Decision-Making

At the heart of the IoHT lies the principle of data-driven decision-making. The IoHT generates immense volumes of data from diverse sources, including medical devices, EHRs, and patient-generated data [17]. Through harnessing advanced analytics techniques like machine learning, artificial intelligence, and predictive modeling, healthcare professionals can derive invaluable insights from these data [7]. These insights can inform clinical decisions, optimize treatment plans, predict potential risks, and support preventive care measures [18]. Utilizing data analytics enables healthcare providers to make informed decisions, ultimately leading to improved patient outcomes and more efficient allocation of resources.

2.3 *Real-Time Monitoring and Proactive Care*

The IoHT enables real-time monitoring of patient's health conditions, vital signs, and treatment adherence. Connected gadgets, including wearable sensors, implantable devices, together with remote patient monitoring systems, continuously gather and transmit data to healthcare providers [4, 5, 19, 20]. This principle of real-time monitoring enables proactive intervention and timely adjustments to treatment plans. By detecting early warning signs or deviations from normal patterns, healthcare professionals can take swift action, preventing potential complications and improving patient outcomes. Real-time monitoring additionally facilitates remote patient care, thereby improving access to healthcare services, particularly in underserved or remote areas [21].

2.4 *Personalized and Patient-Centric Care*

The IoHT embraces the principle of personalized and patient-centric care by empowering individuals to participate actively in their healthcare journey. Connected devices and mobile applications empower patients with the ability to track their health data, monitor their conditions, and engage in self-management practices. By integrating patient-generated data with clinical data, healthcare providers can comprehensively understand each patient's unique needs and preferences [22–25]. This principle fosters a collaborative approach between healthcare professionals and patients, promoting shared decision-making, enhancing treatment adherence, and improving overall patient satisfaction and quality of life.

2.5 *Security, Privacy, and Trust*

Ensuring the security, privacy, and trust of sensitive healthcare data is paramount in the IoHT ecosystem. As healthcare data are highly confidential and personal, strong security measures, such as authentication protocols, encryption, and access controls are essential to safeguard patient information from unauthorized users or cyber criminals [1, 2, 14]. Additionally, adhering to privacy regulations and ethical guidelines is crucial to maintaining patient trust and facilitating the adoption of IoHT technologies. Prioritizing security, privacy, and trust empowers the IoHT environment to foster a secure and trustworthy environment for healthcare delivery.

2.6 *Scalability and Adaptability*

The IoHT must be built on scalability and adaptability to allow the ever-growing number of connected medical devices, escalating data volumes, and evolving healthcare needs. The underlying infrastructure, including communication networks, data storage, and computing resources, should be designed to scale seamlessly as the IoHT ecosystem expands [26, 27]. Furthermore, the IoHT should be adaptable to changing technologies, regulatory frameworks, and healthcare paradigms, ensuring its long-term viability and relevance.

In summary, the foundational principles of the IoHT collectively contribute to optimizing healthcare delivery by enabling efficient data exchange, empowering data-driven decision-making, promoting proactive care, fostering personalized treatment approaches, ensuring data security and privacy, and enabling scalability and adaptability. Embracing these principles empowers the IoHT to transform the healthcare landscape, improve patient outcomes, enhance care coordination, and drive innovation in healthcare services.

3. Components of IoHT in Healthcare

The IoHT consists of a vast ecosystem comprising various components working to revolutionize healthcare delivery. This section explores the components of IoHT, including wearable devices, smart sensors, and interconnected medical devices, detailing how they contribute to a connected and efficient healthcare system.

3.1 Wearable Devices

Wearable devices have emerged as game-changers in IoHT, allowing for non-stop monitoring and instant data collection from patients. This subsection explores some specific examples and their roles.

3.1.1 Fitness Trackers and Smartwatches

These devices have sensors to monitor vital signs such as oxygen levels, blood pressure, and heart rate. They are crucial in promoting healthy lifestyles by tracking physical activity, sleep patterns, and calorie intake. Additionally, they can provide real-time alerts and notifications to users and healthcare providers in case of abnormal readings or emergencies [5, 28].

3.1.2 Continuous Glucose Monitoring (CGM) Devices

For individuals with diabetes, CGM devices like Dexcom and FreeStyle Libre continuously measure glucose levels in the interstitial fluid, providing real-time data and alerts to help manage insulin dosages and prevent complications [5, 29].

3.1.3 Electrocardiogram (ECG) Monitors

Wearable ECG monitors like KardiaMobile[1] and QardioCore[2] enable remote monitoring of heart rhythms, allowing for early detection of arrhythmias and potential cardiovascular events [30].

3.1.4 Smart Clothing

Companies like Hexoskin and Athos have developed smart clothing with integrated sensors to monitor physiological parameters like heart rate, respiration, and muscle activity. These garments are particularly useful for athletes, rehabilitation patients, and individuals with chronic conditions, enabling continuous monitoring during daily activities [3, 5, 31].

3.2 Smart Sensors

Smart sensors serve as the eyes and ears of the IoHT ecosystem, providing valuable insights into environmental conditions, physiological parameters, and patient safety. We highlight specific sensors and their roles in this subsection.

3.2.1 Ambient Sensors

Temperature, humidity, and air quality sensors are crucial in monitoring environmental conditions within healthcare facilities and patient homes [32, 33]. These sensors ensure optimal patient recovery and comfort conditions, enabling predictive maintenance and efficient resource allocation.

3.2.2 Physiological Sensors

Sensors that measure blood glucose, oxygen saturation, respiration, and other physiological parameters are essential for remote patient monitoring and early intervention [34, 35]. For example, continuous positive airway pressure (CPAP) machines equipped with sensors can track sleep apnea and adjust airflow accordingly, improving patient outcomes [36].

3.2.3 Motion Sensors

Fall detection and activity monitoring sensors are particularly useful for elderly patients or those with mobility issues [37]. These sensors can alert caregivers in case of falls or abnormal activity patterns, ensuring timely assistance and preventing potential complications.

---

[1] https://store.kardia.com/products/kardiamobile.

[2] https://www.qardio.com/.

3.2.4 *Pressure Sensors*

Bed occupancy and patient positioning sensors can help healthcare providers monitor patient movements and ensure proper positioning, minimizing the risk of pressure ulcers and enhancing overall patient comfort [38].

3.2.5 *Imaging Sensors*

Amidst the COVID-19 pandemic, thermal cameras and depth sensors were remotely employed to monitor patient vital signs, including respiration rate and body temperature, without direct contact, thereby minimizing the risk of infection transmission [39].

In a nutshell, smart sensors enable remote patient monitoring, early intervention, and predictive analytics. By integrating with other IoHT components, such as wearable and interconnected medical devices, smart sensors provide a thorough view of the patient's condition and environmental factors, enabling data-driven decision-making and optimizing resource allocation.

3.3 *Interconnected Medical Devices*

Interconnected medical devices form the backbone of the IoHT ecosystem, enabling seamless communication and data exchange between various healthcare systems and stakeholders. This subsection explores some examples and their roles.

3.3.1 *Diagnostic Equipment*

Imaging machines like CT scanners, MRI machines, and ultrasound devices generate vast amounts of data that can be seamlessly integrated into EHRs and shared with healthcare professionals for timely diagnosis and treatment planning [40].

3.3.2 *Therapeutic Devices*

Infusion pumps, ventilators, and defibrillators can be remotely monitored and controlled, ensuring precise dosage delivery, optimal ventilation support, and timely emergency intervention [41].

3.3.3 *Monitoring Devices*

Patient and vital sign monitors furnish instantaneous data on a patient's condition, allowing for continuous monitoring and rapid response to changes in health status [41].

3.3.4 Implantable Devices

Pacemakers, insulin pumps, and neurostimulators can be remotely monitored and adjusted, improving patient outcomes and minimizing endless hospital visits [5].

3.3.5 Laboratory Analyzers

Blood and molecular diagnostics equipment can transmit test results directly to EHRs and healthcare providers, enabling faster diagnosis and treatment decisions [5].

The synergy between wearable devices, smart sensors, and interconnected medical devices within the IoHT ecosystem is transforming the healthcare landscape. Utilizing these components, healthcare providers can remotely monitor patients, identify potential issues early, and deliver timely interventions. Additionally, the seamless data exchange between these components enables predictive analytics, personalized care, and optimized resource allocation, eventually resulting into enhanced patient outcomes, enhanced efficiency, and a more sustainable healthcare system [42]. Table 1 summarizes the components of IoHT in healthcare.

Table 1: Summary of the components of IoHT in healthcare.

Component	**Examples**	**Description**	**References**
Wearable Devices	Fitness trackers, smartwatches, CGM devices, ECG monitors, smart clothing	Enable continuous monitoring of vital signs, activity levels, glucose levels, heart rhythms, respiration, muscle activity, etc. Promote patient engagement and remote monitoring.	[5, 28–31]
Smart Sensors	Ambient sensors, physiological sensors, motion sensors, pressure sensors, imaging sensors	Monitor environmental conditions, physiological parameters, patient movements, bed occupancy, and enable remote vital sign tracking without contact. Facilitate predictive analytics and early intervention.	[32–39]
Interconnected Medical Devices	Diagnostic equipment, therapeutic devices, monitoring devices, implantable devices, laboratory analyzers	Enable seamless data exchange between devices and healthcare systems. Includes imaging machines, infusion pumps, ventilators, pacemakers, insulin pumps, blood analyzers, etc. Allows remote monitoring, control, and integration with EHRs for timely diagnosis and treatment.	[5, 40, 41]

4. Architecture of IoHT in Healthcare

The IoHT is a rapidly evolving paradigm integrating various technologies, including the IoT, cloud computing, data analytics, artificial intelligence (AI), and machine learning (ML), to revolutionize the healthcare sector. The architecture of IoHT in healthcare is designed to facilitate seamless data collection, processing, analysis, and decision-making, ultimately leading to improved patient care and personalized healthcare services.

4.1 IoT Devices and Sensors

The IoHT architecture's foundation lies in deploying IoT devices and sensors. These devices collect health-related data, such as sleep patterns, vital signs, activity levels, and environmental conditions. IoT devices in healthcare include wearable devices (e.g., smartwatches and fitness trackers), smart clothes, remote patient monitoring system, ingestible devices, implantable medical devices, and smart hospital equipment [2].

4.2 Data Acquisition and Communication

The collected data from IoT devices and sensors are transmitted securely to a centralized or distributed data repository, typically through wireless communication technologies like Bluetooth, Wi-Fi, or cellular networks. This data acquisition and communication layer ensures reliable and efficient data transfer while adhering to strict privacy and security protocols [16].

4.3 Cloud-Based Data Storage and Management

The healthcare data generated by IoT devices are typically stored and managed in a cloud-based infrastructure. Cloud computing provides scalable, secure, cost-effective storage solutions, enabling efficient data management, backup, and retrieval. Additionally, cloud platforms offer computational resources for data processing and analysis [27, 42].

4.4 Data Analytics and Machine Learning

One key component of the IoHT architecture is the integration of data analytics and machine learning techniques. These technologies extract valuable insights and patterns from the vast healthcare data collected [43, 44]. Data analytics techniques, such as descriptive, predictive, and prescriptive, are employed to uncover trends, identify risk factors, and support informed decision-making [45]. Figure 1 depicts the architecture of IoHT in healthcare.

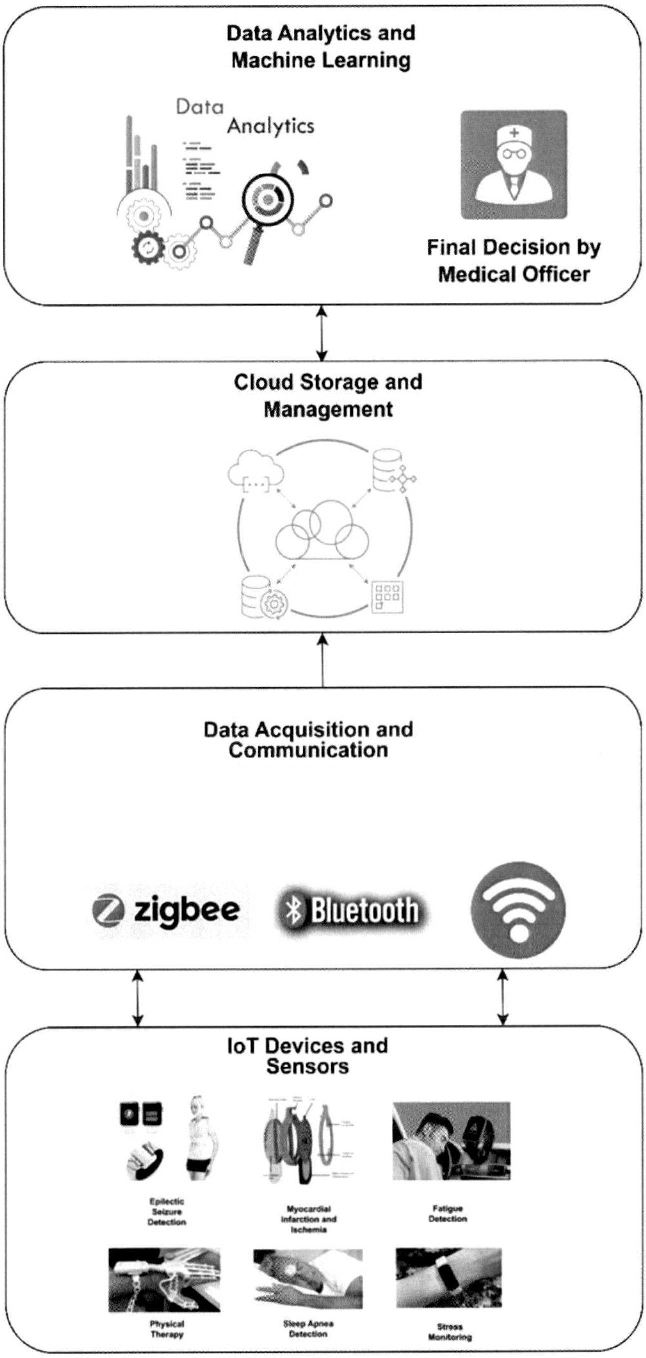

Figure 1: The architecture of IoHT in healthcare.

In summary, the IoHT architecture in healthcare is a complex and multi-layered system that relies on seamlessly integrating various technologies and stakeholders. The IoHT enables informed decision-making, personalized healthcare solutions, and improved patient outcomes by utilizing data analytics and AI-powered techniques.

5. Challenges and Considerations of IoHT in Healthcare

Integrating the IoHT into the healthcare sector can revolutionize delivering and managing medical services. However, as with any technological advancement, significant obstacles and solutions must be addressed to ensure its successful and responsible implementation. This section discusses the challenges of adopting IoHT in healthcare and proposes solutions to mitigate them.

5.1 Data Security and Privacy Concerns

Data security and privacy are among the primary challenges associated with IoHT in healthcare. IoHT devices gather and transmit huge volumes of sensitive medical data, including personal health information, vital signs, and treatment records [46–49]. These data are vulnerable to cyber threats such as hacking, data breaches, and unauthorized access, which could have devastating consequences for patients and healthcare providers. Ensuring the security of these data is crucial, as any compromise could lead to identity theft, financial fraud, or even life-threatening situations if medical devices are tampered with or controlled remotely by malicious actors [2, 50]. Robust encryption protocols, access control mechanisms, and stringent security measures must be implemented at all levels, from device manufacturing to data transmission and storage. Furthermore, patients' medical information privacy is a fundamental right that must be protected. Healthcare providers must adhere with applicable data protection regulations, including the HIPAA in the United States or the GDPR in the European Union, to protect patient confidentiality and prevent unauthorized disclosure or misuse of sensitive data [51].

5.2 Interoperability and Integration Challenges

The healthcare industry comprises various devices, systems, and vendors, each with proprietary protocols and data formats. Achieving interoperability and seamless integration among these diverse components is a significant challenge when implementing IoHT solutions. Lack of interoperability can lead to data silos, inefficient communication, and fragmented workflows, ultimately hindering the potential benefits of IoHT [52, 53]. Standardized protocols, data exchange formats, and open APIs must facilitate seamless data sharing and integration across healthcare systems and devices [54–56]. Additionally, integrating IoHT devices with existing healthcare infrastructure, such as EHRs, hospital information systems (HIS), and clinical decision support systems (CDSS), is crucial for leveraging the full potential of IoHT [57]. This integration requires careful planning, extensive testing, and collaboration among healthcare providers, device manufacturers, and IT professionals.

5.3 *Regulatory and Ethical Considerations*

The healthcare sector is subject to stringent regulation, necessitating IoHT technology introductions to comply with rigorous regulatory frameworks and ethical guidelines. These regulations aim to guarantee patient safety, data privacy, and the responsible use of medical devices and technologies [54]. Compliance with these regulations is essential to mitigate risks and ensure the safe and effective use of IoHT solutions.

Furthermore, ethical considerations must be addressed when implementing IoHT in healthcare. Issues such as informed consent, patient autonomy, and equitable access to healthcare services must be carefully evaluated [58, 59]. Healthcare providers and technology developers must prioritize patients' well-being and rights while ensuring transparency and accountability in the use of IoHT technologies.

5.4 *Infrastructure and Resource Constraints*

The successful deployment of IoHT in healthcare requires a robust and scalable infrastructure, including reliable network connectivity, sufficient bandwidth, and adequate computing resources [60]. In many healthcare facilities, particularly in remote or underserved areas, the existing infrastructure may not be adequate to support the demands of IoHT systems. Upgrading and maintaining this infrastructure is costly and resource-intensive, posing significant challenges for healthcare providers with limited budgets. Additionally, the need for specialized IT personnel with expertise in IoHT technologies and cybersecurity may strain already limited human resources within healthcare organizations.

5.5 *User Adoption and Training*

The successful implementation of IoHT in healthcare relies heavily on user adoption and acceptance. Healthcare professionals and patients may be hesitant to embrace new technologies due to concerns about data privacy, usability issues, or resistance to change. Addressing these concerns through comprehensive training programs, user-friendly interfaces, and effective change management strategies is crucial. Healthcare providers must invest in educating their staff and patients on the benefits and proper use of IoHT devices and applications, fostering a culture of digital literacy and technology adoption [61].

5.6 *Cost and Return on Investment (ROI)*

The deployment of IoHT solutions in healthcare can be a significant financial investment involving the acquisition of devices, software, infrastructure upgrades, and ongoing maintenance costs. Healthcare organizations, particularly those with limited resources, may struggle to justify the upfront costs of IoHT implementation [62]. Demonstrating a clear ROI and quantifying the long-term benefits, such as improved patient outcomes, increased efficiency, and cost savings, is essential to secure buy-in and funding from stakeholders. Conducting comprehensive cost–benefit analyses and piloting IoHT solutions on a smaller scale can help healthcare providers assess the potential ROI and make informed decisions.

In summary, it is crucial to balance technological advancement and ethical responsibility, ensuring that IoHT solutions are implemented securely, interoperable, and patient-centric. Table 2 summarizes the challenges, considerations, and proposed solutions for IoHT in healthcare.

6. Real-World Applications and Case Studies of IoHT in Healthcare

Across various healthcare domains, IoHT is finding practical applications that transform the way healthcare services are delivered and experienced across various healthcare domains. This section examines the practical applications of IoHT across various healthcare domains. Moreover, it highlights the benefits of incorporating IoHT into existing healthcare infrastructures.

6.1 *Philips Remote Patient Monitoring*

Philips' remote patient monitoring solution is a comprehensive IoHT-enabled platform that supports continuous monitoring and care delivery for patients with chronic conditions. The system includes medical-grade biosensors that monitor vital signs including blood pressure, heart rate, respiratory rate, and oxygen saturation.[3] These biosensors are connected to a user-friendly patient interface, typically a tablet or smartphone app, which securely collects and transmits data to healthcare providers. The

[3] https://www.usa.philips.com/healthcare/services/population-health-management/patient-engagement/remote-patient-monitoring.

Table 2: Summary of the challenges, considerations, and proposed solutions for IoHT in healthcare.

Challenge	Summary	Proposed Solutions	References
Data Security and Privacy Concerns	Sensitive medical data collected by IoHT devices are vulnerable to cyber threats and privacy breaches.	Implement robust encryption protocols, access control mechanisms, and stringent security measures. Comply with data protection regulations like HIPAA and GDPR.	[2, 46–51]
Interoperability and Integration Challenges	Lack of interoperability between diverse devices, systems, and vendors can lead to data silos and inefficient communication.	Develop standardized protocols, data exchange formats, and open APIs. Integrate IoHT devices with existing healthcare infrastructure like EHRs, HIS, and CDSS.	[52–57]
Regulatory and Ethical Considerations	IoHT technologies must adhere to stringent regulations and ethical guidelines to ensure patient safety, data privacy, and responsible use.	Comply with applicable regulations and address ethical issues like informed consent, patient autonomy, and equitable access to healthcare services.	[54, 58, 59]
Infrastructure and Resource Constraints	Healthcare facilities may lack the robust infrastructure, network connectivity, and computing resources required for IoHT deployment.	Upgrade and maintain infrastructure, including reliable network connectivity and adequate computing resources. Allocate resources for specialized IT personnel.	[60]
User Adoption and Training	Healthcare professionals and patients may be hesitant to adopt new IoHT technologies due to concerns or resistance to change.	Invest in comprehensive training programs, user-friendly interfaces, and effective change management strategies to foster digital literacy and technology adoption.	[61]
Cost and Return on Investment (ROI)	Deploying IoHT solutions can be a significant financial investment, and healthcare organizations may struggle to justify the costs.	Demonstrate a clear ROI by quantifying long-term benefits, such as improved patient outcomes, increased efficiency, and cost savings. Conduct cost–benefit analyses and pilot IoHT solutions.	[62]

platform also incorporates educational resources and interactive features to promote patient engagement and self-management. Healthcare professionals can access the data through a web-based portal, empowering them to monitor patients' conditions remotely and detect any concerning trends or deviations from established parameters. This allows for timely interventions, such as medication adjustments or scheduling follow-up appointments, without needing in-person visits.

6.2 GE Healthcare's Clinical Command Centers

GE Healthcare's Clinical Command Centers are advanced healthcare facilities that leverage IoHT technology to provide comprehensive patient monitoring and clinical decision support. These command centers integrate data from multiple sources, including medical devices, EHRs, and RTLS. The command centers are staffed by healthcare professionals, including nurses, physicians, and data analysts, who continuously monitor patient data streams. Advanced analytics and predictive algorithms identify potential issues or adverse events before they occur, enabling proactive interventions and preventive measures. For example, the system can detect early signs of sepsis, respiratory distress, or patient deterioration by analyzing vital signs, lab results, and other relevant data points.[4] GE Healthcare's Clinical Command Centers have been implemented in various healthcare systems across the United States, including Johns Hopkins Health System.[5] These facilities have reported significant reductions in hospital lengths of stay, readmission rates, and overall healthcare costs while improving patient outcomes and satisfaction [63].

6.3 Abbott's FreeStyle Libre Continuous Glucose Monitoring System

Abbott's FreeStyle Libre Continuous Glucose Monitoring (CGM) system is an IoHT-enabled device revolutionizing diabetes management by providing real-time glucose monitoring and insights. The system comprises a small, disposable sensor worn on the back of the upper arm, continuously measuring glucose levels in the interstitial fluid. The sensor wirelessly transmits the glucose data to a compatible smartphone app or a dedicated reader device. Patients can conveniently scan the sensor with their smartphone or reader to obtain their current glucose level and

---

[4] https://www.gehccommandcenter.com/.

[5] https://www.gehccommandcenter.com/videos/johns-hopkins-capacity-command-center-improving-efficiency-and-patient-care.

historical trends and patterns.[6] The FreeStyle Libre system also provides customizable alerts and alarms, notifying patients when their glucose levels are approaching high or low thresholds. This real-time feedback enables patients to make informed decisions regarding their diet, exercise, and insulin dosages, enabling better diabetes self-management.

Healthcare providers can access the glucose data through secure cloud-based platforms, allowing them to remotely monitor their patients' glucose levels and provide personalized treatment plans and recommendations. This remote monitoring capability reduces the need for frequent in-person visits, improving patient convenience and reducing healthcare costs.

Abbott's FreeStyle Libre CGM system has been widely adopted globally, with over 4.5 million users across more than 50 countries.[7] Clinical studies have demonstrated its effectiveness in improving glycemic control, reducing hypoglycemic events, and enhancing overall quality of life for individuals with diabetes. Its effectiveness was also tested and proved during the COVID-19 pandemic [64].

6.4 *Propeller Health's Digital Therapy for Asthma and Chronic Obstructive Pulmonary Disease (COPD)*

Propeller Health has developed an innovative IoHT-based platform to improve the management of respiratory conditions such as asthma and COPD. The platform combines connected inhalers, sensors, and a mobile app to provide personalized insights and guidance to patients while enabling healthcare providers to monitor them remotely. The connected inhalers incorporate small sensors that automatically record and transmit data about medication usage, including the time, date, and location of each inhaler activation. These data are then synced with the Propeller Health mobile app, allowing patients to log their symptoms, triggers, and other relevant information.[8] Using this comprehensive data set, the app provides personalized feedback, educational resources, and actionable recommendations to help patients better articulate and manage their well-being. For instance, it can identify potential triggers based on location data and offer strategies to mitigate exposure to those triggers. Additionally, healthcare providers can access a web-based portal to monitor patients' medication adherence without contact, symptom patterns, and overall condition management. This remote monitoring capability allows for timely interventions, such as adjusting treatment plans or scheduling follow-up appointments, without frequent in-person visits.

6 https://www.freestyle.abbott/in-en/home.html.

7 https://www.freestyle.abbott/my-en/blog/freestyle-libre-system-kit.html.

8 https://propellerhealth.com/.

6.5 *Fitbit's Corporate Wellness Pledge Program*

Fitbit, a leading provider of wearable fitness trackers, has collaborated with numerous companies to implement corporate wellness programs that leverage IoHT technology. These programs aim to promote healthy lifestyles, increase physical activity, and improve overall well-being among employees, potentially leading to reduced healthcare costs and increased productivity for employers. The Fitbit corporate wellness pledge program typically involves providing employees with Fitbit wearable devices, such as smartwatches, and access to the Fitbit mobile app and online platform.[9] These devices and applications capture data on physical activity levels, sleep patterns, heart rate, and other health-related metrics. Employees can set personalized fitness goals, participate in company-wide challenges or competitions, and track progress through the Fitbit app and web platform. The program also provides educational resources, healthy habit-building tools, and opportunities for social support and encouragement within the company's employee community.

Employers can access aggregated and anonymized employee health data through a dedicated corporate dashboard, enabling them to gain insights into their workforce's overall health and wellness. These data can inform the development of targeted wellness initiatives, such as on-site fitness classes, healthy food options in the cafeteria, or stress management programs.

6.6 *Omron's VitalSight Remote Blood Pressure Monitoring Solution*

Omron, a leading manufacturer of medical devices, has developed an IoHT-based solution for remote blood pressure monitoring. This system combines connected blood pressure monitors, a mobile app, and a cloud-based platform. It enables individuals to monitor their home blood pressure levels and share the data with healthcare providers. The connected blood pressure monitors are designed to be user-friendly and accurate, providing reliable measurements with each use. These devices automatically transmit the blood pressure data to the Omron mobile app or a dedicated device via Bluetooth or other wireless connectivity.[10]

The mobile app is a central hub, allowing users to track their blood pressure readings over time, visualize trends and patterns, and set reminders for regular monitoring. Additionally, the app provides educational resources and guidance on interpreting blood pressure values and making lifestyle changes to manage hypertension.

[9] https://healthsolutions.fitbit.com/wellness-pledge/.

[10] https://omronhealthcare.com/professionals/remote-patient-monitoring/.

7. Conclusion

In conclusion, this chapter explores the IoHT and underscores its potential to revolutionize healthcare delivery, diagnosis, and management. Through thoroughly examining its foundational principles, including interconnectivity, data analytics, real-time monitoring, personalized care, and security, the chapter elucidates the comprehensive framework necessary for successful IoHT implementation. Moreover, delineating IoHT components, spanning wearable devices, smart sensors, and interconnected medical devices, elucidates the diverse technological landscape contributing to its functionality. Furthermore, the architectural framework outlined, encompassing IoT devices, data acquisition, cloud-based storage, and analytics, provides a structured approach to IoHT deployment. However, the chapter also illuminates the myriad challenges confronting IoHT adoption in healthcare, ranging from data security and interoperability issues to regulatory compliance and resource constraints. Nevertheless, through real-world applications and case studies, such as Philips Remote Patient Monitoring and Abbott's FreeStyle Libre Continuous Glucose Monitoring System, the tangible benefits and transformative potential of IoHT in improving patient outcomes and healthcare delivery are vividly demonstrated. In summary, this chapter serves as a comprehensive guide, delineating the principles, components, architectures, challenges, and real-world applications of IoHT in healthcare, thereby offering valuable insights for researchers, practitioners, and policymakers as they navigate the evolving landscape of digital health technologies.

References

[1] Haghi Kashani, M., M. Madanipour, M. Nikravan, P. Asghari and E. Mahdipour. Oct. 2021. A systematic review of IoT in healthcare: Applications, techniques, and trends. *Journal of Network and Computer Applications,* 192: 103164, doi: 10.1016/J.JNCA.2021.103164.

[2] Verma, H., N. Chauhan and L. K. Awasthi. Nov. 2023. A comprehensive review of 'Internet of Healthcare Things': Networking aspects, technologies, services, applications, challenges, and security concerns. *Comput. Sci. Rev.,* 50: 100591, doi: 10.1016/J.COSREV.2023.100591.

[3] Kalinaki, K., M. Fahadi, A. A. Alli, W. Shafik, M. Yasin and N. Mutwalibi. 2023. Artificial Intelligence of Internet of Medical Things (AIoMT) in Smart Cities: A review of cybersecurity for smart healthcare. In *Handbook of Security and Privacy of AI-Enabled Healthcare Systems and Internet of Medical Things,* 1st Edition., CRC Press, pp. 271–292. doi: 10.1201/9781003370321-11.

[4] Andrade, A., A. T. Cabral, B. Bellini, V. F. Rodrigues, R. da Rosa Righi, C. A. da Costa and J. L. V. Barbosa. Jun. 2024. IoT-based vital sign monitoring: A literature review. *Smart Health,* 32: 100462, doi: 10.1016/J.SMHL.2024.100462.

[5] Fahim, K. E., K. Kalinaki and W. Shafik. 2023. Electronic devices in the Artificial Intelligence of the Internet of Medical Things (AIoMT). In *Handbook of Security and*

Privacy of AI-Enabled Healthcare Systems and Internet of Medical Things, 1st Edition, CRC Press, pp. 41–62. doi: 10.1201/9781003370321-3.

[6] Muzamil Aslam, M., R. Yusuf Zakari, A. Tufail, S. Ali, K. Kalinaki and W. Shafik. 2024. Introduction to industry's fourth revolution and its impacts on healthcare. In *Digital Transformation in Healthcare 5.0*, De Gruyter, pp. 33–66. doi: 10.1515/9783111327853-002.

[7] Kalinaki, K., U. Yahya, O. A. Malik and D. T. C. Lai. 2024. A review of big data analytics and Artificial Intelligence in Industry 5.0 for smart decision-making. In *Human-Centered Approaches in Industry 5.0: Human-Machine Interaction, Virtual Reality Training, and Customer Sentiment Analysis*, pp. 24–47. doi: 10.4018/979-8-3693-2647-3.ch002.

[8] Overmann, K. M., D. T. Y. Wu, C. T. Xu, S. S. Bindhu and L. Barrick. Jun. 2021. Real-time locating systems to improve healthcare delivery: A systematic review. *Journal of the American Medical Informatics Association*, 28(6): 1308–1317, doi: 10.1093/JAMIA/OCAB026.

[9] Kalinaki, K., W. Shafik, S. Namuwaya and S. Namuwaya. 2024. Perspectives, applications, challenges, and future trends of IoT-based logistics. In *Navigating Cyber Threats and Cybersecurity in the Logistics Industry*, IGI Global, pp. 148–171, doi: 10.4018/979-8-3693-3816-2.CH005.

[10] Gupta, S., M. Shabaz, A. Gupta, A. Alqahtani, S. Alsubai and I. Ofori. 2023. Personal HealthCare of Things: A novel paradigm and futuristic approach. *CAAI Trans. Intell. Technol.*, doi: 10.1049/CIT2.12220.

[11] Behmann, F. Jan. 2024. Visibility in Healthcare with IoHT. *The Rise of the Intelligent Health System*, pp. 38–51, doi: 10.4324/9781032690315-3.

[12] Sahu, K. N., R. Ethiraj and P. Jena. Sep. 2021. Applications of IoT in Health Care: Challenges and benefits. *IoT Applications, Security Threats, and Countermeasures*, pp. 177–193, doi: 10.1201/9781003124252-10.

[13] Srinivasan, A., V. Rampur, M. M. S. Rao and R. Singh. Jun. 2024. Implementation of IoT in Healthcare barriers and future challenges. *Advances in Fuzzy-Based Internet of Medical Things (IoMT)*, pp. 271–286, doi: 10.1002/9781394242252.CH18.

[14] Thilakarathne, N. N., H. D. Weerasinghe, A. Welhenge and M. K. Kagita. 2021. Privacy dilemma in Healthcare: A review on privacy preserving medical Internet of Things. *2021 12th International Conference on Computing Communication and Networking Technologies, ICCCNT 2021*, doi: 10.1109/ICCCNT51525.2021.9579933.

[15] Rubí, J. N. S. and P. R. de L. Gondim. Jan. 2020. Interoperable internet of medical things platform for e-Health applications. *Int. J. Distrib. Sens. Netw.*, 16(1), doi: 10.1177/1550147719889591.

[16] Li, C., J. Wang, S. Wang and Y. Zhang. Jan. 2024. A review of IoT applications in healthcare. *Neurocomputing*, 565: 127017, doi: 10.1016/J.NEUCOM.2023.127017.

[17] Putra, K. T., A. Z. Arrayyan, N. Hayati, C. Firdaus Damarjati, A. Bakar and H. Chen. 2024. A review on the application of internet of medical things in wearable personal health monitoring: A cloud-edge artificial intelligence approach. *IEEE Access*, 12: 21437–21452, doi: 10.1109/ACCESS.2024.3358827.

[18] Kadayat, Y., S. Sharma, P. Agarwal and S. Mohan. 2024. Internet-of-Things enabled smart health monitoring system using AutoAI: A graphical tool of IBM Watson Studio, pp. 427–445, doi: 10.1007/978-981-97-0052-3_21.

[19] Wu, X., C. Liu, L. Wang and M. Bilal. Jul. 2023. Internet of things-enabled real-time health monitoring system using deep learning. *Neural Comput. Appl.*, 35(20): 14565–14576, doi: 10.1007/S00521-021-06440-6.

[20] Herfandi, H., S. Sitanggang, M. Rangga, A. Nasution, H. Nguyen and Y. M. Jang. Jan. 2024. Real-time patient indoor health monitoring and location tracking with optical camera communications on the internet of medical things. *Applied Sciences*, 14(3): 1153, doi: 10.3390/APP14031153.

[21] Gupta, D. and R. Jain. Mar. 2024. The Internet of Things in Healthcare: A remote patient monitoring system. *Convergence of Blockchain and Internet of Things in Healthcare,* pp. 68–86, doi: 10.1201/9781003466949-4.

[22] Gibson, R., H. Larijani, P. Mishra and G. Singh. Aug. 2023. Internet of Medical Things Healthcare for sustainable Smart Cities: Current status and future prospects. *Applied Sciences,* 13(15): 8869, doi: 10.3390/APP13158869.

[23] Ray, P. P., D. Dash and N. Kumar. Jul. 2020. Sensors for internet of medical things: State-of-the-art, security and privacy issues, challenges and future directions. *Comput. Commun.,* 160: 111–131, doi: 10.1016/J.COMCOM.2020.05.029.

[24] Aminabee, S. 2024. The future of Healthcare and patient-centric care. In *Emerging Technologies for Health Literacy and Medical Practice,* pp. 240–262. doi: 10.4018/979-8-3693-1214-8.ch012.

[25] Shafik, W., A. F. Hidayatullah, K. Kalinaki and M. M. Aslam. Feb. 2024. Artificial Intelligence (AI)-Assisted Computer Vision (CV) in Healthcare systems. *Computer Vision and AI-Integrated IoT Technologies in the Medical Ecosystem,* pp. 17–36, doi: 10.1201/9781003429609-2.

[26] Alsaeed, N., F. Nadeem and F. Albalwy. Feb. 2024. A scalable and lightweight group authentication framework for Internet of Medical Things using integrated blockchain and fog computing. *Future Generation Computer Systems,* 151: 162–181, doi: 10.1016/J.FUTURE.2023.09.032.

[27] Putra, K. T., A. Z. Arrayyan, N. Hayati, C. Firdaus Damarjati, A. Bakar and H. Chen. 2024. A review on the application of internet of medical things in wearable personal health monitoring: A cloud-edge artificial intelligence approach.*IEEE Access,* 12: 21437–21452, doi: 10.1109/ACCESS.2024.3358827.

[28] Tariq, M. U. 2024. Advanced wearable medical devices and their role in transformative remote health monitoring. In *Transformative Approaches to Patient Literacy and Healthcare Innovation,* pp. 308–326, doi: 10.4018/979-8-3693-3661-8.ch015.

[29] Abubeker, K. M., R. Krishnamoorthy, S. S. B. Gogula, S. Muthu, G. Chellamuthu and K. Subramaniam. Mar. 2024. Internet of Things enabled open source assisted real-time blood glucose monitoring framework. *Scientific Reports,* 14(1): 1–11, doi: 10.1038/s41598-024-56677-z.

[30] Al-Alusi, M. A., E. Ding, D. D. McManus and S. A. Lubitz. Nov. 2019. Wearing your heart on your sleeve: The future of cardiac rhythm monitoring. *Curr. Cardiol. Rep.,* 21(12): 158, doi: 10.1007/S11886-019-1223-8.

[31] Ahsan, M., S. H. Teay, A. S. M. Sayem and A. Albarbar. Mar. 2022. Smart clothing framework for health monitoring applications. *Signals,* 3(1): 113–145, doi: 10.3390/SIGNALS3010009.

[32] Pise, A., B. Yoon and S. Singh. Jan. 2023. Enabling Ambient Intelligence of Things (AIoT) healthcare system architectures. *Comput. Commun.,* 198: 186–194, doi: 10.1016/J.COMCOM.2022.10.029.

[33] Ashraf, S., S. P. Khattak and M. T. Iqbal. Oct. 2023. Design and implementation of an open-source and Internet-of-Things-based health monitoring system. *Journal of Low Power Electronics and Applications,* 13(4): 57, doi: 10.3390/JLPEA13040057.

[34] Kaidi, H. M., M. A. M. Izhar, R. A. Dziyauddin, N. E. Shaiful and R. Ahmad. 2024. A comprehensive review on wireless healthcare monitoring: System components. *IEEE Access,* 12: 35008–35032, doi: 10.1109/ACCESS.2024.3349547.

[35] Kulkarni, M. B., S. Rajagopal, B. Prieto-Simón and B. W. Pogue. May 2024. Recent advances in smart wearable sensors for continuous human health monitoring. *Talanta,* 272: 125817, doi: 10.1016/J.TALANTA.2024.125817.

[36] Pan, Z., S. Liao, W. Sun, H. Zhou, S. Lin, D. Chen, S. Jiang, H. Long, J. Fan, F. Deng and W. Zhang. Feb. 2024. Protocol: Screening and early warning system for chronic obstructive pulmonary disease with obstructive sleep apnoea based on the medical

Internet of Things in three levels of healthcare: protocol for a prospective, multicentre, observational cohort study. *BMJ Open*, 14(2): 75257, doi: 10.1136/BMJOPEN-2023-075257.
[37] Al Dujaili, M. J., H. Z. Dhaam and M. T. Mezeel. Jan. 2024. An intelligent fall detection algorithm for elderly monitoring in the internet of things platform. *Multimed. Tools Appl.*, 83(2): 5683–5695, doi: 10.1007/S11042-023-15820-0.
[38] Mathkor, D. M., N. Mathkor, Z. Bassfar, F. Bantun, P. Slama, F. Ahmad and S. Haque. Apr. 2024. Multirole of the internet of medical things (IoMT) in biomedical systems for managing smart healthcare systems: An overview of current and future innovative trends. *J. Infect. Public Health*, 17(4): 559–572, doi: 10.1016/J.JIPH.2024.01.013.
[39] Rohmetra, H., N. Raghunath, P. Narang, V. Chamola, M. Guizani and N. R. Lakkaniga. Apr. 2023. AI-enabled remote monitoring of vital signs for COVID-19: Methods, prospects and challenges. *Computing*, 105(4): 783–809, doi: 10.1007/S00607-021-00937-7.
[40] Banerjee, A., C. Chakraborty and M. Rathi. Jan. 2020. Medical imaging, Artificial Intelligence, Internet of Things, wearable devices in terahertz healthcare technologies. *Terahertz Biomedical and Healthcare Technologies: Materials to Devices*, pp. 145–165, doi: 10.1016/B978-0-12-818556-8.00008-2.
[41] Babu, B. K. and B. A. 2021. Application of equipment utilization monitoring system for ICU equipment using Internet of Things (IoT). *Lecture Notes in Electrical Engineering*, 796: 57–83, doi: 10.1007/978-981-16-5078-9_6.
[42] Kalinaki, K., M. Abdullatif, S. A.-K. Nasser, R. Nsubuga and J. Kugonza. Jan. 2024. Paving the path to a sustainable digital future with green cloud computing. *Emerging Trends in Cloud Computing Analytics, Scalability, and Service Models*, pp. 44–66, doi: 10.4018/979-8-3693-0900-1.CH002.
[43] Kalinaki, K., O. A. Malik, U. Yahya and D. T. C. Lai. 2024. Federated learning challenges and risks in modern digital healthcare systems. In *Federated Learning for Digital Healthcare Systems*, Elsevier, pp. 283–300, doi: 10.1016/B978-0-443-13897-3.00004-7.
[44] Kalinaki, K., A. A. Alli, B. Asuman and R. Y. Zakari. 2024. Secure federated learning in the Internet of Health Things for improved patient privacy and data security. In *Federated Learning for Digital Healthcare Systems*, Elsevier, pp. 387–408. doi: 10.1016/B978-0-443-13897-3.00003-5.
[45] Aminizadeh, S., A. Heidari, S. Toumaj, M. Darbandi, N. J. Navimipour, M. Rezaei, S. Talebi, P. Azad and M. Unal. Nov. 2023. The applications of machine learning techniques in medical data processing based on distributed computing and the Internet of Things. *Comput. Methods Programs Biomed.*, 241: 107745, doi: 10.1016/J.CMPB.2023.107745.
[46] Kalinaki, K., N. N. Thilakarathne, H. R. Mubarak, O. A. Malik and M. Abdullatif. 2023. Cybersafe capabilities and utilities for Smart Cities. In *Cybersecurity for Smart Cities*, Springer, Cham, pp. 71–86, doi: 10.1007/978-3-031-24946-4_6.
[47] Abba Ari, A., O. K. Ngangmo, C. Titouna, O. Thiare, A. M. Kolyang and A. M. Gueroui. Jan. 2024. Enabling privacy and security in Cloud of Things: Architecture, applications, security & privacy challenges. *Applied Computing and Informatics*, 20(1-2): 119–141, doi: 10.1016/J.ACI.2019.11.005.
[48] Singhai, R. and R. Sushil. Jan. 2023. An investigation of various security and privacy issues in Internet of Things. *Mater Today Proc.*, 80: 3393–3397, doi: 10.1016/J.MATPR.2021.07.259.
[49] Alli, A. A., K. Kassim, N. Mutwalibi, H. Hamid and L. Ibrahim. 2021. Secure fog-cloud of things: Architectures, opportunities and challenges. pp. 3–20. *In*: Ahmed, M. and P. Haskell-Dowland (eds.). *Secure Edge Computing*, 1st ed., CRC Press, pp. 3–20. doi: 10.1201/9781003028635-2.
[50] Alabdulatif, A., N. N. Thilakarathne and K. Kalinaki. Jun. 2023. A novel cloud enabled access control model for preserving the security and privacy of medical big data. *Electronics (Basel)*, 12(12): 2646, doi: 10.3390/electronics12122646.

[51] Said, A., A. Yahyaoui and T. Abdellatif. 2024. HIPAA and GDPR Compliance in IoT Healthcare Systems, pp. 198–209, doi: 10.1007/978-3-031-55729-3_16.

[52] Osama, M., O. K. Ngangmo, C. Titouna, O. Thiare, A. M. Kolyang and A. M. Gueroui. Aug. 2023. Internet of Medical Things and Healthcare 4.0: Trends, requirements, challenges, and research directions. *Sensors*, 23(17): 7435, doi: 10.3390/S23177435.

[53] Kumar, M., A. Kumar, S. Verma, P. Bhattacharya, D. Ghimire, S. H. Kim and A. S. Hosen. Apr. 2023. Healthcare Internet of Things (H-IoT): Current trends, future prospects, applications, challenges, and security issues. *Electronics*, 12(9): 2050, doi: 10.3390/ELECTRONICS12092050.

[54] Philip, N. Y., J. J. P. C. Rodrigues, H. Wang, S. J. Fong and J. Chen. Feb. 2021. Internet of Things for in-home health monitoring systems: current advances, challenges and future directions. *IEEE Journal on Selected Areas in Communications*, 39(2): 300–310, doi: 10.1109/JSAC.2020.3042421.

[55] Islam, M. M., S. Nooruddin, F. Karray and G. Muhammad. Feb. 2023. Internet of Things: Device capabilities, architectures, protocols, and smart applications in healthcare domain. *IEEE Internet Things J.*, 10(4): 3611–3641, doi: 10.1109/JIOT.2022.3228795.

[56] Chemisto, M., T. J. Gutu, K. Kalinaki, D. M. Bosco, P. Egau, K. Fred, I. T. Oloya and K. Rashid. Sep. 2023. Artificial Intelligence for improved maternal healthcare: A systematic literature review. *2023 IEEE AFRICON*, pp. 1–6, doi: 10.1109/AFRICON55910.2023.10293674.

[57] Gou, H., G. Zhang, E. P. Medeiros, S. K. Jagatheesaperumal and V. H. C. de Albuquerque. Jan. 2024. A cognitive medical decision support system for IoT-based human-computer interface in pervasive computing environment. *Cognit. Comput.*, pp. 1–16, doi: 10.1007/S12559-023-10242-4.

[58] Jokinen, A., M. Stolt and R. Suhonen. Mar. 2021. Ethical issues related to eHealth: An integrative review. *Nurs Ethics*, 28(2): 253–271, doi: 10.1177/0969733020945765.

[59] Wakili, A. and S. Bakkali. 2024. Ethical considerations in the integration of Internet of Things (IoT) technologies within digital health: A comprehensive framework for evaluation. *Lecture Notes in Networks and Systems*, vol. 905 LNNS, pp. 219–231, 2024, doi: 10.1007/978-3-031-52385-4_21.

[60] Aghdam, Z. N., A. M. Rahmani and M. Hosseinzadeh. Feb. 2021. The role of the Internet of Things in Healthcare: Future trends and challenges. *Comput. Methods Programs Biomed.*, 199: 105903, doi: 10.1016/J.CMPB.2020.105903.

[61] Koohang, A., C. S. Sargent, J. H. Nord and J. Paliszkiewicz. Feb. 2022. Internet of Things (IoT): From awareness to continued use. *Int. J. Inf. Manage*, 62: 102442, doi: 10.1016/J.IJINFOMGT.2021.102442.

[62] Ahmed, S. F., M. S. Bin Alam, S. Afrin, S. J. Rafa, N. Rafa and A. H. Gandomi. Feb. 2024. Insights into Internet of Medical Things (IoMT): Data fusion, security issues and potential solutions. *Information Fusion*, 102: 102060, doi: 10.1016/J.INFFUS.2023.102060.

[63] Small, S. M. Feb. 2024. Mission control: Incorporating operations centers in hospital pharmacy design. *American Journal of Health-System Pharmacy*, doi: 10.1093/AJHP/ZXAE034.

[64] Jaques-Albuquerque, L. T., E. dos Anjos-Martins, L. Torres-Nunes, A. G. Valerio-Penha, A. C. Coelho-Oliveira, V. L. da Silva Sarandy, A. Reis-Silva, A. Seixas, M. Bernardo-Filho, R. Taiar and D. C. de Sa-Caputo. Apr. 2023. Effectiveness of using the FreeStyle Libre® system for monitoring blood glucose during the COVID-19 pandemic in diabetic individuals: Systematic review. *Diagnostics*, 13(8): 1499, doi: 10.3390/DIAGNOSTICS13081499.

Section II

Cyber Security Challenges for Internet of Health Things

DOI: 10.1201/9781003483267-3

Chapter 2

Data Breaches and Trends in Internet of Health Things

Mohammad Manzurul Islam,[1,*] *Md. Adnan Morshed,*[1] *Saleh Masum,*[2] *Md. Hasanul Ferdaus,*[1] *Maheen Islam,*[1] *Md. Sawkat Ali*[1] and *Taskeed Jabid*[1]

1. Introduction

The changes in the contemporary way of living cannot be overemphasized, thanks to the rise of the digital age coupled with the rise of connectivity. The phrase Internet of Health Things (IoHT) also refers to the infrastructure that supports it and connects previously unconnected platforms and devices in the healthcare industry [1, 2].

IoHT can be first understood as an information system that incorporates various systems and services, software applications, and medical devices. It is simply the Internet of Things (IoT), but as implemented in healthcare to bring about delivery of healthcare services. The IoHT is broad in scope, ranging from wearable health devices to electronic and institutional health devices and systems [1, 3].

[1] Department of Computer Science and Engineering, East West University, Aftabnagar, Dhaka, Bangladesh.
[2] Department of Information and Communication Engineering, University of Rajshahi, Rajshahi, Bangladesh.
Emails: adnansadat4@gmail.com, salehmasum@gmail.com, hasanul.ferdaus@ewubd.edu, maheen@ewubd.edu, alim@ewubd.edu, taskeed@ewubd.edu
* Corresponding author: mohammad.islam@ewubd.edu

DOI: 10.1201/9781003483267-4

Someone looking at the internet of health technology devices and systems would come across basic wearables like fitness or health monitors that include heart, blood pressure, and oxygen monitoring, to high-end technology like automated insulin diabetic pumps, stroke prediction software, and remote patient monitoring systems [4]. Some more systems with higher levels of complexities are more advanced fusion of communication platforms in telemedicine where patients can consult doctors in time and the sections of smart hospital rooms that have beds and active patient-helping systems that are able to collect and inform medical specialists what to do at that moment [5].

Furthermore, the significance and advantages of IoHT cannot be understated in any conversation about its application in healthcare. IoHT devices, on the one hand, provide real-time information on numerous health indicators to customers, empowering them to take an active role in their own health management. Conversely, IoHT makes therapy and care more precise, efficient, and customized [6]. Health service providers benefit greatly from it because of its many advantages, which include improved patient care, more accurate disease diagnosis, treatment, and management, and lower healthcare costs. Also, because it provides a more comprehensive picture of a person's health, it can help in the detection and prevention of ailments at a much earlier stage [7]. Figure 1 illustrates an IoHT system where wearable health devices, mobile apps, cloud storage, and healthcare providers connect via secure networks to monitor, store, and manage patient data in real time. IoHT, as a field of medicine, has rich patient data that are hidden and stay in the interconnectivity skirt of devices and systems.

Having said that, these gadgets gather an immense amount of data and provide real-time patient monitoring, which enables the customization of interventions. Additionally, these gadgets are easy targets for hackers, which may result in unlawful access, data compromise, and medical record manipulation. New and important challenges, particularly those pertaining to the security and privacy of the data gathered from the devices, have been brought up by the IoT explosion. It is impossible to stress how important these problems are, especially in light of the availability of data security solutions. It should be mentioned that safeguarding patient data is crucial for maintaining trust in developing medical technology and the security of medical equipment, in addition to being significant from a risk prevention and legal standpoint. IoHT's benefits run the risk of diminishing patient happiness and eroding carers' confidence in these new technologies if security, especially cyber security, is lacking [8, 9].

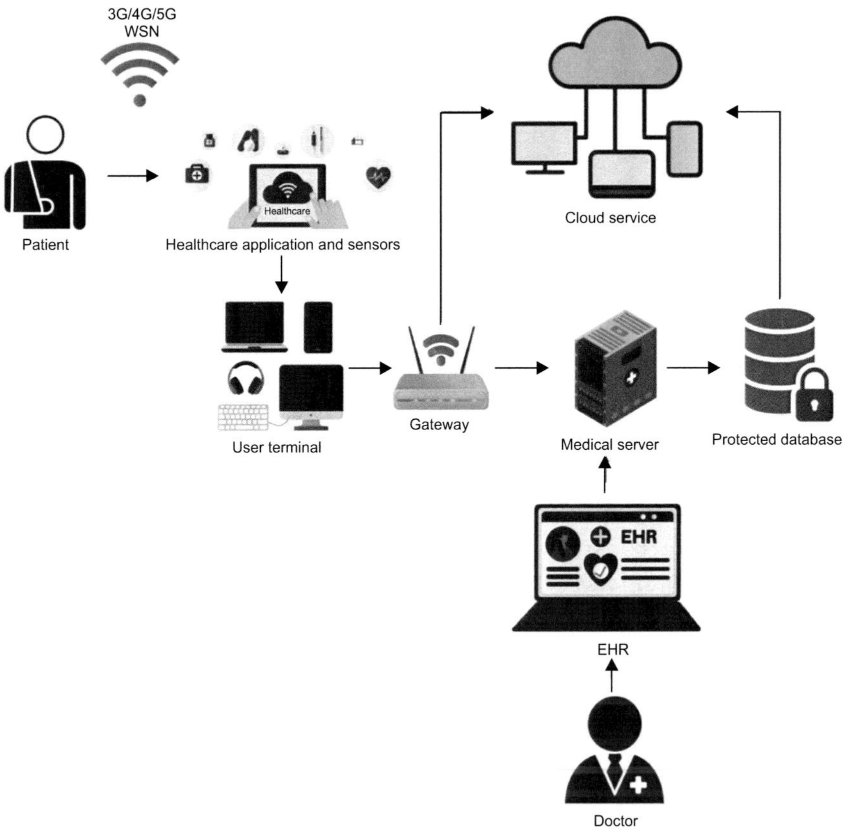

Figure 1: Illustration of an IoHT solution architecture.

This chapter addresses critical aspects of IoHT: presenting the main contributions focused on understanding its architecture, identifying vulnerabilities, data breach analysis, and proposing strategies for enhanced security. The main contributions are as follows:

- Provided the overall concept of IoHT architecture and integrated it into Healthcare.
- Categorized and identified major vulnerabilities based on device level, network level, and data-related risks.
- Researched ongoing data breaches and, by using real-life case studies, pointed out the consequences to healthcare systems.
- Analyzed implications of IoHT data breaches, regarding privacy, financial, and regulatory challenges.

- Examined such emerging security trends as blockchain, AI, and global regulations that handle IoHT vulnerabilities.
- Proposed measures that would help avert data breaches include device security, encryption of data, and user education.

The chapter starts with Section 1: Introduction, where IoHT is identified as one of the most important subjects in current healthcare; thus, its significance and challenges are presented, as well as the purposes of the discussion. Section 2 defines IoHT, architecture, and applications regarding wearables, remote patient monitoring systems, and smart implants, including a presentation of device, network, and data-level vulnerabilities. The next section, Section 3, describes the most common IoHT data breaches and is supported by case studies on unauthorized access, man-in-the-middle attacks, ransomware, and DDoS incidents. Consequences stemming from these breaches are explored in detail in Section 4, with an emphasis on the impact on patient privacy, financial stability, reputational damage, and compliance with regulatory frameworks such as Health Insurance Portability and Accountability Act (HIPAA) and General Data Protection Regulation (GDPR). Then, in Section 5, the discussion moves on to introduce a few of the emerging security technologies, namely blockchain, AI, and end-to-end encryption, while also focusing on global regulatory trends and collaborative efforts by public and private stakeholders to increase IoHT security. Section 6 portrays the IoHT security challenges in the near future: a continuously increasing number of interconnected devices; striking a balance between innovation and security; and ethical and privacy concerns. Section 7 gives some practical ways of preventing data breaches. It focuses on security regarding devices, encryption of data, and the education of users. Finally, Section 8: Conclusion summarizes the presented key takeaways from this paper and concludes that proactive measures are called for so as to ensure both security and sustainability within the IoHT ecosystem.

2. Understanding IoHT and its Vulnerabilities

The IoHT will revolutionize healthcare by interconnecting medical devices and systems for monitoring and exchanging data in real time. This section initiates an architectural overview related to the IoHT, which shows very clearly how sensors, devices, and cloud-based systems are integrated into the system for better healthcare delivery. Next, we introduce different IoHT devices and applications, such as wearable health gadgets, remote patient monitoring systems, and smart implants that support continuous health monitoring and management. On the other hand, these developments are associated with serious security issues. Respectively, the key weaknesses in IoHT systems are placed into three areas: data transmission and storage vulnerabilities that result in sensitive patient data breaches. Further discussion of these vulnerabilities and implications will be done in the subsequent sections, which will aim to discuss in-depth possible security measures to mitigate these risks.

2.1 Definition and Architecture of IoHT

The IoT of healthcare can be defined as the connectivity of devices and applications interconnected and used within healthcare to record, process, and communicate information about health. Such will include wearable technologies, medical devices, and health monitoring systems in conjunction with the communication of these with each other and with healthcare professionals with an aim of improving the quality of care provided and improving operational efficiencies. The IoHT architecture typically consists of:

- **Perception Layer:** It typically comprises sensors and devices that perceive different parameters in the physical world. Some very common examples include wearable health monitoring devices, high-end medical instruments, and environmental monitoring sensors.
- **Network Layer:** This is the layer that has to transmit the data re-received from the perception layer. It makes use of different communication technologies such as Wi-Fi, Bluetooth, and cellular networks.
- **Processing Layer:** This includes the basic processing functions along with storage. It integrates cloud computing platforms and numerous data analytic tools for the processing and analysis of the data received.
- **Application Layer:** This will provide a platform that can be used by both the users and the healthcare provider to interact with the IoHT system. It will comprise remote patient monitoring applications, telemedicine, and health data management applications.

These are the basic components of IoHT architecture [10]. Figure 2 shows the 4-layer IoHT architecture outlines how healthcare data flow from devices (Perception Layer), through networks (Network Layer), to be processed (Processing Layer), and finally presented or used in healthcare applications (Application Layer).

2.2 Common IoHT Devices and Applications in Healthcare

This subsection will outline a few of the most pervasive IoHT devices and applications that are changing patient care and clinical practice. Wearable health monitoring devices, with their specific developments in the form of fitness tracking devices and smartwatches, can measure

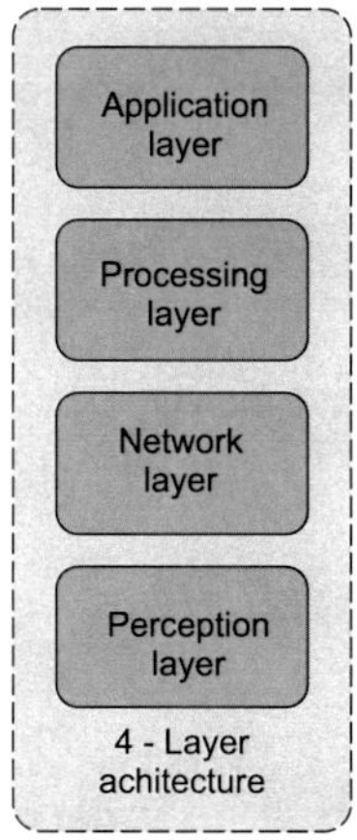

Figure 2: 4 - Layer IoHT architecture.

an individual's vital signs—for instance, heart rate and physical activity. Remote patient monitoring systems track the condition of a patient from a distance without the need for house calls. Other innovative medical devices, such as smart implants, provide more accurate solutions for the long-term management of chronic conditions, hence improving results in patients. These emerging technologies take care of further enhance patient-centered care while optimizing medical decision-making. The second section shows how applications developed around IoHT make a difference in healthcare delivery and patient management.

2.2.1 *Wearable Health Devices*

Wearable health technologies are designed to be attached to the body for continuous monitoring of various parameters of health. Devices that come under it include: All the gadgets seem to be covered, from Fitbit and Apple Watches to other wearables that keep tabs on sleep, exercise, heart rate, and more. A fitness tracker is a small gadget that keeps an eye on different fitness stats, like how many steps you've taken and how many calories you've burned. People with diabetes use Continuous Glucose Monitors to check their blood sugar levels right away. Portable ECG monitors help to spot irregular heartbeats and figure out heart problems [11].

2.2.2 *Remote Patient Monitoring Systems*

These remote patient monitoring systems enable health professionals to monitor patients' health information from a distance. The list includes: Blood pressure monitors are instruments specifically engineered to assess blood pressure levels and subsequently relay this information to healthcare providers. Glucose Monitoring Devices: Continuous monitoring of glucose levels in the blood and subsequent delivery to practitioners. Telehealth systems also include frameworks designed to support video-mediated consultations and enable the remote monitoring of patients through various digital health records [12].

2.2.3 Smart Implants and Medical Equipment

Smart implants and medical equipment are excellent goods with network and sensor capabilities. Their goal is to monitor patients closely and improve their quality of life. These include, for instance, smart knee implants with sensors that monitor the status of the knee joint and provide clinicians with precise information, and bioelectronic bone implants with systems to initiate therapy and sense what's happening at the bone–implant interface. Scaffolds created using 4D technology that can adapt to stimuli and function effectively with living tissues [13].

2.3 *Key Vulnerabilities in IoHT Systems*

The IoHT comprises various entry points, either directly at the device level or from network-level vulnerabilities. On the device level, these relate to the lack of sufficient security in wearable devices and smart implants. These are then vulnerable to unauthorized access and subsequent exploitation. On the other side, network-level vulnerabilities arise due to the use of insecure protocols for communication, where data are, therefore, exposed during transmission, in which malicious actors may intercept or manipulate information. The other risks associated with sending and storing data are those that result from poor encryption, which leads to breaches and loss of sensitive health information. We will continue to discuss various types of IoHT data breaches in more detail, together with several case studies involving the consequences of such vulnerabilities to patient privacy and healthcare institutions. Table 1 shows the key vulnerabilities in IoHT systems.

Table 1: Key vulnerabilities in IoHT systems.

Vulnerability Type	Description
Device-Level Vulnerabilities	Outdated firmware, weak authentication (default or guessable passwords), physical tampering, and limited resources restricting security measures.
Network-Level Vulnerabilities	Insecure communication protocols, poor encryption, weak network segmentation enabling lateral attacks, and vulnerability to DoS attacks.
Data Transmission and Storage Risks	Unencrypted data during transmission and storage, insecure cloud services, and risks of data tampering affect integrity.

2.3.1 Device-Level Vulnerabilities

Intrinsic IoHT device-level vulnerabilities are shared between hardware and software, making them very appealing targets for cyberattacks. Among the very common problems are insecure firmware outdated or lacking any updates and poor authentication mechanisms, such as using default passwords or those which can be easily guessed. Another problem is physical security itself: IoHT devices can be tampered with for unauthorized access [14]. Besides this, the scarcity of computational resources related to processing power and memory restricts the implementation of strong security measures, hence further increasing the chances of their exploitation.

2.3.2 Network-Level Vulnerabilities

The main cause of IoHT's network-level vulnerabilities is weaknesses in communication protocols and network infrastructure. Such security issues include insecure protocols of communication, where encryption might be lacking or cannot keep up with the newest requirements of security [15]. Poor network segmentation may also allow an intruder to have lateral movement capabilities inside a system once he has compromised one device. Besides, IoHT devices are much more prone to DoS attacks, which disrupt the functionality and availability of such devices, hence imposing a critical risk to healthcare operations.

2.3.3 Data Transmission and Storage Risks

Data transmission and storage within IoHT systems are open to several forms of vulnerabilities that could compromise sensitive health information. Unencrypted data transmitted are accessed by unauthorized parties at the instance of its transfer between devices. Insecure data storage, either on IoHT devices or on cloud services, is surely leading to breaches if proper encryption and other security measures are not implemented [16]. Besides, the integrity of the data should be secured to avoid any tampering during transmission and storage so that the information obtained is correct and reliable.

3. Types of Data Breaches in IoHT

This section discusses topics ranging from various IoHT data breaches to consequences for patient privacy and healthcare systems. It looks first at some general breaches in IoHT: unauthorized access and theft of data, whereby malicious actors leverage weak security to take advantage of sensitive health information. The following ones concern the analyses of man-in-the-middle attacks, where the communications between devices are intercepted, thus allowing manipulations. It also points to critical vulnerabilities of ransomware and malware infections that can lock critical data in and disrupt healthcare operations. DDoS attacks are discussed in the way they overwhelm systems to cause great service disruption. It concludes this section through specific examples of such threats through case studies of some major IoHT data breaches, including incidents of healthcare monitoring devices and smart hospital system compromises, thereby showing the real-life impact of such vulnerabilities.

3.1 Common Types of Data Breaches in Healthcare IoT

As we delve deeper into the dynamics of the IoHT, it becomes imperative to tackle one of the most challenging issues associated with this domain—data breaches. As the IoHT continues to yield enormous amounts of sensitive and highly valued data, this makes it a prime target for unscrupulous parties, which in turn, raises the specter of data breaches [17, 18]. In the context of IoHT, data breaches can be defined as the unauthorized access, disclosure, or sharing of healthcare-acquired, patient-connected, data. The data in question may include personal identification information, health and genetic information, and medical records. The types of breaches can vary broadly, ranging from physical theft to more sophisticated forms like hacking, malware attacks, and ransomware, to insider threats and misconfigurations [19–21]. Table 2 summarizes the IoHT Data Breaches.

Table 2: Summary of IoHT Data Breaches and case studies.

Type of Data Breach	Description
Unauthorized Access and Data Theft	Exploiting weak security or phishing to gain unauthorized access, stealing personal, financial, or sensitive health data.
Man-in-the-Middle (MITM) Attacks	Intercepting communications between two parties to manipulate or steal data; methods include packet sniffing and SSL stripping.
Ransomware and Malware Infections	Encrypting data and demanding ransom for decryption; includes viruses, worms, and trojans disrupting healthcare operations.
Distributed Denial of Service (DDoS)	Overloading systems with traffic using botnets to cause service disruptions and financial damage to institutions.

3.1.1 Unauthorized Access and Data Theft

Unauthorized access and data theft involve unauthorized access by an attacker to a system or network, from where sensitive information is usually stolen. The access can be due to software vulnerabilities being exploited, phishing attacks, or the use of credentials of other, legitimate users. Once inside, they could steal personal data, financial information, or intellectual property [22].

3.1.2 Man-in-the-Middle Attacks (MITM)

The basic concept behind any MITM attack is that an intruder will intercept and likely the communication of two parties unbeknownst to either. Such tampering could lead to a data breach, unauthorized transactions, and so on. Packet sniffing, session hijacking, and SSL stripping are some of the methods used by an attacker to execute an MITM attack [23].

3.1.3 Ransomware and Malware Infections

Ransomware is a kind of malware that encrypts the victim's data and then offers to sell the decryption key. A malware infection can also involve viruses, worms, and trojans that will probably cause no small amount of damage to the systems and data. This could bring organizations to their knees by making them unable to access any business data until the ransom is paid in ransomware attacks [24, 25].

3.1.4 Distributed Denial of Service (DDoS) Attacks

DDoS overloads a targeted service with traffic from more than one source, and in this way, it makes services unavailable. This attack causes denial of services, damages the economy quite significantly, and could be costly to the targeted institution. Attackers use a botnet to generate bulks of traffic that flood the targeted system [26].

3.2 Case Studies of Notable IoHT Data Breaches

Various practical examples of major data breaches within the IoHT ecosystem are discussed in this subsection. In this case study, we review breaches in health monitoring devices that utilized vulnerabilities in wearable health devices and remote patient monitoring systems to facilitate unauthorized access and exposure of sensitive patient data. The second case study is the smart compromised hospital system; it will provide an idea about how security vulnerabilities in connected medical equipment and within hospital networks are used by the attacker to cause widespread disruption of safety. These case studies will provide concrete, realistic insights into IoHT system risks and real-life consequences of not having sufficient security measures in place.

3.2.1 Case Study: Breach of Healthcare Monitoring Devices

In late 2014, Anthem, the country's second-largest health insurer, was one of the worst cyberattack victims ever. It was perpetrated by Deep Panda group of highly sophisticated cybercriminals. The attackers accessed the Anthem network courtesy of a phishing email whereby one employee was tricked into clicking on a malicious link; that is how the attackers installed malware on the employee's computer. The malware allowed the attackers to conduct a lateral movement in Anthem's network and perform privilege escalation to reach sensitive parts of the network, including the company's data warehouse. Almost 80 million people had their personal information compromised, including names, dates of birth, Social Security numbers, and addresses. This put identity theft and fraud at risk; several lawsuits have been filed, with major costs to Anthem in the form of credit monitoring services provided to affected individuals [27].

3.2.2 Case Study: Compromised Smart Hospital Systems

An APT group utilized this vulnerability in the OpenSSL cryptographic software library, with the help of the infamous Heartbleed bug, by stealing data from the memory of affected systems to deploy advanced malware for deeper intrusion into CHS's network. They had accessed and stolen sensitive data of approximately 4.5 million patients, which included their names, birthdates, Social Security numbers, phone numbers, and addresses. This breach underlined the most important need that was required for cyber security measures in healthcare and plagued CHS to increase the pace of security protocols and become the center of regulatory scrutiny [28].

4. Consequences of IoHT Data Breaches

Data breaches in the IoHT can have severe consequences, affecting individuals, organizations, and broader societal structures. The vulnerabilities inherent in IoHT devices can lead to unauthorized access, data leakage, and denial-of-service attacks, which pose significant risks to personal privacy and public safety [29]. In the following section, different consequences of IoHT are discussed.

4.1 Patient Privacy and Confidentiality Risks

The IoHT is the interconnection of all medical devices to capture, transmit, and store sensitive patient information. Thus, IoHT provides a huge opportunity to improve healthcare. Connectivity in the same way creates significant risks related to the privacy and confidentiality of patients. Breaches will be fully packed with a lot of risks: security protocol lapse, software bugs, or sophisticated cyberattacks leading to the leakage of sensitive information regarding the patients' medical history, personal identification, and financial information. In addition to breaches, there is also malicious editing to the patient record crime that would trigger misdiagnosis or improper treatment and destroy confidence in healthcare systems. This also presents another risk of unauthorized sharing of data to third parties without patient consent, hence breaching privacy laws like HIPAA—a US law protecting health information that sets benchmarks for electronic protected health information (ePHI), and eroding trust from the patients. While most IoHT devices are just not up to snuff when it comes to security features, the vulnerabilities in hacking make them such that this could compromise not only an individual device but even healthcare networks. These risks make acute measures involving security, encryption, and consent mechanisms quite imperative in nature for the protection of patient data in the IoHT landscape [30].

4.2 *Financial and Reputational Impact on Healthcare Institutions*

Serious consequences of a security breach may be caused in IoHT system security, including the financial and reputational status of the healthcare institution. Financial loss due to a breach can be very significant, since there are major regulatory fines a healthcare provider has to pay, typically associated with HIPAA, apart from the costs related to breach mitigation, litigation fees, and compensation to affected patients. Operational disruption is a common consequence of such cyberattacks as ransomware, locking critical systems; it causes delays in medical procedures, cutting off access to patient records and therefore increasing the costs of operations. These not only affect patient care but also stretch resources further for recovery. The reputational damage can last a long time since trust is a critical entity in healthcare. The breach may shave off the confidence of patients in that facility, translating to reduced numbers of patients. During the rebuilding process for a tarnished reputation, the process usually is very expensive and time-consuming. In addition, security breaches invite regulatory scrutiny, ensuring that there will be more vigorous audits with heavy oversight, and demands for more compliance requests that put extra burdens on the institution both financially and operationally [31].

4.3 *Regulatory and Legal Repercussions*

The regulatory and legal challenges for the IoT and smart home technologies are multifaceted and significant. One of the primary issues is the inadequacy of existing legal frameworks, such as the GDPR, which may not fully encompass the unique functionalities and risks associated with IoT devices. This gap can lead to insufficient protection for users' personal data and privacy [32]. Additionally, the diverse types of data collected by these devices complicate the classification of personal information, making it challenging to determine the applicability of data protection laws. User awareness is another critical challenge, as many individuals are often unaware of the extent of data collection and processing by IoT devices. This lack of transparency undermines users' ability to provide informed consent and exercise control over their personal data, which is a fundamental requirement of data protection regulations. The rapid evolution of technology requires that regulatory frameworks adapt continuously to address new functionalities and risks. This ongoing change makes it difficult for regulators to keep pace with the innovations in IoT and smart home technologies, potentially leaving users vulnerable to emerging threats [32].

IoHT consequently falls directly within the legal and regulatory environment that governs the use of personal health information. Two major regulations involve the HIPAA of the United States and the GDPR of the European Union. HIPAA dictates stringent standards to protect sensitive patient information, laying down rules that any healthcare organization is expected to adhere to. Most notably, GDPR focuses on individual control over personal data by elaborating on data management principles and rights of individuals. Both regulations have huge fines depending on the gravity of violations. However, IoHT cannot easily comply for the simple reason that its technology keeps on changing, which frequently runs ahead of existing legislation. Besides, the integration of multiple devices within various geographies further develops the complexity regarding meeting regulatory compliances [31, 33].

Non-compliance with such regulations, like HIPAA and GDPR, could result in significant financial and legal consequences for healthcare organizations in case of data breaches. The laws require heavy punishments against such organizations for their failure to protect patient data accordingly. In the event of security breaches that may result in the leakage of sensitive information, the imposed fines include other additional costs, which may also include being taken to court by the affected people or class-action lawsuits. Besides fines, legal scrutiny possibly with sanctions also includes damage to the organization's reputation; hence, compliance and adequate security measures on the part of a health provider are very crucial.

HIPAA fines are considered quite significant, and the fines themselves are divided into four tiers depending on the level of the breach in culpability. For example, a Tier 1 breach is due to reasonable cause; the fines range between $137 and $68,928 for every violation with a yearly limit of $2,067,813. More serious types of breaches, such as Tier 4, consist of willful neglect that has not been corrected within 30 days from the first day it was known, and these can be fined $68,928 per violation, with the same annual limit [34].

Under GDPR, fines are divided into two tiers, with the lower tier allowing for fines of up to €10 million or up to 2% of annual global turnover from the preceding financial year, whichever amount is greater. Among other areas of violation, this is a breach for not notifying the supervisory authority and the data subjects about the breach. The upper limit may be €20 million or, in the case of an undertaking, up to 4% of the total worldwide annual turnover within a financial year, whichever is greater, for grave breaches: infringement of the basic principles for processing, including conditions for consent [35].

5. Trends in IoHT Security

The IoHT is swiftly progressing, propelled by the necessity for interconnected medical devices, wearable health surveillance systems, and intelligent hospital infrastructures. As these innovations develop, guaranteeing robust security becomes crucial to safeguard sensitive patient information and uphold system integrity. A prominent trend in IoHT security is the utilization of end-to-end encryption to protect data as they traverse various devices and networks. Furthermore, blockchain technology is acquiring momentum for its capacity to establish immutable and secure ledgers for patient records and device interactions. AI-driven anomaly detection systems are being incorporated to discern and respond to dubious activities in real time, augmenting proactive defense mechanisms. The execution of zero-trust architectures, where devices are perpetually validated, has also surfaced as an essential methodology to reduce vulnerabilities within healthcare networks. Secure device authentication employing advanced cryptographic techniques ensures that only sanctioned devices can access the network. Moreover, privacy-preserving algorithms, such as federated learning, are facilitating data analysis to be performed without direct data sharing, thereby minimizing exposure. Another significant trend is adherence to global regulations like HIPAA and GDPR, which enforce rigorous data protection protocols. Ultimately, ongoing collaborative endeavors between medical institutions, technology providers, and regulatory bodies are facilitating the development of comprehensive security frameworks that address both present and future challenges in IoHT. In the subsections, some of the emerging IoHT security technologies are discussed.

5.1 Emerging IoHT Security Technologies

Innovative security technologies are being formulated to address the escalating necessity for data protection and device integrity in IoHT. Blockchain has emerged as a pivotal element, facilitating immutable and decentralized ledgers that guarantee transparency and security in the transmission of patient data among devices and healthcare entities. Furthermore, the integration of AI and machine learning enables sophisticated algorithms to scrutinize extensive data flows, identifying anomalies, anticipating security breaches, and adapting defenses in real time, thus fortifying IoHT systems against sophisticated cyber threats. Furthermore, zero-trust models are being embraced throughout healthcare IoT networks. In contrast to conventional security methodologies that presume trust within a network perimeter, zero trust mandates continuous verification of each user and device attempting to access resources. Collectively, these technologies constitute a holistic security infrastructure that addresses the diverse challenges observed by IoHT systems. In the subsections, these issues are elaborated.

5.1.1 Blockchain for Secure Data Sharing

Blockchain technology ensures huge scope for security enhancement in IoHT due to its very principal idea of logging and decentralized data accounting. In healthcare, this ensures that highly sensitive medical information is safely shared by the subject to doctors, hospitals, and patients without any scope for interference or unauthorized access. The cryptographic attributes of blockchain ensure data integrity, as once recorded, the information can neither be changed nor erased [36]. This may further facilitate transparency in all transactions. Thus, any dependency on a centralized authority can be minimal, and other vulnerabilities related to cyberattacks can also be minimized in order to create trust in data sharing. Access controls can be mechanized and compulsively enforced with smart contracts; therefore, the process is further secured. In general, this Blockchain guarantees a promising solution toward safeguarding health information in the exponentially increasing connected IoHT ecosystem [37].

5.1.2 AI and Machine Learning in Threat Detection

In security related to IoHT, AI and ML algorithms identify huge volumes of data with a view to checking for real-time anomaly detection and threat incident hints. These intelligent systems would thereby trace the unusual pattern in network behavior, device activities, or even flows of data that indicate unauthorized access or malicious attacks. AI-powered threat detection systems learn from continually improving their predictions against emerging cyber threats and even sophisticated ones that change with time. This, in turn, allows quick and automated detection of threats and thus the ability to respond quicker than when using manual procedures, limiting the potential damage at hand. Such approaches ensure security and integrity at both IoHT devices and networks. This corresponds to the fact that AI-powered security solutions will become crucial with increasingly sophisticated cyberattacks on healthcare infrastructures to protect sensitive medical data and connected devices [38, 39].

5.1.3 End-to-End Encryption and Zero Trust Models

E2EE and Zero Trust are two major components when it comes to IoHT for data and device security. E2EE makes sure sensitive healthcare data are encrypted right at the generation point to when it reaches the intended recipient while preventing any interception or unauthorized access in the process of transmission. Only the authorized parties would be able to decrypt such data, hence making it highly secure. Complementary to this, the Zero Trust model assumes that no user, whether inside or outside the network, is to be taken inherently as trusted; there needs to be continuous verification of devices and users and their levels of access at every stage. This means that any layer within this model is strictly verified and validated; if there is any breach of any layer, all further access to sensitive data or devices will be invalidated without the same kind of continuous validation. Each forms a strong foundation for IoHT ecosystem security against cyber threats [40].

5.2 Regulatory Trends and Security Frameworks

As the IoHT evolves, ensuring robust data security and privacy has emerged as a concern for governmental entities and regulatory agencies, and healthcare institutions on a global scale. The international regulatory framework governing IoHT is fluid, with diverse regions instituting comprehensive data protection statutes and regulations aimed at establishing rigorous benchmarks for the management of patient information. These legal stipulations necessitate that healthcare practitioners and IoHT developers conform to elevated standards of data governance, thereby preempting unauthorized access, data breaches, and the inappropriate handling of sensitive information. Adherence to such regulatory requirements not only cultivates trust among patients but also shields healthcare providers from prospective legal liabilities and reputational damage. In conjunction with these regulations, there exist established security frameworks that delineate best practices for the security of IoHT. These frameworks underscore the significance of risk management, ongoing surveillance, and prompt incident response, thereby enabling organizations to construct secure infrastructures that maintain data integrity, confidentiality, and availability. The implementation of these security protocols is crucial for alleviating risks and protecting IoHT systems within an increasingly intricate and interconnected healthcare landscape.

5.2.1 Global Regulatory Landscape for IoHT

It is worth noting that the IoHT regulatory landscape at a global level is dynamic; it keeps on evolving whereby governments and bodies of regulation are yet working toward securing healthcare data security and privacy. To such an end, a number of countries around the world have implemented various regulations concerning IoHT—for instance, the GDPR in Europe, and the HIPAA in the United States—which do involve strict requirements for protecting the information of patients. These regulations are intended to make health professionals and IoHT developers maintain high standards of data protection, without unauthorized access to personal information, data breaches, or improper handling of sensitive health data. The need to observe such laws arises because the compliance that comes with them engenders trust in patients and can keep the facilities and caregivers away from legal penalties. Consequently, as IoHT grows day in and day out, this renders understanding the regulations crucial for the security and responsible use of connected health devices and systems in the various global markets [41].

5.2.2 Security Frameworks and Best Practices (NIST, ISO)

The security frameworks, such as NIST and ISO, ensure that steps are followed with best practices to provide security to the IoHT system. These sets of frameworks offer a holistic approach to IoHT security: risk management, incident response, and continuous monitoring. For instance, the vulnerability testing of information, protection of sensitive data, and quick response in case of a potential breach are provided by guidelines such as NIST's Cybersecurity Framework and ISO's 27001 standard. With such recommendations, health organizations and IoHT developers are well-placed in implementing adequate security infrastructures that secure patient information through observance of set regulations within the industry. These practices and measures, if implemented, would go a long way in ensuring that IoHT systems remain intact with integrity, confidentiality, and availability, hence reducing risks within an increasingly complex landscape of connected healthcare technology [42].

5.3 Collaboration between IoT and Healthcare Stakeholders

Collaboration between IoT and healthcare stakeholders is essential to harness the full potential of connected technologies. This collaboration involves close partnerships among technology developers, healthcare providers, regulatory authorities, and patients to ensure that IoT solutions align with clinical needs, safety standards, and data privacy requirements. Joint efforts facilitate the development of interoperable systems, secure data exchange protocols, and innovative applications tailored to medical settings. The subsections elaborate this discussion.

5.3.1 Public–Private Partnerships for Securing IoHT

In developing IoHT systems' security, much-needed collaboration among governments, healthcare providers, and private businesses has to be carried out with the help of public–private partnerships. Such partnerships allow for resource hoarding, expertise, and innovation to devise comprehensive security strategies that can tackle evolving complexities in IoHT devices and network protection. Government agencies provide regulatory guidance and funding, while private companies bring into play advanced technologies and cybersecurity expertise. Healthcare providers contribute a wide variety of real-world challenges and needs in the medical environment. Each of these stakeholders working together on such initiatives as developing secure IoHT standards, sharing threat intelligence, and promoting research into advanced security solutions will be effective in yielding results [43]. Therefore, it would be proper to deduce that in public–private collaboration, consideration of the security infrastructures would be resilient and efficient enough to provide protection for IoHT systems against cyber threats that keep evolving.

5.3.2 Role of Government and Healthcare Providers

Government agencies provide the regulatory guidance and funding, while private companies bring into play advanced technologies and cybersecurity expertise. The healthcare providers contribute a wide variety of real-world challenges and needs in the medical environment. Each of these stakeholders working together on such initiatives as developing secure IoHT standards, sharing threat intelligence, and promoting research into advanced security solutions will be effective in yielding results. Therefore, it would be proper to deduce that in public–private collaboration, consideration of the security infrastructures would be resilient and efficient enough to provide protection for IoHT systems against cyber threats that keep evolving [44].

6. Future Challenges in Securing IoHT

Although IoHT promises significant advancements in healthcare through enhanced connectivity and data sharing among medical devices, patients, and providers, securing this ecosystem presents formidable challenges. As the adoption of IoHT devices increase, ensuring robust cybersecurity becomes important to protect sensitive patient data from breaches and unauthorized access. Additionally, the diversity of devices and their varying security protocols complicates the establishment of a unified security framework. The potential for device vulnerabilities to be exploited can lead to severe consequences, including compromised patient safety and trust in healthcare systems. Furthermore, regulatory compliance and the need for continuous monitoring and updates pose ongoing challenges for healthcare organizations in safeguarding IoHT infrastructures. Addressing these issues will be critical to fully realizing the benefits of IoHT while minimizing risks. The challenges in securing of IoHT are detailed in subsection.

6.1 *Increasing Complexity and Interconnectedness of Devices*

As the ecosystem of IoHT devices is rapidly growing—from wearable health monitors to smart medical implants and networked hospital systems—the security challenges are aplenty in themselves. Each added device opens a window of vulnerability that can be used by the attacker. The complexity arises because all these devices operate on different operating systems, use various communication protocols, and have different security capabilities. Interoperability with highly viable security measures is perhaps the most important task at hand [45]. Moreover, there are lots of data coming out of these connected devices; these, too, provide a big test in data management and protection to avoid unauthorized access and breaches.

6.2 *Balancing Innovation with Security in IoHT*

IoTs in healthcare are rapidly innovative in their ways of creating better outcomes for patients, enhancing healthcare delivery, and reducing overall costs. Such rapid innovation outpaces the development of security measures, as new devices and applications are being launched very frequently without proper security testing. It leaves hackers with many opportunities to exploit, as balancing such a drive for innovation with robust security is a great challenge. Healthcare providers and device manufacturers shall develop a philosophy of security-by-design, integrate security at the earliest stages of development, deliver periodic updates and patches, use secure communication protocols, and conduct thorough risk assessments that expose potential threats [46].

6.3 *Ethical and Privacy Issues with IoHT Adoption*

Therefore, in IoHT ethics and privacy issues may arise. Massive volumes of sensitive personal health data are being collected, stored, and analyzed, and may pose a serious privacy risk if not handled and managed appropriately. As the nature of the information handled is highly sensitive to health, the information of patients may always be vulnerable to breaches and unauthorized access for prospective misuse. The ethical issues that become debatable are related to informed consent, ownership of data, and the right to privacy. Informed consent about data usage and protection should be asked from the patients by taking them into confidence [47]. In addition, the challenge of ethics and privacy needs to evolve through regulatory frameworks so that benefits can be reaped from IoHT without losing patients' trust and confidentiality.

7. Best Practices for Preventing Data Breaches in IoHT

As the IoHT continues to transform healthcare through improved connectivity and data sharing, the importance of safeguarding sensitive patient information has never been greater. Data breaches in this ecosystem can have serious consequences, including compromised patient safety and loss of trust in healthcare providers. To mitigate these risks, implementing best practices for preventing data breaches is essential. This includes adopting robust security measures, promoting employee awareness, and ensuring regular updates and monitoring of connected devices. By prioritizing these practices, healthcare organizations can effectively protect patient data and enhance the overall security of the IoHT landscape.

7.1 Strengthening Device Security

Strengthening device security is a critical best practice for preventing data breaches in the IoHT. With the increasing number of connected medical devices, each presents a potential entry point for cyberattacks, making robust security measures essential. Implementing comprehensive security protocols, such as end-to-end encryption, regular software updates, and strong authentication mechanisms, can significantly reduce vulnerabilities and ensure that sensitive patient data remain protected. Moreover, conducting thorough risk assessments and penetration testing can help identify and address weaknesses before they are exploited, allowing organizations to proactively mitigate risks.

It is also important to establish a robust incident response plan that enables healthcare providers to respond swiftly to any security breaches, minimizing potential damage and restoring trust. Organizations should also promote a culture of security awareness among employees, providing training on recognizing phishing attempts and adhering to security best practices. Healthcare organizations can enhance their resilience against cyber threats by integrating security considerations into the entire lifecycle of IoHT devices. Furthermore, collaborating with manufacturers to ensure that devices are designed with security in mind will contribute to an overall safer IoHT ecosystem. By prioritizing device security, healthcare providers can safeguard patient information, maintain regulatory compliance, and foster trust in the rapidly evolving landscape of IoHT, ultimately leading to improved patient outcomes and greater confidence in digital health solutions. Some security best practices are discussed in subsections.

7.1.1 Secure Boot and Device Authentication

Secure boot and device authentication will be two important securities that will help protect the devices from most of the IoHT. Secure boot helps make sure that a device only executes firmware and software that has been verified and trusted by the manufacturer; it blocks malicious code from executing during boot. This will help block potential threats at the earliest stage of operation and safeguard the integrity of a device. On the other side, device authentication makes sure that only devices with proven identities have access to the network, in order not to allow unauthorized devices to access sensitive healthcare data and system resources [48]. Together, these are powerful technologies that create a robust layer of security, keeping unauthorized devices or compromised code from gaining entry to the network and protecting, if only by that fact, the whole IoHT ecosystem from possible cyberattacks.

7.1.2 Firmware and Software Updates

It is for this reason that the most critical security actions to be carried out on an ongoing basis with IoHT devices are firmware and software updates. These often provide corrections for newly discovered vulnerabilities in software and firmware, offering better protection. Since cyber threats are continually evolving, device manufacturers regularly provide updates to fix security gaps, improve functionality, and strengthen device defenses. These updates are going to be effective, with automation that minimizes the probability of human mistakes or tardiness and is verified to ensure their proper application without introducing new vulnerabilities. The process here involves cryptographic checks, which authenticate the source and integrity of an update to prevent tampered or malicious software from installing. Practically, with timely and secure updates, health providers can reduce significantly the risks of cyberattacks in IoT health [16].

7.2 *Protecting Data at Rest and in Transit*

In IoHT, protecting sensitive medical data both in transit and on storage is critical to ensuring patient privacy and security. Two key approaches in achieving this protection are effective data encryption techniques and robust cloud storage security measures. These are elaborated in subsections.

7.2.1 Data Encryption Techniques

Encryption of data in IoHT systems, either at rest or in motion, is very important in securing sensitive medical information from any unauthorized access or tampering. Data at rest may include data stored in the form of patient records in databases; it could be encrypted through techniques like AES that ensure strong protection through conversion into unreadable formats that can be decrypted with the right key. For this reason, TLS is widely applied for securing data in transit by creating an encrypted connection during the real-time communications of devices or servers without wiretapping or manipulation on the way [49]. These are a set of encryption techniques that set a barrier that makes it hard to break through cyber threats and ensure data privacy and integrity in IoHT ecosystems.

7.2.2 Securing Cloud Storage Systems

Sensitive data need to be secured from a breach of cloud storage against unauthorized access. Data to be stored on the cloud need to be strongly encrypted before their uploading in such a way that even in the event of a breach of storage, the data remain inaccessible without the correct decryption key. Strong access controls, including MFA and role-based permissions, provide an additional layer of security so that only the personnel who have been granted access can access such data, minimizing both internal and external breaches. Regular security audits and monitoring identify issues related to vulnerability and compliance with security protocols for continued protection [50]. Aggregately, encryption, access controls, and audits are comprehensive strategies to safeguard cloud-stored data.

7.3 *User Education and Training*

User education and training play an important role in preventing data breaches in IoHT by equipping healthcare personnel with the knowledge and skills needed to recognize and respond to security threats. Comprehensive training programs can raise awareness about common cyber risks, such as phishing attacks and weak password practices, emphasizing the importance of safeguarding sensitive patient information. By fostering a culture of security consciousness, users become vigilant against potential breaches and are more likely to adhere to established security protocols. Regular training updates ensure that staff stay informed about the latest threats and security measures, ultimately reducing the likelihood of human errors that could compromise IoHT systems. Thus, investing in user education is a fundamental strategy for enhancing the overall security posture of IoHT environments.

7.3.1 Raising Awareness among Healthcare Professionals

The education of health professionals on cybersecurity is, therefore, an important component in protecting patient data and should continue particularly when IoHT devices increase. Training on topics such as identifying phishing attacks as an avenue of entry for cybercriminals along with the use of strong and unique passwords to prevent unauthorized access to systems, among others, is critical. They also have to be very aware of the specific risks that IoHT devices face, which, if their security is not addressed, might easily be subjected to hacking. By creating a cybersecurity culture within an organization, it can reduce data breach incidents significantly [16].

7.3.2 Regular Security Audits and Penetration Testing

Security audits and penetration testing in maintaining security in IoHT systems should be routine in nature through the unmasking of hidden vulnerabilities an attacker may use. This would involve a deep review of the existing securities to see whether they are compliant with recent standards and best practices. It will simulate a cyberattack on computer systems, networks, or web applications to find weak points before malicious actors can use them [49]. The integration of all these practices will help keep the security features updated and reduce the chances of a data breach so that IoHT can remain resilient against emerging cybersecurity threats.

8. Conclusion

IoHT redesigned healthcare and can easily be connected with wearables, remote monitoring systems, and smart medical devices. This latest advancement, on the other hand, is giving a boost to different critical vulnerabilities in devices and networks, data transmission, and storage. All of these IoHT systems are susceptible to unauthorized access, ransomware attacks, and data theft among other critical cyber threats that might have serious repercussions for patient privacy and health institutions. In this regard, over the last couple of years, some of the new technologies to emerge for IoHT protection include blockchain and AI, along with refining regulatory frameworks such as HIPAA and GDPR against evolving threats. However, the security of IoHT is destined to be an upward struggle so long as these systems continue on their trajectory of increasing in complexity.

The fight against IoHT data breach is a multi-stakeholder approach wherein the healthcare organization, technology developers, and their respective regulatory bodies must work in collaboration. Considering IoHT is of a rapidly changing nature, there is a need for increased collaboration among all parties through the adoption of secure device design, robust encryption techniques, and deep incident response plans. Public–private partnerships shall be pivotal in developing global security standards and enforcing compliance that would prevent data breaches. This also implies considerable investment by the healthcare provider in continuous monitoring, training of staff, and security audits. Only when efforts are combined can the benefits of IoHT be materialized without losing privacy and security of healthcare data, thus enabling the road to safer and more efficient healthcare systems in the future.

References

[1] Natraj, N., S. Mitra and G. G. Hallur. 2023. An investigative study on internet of things in healthcare. In: *Handbook of Research on Machine Learning-Enabled IoT for Smart Applications Across Industries*, IGI Global, pp. 116–126.

[2] Ejiyi, C., Z. Qin, M. B. Ejiyi, G. U. Nneji, H. N. Monday, F. A. Agu, T. U. Ejiyi, C. Diokpo and C. O. Orakwue. 2023. The internet of medical things in healthcare management: A review. *Journal of Digital Health*, 30–62.

[3] Rana, A., C. Chakraborty, S. Sharma, S. Dhawan, S. K. Pani and I. Ashraf. 2022. Internet of medical things-based secure and energy-efficient framework for health care. *Big Data*, 10(1): 18–33.

[4] Kumaran, D., K. Prasad and K. Rohith. 2023. Internet of medical things (IoMT) for cardio-vascular disease. *International Journal for Research in Applied Science and Engineering Technology*, 11(5): 2651–2663.

[5] Jagannath, D. J., R. J. Dolly, G. S. Let and J. D. Peter. 2022. An IoT-enabled smart healthcare system using deep reinforcement learning. *Concurrency and Computation: Practice and Experience*, 34(28): e7403.

[6] Rajdhev, M. and D. S. David. 2017. Internet of things for health care. *International Journal of Scientific Research in Computer Science, Engineering and Information Technology (IJSRCSEIT), ISSN*, 2456–3307.

[7] Mehboob, R. 2023. Technology in advancing medical practice. *Pakistan BioMedical Journal*, 01–01.

[8] Haris, M. A. H. B., M. I. H. B. Yahya and M. N. B. Ibrahim. 2023. Security and privacy issues in internet of things (IoT). *Authorea Preprints*.

[9] Khatiwada, P. and B. Yang. 2022. An overview on security and privacy of data in iomt devices: Performance metrics, merits, demerits, and challenges. *pHealth*, 126–136.

[10] Di Martino, B., M. Rak, M. Ficco, A. Esposito, S. A. Maisto and S. Nacchia. 2018. Internet of things reference architectures, security and interoperability: A survey. *Internet of Things*, 1: 99–112.

[11] Lu, L., J. Zhang, Y. Xie, F. Gao, S. Xu, X. Wu and Z. Ye. 2020. Wearable health devices in health care: Narrative systematic review. *JMIR mHealth and uHealth*, 8(11): e18907.
[12] Islam, S. R., D. Kwak, M. H. Kabir, M. Hossain and K. -S. Kwak. 2015. The internet of things for health care: A comprehensive survey. *IEEE Access*, 3: 678–708.
[13] Jovanov, E., A. Milenkovic, C. Otto and P. C. De Groen. 2005. A wireless body area network of intelligent motion sensors for computer assisted physical rehabilitation. *Journal of NeuroEngineering and Rehabilitation*, 2: 1–10.
[14] Siwakoti, Y. R., M. Bhurtel, D. B. Rawat, A. Oest and R. Johnson. 2023. Advances in IoT security: Vulnerabilities, enabled criminal services, attacks, and countermeasures. *IEEE Internet of Things Journal*, 10(13): 11224–11239.
[15] Kandasamy, K., S. Srinivas, K. Achuthan and V. P. Rangan. 2020. IoT cyber risk: A holistic analysis of cyber risk assessment frameworks, risk vectors, and risk ranking process. *EURASIP Journal on Information Security*, 2020: 1–18.
[16] Stellios, I., P. Kotzanikolaou, M. Psarakis, C. Alcaraz and J. Lopez. 2018. A survey of IoT-enabled cyberattacks: Assessing attack paths to critical infrastructures and services. *IEEE Communications Surveys & Tutorials*, 20(4): 3453–3495.
[17] Czekster, R. M., P. Grace, C. Marcon, F. Hessel and S. C. Cazella. 2023. Challenges and opportunities for conducting dynamic risk assessments in medical IoT. *Applied Sciences*, 13(13): 7406.
[18] Kumar, A. and I. Sharma. 2023. Enhancing data privacy of IoT healthcare with keylogger attack mitigation. In: *2023 4th International Conference for Emerging Technology (INCET), IEEE*, pp. 1–6.
[19] Almulihi, A. H., F. Alassery, A. I. Khan, S. Shukla, B. K. Gupta and R. Kumar. 2022. Analyzing the implications of healthcare data breaches through computational technique. *Intelligent Automation & Soft Computing*, 32(3).
[20] Ganai, P. T., A. Bag, A. Sable, K. H. Abdullah, S. Bhatia and B. Pant. 2022. A detailed investigation of implementation of internet of things (IoT) in cyber security in healthcare sector. In: *2022 2nd International Conference on Advance Computing and Innovative Technologies in Engineering (ICACITE), IEEE*, pp. 1571–1575.
[21] Djenna, A. and D. E. Säidouni. 2018. Cyber attacks classification in IoT-based healthcare infrastructure. In: *2018 2nd Cyber Security in Networking Conference (CSNet), IEEE*, pp. 1–4.
[22] Subashini, S. and V. Kavitha. 2011. A survey on security issues in service delivery models of cloud computing. *Journal of Network and Computer Applications*, 34(1): 1–11.
[23] Al-Shareeda, M. and S. Manickam. 2022. Man-in-the-middle attacks in mobile ad hoc networks (MaNets): Analysis and evaluation. *Symmetry*, 14: 1543.
[24] Maglaras, L. and I. Kantzavelou. 2021. *Cybersecurity Issues in Emerging Technologies*. CRC Press.
[25] Yuryna Connolly, L., D. S. Wall, M. Lang and B. Oddson. 2020. An empirical study of ransomware attacks on organizations: an assessment of severity and salient factors affecting vulnerability. *Journal of Cybersecurity*, 6(1): tyaa023.
[26] Srinivasan, K., A. Mubarakali, A. S. Alqahtani and A. Dinesh Kumar. 2020. A survey on the impact of DDoS attacks in cloud computing: prevention, detection and mitigation techniques. In: *Intelligent Communication Technologies and Virtual Mobile Networks: ICICV 2019, Springer*, pp. 252–270.
[27] Young, K. 2021. Cyber case study: Anthem data breach, CoverLink InsuranceCase Study, Cyber Liability Insurance (September 2021). URL https://coverlink.com/case-study/anthem-data-breach/.
[28] Kost, E. 2022. 10 biggest healthcare data breaches (updated for February 2022), UpGuardAccessed: Oct. 03, 2024 (August 2022). URL https:// www.upguard.com/blog/ biggest-data-breaches-in-healthcare.

[29] Vallabhaneni, R. 2024. Effects of data breaches on internet of things (IoT) devices within the proliferation of daily-life integrated devices. *Engineering and Technology Journal*, 09(07). doi:10.47191/etj/v9i07.13.

[30] ISACA. 2022. Addressing security risks to medical iot devices, accessed: Oct. 03, 2024. URL https://www.isaca.org/resources/news-and-trends/isaca-now-blog/2022/addressing-security-risks-to-medical-iot- devices.

[31] A comparative audit of privacy policies from healthcare organizations in USA, UK and India. Accessed: Oct. 03, 2024 (2023). doi:10.48550/ arxiv.2306.11557.

[32] Vojković, G., M. Milenković and T. Katulić, 2020. IoT and smart home data breach risks from the perspective of data protection and information security law. *Business Systems Research*. doi:10.2478/BSRJ- 2020-0033.

[33] Balde, G., A. Singh, N. Ganguly and M. Mondal. 2023. A comparative audit of privacy policies from healthcare organizations in USA, UK and India. *arXiv preprint arXiv:2306.11557*.

[34] HIPAA Journal. HIPAA violation fines, accessed: Oct. 03, 2024. URL https:// www.hipaajournal.com/hipaa-violation-fines/.

[35] Watson, R. M. 2022. Healthcare data breach statistics. HIPAA Journal. Accessed: Oct. 03, 2024. URL https://www.hipaajournal.com/healthcare-data-breach-statistics/.

[36] Yang, W., C. Hou, Z. Zhang, X. Wang and S. Chen. 2024. Secure and efficient data sharing for IoT based on blockchain and reputation mechanism. *IEEE Internet of Things Journal*.

[37] IoT Business News, 2024. IoT evolution: Cybersecurity, AI, and emerging technologies transforming the industry, IoT Business News. Accessed: Oct. 03, 2024 (December 2023). URL https://iotbusinessnews.com/ 2023/12/21/63546-2024-iot-evolution-cybersecurity-ai-and-emerging-technologies-transforming-the-industry/.

[38] World Economic Forum, Is cybersecurity keeping pace with evolving IoT threats?, accessed: Oct. 03, 2024 (August 2021). URL https:// www.weforum.org/agenda/2021/08/threats-to-iot-devices-are-constantly-evolving-but-is-security-keeping- up/.

[39] Salem, A. H., S. M. Azzam, O. Emam and A. A. Abohany. 2024. Advancing cybersecurity: A comprehensive review of AI-driven detection techniques. *Journal of Big Data*, 11(1): 105.

[40] Bast, C. and K. -H. Yeh. 2024. Emerging authentication technologies for zero trust on the internet of things. *Symmetry*, 16(8): 993.

[41] Secureframe, 15 regulatory and security compliance frameworks to secure your business, accessed: Oct. 03, 2024 (2024). URL https:// secureframe.com/hub/grc/compliance-frameworks.

[42] Bonnie, E. Jan. 2024. Essential guide to security frameworks & 14 examples, Secureframe. Accessed: Oct. 03, 2024. URL https:// secureframe.com/blog/security-frameworks.

[43] Robert, N. 2021. The promise and perils of health internet of things (HIoT). *OJIN: The Online Journal of Issues in Nursing*, 26(3).

[44] i-SCOOP. 2024. The future of healthcare facilities: collaboration and facility intelligence, accessed: Oct. 03, 2024. URL https://www.i-scoop.eu/internet-of-things-iot/facility-management-iot-smart-buildings/ collaboration- iot-ai-the-future-healthcare-facilities/.

[45] Thales, IoT security issues in 2021: A business perspective, accessed: Oct. 03, 2024 (February 2022). URL https://www.thalesgroup.com/ en/markets/digital-identity-and-security/iot/magazine/internet-threats.

[46] Mamdouh, M., A. I. Awad, H. F. Hamed and A. A. Khalaf. 2020. Outlook on security and privacy in IoHT: Key challenges and future vision. In: *Proceedings of the International Conference on Artificial Intelligence and Computer Vision (AICV2020)*, Springer, 2020, pp. 721–730.

[47] Kumar, M., A. Kumar, S. Verma, P. Bhattacharya, D. Ghimire, S. -h. Kim and A. S. Hosen. 2023. Healthcare internet of things (HIoT): Current trends, future prospects, applications, challenges, and security issues. *Electronics*, 12(9): 2050.
[48] Fortinet. 2023. IoT security best practices? How to protect IoT devices, accessed: Oct. 03, 2024. URL https://www.fortinet.com/resources/ cyberglossary/iot-best-practices.
[49] Seletskiy, I. Aug. 2024. Council post: Best practices for protecting IoT devices from security threats, Forbes. Accessed: Sep. 19, 2024. URL https://www.forbes.com/councils/ forbestechcouncil/2020/10/22/best-practices-for-protecting-iot-devices-from- security-threats/.
[50] dig8ital, Securing IoT networks: Best practices for ensuring data protectoin accessed: Oct. 03, 2024 (March 2024). URL https://dig8ital.com/post/iot-network-security/.

Chapter 3

An Investigation of Vulnerabilities in Internet of Medical Things (IoMT) and Development of a Benchmark Dataset Using Smartwatch

*Kin Hei Look** and *Wai Kin Fung Ritz*

1. Introduction

1.1 Background

The integration of internet-connected medical devices, known as the Internet of Medical Things (IoMT), has transformed healthcare delivery. The increased adoption of IoMT in healthcare necessitates heightened awareness of cyberthreats. A Cynerio 2022 [1] report highlights the prevalence of ransomware attacks targeting IoMT devices, leading to financial losses and potentially even human lives.

As the healthcare sector relies more heavily on connected devices and services, IoMT security becomes paramount. Hospitals and clinics storing patient data in cloud servers are vulnerable to ransomware attacks. Furthermore, cybercriminals could potentially manipulate devices like thermometers or blood pressure monitors, leading to inaccurate readings.

School of Science, Edith Cowan University, Australia.
Email: kin26916934@gmail.com
* Corresponding author: kenexlookau@gmail.com

DOI: 10.1201/9781003483267-5

By addressing IoMT vulnerabilities, this project can empower the medical industry to become more cyber-resilient. Stakeholders will benefit from secure IoMT systems, protecting them from financial losses, data breaches, and service disruptions. Ultimately, robust IoMT security safeguards the user privacy, ensures reliable healthcare services, and potentially even saves lives.

1.2 Security Challenges

First, many IoMT devices were not designed with robust security in mind, leaving them susceptible to cyberattacks. Weak encryption, insecure communication protocols, and outdated software create vulnerabilities that attackers can exploit to steal sensitive patient data or disrupt critical healthcare services [2]. Second, limited cybersecurity awareness among healthcare professionals and patients can be a significant security risk. Phishing attacks, social engineering scams, and poor password hygiene practices can compromise security measures [3]. Furthermore, cybercriminals are constantly developing new attack vectors to target IoMT devices. This necessitates continuous vigilance and proactive measures to address emerging threats and vulnerabilities [4].

1.3 Common Vulnerabilities in IoMT Devices

The interconnected nature of the IoMT devices introduces a new set of security challenges [5]. These devices collect and transmit sensitive patient data, making them attractive targets for cyberattacks. Common vulnerabilities found in the device include weak encryption, insecure communication protocols, software vulnerabilities, poor password management, physical security issues, and supply chain attacks [2, 3, 5–7].

Weak encryption, for instance, allows attackers to intercept and decipher data transmitted between devices [5]. This can lead to breaches of patient confidentiality and even the manipulation of critical medical data. Insecure communication protocols, like unencrypted Bluetooth connections, can also be exploited by attackers to gain unauthorized access to devices or tamper with data transmissions [2].

(1) Unpatched software vulnerabilities in the devices create openings for attackers to inject malicious code, take control of devices, or disrupt their functionality [3].
(2) Weak or default passwords on the medical devices are another security risk, as they can be easily guessed or cracked, granting unauthorized access to sensitive data [6].
(3) Inadequate physical security measures can also leave on the devices vulnerable. If devices that lack of tamper detection mechanisms,

attackers may be able to gain physical access and steal data or implant malicious firmware [7].

(4) Vulnerabilities within the devices supply chain can also introduce risks. Malicious actors could introduce compromised components during manufacturing or exploit weaknesses in software updates [2].

These vulnerabilities can have serious consequences, including data breaches, disrupted healthcare services, and even the manipulation of medical treatment [5]. Data breaches can expose sensitive patient information, such as medical history, medication details, and vital signs. Cyberattacks can disrupt critical healthcare services, potentially delaying diagnoses and endangering patient lives. Infiltration of the devices could allow attackers to manipulate medication delivery or other treatment parameters, putting patients at risk. The security of IoMT devices is critical to ensure patient safety and privacy. By addressing these vulnerabilities, healthcare providers can help to mitigate the risks associated with cyberattacks.

1.4 Cybersecurity Threats to IoMT Devices

The interconnected nature of IoMT devices introduces a unique set of cybersecurity threats that can have serious consequences for patient safety and healthcare operations. Here's a breakdown of some prominent threats facing the IoMT devices:

Unauthorized Access: Hackers can exploit vulnerabilities in IoMT devices to gain unauthorized access and steal sensitive patient data like medical history, medication details, and vital signs. This stolen data can be used for identity theft, extortion, or even sold on the black market [3].

(1) **Data Breaches:** Weak encryption protocols or insecure communication channels can leave data transmissions vulnerable to interception. Hackers can intercept these data and gain access to confidential patient information [5].

(2) **Denial-of-Service (DoS) Attacks:** These attacks can overwhelm IoMT devices with traffic, rendering them unavailable to healthcare providers. This can disrupt critical healthcare services and delay treatment for patients [2].

(3) **Ransomware Attacks:** Malicious actors can deploy ransomware to lock healthcare providers out of their IoMT devices and demand a ransom payment to regain access. This can significantly disrupt operations and delay critical treatments [7].

(4) **Man-in-the-Middle (MitM) Attacks:** Cybercriminals can intercept communication between IoMT devices and other devices or systems,

allowing them to eavesdrop on data transmissions or even manipulate data in transit [8].

(5) **Firmware Attacks:** Hackers can target the firmware of IoMT devices, potentially taking complete control of the device and altering its functionality. This could have devastating consequences, especially for devices like pacemakers or insulin pumps [6].

(6) **Supply Chain Attacks:** Vulnerabilities within the IoMT devices supply chain can create security risks. Malicious actors could introduce compromised components during manufacturing or exploit weaknesses in software updates [2].

(7) **Social Engineering Attacks:** Healthcare staff can be targeted by social engineering scams, tricking them into revealing sensitive information or clicking on malicious links that can compromise the IoMT devices security [3].

1.5 Relevant Known Vulnerabilities

(1) Insecure Communication:

Vulnerability: Smartwatches often rely on Bluetooth Low Energy or Wi-Fi for communication. Weak encryption protocols or insecure pairing mechanisms could allow attackers to intercept data transmissions (e.g., eavesdropping on heart rate data).

CVE-2018-5389: This vulnerability, while not specific to smartwatches, affects Bluetooth implementations and could allow attackers to remotely intercept data transmitted via Bluetooth Low Energy (BLE) [9].

(2) Unsecured App Stores and Applications:

Vulnerability: Downloading apps from untrusted sources or app stores with lax security measures could expose smartwatches to malware or malicious code. This code could steal user data, manipulate watch functions, or even launch attacks against connected smartphones.

CVE-2019-8564: This vulnerability affects an Android library used by many apps and could allow attackers to bypass security restrictions and gain unauthorized access to sensitive data or functionalities [10].

(3) Weak Authentication Mechanisms:

Vulnerability: Smartwatches often rely on PINs or simple passwords for user authentication. Weak credentials or lack of multi-factor authentication could allow unauthorized access to sensitive data like health information or payment details.

CVE-2020-7293: This vulnerability affects a fingerprint sensor library used in various devices and could allow attackers to bypass fingerprint authentication [11].

(4) Insecure Data Storage:

Vulnerability: Sensitive data collected by smartwatches, like health information or GPS location, might be stored on the device itself or transmitted to the cloud. Weak encryption or insecure storage practices could expose these data to unauthorized access or breaches.

CVE-2022-3007: This vulnerability allows attackers exploit target, perform OTA updates, reboot system, and manipulate data [39].

1.6 Dataset Comparison

Dataset	Year	Protocol	Network Intrusion Detection Evaluation	Healthcare	IOT	Smartphone	Smartwatch
DARPA [27]	1998	Network	yes	no	no	no	no
NSL-KDD [28]	1999	Network	yes	no	no	no	no
KDDCup99 [29]	1999	Network	yes	no	no	no	no
Kyoto [30]	2008	Network	yes	no	no	no	no
Wustl-EHMS [31]	2020	Network	yes	yes	no	no	no
UNSW-NB15 [32]	2015	Network	yes	no	no	no	no
Bot-IoT [33]	2019	Network	yes	no	yes	no	no
ISCXIDS2012 [34]	2012	Network	yes	no	no	no	no
ECU-IoHT [35]	2021	Network	yes	yes	yes	no	no
BlueTack [36]	2022	Bluetooth	yes	yes	yes	no	no
CCICIoMT [37]	2024	Bluetooth & Network	yes	yes	yes	no	no
BLE-WBAN [38]	2024	Bluetooth	yes	yes	yes	yes	no
BLE-KSW	2024	Bluetooth	yes	yes	yes	yes	yes

Related dataset:

DARPA 1998

The DARPA 1998 dataset is widely used for benchmarking and evaluating the performance of intrusion detection machine learning models. It primarily focuses on network data, providing a foundational dataset for the development and testing of IDS [27].

KDDCup99

KDDCup99, originated in 1999 by MIT Lincoln Labs [28], provided a benchmark dataset for network intrusion detection systems (IDS) in the context of data mining. This dataset offered a structured review of intrusion detection models, setting a standard for subsequent research in the field.

NSL-KDD

The NSL-KDD dataset was developed to address some of the inherent issues found in the original KDD'99 dataset. It aims to provide a more reliable benchmark for evaluating network intrusion detection systems (IDS). Unlike its predecessor, NSL-KDD eliminates redundant records, which helps prevent classifiers from being biased toward more frequent records. This improvement ensures that the evaluation results of different research works are consistent and comparable [29].

Kyoto Dataset

The Kyoto University Benchmark Data [30] is a specialized dataset created to enhance the evaluation of intrusion detection systems. Developed by researchers at Kyoto University, it includes 24 statistical features derived from network traffic data captured by honeypot systems. These features are divided into 14 conventional features, based on the widely used KDD Cup 99 dataset, and 10 additional features that provide deeper insights into network activities. This dataset captures various aspects of network connections, such as duration, service type, and error rates, as well as specific indicators of malicious activities like IDS alerts and malware detection. It serves as a comprehensive resource for researchers aiming to develop and test sophisticated network security solutions.

Wustl-EHMS

Hady et al. [31] conducted a study using a machine learning model for intrusion detection systems (IDS) targeting injection attacks in healthcare

IoMT. The results indicated poor performance of the models, with high error rates, highlighting the challenges in detecting such sophisticated attacks in healthcare environments.

UNSW-NB15

Moustafa & Slay [32] developed the UNSW-NB15 dataset to address the limitations of outdated datasets like KDD98, KDDCup99, and NSLKDD. This new benchmark dataset focuses on network intrusion attacks, providing a more contemporary and comprehensive resource for evaluating IDS.

Bot-IoT

The Bot-IoT dataset, also developed by Moustafa & Slay in UNSW Canberra [33], is a valuable resource for researchers focusing on network security and IoT. It simulates a realistic network environment with a mix of normal and malicious traffic, including various attack types such as DDoS, DoS, and data exfiltration.

ISCXIDS2012

The ISCXIDS2012 dataset is a valuable resource developed by the team of Shiravi et al. [34] at the University of New Brunswick. It provides seven days of network traffic data, including both normal and malicious activities across various protocols like HTTP, SMTP, and FTP. This dataset is designed to simulate real-world network conditions, featuring a range of attack scenarios such as DoS and brute force attacks, making it an essential tool for researchers developing and testing intrusion detection systems.

ECU-IoHT

Ahmed et al. [35] highlighted the development of a cybersecurity dataset specifically for the healthcare field. This dataset was created from network-based attacks targeting a real-life healthcare device called My-Signal. After the dataset was developed, anomaly detection techniques were applied to identify irregularities and potential threats within the data.

BlueTack

Zubair et al. [36] introduced the BlueTack dataset, which provides valuable insights into the Bluetooth protocol and its applications in the healthcare sector. The dataset was generated by launching cyberattacks on multiple healthcare devices. Machine learning analysis was then used to evaluate the dataset, offering a comprehensive understanding of Bluetooth security in healthcare environments.

CCICIoMT

Dadkhah et al. [37] presented datasets for multi-protocol environments, establishing a robust benchmark for both network and Bluetooth protocols. These datasets were generated from various healthcare devices subjected to different types of cyberattacks. The results were evaluated using common machine learning algorithms, demonstrating the effectiveness of these datasets in benchmarking security measures.

BLE-WBAN

The Bluetooth Low Energy (BLE) RF Dataset for Machine Learning in WBANs by Kashani et al. [38] is a comprehensive dataset designed to facilitate research in Wireless Body Area Networks (WBANs). It includes 100 MSps radio signal recordings from 13 ESP32 IoT nodes, captured in both on-body and off-body settings within an anechoic chamber. The dataset covers the entire 2.4 GHz ISM band and provides high-resolution raw In-phase (I) and Quadrature (Q) components. It features data recorded at different transmission power levels (9 dBm and 3 dBm) and includes nanosecond-order synchronization across nodes. Additionally, the dataset is accompanied by a Python tool for processing and analyzing the data, making it valuable for developing machine learning models for authentication, localization, and other WBAN-specific applications.

BLE-KSW

Our developed BLE-KSW dataset will provide insight from Bluetooth data link layer dataset generated from real-life example, smartwatch and a smartphone. The research papers in healthcare domain were focused only on the healthcare devices. However, nowadays smartphones are part of the ecosystem. This paper will consider smartphone in the ecosystem and provide a benchmark dataset with detection machine learning results.

2. Research Dataset Development on Smartwatch Ecosystem

2.1 *Research Environment*

The computing environment used for developing the IOMT dataset constituted a Windows 10 and Kali Linux instance, a mobile Wi-Fi hotspot, a nrf52480 BLE USB dongle.

Attacking terminal local environment is a Mac OSX MacBook with a USB Bluetooth dongle and Kali Linux instance. There was also an AWS kali cloud terminal being setup.

The Samsung Galaxy A20 smartphone and Kmart smartwatch were selected to create the IOMT test bed. The Kmart smartwatch provides health data such as heart rate, sleep data, walking steps, etc. The smartwatch connects to a Gloryfit app installed in the Samsung phone. The data were transmitted to the phone by Bluetooth only. The device and data are compatible with iPhone and Android applications.

2.2 *Test Bed Setup with Smartwatch*

The Kmart smartwatch was Bluetooth connected to the smartphone A20 and was also connected to a Wi-Fi hotspot. The Bluetooth data transferring between the smartwatch and smartphone was sniffing via Wireshark with an nfr52480 dongle. A local attacking laptop (MacBook) was using a Bluetooth dongle attempting to attack the smartwatch and the smartphone. The AWS kali cloud attacking terminal was used attempting to launch attack toward the smartphone from backdoor.

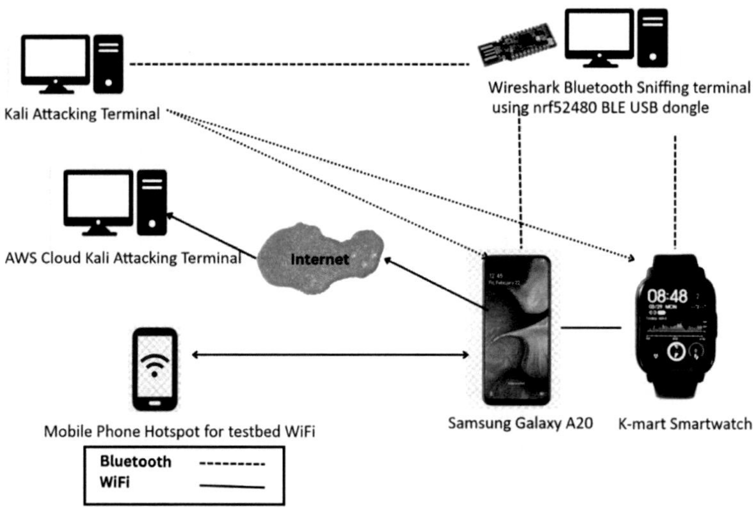

Figure 1: Test bed diagram.

2.3 *Cyberattacks Launched toward Smartwatch Ecosystem*

In the process of the penetration testing, we tried to perform the smurfing attack (DDOS), Bettercap attack, and Keystroke Injection attack.

In these three attacks, we found the below actual vulnerabilities and potential vulnerabilities in our testing.

2.4 *Actual Vulnerabilities Found*

The team found out a vulnerability CVE-2023-45866 [26] in the Keystroke Injection attack, where the attacker's terminal could impersonate a human interface device, such as a wireless keyboard, through a Bluetooth connection. The team implemented the "Blue Ducky" tool in the testing [12]. One significant advantage is its capability for genuine automation. By modifying the script, it can be set up to autonomously identify devices and attempt exploitation, systematically recording the outcomes of each attempt. Therefore, the team can be controlled by the phone remotely that we can download, execute instruction, or make a phone call remotely. Also, we preformed the DDOS attack against the phone and smartwatch. We succeeded in performing the DDOS attack against the devices. Although we can't stop the operation of the devices, we can make the device slowdown 1 to 2 seconds.

Finally, we performed the Bettercap attack [13] against the devices. We acquired the UUID service code from the device which can perform the attack based on the UUID services. However, the UUID decoding did not bring any related results.

Result of the attacking of the smartphone:

The paring time between smartphone and the smartwatch is expected to be delayed 0.5 second compared to normal state. Syncing data between smartphone and smartwatch are also delayed 0.5 second compared to normal state. Due to limited resources, we cannot test with multiple attacking terminals to launch large-scale DDOS attack together at the same time. But it is expected to delay the paring time and syncing time will increase in relation to the attacking terminals increases and launching attack at the same time.

Result of the attacking of the smartwatch itself:

Overall, it is not feasible to launch the DDOS attack only on the smartwatch. DDOS attack is only able to connect the smartwatch when it is not connected to the smartphone (i.e., Bluetooth of the smartphone is off). However, the security level of the BLE standard is high, the watch will disconnect itself when it receives multiple packet transmissions. Besides, when the smartwatch is connected to the smartphone, the smartwatch is only connected to one device. On the attack terminal will be showing "host is down" which is not reachable and launch attack.

2.5 *Dataset Development*

Data Exportation

In the research experiment, an extensive data collection process was conducted to capture Bluetooth traffic under both normal and attack conditions. This phase, termed "Data Exportation," was meticulously executed over an 8-minute time interval, during which Bluetooth communication activities were monitored and recorded using Wireshark, a widely used network protocol analyzer.

The data collection strategy was structured to encompass two primary scenarios: normal Bluetooth traffic and instances of potential attacks. Under normal conditions, the aim was to capture routine interactions between Bluetooth-enabled devices, including typical pairing, data exchange, and device discovery processes. This served as a baseline for understanding the standard behavior of devices within the Bluetooth network. In parallel, the research experiment also sought to simulate and capture instances of potential security threats or attacks. Three specific types of attacks were targeted: Keystroke Injection, Bettercap sniffing, and L2ping Request. These attack scenarios were selected based on their relevance and potential impact on Bluetooth-enabled devices. Keystroke Injection involves injecting malicious keystrokes into the Bluetooth communication stream, potentially leading to unauthorized access or control over devices. Bettercap sniffing is a versatile network attack tool used for network monitoring, spoofing, and other malicious activities, posing a significant threat to Bluetooth security. L2ping Request involves sending flooding of Echo Request packets to devices within the Bluetooth network, potentially leading to network disruptions or security breaches.

By recording Bluetooth traffic during both normal and attack conditions, the research experiment aimed to gather comprehensive data that could be analyzed to discern patterns, anomalies, and vulnerabilities within the Bluetooth network. This rich dataset serves as the foundation for subsequent phases of the research, enabling in-depth analysis, evaluation of security protocols, and the development of effective countermeasures to mitigate potential risks and safeguard Bluetooth-enabled devices against security threats. Through meticulous data exportation and capture using Wireshark, the research experiment lays the groundwork for valuable insights and advancements in the realm of Bluetooth security research and cybersecurity.

2.6 Data Collection

In the research experiment, a meticulous data collection phase, termed "Data Collection," was conducted to gather Bluetooth traffic data under various conditions, including normal operation and potential attack scenarios. This phase involved capturing and selecting specific features from the Bluetooth traffic data using Wireshark, a robust network protocol analyzer. The chosen features, meticulously curated for their variability and significance, were intended to provide insights into the behavior of Bluetooth-enabled devices and the potential presence of security threats.

The selection of features was guided by the objective of capturing diverse aspects of Bluetooth communication, allowing for comprehensive analysis and identification of patterns. Among the selected features were Source and Destination addresses, Protocol type, Packet Length, Packet Header, PDU (Protocol Data Unit) Type, CRC (Cyclic Redundancy Check), Length of payload, Advertising Header Length, and Packet time (start to end). Each of these features offers unique insights into the characteristics and attributes of the captured Bluetooth packets.

- **Source and Destination Addresses:** These fields indicate the source and destination devices involved in the Bluetooth communication, providing essential context for understanding the origin and destination of data packets.
- **Protocol Type:** This feature specifies the protocol used for the communication, such as Bluetooth Low Energy (BLE), Bluetooth Classic, or other relevant protocols, facilitating protocol-specific analysis.
- **Packet Length:** The length of the packet in bytes provides information about the size of the data being transmitted, which can vary depending on the type of communication and payload content.
- **Packet Header:** The packet header contains metadata and control information about the packet, including sequence numbers, acknowledgment flags, and other protocol specific details.
- **PDU Type:** The PDU Type field identifies the type of Protocol Data Unit being transmitted, such as an advertising packet, data packet, or control packet, allowing for classification and analysis of different types of Bluetooth traffic.
- **CRC (Cyclic Redundancy Check):** This field contains error-checking information used to detect errors in the transmitted data and ensure data integrity during transmission.
- **Length of Payload:** The length of the payload indicates the size of the actual data payload within the packet, excluding header and control information.
- **Advertising Header Length:** For advertising packets, this field specifies the length of the advertising header, which contains information about the advertising device and its capabilities.
- **Packet Time (Start to End):** This feature records the duration of time taken for the packet transmission, providing insights into the timing and duration of Bluetooth communication events.

In addition to selecting these features, the data collection process encompassed the recording of Bluetooth traffic under both normal conditions and specific attack scenarios. Malicious Bluetooth traffic was simulated through Keystroke Injection Attack, Bettercap sniffing Attack, and Ping Request, while normal traffic was captured during periods of regular operation without any active attacks. This comprehensive approach enabled the acquisition of a diverse dataset encompassing various forms of Bluetooth communication, facilitating in-depth analysis and identification of anomalous behavior associated with security threats.

Overall, the Data Collection phase was instrumental in gathering high-quality Bluetooth traffic data, encompassing a wide range of features and scenarios, to support subsequent analysis and evaluation of Bluetooth security protocols and countermeasures.

2.7 *Dataset Development*

The dataset features Table 1 is showing result of the data collection process in the flow of cumulative statistics. Different features of the dataset are provided, such as Source MAC address, destination MAC address, protocol, packet length, packet header, PDU type, CRC, length of payload, Advertising Header Length, packet time (start to end), info, and counts of unique MAC address. Packets Link layer of the Bluetooth protocol is captured in the whole process of Bluetooth sniffing process. We go through in packet frame in Wireshark and selected the components in the packet. Referring to the Bluetooth LE packet structure, the most important data are in the PDU, packet header, PDU type and length are representing the whole PDU. Selected features will be shown into columns in Wireshark, and then we exported the data into CSV. After that, we differentiated the data traffic in relation to specific time intervals that refer to normal interval and another 3 types of attacking activities intervals using Microsoft Excel to add two more columns: "Type" and "Type of Attack"

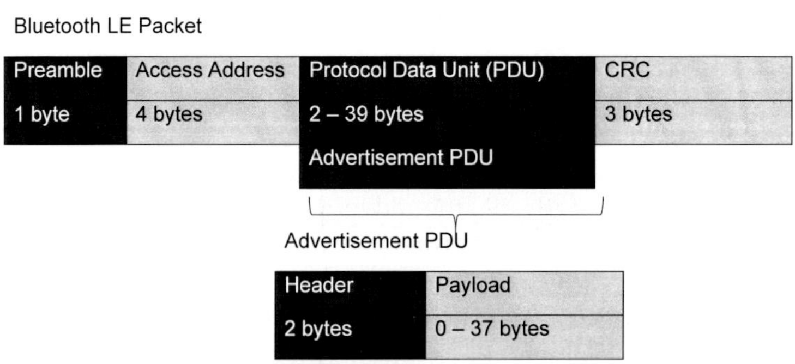

Figure 2: Bluetooth LE Packet structure [25].

to the dataset. This is the final output of the dataset that is used in later machine learning process. Figures 3 and 4 will give you a visualized view in the dataset related to the distribution of the attacking activities and normal activities.

Table 1: Dataset features.

Feature Types	**Feature Count (in 8 mins)**
Source MAC Address	104,638
Destination MAC Address	104,638
Protocol - LE LL	105,136
Protocol - BT Mesh	14
Protocol - BT Mesh PB-ADV	9
Protocol - BT Mesh Beacon	2
Packet Length	105,161
Packet Header	105,161
PDU Type	105,161
CRC	103,175
Length of payload	105,161
Advertising Header Length	105,161
Packet time (start to end)	105,161
Info - ADV_NONCONN_IND	54,423
Info - ADV_IND	29,933
Info - ADV_SCAN_IND	7,443
Info - SCAN_REQ	4,985
Info - Malformed Packet	4,953
Info - SCAN_RSP	2,803
Info - Unknown	458
Info - ADV_DIRECT_IND	139
Info - CONNECT_IND	10
Info - Others	9
Type of Attack - No_attack	86,965
Type of Attack - Keystroke_injection	10,200
Type of Attack - bettercap_sniffing	4,490
Type of Attack - DDOS_l2ping	3,506
Unique Source MAC Address	4,357
Unique Destination MAC Address	358

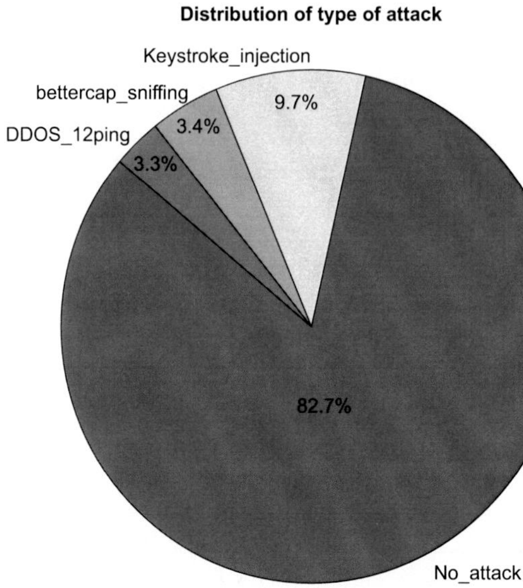

Figure 3: Distribution of types of attacks.

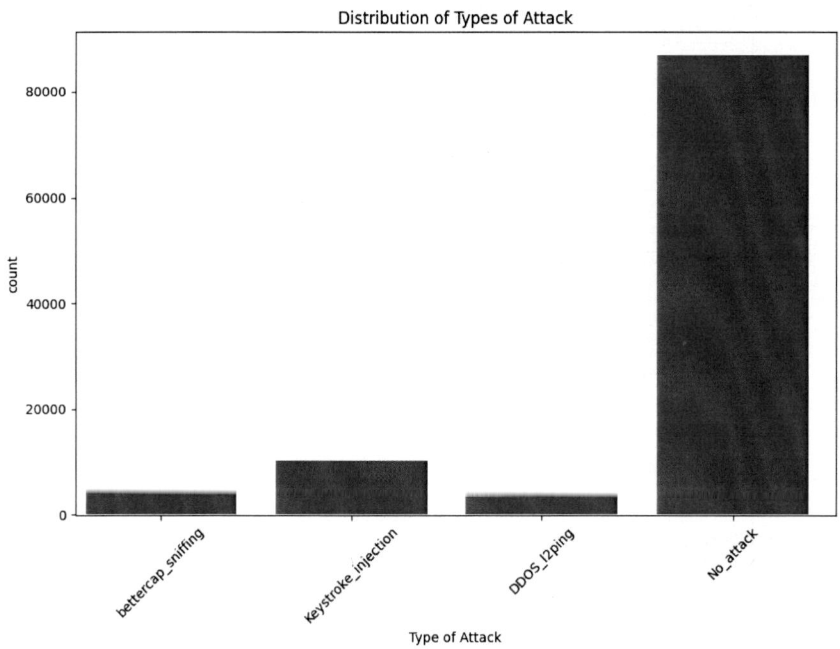

Figure 4: Distribution of types of attacks.

3. Abnormality Detection on the Dataset

3.1 Machine Learning Algorithm Selection

The selected machine learning algorithm combines supervised and unsupervised approaches. It was chosen to evaluate the quality of the dataset serving as the research's benchmark, which aligns with its primary goal. Not only does this test validate the quality of the benchmark, but it also demonstrates what algorithm performs best in identifying vulnerabilities in Bluetooth IoMT supervised learning.

- **Logistic Regression** is excellent for analyzing Bluetooth data with linear relationships between features and outcomes. As a supervised learning method, it effectively manages binary and multiclass classification tasks, helping identify legitimate or malicious connections. Its interpretability and efficiency allow for swift analysis of Bluetooth data while offering insights into feature importance [14].
- **Random Forest** provides high predictive performance in supervised classification and regression tasks by leveraging multiple decision trees. For analyzing Bluetooth traffic, its robust ensemble learning accurately classifies packets and identifies malicious activity, offering adaptability and high-quality results even in the presence of noisy data [15].
- **K-Nearest Neighbors (KNN)**, a supervised learning method, compares unknown signals to known patterns for both classification and regression tasks. It can quickly identify known attack patterns or normal traffic behaviors through the majority voting of neighbors, making it suitable for distinguishing Bluetooth traffic [16].
- **AdaBoost with Decision Trees** is effective for enhancing the performance of decision trees in classification tasks by focusing sequentially on difficult instances. By adjusting parameters like the number of estimators and learning rate, it effectively boosts weak learners, making them suitable for complex datasets where simple models fail to perform adequately [17].
- **Naive Bayes classifier,** a probabilistic model based on Bayes' theorem, performs well despite its independence assumptions. It classifies Bluetooth signals rapidly, distinguishing normal from malicious patterns while providing probabilistic outputs that quantify classification certainty [18, 19].
- **Isolation Forest,** an unsupervised anomaly detection algorithm, is proficient at isolating outliers by recursively partitioning the data.

This makes it ideal for finding anomalies in Bluetooth traffic patterns and detecting compromised devices due to unexpected network behavior [20].

- **DBSCAN** (Density-Based Spatial Clustering of Applications with Noise) can detect clusters within Bluetooth traffic data without requiring a predefined number of clusters. It is particularly effective in grouping devices, identifying dense patterns, and recognizing sparse anomalous connections, making it suitable for detecting security issues in Bluetooth networks [21].
- **Local Outlier Factor** (LOF) compares the local density of each point with its neighbors. This unsupervised anomaly detection method excels in detecting subtle anomalies in Bluetooth traffic, like compromised devices or unusual patterns, by evaluating density differences that would be missed with traditional clustering [22].
- **RPCA (Robust Principal Component Analysis)** reduces dimensionality and detects anomalies by separating data into low-rank and sparse components. RPCA isolates noise and redundant features from Bluetooth traffic, enhancing the ability to identify irregular patterns efficiently [23].
- **K-Means** clustering is effective for segmenting Bluetooth devices based on their communication patterns. Despite sensitivity to initialization, its simplicity and speed help categorize different communication patterns and devices, making it suitable for traffic analysis [24]. These algorithms, each with their unique capabilities, offer effective solutions for recognizing, classifying, and understanding various aspects of Bluetooth traffic behavior.

3.2 Benchmark Dataset Evaluation Criteria

We are using a dataset comprising of 100,000 of rows and 11 distinct features. We selected the features, based on Gini Impurity Score. And found that "Source" and "Destination" features have a negligible impact to the dataset. We are using 80% for training and 20% for testing.

The research on machine learning and result evaluation aimed to assess all 10 machine learning algorithms based on specific parameters. This was done not only to determine which algorithm performs best but also to demonstrate the quality of the obtained data benchmark.

- Overall Accuracy
- Tuning Parameters and Their Result
- Confusion Matrix

- Precision
- Recall
- F-Score
- Cross-Validation

3.3 Machine Learning Algorithm and Result Evaluation

Good Models

These models show high performance across most metrics provided:

Random Forest, KNN (K-Nearest Neighbors), and Naive Bayes Classifier show it is the best performer in this dataset. The three algorithms are showing superior results on overall accuracy, precision, recall, F-score. Besides, their CV score value is around 90, which are excellent results. Each with distinct strengths makes them suitable for different types of classification tasks and handling of nonlinear relationships in data.

Logistic regression demonstrated strong performance with this dataset. The algorithm achieved overall accuracy, precision, and recall of approximately 80%, and an F-score of 78%, indicating reliable results. Its cross-validation score exceeded 80%, further confirming its effectiveness in distinguishing between four classes of attacking traffic and normal traffic.

AdaBoost is another good performer, which provided outstanding result on the overall accuracy at 94%. However, the performance of precision, recall, F-score is a bit poorer than the previous ones. It may have a good

Table 2: Comparing algorithms performances after parameter tuning.

	Overall Accuracy	Precision weighted Average	TP = Recall weighted Average	F-Score weighted Average	CV/ Silhouette Score
Logistic Regression	0.84	0.83	0.84	0.78	0.8414
Isolation Forest	0.57	0.59	0.57	0.55	0.46
Random Forest	0.97	0.98	0.98	0.98	0.93
DBSCAN	0.61	0.74	0.61	0.66	0.95
Local Outlier Factor	0.66	0.65	0.66	0.65	0.98
RPCA	0.33	0.24	0.33	0.24	0.33
K-Means	0.29	0.67	0.26	0.35	0.29
KNN	0.98	0.99	0.98	0.98	0.95
AdaBoost	0.95	0.75	0.74	0.76	0.95
Nave Bay Classifier	0.92	0.94	0.92	0.92	0.90

classification between classes, but the performance is not as reliable as random forest and KNN. The high CV score at 95 means the model is consistent in prediction.

Poor Models

RPCA, K-Means exhibit lower performance across the critical metrics:

RPCA shows very low performance in all aspects around 30, indicating it might not be suitable for this dataset. And K-Means is showing moderate precision at 0.67, but other results are below 40, which is worse than a coin flip. It indicates that K-Means does not effectively capture the certain patterns of the dataset.

Models with Moderate Results

LOF shows a high level of effectiveness in clustering or anomaly detection as indicated by the silhouette score at 0.98, making it suitable for datasets where anomalies form noticeable separate clusters. But the result in classification is just moderate in the range of 60–70.

Isolation Forest, potentially useful in anomaly detection, with its lower CV score at 0.46, might struggle with complex datasets where anomalies do not follow a clear isolation pattern and classify them as anomalies. This model performed moderate only with values around 60 even after significant parameter tuning or may be not suitable to the characteristics of the dataset being used.

DBSCAN, 95 in silhouette score, is successfully clustering the dataset by different types of attack. However, the performance metrics is showing

Table 3: Parameters used by anomaly detection algorithms.

Algorithm	**Parameter**
KNN	Number of neighbors considered (k)
K-Means	Number of cluster (k)
RPCA	Amount of contamination, i.e., proportion of outliers (n)
LOF	Minimum and maximum number of neighbors (k min and k max)
Isolation Forest	Number of isolation trees & proportion of outliners contamination (n)
Random Forest	Number of trees (n)
Nave Bay	Smoothing value (α)
Logistic Regression	Controls the strength of the regularization (C)
DBSCAN	Value of epsilon and minimum Points
AdaBoost	Rate of learning and No. of weak learners (n)

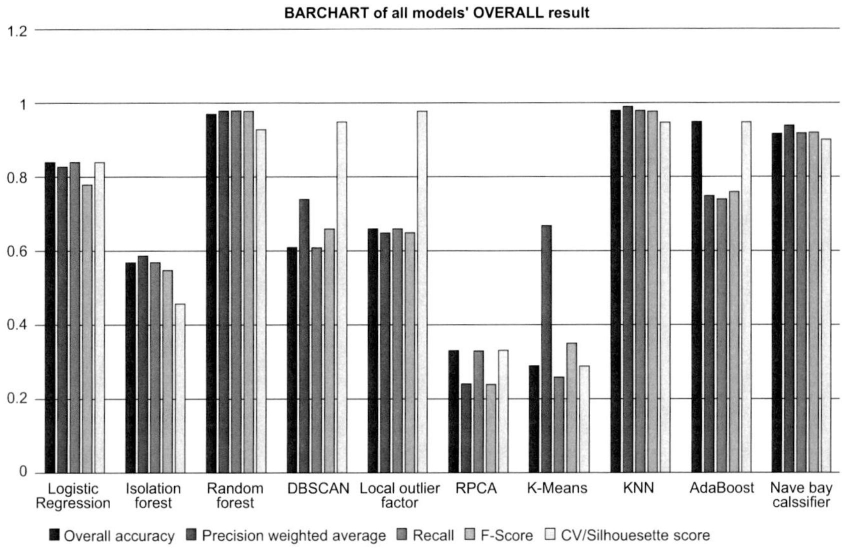

Figure 5: BARCHART of all models' OVERALL result.

around 60–70. This model is still useful in predicting attacking activities. But it is not performing best in this dataset.

In short, future researcher might need to avoid using RPCA and K-Means in this dataset. Furthermore, complex, non-linear, and high dimensional data are not suitable for the nature of these two models.

4. Conclusion

Since the global crimes are still rapidly growing on smartphones and wearable medical devices, cyberattacks against these devises are also increasing. This paper suggests security update on the Bluetooth protocol. The security of Bluetooth protocol is always overlooked, since the world is mainly focusing on internet security which allows vulnerability of our close distance devices, medical things especially becoming potentially vulnerable. However, with this paper with Bluetooth datasets in the medical things' domain, it is an attempt to fill the gap by providing dataset within the link layer of the Bluetooth protocol which could help identifying vulnerabilities of current exploits. In the future, other layers of Bluetooth protocol dataset could be also developed that allow us to have a broader overview of the Bluetooth security.

References

[1] Cynerio. 2022. Ponemon Survey: Insecurity of Connected Devices in Healthcare, 2022. [Online]. Available: https://www.cynerio.com/ponemon-survey-insecurity-of-connected-devices-in-healthcare-2022.

[2] Radcliffe, A. J. and S. Sanchez. 2022. Cybersecurity in Healthcare: A systematic review of the global landscape. *International Journal of Medical Informatics*, 168: 104592. [Online]. Available: https://doi.org/10.3233/THC-161263.

[3] Huang, Y., Y. Liu and H. Yang. 2023. The security challenges and countermeasures of Internet of Medical Things in Healthcare. *Sustainable Computing: Informatics and Systems*, 33: 101329.

[4] Sengar, S. K., S. Jain and P. K. Sharma. 2023. A survey on Advanced Persistent Threats (APTs) targeting healthcare systems. *Journal of Network and Computer Applications*, 222: 103827.

[5] Mittal, S., M. Gupta, J. Reissman and A. Wadhera. 2019. Why securing medical devices is more important than ever. *Communications of the ACM*, 62(1): 78-85.

[6] Laskowski, A. 2013. Insulin pump security: A delicate balance. *IEEE Security & Privacy*, 11(6): 78–82. [Online]. Available: https://standards.ieee.org/beyond-standards/addressing-the-need-for-protectingcybersecurity-in-connected-diabetes-devices/.

[7] Sengupta, S., S. Banerjee and J. Mukhopadhyay. 2019. Internet of Things-Based Healthcare systems: A taxonomy of security vulnerabilities, attacks and countermeasures. *Journal of Ambient Intelligence and Humanized Computing*, 10(8): 3427–3453.

[8] Salem, O., K. Alsubhi, A. Shaafi, M. Gheryani, A. Mehaoua and R. Boutaba. 2022. Man-in-the-middle attack mitigation in Internet of Medical things. *IEEE Transactions on Industrial Informatics*, 18(3): 1649–1657. [Online]. Available: https://doi.org/10.1109/TII.2021.3089462.

[9] National Institute of Standards and Technology (NIST). 2024. CVE-2018-5389. National Vulnerability Database. [Online]. Available: https://nvd.nist.gov/vuln/detail/CVE-2018-5389.

[10] National Institute of Standards and Technology (NIST). 2020. CVE-2019-8564. National Vulnerability Database. [Online]. Available: https://nvd.nist.gov/vuln/detail/CVE-2019-8564.

[11] National Institute of Standards and Technology (NIST). 2023. CVE-2020-7293. National Vulnerability Database. [Online]. Available: https://nvd.nist.gov/vuln/detail/CVE-2020-7293.

[12] Baran, G. 2024. BlueDucky: A new tool exploits bluetooth vulnerability with 0-Click code execution. *Cyber Security News*, Mar. 27, 2024. [Online]. Available: https://cybersecuritynews.com/blueducky-exploitsbluetooth-vulnerability/.

[13] Bettercap. BLE Module. *Bettercap*. [Online]. Available: https://www.bettercap.org/modules/ble/.

[14] James, G., D. Witten, T. Hastie and R. Tibshirani. 2013. *An Introduction to Statistical Learning: With Applications in R*, vol. 112. New York: Springer.

[15] Breiman, L. 2001. Random forests. *Machine Learning*, 45(1): 5–32.

[16] Altman, N. S. 1992. An introduction to kernel and nearest-neighbor nonparametric regression. *The American Statistician*, 46(3): 175–185.

[17] Freund, Y. and R. E. Schapire. 1997. A decision-theoretic generalization of on-line learning and an application to boosting. *Journal of Computer and System Sciences*, 55(1): 119–139. [Online]. Available: https://www.sciencedirect.com/science/article/pii/S002200009791504X.

[18] Zhang, H. 2004. The optimality of Naive Bayes. In *Proceedings of the Seventeenth International Florida Artificial Intelligence Research Society Conference*, pp. 562–567. [Online]. Available: https://aaai.org/papers/flairs-2004-097/.

[19] Zhang, H. and W. Zhang. Naive Bayes Text Classification for Imbalanced Classes. [Online]. Available: https://link.springer.com/chapter/10.1007/11871637_49.

[20] Liu, F. T., K. M. Ting and Z. H. Zhou. 2008. Isolation forest. In *2008 Eighth IEEE International Conference on Data Mining*.

[21] Ester, M., H. -P. Kriegel, J. Sander and X. Xu. 1996. A density-based algorithm for discovering clusters in large spatial databases with noise. In *Proceedings of the 2nd International Conference on Knowledge Discovery and Data Mining*, pp. 226–231. AAAI Press.

[22] Breunig, M. M., H. -P. Kriegel, R. T. Ng and J. Sander. 2000. LOF: Identifying density-based local outliers. In *Proceedings of the 2000 ACM SIGMOD International Conference on Management of Data*, pp. 93–104. [Online]. Available: https://dl.acm.org/doi/10.1145/335191.335388.

[23] Candes, E. J., X. Li, Y. Ma and J. Wright. 2011. Robust principal component analysis? *Journal of the ACM (JACM)*, 58(3): 1–37.

[24] MacQueen, J. 1967. Some methods for classification and analysis of multivariate observations. In *Proceedings of the Fifth Berkeley Symposium on Mathematical Statistics and Probability*, 1: 281–297. University of California Press.

[25] Nordic Semiconductor Academy. 2024. Bluetooth Low Energy Fundamentals. DevAcademy. [Online]. Available: https://academy.nordicsemi.com/courses/bluetooth-low-energy-fundamentals/.

[26] National Institute of Standards and Technology (NIST). 2024. CVE-2023-45866. National Vulnerability Database. [Online]. Available: https://nvd.nist.gov/vuln/detail/CVE-2023-45866.

[27] Lippmann, R., J. W. Haines, D. J. Fried, J. Korba and K. Das. 2000. The 1999 DARPA off-line intrusion detection evaluation. *Computer Networks*, 34(4): 579–595. [Online]. Available: https://doi.org/10.1016/S1389-1286(00)00139-0.

[28] Dua, D. and C. Graff. 2017. *UCI Machine Learning Repository: KDD Cup 1999 Data*. University of California, Irvine, School of Information and Computer Sciences. [Online]. Available: https://kdd.ics.uci.edu/databases/kddcup99/kddcup99.html.

[29] Tavallaee, M., E. Bagheri, W. Lu and A. A. Ghorbani. 2009. A detailed analysis of the KDD CUP 99 data set. In *IEEE International Conference on Communications, 2009. ICC '09*, pp. 1–5. [Online]. Available: https://doi.org/10.1109/ICC.2009.5194111.

[30] Song, J., H. Takakura and Y. Okabe. 2008. Kyoto University Benchmark Data. National Institute of Information and Communications Technology (NICT), Japan. [Online]. Available: https://www.takakura.com/Kyoto_data/.

[31] Hady, A. A., A. Ghubaish, T. Salman, D. Unal and R. Jain. 2020. Intrusion detection system for healthcare systems using medical and network data: A comparison study. *IEEE Access*, 8: 106576–106584. [Online]. Available: https://doi.org/10.1109/ACCESS.2020.3000421.

[32] Moustafa, N. and J. Slay. 2015. UNSW-NB15: A Comprehensive Data Set for Network Intrusion Detection Systems (Version 1.0) [Data set]. UNSW Canberra. [Online]. Available: https://doi.org/10.4225/75/57b3d94bfb3ea.

[33] Moustafa, N. and J. Slay. 2019. The Bot-IoT Dataset. UNSW Canberra Cyber. [Online]. Available: https://research.unsw.edu.au/projects/bot-iot-dataset.

[34] Shiravi, A., H. Shiravi, M. Tavallaee and A. A. Ghorbani. 2012. ISCXIDS2012 Dataset. Information Security Centre of Excellence, University of New Brunswick. [Online]. Available: https://www.unb.ca/cic/datasets/ids.html.

[35] Ahmed, M., S. Byreddy, A. Nutakki, L. F. Sikos and P. Haskell-Dowland. 2021. ECU-IoHT: A dataset for analyzing cyberattacks in Internet of Health Things. *Ad Hoc Networks*, 122: Article 102621. [Online]. Available: https://doi.org/10.1016/j.adhoc.2021.102621.

[36] Zubair, M., A. Ghubaish, D. Unal, A. Al-Ali, T. Reimann, G. Alinier, M. Hammoudeh and J. Qadir. 2022. Secure bluetooth communication in smart healthcare systems: A novel community dataset and intrusion detection system. *Sensors,* 22(21): 8280. [Online]. Available: https://doi.org/10.3390/s22218280.

[37] Dadkhah, S., E. C. Pinto Neto, R. Ferreira, R. C. Molokwu, S. Sadeghi and A. A. Ghorbani. 2024. CICIoMT2024: A benchmark dataset for multi-protocol security assessment in IoMT. *Internet of Things,* 28: Article 101351. [Online]. Available: https://doi.org/10.1016/j.iot.2024.101351.

[38] Kashani, S., S. Sherazi, A. Khokhar, S. W. Kim and F. Nait-Abdesselam. 2024. Bluetooth Low Energy (BLE) RF dataset for machine learning in WBANs. In *2024 IEEE Wireless Communications and Networking Conference (WCNC).* [Online]. Available: https://ieeexplore.ieee.org/abstract/document/10571027.

[39] National Institute of Standards and Technology (NIST). 2024. CVE-2022-3007. National Vulnerability Database. [Online]. Available: https://nvd.nist.gov/vuln/detail/CVE-2022-3007.

Chapter 4

Safeguarding Patient Records in the Information Age

*Michael Otradovec** and *Nazim Choudhury*

1. Introduction

Cybersecurity threats are an increasingly common occurrence. The advent of Internet of Health Things (IoHT) is transforming healthcare delivery by enhancing patient monitoring, diagnostics, and personalized care. However, the rapid adoption of IoHT in the Information Age has also introduced significant cybersecurity challenges. Despite the rise in technological advancements to both cyberattacks and techniques used to combat them, the digital healthcare sector has, to some degree, neglected to mirror and implement these advancements in its security measures. This has left valuable electronic patient data integrated in the IoHT vulnerable.

The term IoHT, a subset of the broader Internet of Things (IoT), refers to the interconnection of medical devices and sensors that are used to collect, store, and transmit patient health data [32]. The objective is to improve healthcare outcomes. The use of electronic patient records in the IoHT involves managing and processing health data through interconnected devices and systems [30, 33]. The IoHT combines the IoT with healthcare applications to

University of Wisconsin, Green Bay, WI, 54311.
* Corresponding author: otramj10@uwgb.edu

DOI: 10.1201/9781003483267-6

create an ecosystem that enhances patient care, monitoring, and management. The purpose of this work is to inform the reader about cyberattacks that are performed on patient record databases in IoHT, as well as applicable attacks on its infrastructure. An applicable attack does not directly attack the patient database. It leaves the database vulnerable to being easily accessed and breached as a byproduct of the initial attack. For example, an attack on a diagnostic IoHT device such as an ECG that captures and stores data to be shared in the patient database. The paper will discuss recent attacks and explain the repercussions faced by healthcare providers, security providers, and patients. Finally, the paper will present current techniques that hospitals and security providers use to protect patient data.

This paper used search keywords such as "cybersecurity," "Internet of Health Things," "cyberattacks," "hospitals," and "patient data" to gather journal articles from 2019 to the present, especially regarding current techniques employed by cybercriminals and cybersecurity professionals to attack and defend patient records and IoHT infrastructure. These papers cited other scholarly articles that (i) synthesized related information, (ii) performed interviews on security professionals who work in the healthcare sector, and (iii) studied databases regarding attacks on healthcare infrastructures and patient records to show the trends of current cyberattacks on patient records.

2. History

As healthcare systems entered digitization, they lessened the need for hard copies that could be easily stolen or lost. However, they opened patient data to vulnerabilities online, which malicious hackers exploit almost daily. This section will include a brief history of recent and notable attacks on healthcare databases.

To begin with, the largest breach of healthcare data was done in February of 2024. Change Healthcare, owned by the UnitedHealth Group, was the victim of a ransomware attack, specifically ALPHV Black Cat [2]. Change Healthcare was a middleman between healthcare providers and insurance payers. Therefore, they had a large set of data that dealt with patient information in the context of using that information to submit insurance claims. While this information was not directly stolen from a hospital, it is still applicable because patient data was stolen. Researchers have attributed the attack to neglect in implementing multifactor authentication onto a legacy server. This directly resulted in many healthcare providers and medical facilities such as pharmacies being unable to secure payments or submit claims. As a result, many of these sites were unable to provide care and faced financial disasters [13].

According to experts, an estimated 100 million Americans had sensitive healthcare information directly leaked onto the dark web, where it could be sold or accessed by anyone. United Health was also required to pay $22 million in Bitcoin [26]. Effects on the hospitals in this case were mainly financial. While the attacks, for the most part, didn't slow important healthcare for patients, insurance verifications and reimbursements to healthcare organizations were blocked. This meant that in many cases hospitals owed patients money but didn't have the reserves to pay these claims before insurance was able to resume payments. This case highlights a ransomware attack, that while not directly coming from a hospital, resulted in the release of over one hundred million Americans' vital healthcare information.

Another recent attack was conducted on Community Health Systems, where a zero-day software vulnerability resulted in hackers exploiting almost 1 million patients' private data. Information stolen included names, addresses, medical billings, insurance information, birth dates, social security numbers, and medical diagnoses and medication [17]. In this case, Community Health Systems held their patient records in the third-party security system "Fotra." This case is an example of a database breach due to a software vulnerability that was exploited before it could be found and patched. Following the attack "Fotra" applied a patch and took steps to "harden the security" on the "GoAnywhere" platform that was exploited [17].

These situations highlight that even now with so many technological advancements, attacks still occur and mistakes in security are made. They also showcase the severity of the effects that attacks bring, with millions of Americans having extremely sensitive patient data stolen in just these two attacks.

3. Importance of Electronic Health Records

One important aspect about Electronic Health Records that makes them more susceptible to breaches is their interoperability. This refers to the ability of different healthcare organizations and providers to exchange and use patient health information securely. Due to healthcare information being exchanged across multiple platforms, devices, and sites, risks of unauthorized access to them and larger-scale breaches are much more significant. In the IoHT, many different devices and applications coexist, and the safe exchange of data among them is key. Security of patient data is necessary among all steps of delivery and reception, and the benefits of patient record interoperability are also an immense risk factor.

When storing Electronic Health Records, it is also important to comply with government and sector regulations. In the US, HIPAA, the Health

Insurance Portability and Accountability Act, addresses the security of electronic protected health information. It requires security such as firewalls, access control systems, data encryption, backup and recovery, as well as employee training to prevent cyberattacks or unauthorized access. It also requires the auditing of data, ensuring that in the event of a security breach, the organization can investigate the attack more easily.

4. What Can Cybercriminals Do After Breaching Patient Data?

When understanding why it is so important to protect patient data, it is important to look at exactly what patient data entail. While the specific details included in patient data may vary case-by-case, for the most part, it may include the patient's name, age, gender, social security number, blood type, medical history, insurance provider, dates of admission and discharge, medication received, test results, care giver names and the hospital they received care from. It may also include more specific information such as notes, vitals, and imaging results from applicable visits. This means that hackers can access and exploit a variety of information when breaching a hospital's patient database, with a variety of uses.

4.1 Identity Theft

Among the vast information hospitals hold on record for patients, one of the most valuable to hackers is personal identification information, including names, addresses, contact information, social security numbers, and date of birth. After stealing this information from patients, hackers can use it for a variety of malicious purposes, including opening credit cards or loans, draining bank accounts, or filing fraudulent tax returns. In some cases, such as the Anthem security breach in 2015, hackers were able to gain access to all this information, as well as the employment data, income data, and medical IDs of as many as 80 million enrollees [6]. Those whose information was breached were instructed to be wary of suspicious emails or texts. In cases such as this one where medical ID numbers are stolen, patients are opened up to medical fraud. Medical fraud occurs when an individual deceives a healthcare provider or insurance company to benefit from healthcare programs or insurance claims. After stealing this information, hackers could use it to obtain medical services as a legitimate patient, obtain prescription drugs, or submit false claims to government healthcare programs and receive benefits.

4.2 Disrupting Healthcare Services

A worst-case scenario for hospitals during a cyberattack is to have critical services delayed or halted. It is one thing to have thousands of individuals' information leaked, but to also have that data inaccessible to healthcare providers is incredibly destructive to hospital functions. By hacking a patient record database and installing ransomware, cybercriminals can encrypt the data on record and deny the hospital access to it. This results in a delay or inaccuracy in patient treatment or diagnosis that could be dangerous in the case of emergency treatments. It also could lock employees out of medical equipment that requires account verification. In one example, a hospital's radiology center had to implement hard copies of patient information using written orders, reports, and DVDs to store related images. While no serious consequences such as deaths or misdiagnoses were reported, the hospital took months to recover from the attack, and patient appointments had to be rescheduled [7]. A separate study by the University of Minnesota School of Public Health done on 374 ransomware attacks found disruptions due to the attack were present in 44% of the attacks, and may have contributed to an estimated 42–67 patient deaths [19]. These studies show the severity of ransomware attacks, especially when they disrupt critical healthcare infrastructure.

4.3 Capture Phishing Data

Hackers can also use personal information stolen to send phishing messages to patients, rather than using it to steal their identity. Phishing is when criminals use social engineering to trick victims that a message sent to them is from a trusted source, while the motive is to plant malware or capture user credentials. Using a patient's email or phone number, a hacker could send an email or message pretending to be from a legitimate source, such as from the patient's healthcare provider. They could claim the user's login information needs to be updated, then ask the user for their current username and password. Should the user be unable to recognize this as a phishing scam, they might share that private information, thereby giving cybercriminals access to information such as full patient records, medical histories, and insurance information. While reports of unique phishing email campaigns and websites detected have been declining since 2016, over 100,000 new phishing email campaigns were employed in 2019, and over 200,000 unique phishing websites were detected [12]. Phishing campaigns are widespread emails or messages sent to many users in attempts to divulge sensitive information. However, these patient data are prime information for implementing spear phishing attacks. Unlike regular phishing, spear phishing is not sent to mass quantities of users, rather, targets are specifically selected after evaluating the probability of being able to exploit them based on information collected on them. Messages are then sent to individuals impersonating trusted entities such as friends or organizations, and often include more specific details and elaborately crafted schemes than a normal phishing attack would. These finely tuned phishing attacks are much more successful than normal large-scale phishing, a report found that around 97% of targeted individuals fell victim to spear-phishing attacks [27].

4.4 *Selling Data*

A final use of stolen patient data is selling or trading that private data on sites such as the Dark Web or through data brokers. Data can also be sold to healthcare data mining companies. In some cases, cybercriminals do not use the data they steal to commit identity theft, create phishing campaigns, or disrupt healthcare services. Rather, they sell it to users on illegal underground sites, or legal data mining companies [25]. Similarly, some cyber criminals do not specialize in hacking and stealing data from databases, instead they use that data for malicious purposes. Patient data are known to be extremely valuable as they include private information similar to a bank and can be more valuable in certain situations. After purchasing these data, criminals can use it to create phishing attacks, commit identity theft, and much more.

5. Effects of Patient Record Data Breaches

There are many direct and indirect effects of patient data being breached, which can mainly be divided into two groups: effects seen by hospitals, and effects seen by patients. I will be going over several qualitative and quantitative effects seen after a breach.

5.1 *Effects on Hospitals*

5.1.1 Reputational Impact

The reputation of a hospital is of utmost importance as they oversee sensitive data and procedures, and often hold the lives of individuals in their care. Patients should have confidence that their data are secured, and not having any are often grounds for seeking care services elsewhere. A study showed that attacks on a healthcare system can dissolve this trust. It surveyed consumers and found 44% reported switching companies to ensure their data were secure [19]. Maintaining patient trust and having a reputation for keeping their information secure is key to keeping business. Having that data breached not only jeopardizes the business of current patients but also prospective ones who could judge them based on a recent attack.

5.1.2 Financial Impact

Aside from simply losing the business of current and possible patients, hospitals could also incur other financial losses such as ransom payments, and increased insurance premiums.

The average cost of a data breach in the healthcare industry is $4.88 million, and the average cost per breached record is $429 [8]. This could be much more dependent on the attack. The number of records released has a significantly positive correlation to the cost of the attack [29].

5.1.3 Operational Disruptions

As previously stated, operational disruptions can be a particularly costly effect, qualitatively and quantitatively. Cyberattacks on patient data can lock doctors out of access to important medical devices and leave patient databases inaccessible, ultimately causing delays in treatment or loss of patient medical history. Many of these operational disruptions are caused by ransomware which encrypts patient data, making them inaccessible to doctors when they need them, such as during appointments. When these ransomware attacks occur for extended periods, hospitals continually are unable to access electronic health records and may have to turn to physical paper records if they can continue admitting patients. In a ransomware attack at the Hillel Yaffe Medical Center in Israel, doctors were unable to log in to computer systems, and patient data were encrypted. The staff were unable to check appointments and the patient list, and documentation such as EMRs, lab images, patient lists, and more were lost [1].

5.1.4 Legal Impacts

In some cases, hospitals or other healthcare providers may be required to pay settlements after having patient data breached. Often lawsuits state the hospital's negligence in implementing adequate security measures. Patients often request compensation including credit monitoring, identity theft protection, and general settlement payments. Hospitals are also strictly required to comply with the Health Insurance Portability and Accountability Act (HIPAA) which manages patient data security. HIPAA and applicable state laws may require an investigation into the attack to decide if the hospital or security provider was at fault, and if they were following guidelines. In the 2014 Premera Blue Cross attack, Premera was required to pay $5.4 million to the Washington State Office of the Attorney General, and $4.6 million to a group of state attorneys general [23]. In addition to this, they settled to pay a $74 million class action settlement. $32 million went to Class members who are also entitled to a maximum $10,000 payment and free credit monitoring service. The remaining $42 million was required to be used for improving security by implementing new encryption, increasing monitoring, and creating a 24/7 security operations center [22].

5.2 *Effects on Patients*

5.2.1 Stolen Personal Information and Increased Vulnerability

This section corresponds with the identity theft and spear phishing sections earlier in the presentation. Again, identity theft can result in financial fraud, insurance fraud, and medical fraud. Having these patient data accessible to hackers can result in spear phishing emails which further gain access to accounts. In addition to this, weak passwords can result in brute-force access to medical and financial accounts. Many users often repeat passwords, meaning successfully finding one set of credentials could open your other accounts to hackers. It is also important to note that should hackers gain access to a user's email account, they could receive verification emails from sites with different passwords and change them, locking the user out. This and the fact that patient data often include email addresses and phone numbers shows once again how valuable patient data are.

5.2.2 Financial Impact

Patients affected by hospital data breaches could stand to lose a significant amount of money depending on the amount of credit card and banking information on record. Avoiding phishing scams and having strong passwords or other forms of authentication are also key to avoiding financial loss after a data breach. Even with secure accounts, patients can still bear a financial burden. In the case of the Integris Data breach, individuals affected were contacted by the cybercriminals and charged $3 to view their stolen data, and $50 to have it deleted from their records. 4.674 million records were listed on the extortion site, while 2.39 million individuals were confirmed to have been affected [3]. This case shows that even when patient accounts are kept secure, they still could face a negative financial impact.

5.2.3 Health Impact

When hospitals face operational disruptions, patients can face health impacts. They may experience canceled appointments, delays in medical treatment, or a mishandling of their data that results in a misdiagnosis. According to a 2021 survey of 600 healthcare institutions in Mexico, 70% stated patients had delayed medical procedures or tests, and saw longer hospital stays during ransomware attacks. Additionally, 22% recognized a higher mortality rate, and 36% faced an increase in medical complications following a procedure [9].

6. Common Attack Strategies or Reasons for Breach

6.1 Social Engineering and Phishing

Social engineering and phishing are perhaps the most common ways hackers gain access to a patient database, and the HIPAA journal repeatedly reports email as one of the most common locations for accessing breached healthcare data [4]. Social engineering is a broader term that involves the manipulation of an individual such as an employee into breaking security protocols. Phishing is a form of this that involves sending fraudulent messages (normally emails) that appear to be from reliable or trusted sources. After clicking links, malware or spyware may be downloaded onto your device which can expose data or key log user credentials. These are particularly dangerous because they exploit individuals rather than security systems. They also are likely the first phase of an attack which can result in malware, ransomware, or other viruses.

6.2 Malware and Ransomware

Malware and Ransomware have been identified as some of the most common and effective strategies when hacking patient data. Malware is any malicious software that can infiltrate and damage a system, while ransomware specifically encrypts patient data, rendering them useless to hospitals. Often, infection of ransomware is done through phishing emails, which as explained above trick employees or patients into opening malicious links and downloading the ransomware to the network. They could also exploit vulnerabilities in the hospital's network to install this malicious malware. Only after this can hackers steal and encrypt the patient data that has been breached. A study done on almost 1600 attacks in the MED sector found that between 2015 and 2019, 35% of attacks were done by hacking, a section that included phishing, malware, or ransomware. However, during this same period, these attacks accounted for over 92% of records exposed, meaning that they are much more successful in exposing larger amounts of patient data [19]. While ransomware is not a way to initially access a hospital's patient database, using it as a follow-up is extremely detrimental to the database and hospital functions.

6.3 Credential Access

Credential access is more of a category, as hospital credentials such as those owned by doctors can be accessed in many ways. For the most part, these include password intrusion, weak or no authentication schemes, unauthorized access, and man-in-the-middle attacks. Password intrusion is an attack that accesses the hospital's system using stolen credentials. According to a review, brute force is one of the most common techniques used [5]. Weak Authentication Exploitation is when medical or other endpoint devices the hospital employs have a lack of strength in authentication mechanisms. In some cases, there may be no authentication mechanisms at all [20]. Having weak or no authentication mechanisms to add defense layers dramatically increases the success of password intrusion. Unauthorized access is different from password intrusion because devices included in this section may have no password. Devices such as insulin pumps, smartwatches, and medical imaging devices are all susceptible to these attacks [28]. Man-in-the-middle attacks are those that attach themselves to the network, capturing communication which could be in the form of test or monitoring results and employee credentials between devices and the network. They not only steal these data, but may also alter them [16].

7. Common Defense Strategies

This section will present common strategies cybersecurity and healthcare providers employ to secure their patient data. While some of these strategies are exclusively seen and used by the cybersecurity team, others rely on the cooperation of on-site employees.

7.1 Access Control and Authentication

In hospitals, implementing role-based access controls is standard practice to prevent unauthorized individuals from accessing some patient's data. For example, doctors, nurses, technicians, and other employees are only given access to the data and systems that are required by their roles. Nurses may only be able to view notes on a specific patient visit, and only records of those assigned to them. This information could be on the procedure they will be assisting or performing on the patient, such as giving antiviral medications. However, a doctor may be able to access the same patient's entire medical history. In conjunction with role-based access controls, it is important to authenticate these roles and ensure that an unauthorized employee is not accessing private patient data with an authorized employee's credentials. Using multi-factor authentication does just that by requiring employees to validate their credentials with a one-time password, smart card, token, or biometric ID. Lee proposes a three-factor authentication process requiring login credentials, a smart card, and biometrics. It also includes a random one-time key between the gateway and control server. This model was able to defend the system from the ten attacks tried upon it [14]. When the "what you know, what you have, and what you are" model is shown in Mohamed's article on multifactor authentication, we see that the password constitutes what you know, the smartcard is what you have, and the biometric key is what you are [18]. By implementing all layers of the model, authentication is much more secure, which is incredibly important with the valuable nature of patient data.

7.2 Network Monitoring/Intrusion Detection Systems

When looking at cyberattacks, a common theme is cybersecurity professionals recognizing attacks in progress and shutting down the network [6, 13]. Recognizing these attacks in progress and denying more access is key to remediation efforts and minimizing the loss of attacks. Recognition can come in the form of traffic analysis, which can track performance, usage, and connectivity to ensure only valid processes are being run. Intrusion detection systems are key to detecting these breaches as soon as possible, limiting damage. Items that could be detected include unusual access requests, login attempts, or unauthorized software usage. Machine learning algorithms such as those detailed in IEEE's article are incredibly useful, achieving a 93.2% accuracy with their bagged decision tree network algorithm, specifically on data traffic collected from the Internet of Medical Things [24].

7.3 Blockchains

A notable technology in databases themselves, blockchain technology is becoming increasingly researched and implemented in databases. Blockchain usage in electronic health records could see increasing usage in upcoming years due to its security and interoperability. It also features immutable records, meaning that after data have been recorded on a ledger, they cannot be removed and instead a new upload must be created, keeping the original and new version as a record. Dwivedi proposes a modified blockchain for IoT in healthcare, aimed at preserving privacy. It improves the scalability of blockchain-based systems and suggests using cloud servers to store encrypted data blocks [31]. Despite the high cost of blockchains, they provide a secure and quick transfer of data which is key in hospitals.

7.4 Employee Training

Training employees on how to protect their credentials is incredibly important. Companies can implement training through required classes, and many companies offer online training through videos and quizzes. This training should include effective password management by varying passwords and choosing long enough ones. It should also train employees to recognize phishing emails and report them. Finally, the security team should be well versed in recognizing a cyberattack in progress, and regular drills are essential to ensuring employees are quick and efficient in response.

8. Are Hospitals Doing Enough?

While it is true that no network or database is one hundred percent secure, this paper has presented many important safety measures to protect electronic health records, and many more are also in use. However, hospitals and protectors of patient data may not be implementing these strategies to a sufficient degree. According to a survey study in 2020, 82% of CIOs at hospitals with under 150 beds state they are not spending adequate capital to protect patient records from a breach. 80% of healthcare organizations surveyed have not completed an incident response drill to a cyberattack, and 73% felt their infrastructures were unprepared to respond to cyberattacks [10]. The government accountability office also recommends that Centers for Medicare and Medicaid Services which hold important electronic health records should develop guidance for researchers on implementing security controls, as well as to track and assess results on more security controls [15]. In many cases, this is due to a lack of funding for cybersecurity at hospitals. Especially in smaller organizations with fewer resources, they are more likely to look at hosted solutions and focus on existing solutions implemented at their facilities rather than develop additional solutions. Resources are often spent elsewhere and subjects in a survey stated that healthcare doesn't receive proper funding in general, meaning revenue is less likely to go to cybersecurity [11]. Another issue is that hospitals often employ legacy systems, which may be rooted in existing hospital infrastructure, making them difficult or expensive to replace [21]. It may not be feasible to allocate more resources to the cybersecurity division at hospitals. Therefore, security professionals must be efficient and strategic with their upgrades.

9. Conclusion

With the incredible sensitivity and value of electronic health records, it is incredibly important to ensure hospitals are taking the necessary steps to protect these data. Patients place a substantial amount of trust in hospitals and other healthcare providers when they seek treatment, and the effects of having their information stolen or ransomed are exceptionally destructive. With many devices operating together in the IoHT, it is all the more important to ensure security among these devices and patient databases. While it is important to ensure organizations are complying with governmental and industry regulations, it is just as important to ensure they are implementing a comprehensive security strategy, using multiple layers of defense such as multi-factor authentication and intrusion detection systems. No singular defense strategy is all-encompassing, rather it is most important to use several strategies in conjunction. It is also essential to ensure security professionals are prepared to recognize and deal with cyberattacks in an efficient and timely manner, which can be done with extensive employee training and regular drills. Patient databases hold some of the most sensitive data, and hospitals need to recognize this and treat the security of that data accordingly.

References

[1] Abbou, B., B. Kessel, M. Ben Natan, R. Gabbay-Benziv, D. Dahan Shriki, A. Ophir, N. Goldschmid, A. Klein, A. Roguin and M. Dudkiewicz. 2024. When all computers shut down: The clinical impact of a major cyber-attack on a general hospital. *Front. Digit. Health*, 6: 1321485.

[2] Alder, S. 2024a. Healthcare Data Breach Statistics. *Hipaa Journal*. www.hipaajournal.com/healthcare-data-breach-statistics/, accessed on Dec 20th, 2024.

[3] Alder, S. 2024b. Integris Health Confirms 2.39 Million Individuals Affected. *Hipaa Journal*. www.hipaajournal.com/integris-health-data-breach, accessed on Dec 20th, 2024.

[4] Alder, S. 2024c. December 2019 Healthcare Data Breach Report. *Hipaa Journal*. www.hipaajournal.com/december-2019-healthcare-data-breach-report, accessed on 20th Dec, 2024.

[5] Martínez, A., M. Pérez and A. Martínez. 2023. A Comprehensive review of the state-of-the-art on security and privacy issues in healthcare. *ACM Comput. Surv.*, 55(12).

[6] Balber, C. 2015. Diagnosing the Anthem data breach. *San Fernando Valley Business Journal*, 20(4): 45.

[7] Chen, P. -H., R. Bodak and N. S. Gandhi. 2021. Ransomware recovery and imaging operations: Lessons learned and planning considerations. *Journal of Digital Imaging*, 34(3): 731–740.

[8] Crume, J. 2024. Cost of Data Breach 2024, *IBM*. www.ibm.com/sg-en/security/data-breach, accessed on 20th Dec, 2024.

[9] Cyberattacks on hospitals increase deaths, study says. 2021. In *CE Noticias Financieras* (English ed.). ContentEngine LLC, a Florida limited liability company. Translated by Content Engine LLC.

[10] Drees, J. 2020. Cyberattacks on healthcare providers expected to triple next year: Black book report. *Becker's Hospital Review* www.beckershospitalreview.com/cybersecurity/cyberattacks-on-healthcare-providers-expected-to-triple-next-year-black-book-report.html, accessed on 20th Dec, 2024.

[11] Jalali, M. S. and J. P. Kaiser. 2018. Cybersecurity in hospitals: A systematic, organizational perspective. *Journal of Medical Internet Research*, 20(5): e10059–e10059.

[12] Jampen, D., G. Gür, T. Sutter and B. Tellenbach. 2020. Don't click: Towards an effective antiphishing training. A comparative literature review. *Human-Centric Computing and Information Sciences*, 10(1).

[13] Kanter, G. P., J. R. Rekowski and J. T. Kannarkat. 2024. Lessons from the change healthcare ransomware attack. *JAMA Health Forum*, 5(9): e242764.

[14] Lee, J., S. Yu, K. Park, Y. Park and Y. Park. 2019. Secure three-factor authentication protocol for multi-gateway IoT environments. *Sensors (Basel, Switzerland)*, 19(10): 2358.

[15] Marinos, N. 2018. Electronic Health Information: CMS Oversight of Medicare Beneficiary Data Security Needs Improvement. *GAO.gov*.

[16] Mallik, A. 2019. Man-in-the-middle-attack: Understanding in simple words. *Cyberspace: Journal Pendidikan Teknologi Informasi*, 2(2): 109–134.

[17] McGee, M. and R. Ross. 2023. CHS to Notify 1 Million in Breach Linked to Software Flaw. *Bank Information Security*. www.bankinfosecurity.com/chs-to-notify-1-million-in-breach-linked- to-software-flaw-a-21405, accessed on 20th Dec, 2024.

[18] Mohamed, Tamaara. 2014. *Security of Multifactor Authentication Model to Improve Authentication Systems*. www.researchgate.net/publication/336642009_Security_of_Multifactor Authentication_Model _to_Improve_Authentication_Systems, accessed on 20th Dec, 2024.

[19] Neprash, H. T., C. C. McGlave, D. A. Cross, B. A. Virnig, M. A. Puskarich, J. D. Huling, A. Z. Rozenshtein and S. S. Nikpay. 2022. Trends in ransomware attacks on US Hospitals, clinics, and other health care delivery organizations, 2016–2021. *JAMA Health Forum*, 3(12): e224873–e224873.

[20] Newaz, A., A. Sikder, M. Rahman and S. Uluagac. 2021. A survey on security and privacy issues in modern healthcare systems: Attacks and defenses. *ACM Transactions on Computing for Healthcare*, 2(3).

[21] Pal, D., S. Chitta and V. Saini. 2018. Addressing legacy system challenges through EA in healthcare. *Distrib. Learn Broad Appl. Sci. Res.*, 4: 180–220.

[22] Top Class Actions. 2019. Premera Blue Cross Security Incident Class Action Settlement, https://topclassactions.com/lawsuit-settlements/closed-settlements/premera-blue-cross-security-incident-class-action-settlement/, Top Class Actions LLC, accessed on 20th Dec, 2024.

[23] Cruz, D. R. 2019. Premera blue cross to pay $10M over data breach. *The SNL Insurance Daily*, Charlottesville.

[24] Saba, T. 2020. Intrusion detection in smart city hospitals using ensemble classifiers. *2020 13th International Conference on Developments in eSystems Engineering (DeSE)*, 418–422.

[25] Tanner, A. 2017. *Our Bodies, Our Data*. Beacon Press.

[26] What We Learned: Change Healthcare Cyber Attack. 2024. *Energy &Commerce*, https://energycommerce.house.gov/posts/what-we-learned-change-healthcare-cyber-attack, accessed on 20th Dec, 2024.

[27] Xu, T., K. Singh and P. Rajivan. 2023. Personalized persuasion: Quantifying susceptibility to information exploitation in spear-phishing attacks. *Applied Ergonomics*, 108.

[28] Yaqoob, T., H. Abbas and M. Atiquzzaman. 2019. Security vulnerabilities, attacks, countermeasures, and regulations of networked medical devices—A review. *IEEE Communications Surveys and Tutorials*, 21(4): 3723–3768.

[29] Yeo, L. H. and J. Banfield. 2022. Human factors in electronic health records cybersecurity breach: An exploratory analysis. *Perspectives in Health Information Management*, 19(Spring).

[30] Huang, C., J. Wang, S. Wang and Y. Zhang. 2023. Internet of medical things: A systematic review. *Neurocomputing*, 126719.

[31] Meena, D. K., R. Dwivedi and S. Shukla. 2019. Pre-serving patient's privacy using proxy re-encryption inpermissioned blockchain. In *2019 Sixth InternationalConference on Internet of Things: Systems, Managementand Security (Iotsms)* (pp. 450–457).

[32] Terry, N. P. 2016. Will the internet of things transformhealthcare. *Vand. J. Ent. & Tech. L.*, 19: 327.

[33] Verma, H., N. Chauhan and L. K. Awasthi. 2023. A comprehensive review of 'Internet of Healthcare Things': Networking aspects, technologies, services, applications, challenges, and security concerns. *Computer Science Review*, 50: 100591.

Section III

Sustainable Solutions to Enhance IoHT Cyber Security

DOI: 10.1201/9781003483267-7

Chapter 5

An Overview of Authentication Protocols for Critical Infrastructure

Taylah Griffiths

1. Introduction

Critical infrastructure is any structure when impaired would have significant consequences on Australia socially and economically. The Security of Critical Infrastructure (SOCI) Act 2018 outlines 11 sectors, which include healthcare, energy, and communications. Due to the importance of these sectors, their security is of a high priority [1].

Each sector is rapidly evolving worldwide by upgrading to traditional devices to smart devices which enables two-way communication. However, this increases their vulnerability to cyberattacks. The health sector is one example, starting to incorporate smart health devices, known as Internet of Health Things (IoHT), that allows the transfer of patient data across networks to their respective medical professionals for benefits such as a decrease in the number of require visits. The energy sector is also being incorporated into the smart device upgrade, making it all the more important as most other sectors are connected to it for power. Kamal, Aljohani [2] gave an example of health patient data being

School of Science, Edith Cowan University, Perth, Australia.
Email: t.griffiths@ecu.edu.au

DOI: 10.1201/9781003483267-8

transferred between devices and an interruption in the grid could cause major problems for that data. Ud Din, Ali [3] proposes a protocol for communication between a patient and medical professional. The authors use a similar architecture to the smart grid for the consumer healthcare architecture. This shows the relevance of smart grid authentication protocols to the IoHT infrastructure. Authentication protocols are being developed by many authors to protect both the IoHT and smart grid from cyberattacks.

Most commonly spoken about in smart grid literature is the attack on the Ukrainian smart grid [4]. In December 2015, over 230,000 electricity users were affected by the attack targeted on 30 substations. The effect of cyberattacks on the energy sector has been investigated by researchers, including more well-known attacks such as MITM attacks and newer attacks such as FDI attacks. FDI attacks were first found to affect the state estimation in the power grid, one of the first recorded being the Ukrainian attack [5]. Ud Din, Ali [3] mentions some attacks affect the health sector. These include Distributed Denial of Service (DDoS) attacks and MITM attacks, both of which also affect the energy sector. Ahmed and Pathan [6] talk about the FDI attacks and their potential effect on the health sector by manipulating health records and misleading medical professionals of their patient's health, such as blood type or diabetic type. These review papers also propose solutions to increasing the security of the grid. Nafees, Saxena [4] and Khoei, Slimane [7] both proposed Intrusion Detection Systems (IDSs) to improve the security of the smart grid. Gunduz and Das [8] and Faquir, Chouliaras [9] both mention authentication and data encryption to increase security. Ahmed and Pathan [6] refer to many countermeasures, including deep learning, blockchain, and public key cryptography. They also mention that little effort would be needed to integrate the countermeasures from smart grid to other sectors.

This review will focus on evaluating authentication protocols proposed in recent literature. It is an expanded review from a previous work in progress paper [10]. Authentication is important to validate entities to ensure the data transferred across the smart grid system are travelling to a legitimate source. There are many papers that propose their own authentication protocols for device or user validation and creating session keys to be used for data encryption to secure the transfer of the data. However, a drawback arises when these protocols are evaluated. A protocol proposed for the smart grid is measured against computational efficiency, mitigation of cyberattacks, and secure data transmission based on analyses from trusted sources. The evaluation metrics differ across recent literature, causing difficulties in comparing and fully evaluating each protocol.

The purpose of this review is to review recent literature to outline possible cyberattacks within the smart grid, compare the metrics used within recent authentication literature, highlight the gaps with the metrics, and outline possible future work.

2. Internet of Health Things and Smart Grid

Ud Din, Ali [3] proposed a model that displays the connectivity between Internet of Health Things (IoHT) and the smart grid. Their scheme utilizes the bandwidth of the grid communications to connect patient data with the cloud of the hospital. This further displays how the vulnerabilities of the smart grid can impact not only itself, but other critical infrastructure sectors as well.

The smart grid upgrades the traditional electrical grid by implementing smart versions of devices that allow two-way communication between devices. Some of the advantages of the newer grid include storage of electricity, reduction in carbon emissions, and blackouts. The National Institute of Standards and Technology (NIST) developed a smart grid conceptual model which is utilized by many papers to outline the various domains of the smart grid. The different domains are Customer, Service Provider, Operations, Markets, Transmission, Distribution, and Generation [11].

The domains in the conceptual model all manage different services for the smart grid. The customer uses the electricity running through the grid; however, with the new smart devices consumer can also generate (solar panels), manage (smart meters), and store (smart batteries) their own electricity. Service providers provide the electricity to the consumers. However, the transferal of electricity is managed by operations, and the actual transmission is managed by the transmission domain. The transmission and customer domains are connected via distribution, which distributes the electricity from the domains, respectively, while the creation of the electricity is performed by the generation domain [11].

The majority of recent smart grid authentication papers focus on the customer domain, more specifically the Advanced Metering Infrastructure (AMI). The AMI is essential in the smart grid processes to monitor power usage in households, including home appliances, gas meters, and photovoltaic panels [7]. The smart meter monitors the power usage within households and has connection to other parts of the smart grid, to communicate the measurement data that get sent onto the service provider or other authorized entity [8]. Typically, the protocols designed are to secure between a smart meter and service provider, or smart meter and a gateway.

Other parts of the smart grid include: the Supervisory Control and Data Acquisition (SCADA), this monitors and controls the transmission network [4]; energy management systems which allow power to be transmitted [12]; phasor measurement units which measure voltage, current, and frequency within the smart grid [4]; and distribution management systems to distribute the power across the grid [12]. All these systems require communication between devices to work efficiently.

Two-way communication allows the domains within the smart grid to provide, use, and manage electricity more effectively. There are smaller networks within the grid, such as the Home Area Network (HAN) or the Building Area Network (BAN). The types of communication technologies used in these areas include well-known technology, Wi-Fi, Ethernet, and Bluetooth, or lesser known ones, ZigBee and ZWave [13]. The Wide Area Network (WAN) is a lot larger than the HAN or BAN and is for the larger domains, such as distribution, generation, and transmission. The WAN encompasses much larger areas such as entire cities, containing multiple HANs and BANs, meaning the smaller communication technologies would not work, so cellular, fiber optics, and WiMAX are some technologies that are used [9].

2.1 *Potential Attacks on the Smart Grid*

Enabling two-way communication has some drawbacks including potential cyberattacks. To mitigate these attacks three main security objectives are followed by most security professionals known as the CIA triad. The triad consists of Confidentiality, Integrity, and Availability. Confidentiality ensures that the data within the system are not accessed by unauthorized parties. Integrity provides protection from data tampering within the system. Lastly, Availability is ensuring the system is available as needed, for the smart grid this is at all times [8].

Multiple papers all mention cyberattacks that target the confidentiality of systems. These include intrusion, brute force, masquerading, traffic analysis, password, eavesdropping, side-channel, and social engineering [7–9]. Three papers talk about cyberattacks that target the integrity, including MITM, time synchronization, replay, and injection attacks, more specifically FDI attacks to target smart grids [4, 7, 8]. DoS attack was identified by each paper [4, 7–9], to impact the availability, as well as jamming attacks and wormhole attacks.

These papers also provide some solutions to aid in the mitigation of the attacks outlined. Some of the confidentiality-based solutions include data encryption, authentication, saturated channel detection [8]; malware protection, network intrusion prevention and detection systems, virtual private networks [9]; AI-based techniques and education

[7]; Nafees et al. [4] outlined different intrusion detection systems, for example, host-based, cloud-based, and machine learning-based. Multiple papers all identified authentication schemes as a preventative technique for integrity-based attacks [7–9]. Khoei, Slimane [7] also outlined spread spectrum as a possible mitigation solution for integrity-based attacks, while Gunduz and Das [8] mentioned end-to-end encryption. Gunduz and Das [8] was the only paper to outline some solution that pertained to availability-based attacks, traffic filtering, and anomaly detection. Solutions were outlined by papers that did not necessarily fit to one type of attack, security operation centers, game theory-based techniques, and risk and maturity assessments [4, 7, 9].

One mitigation technique that appeared multiple times throughout the four smart grid vulnerability papers was authentication.

2.2 *Authentication Protocols*

As outlined by the papers above authentication is a protective technique for mitigating the risk of cyberattacks. When an entity is authenticating with another entity, they are proving their identity is the same to one already registered. After the entities have authenticated, typically, a secret key will be generated between them for secure data transferral [14]. Cryptographic techniques are used with the protocols to authenticate both devices and create the session key [13]. In recent literature, numerous authentication protocols have been proposed by researchers to enhance the security of the smart grid.

3. Other Smart Grid Authentication Reviews

Similar articles exist that have reviewed authentication protocols for the smart grid, although their main points differ from this paper.

Agarkar and Agrawal [13] reviewed authentication and privacy preservation schemes, with a larger focus on the latter, for the smart grid and Internet of Things (IoT). They presented an overview of ECC-based, homomorphic encryption, and lattice cryptography.

Benmalek, Challal [15] presented some of the major cyberattacks to the smart grid. From this they outline some objectives for security within the AMI. They provided a review of authentication schemes, focusing on objectives, pros, and cons. They concluded that their outlined objectives were yet to be met by a proposed authentication protocol.

Qasaimeh, Turab [16] systemically review the literature to evaluate proposed authentication protocols for the smart grid. They identified five approaches used to form the protocols, they were: cryptography-based; password-based; hardware-based; signature-based; and biometric-based.

They found the most common attack mitigated was MITM, with replay as the second most mitigated.

Je, Woo [17] described some security threats to the smart grid by separating them into different types: control system threats; network threats; and consumer security threats. They review countermeasures proposed in literature for security threats in the smart grid. They then developed their own authentication technique utilizing a proposed group signature technique.

Mall, Amin [18] reviewed the literature proposing authentication protocols, specifically using Physically Unclonable Functions (PUFs). They analyzed the literature surrounding the smart grid, wireless sensor networks, and IoT. In their paper, they analyzed each piece of literature based on the computational cost, communication cost, and the cyberattacks mitigated. They concluded that all the protocols were susceptible to PUF-modeling attacks and performance could be impacted due to temperature.

El Makhtoum and Bentaleb [19] outlined some privacy issues within the AMI and review literature that specifically creates authentication schemes using the one-time password technique. The review of each paper is separated based on a set of attacks they protect against, a set of security features, and on the computational and communication cost of the protocol. They concluded that future research is needed for authenticating smart grid devices with one-time password schemes.

Table 1 outlines the similar articles and their topics discussed in regard to the topics discussed in this paper. The columns in the table represent the main points included within the papers as compared to this chapter. Cryptographic techniques represent the papers outlining the different techniques utilized in the authentication protocols. Security vulnerabilities meaning the papers have referred to the different types of vulnerabilities in the grid. Evaluation metrics means the papers discuss the evaluation

Table 1: Summary of similar articles.

References	Cryptographic Techniques	Security Vulnerabilities	Evaluation Metrics
[13]	Y	Y	N
[15]	N	Y	N
[16]	Y	N	N
[17]	N	Y	N
[18]	N	Y	Y
[19]	N	Y	N
This paper	Y	Y	Y

used for the protocols reviewed. The table shows this chapter as the only one that outlines all three of these topics.

4. Review of Authentication Protocols

When reviewing the literature, there were recurring techniques used within the protocols that were broken into different types. The types identified were Elliptic Curve Cryptography (ECC), PUFs, Blockchain, and Biometrics. The literature was separated into these types for comparison. Some papers used multiple techniques, for example, Badshah et al. [20] utilize blockchain, PUFs, and ECC. These papers were put into a category based on the technique thought to be the dominant one used.

The majority of papers reviewed evaluated their protocols with three different metrics. They have been titled security analysis, trusted analysis, and performance analysis. Security analysis was fulfilled by the protocol being analyzed logically to find the attacks mitigated and security features (e.g., mutual authentication). Trusted analysis was performed with a defined set of logic or authentication protocol analysis software that is widely trusted to evaluate the security of authentication protocols. Finally, performance analysis evaluated the computational cost of the protocol on the specified devices, as well as the communication cost, and in some cases the storage cost.

4.1 Elliptic Curve Cryptography

ECC uses an elliptic curve graph and points on the graph to create a secure public/private key for use within a system. When $k.P$ is computed the result is another point on the curve, Q. In order to recover k when given the points P and Q have been named the Elliptic Curve Discrete Logarithm Problem (ECDLP). This is why ECC is used for keys generation, the problem cannot be solved in a timely manner. This means generating a key with ECC cannot be calculated given the points on the graph. ECC is a lightweight algorithm, the number of bits required for a secure key is 384 [21]. Figure 1 shows an elliptic curve adapted from [22].

All the papers reviewed utilized ECC to create keys. Majority of them created private keys and subsequent public keys. The keys were used within the authentication phases for secure data transmission, which then led to the creation of the session key for secure data transfer after successful authentication. Other information obtained from ECC that was utilized within the protocols was random values and in some cases identifiers.

Table 2 displays a summary of the papers performance analyses. Majority of the papers calculated the computational cost based on a

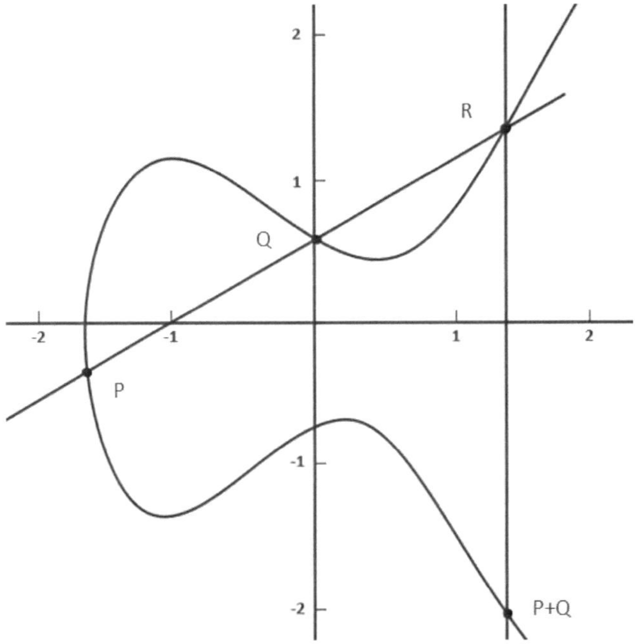

Figure 1: Example of an elliptic curve, adapted from [22].

different paper's execution time of the cryptographic techniques. However, not every paper used the same reference to calculate the execution time of their techniques. The communication cost for each paper was calculated in a similar way the computation cost but differed by using the size of the data transferred. The size of the data differed between papers, for example, Egide and Li [23] calculated 32 bits for the identifier, while Safkhani et al. [24] calculated 32 bits, and Nkurunziza et al. [25] calculated 160 bits. Goel, Gupta [26] did not calculate a computational or communication cost, while Zhai et al. [27] did but only gave the equations for the costs, not the specific numbers. The other performance analysis only performed by two of the papers was the Energy, Garg et al. [28] calculated their energy in microjoules, which has been converted into millijoules, the same measurement used by Safkhani et al. [24].

Figure 3 is a word cloud showing the different software and logic utilized. Most papers utilized different trusted analyses with some using software such as AVISPA or Proverif. Others used logic and models, such as the ROR Model or GNY Logic, as the trusted analysis, and some papers incorporated two different types of trusted analyses. There were three papers that did not perform a trust analysis, which could mean their protocol is less trustworthy than those that did.

The last analysis performed by every paper was the security analysis. Majority of the protocols mitigated replay, MITM, and impersonation attacks, while some attacks were only investigated by one paper, such as the secret disclosure attack mentioned by Hosseinzadeh et al. [29]. Figure 2 shows each attack investigated by the papers and the number of the papers that investigated each attack. As seen, many attacks are investigated but majority of them are only investigated by two to four of the papers.

This table shows that the comparison between the protocols is difficult to find the most efficient or best at mitigation as there are metrics that are not measured and metrics that are measured differently across all the articles.

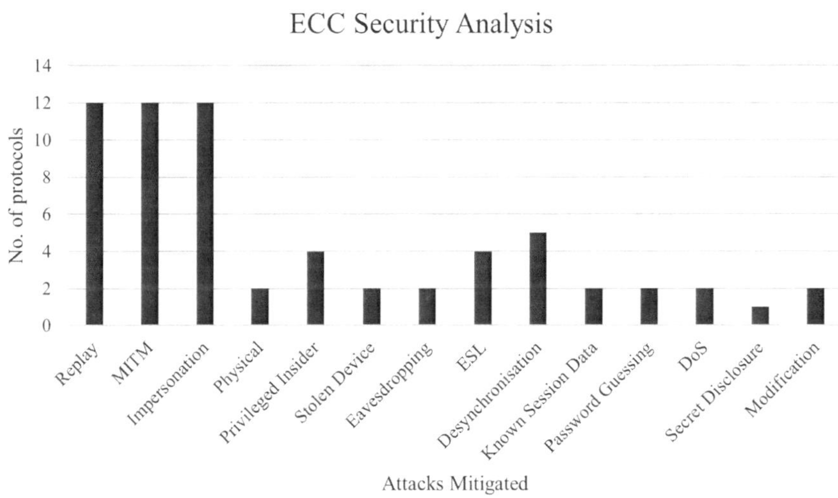

Figure 2: Summary of ECC-based protocols security analysis.

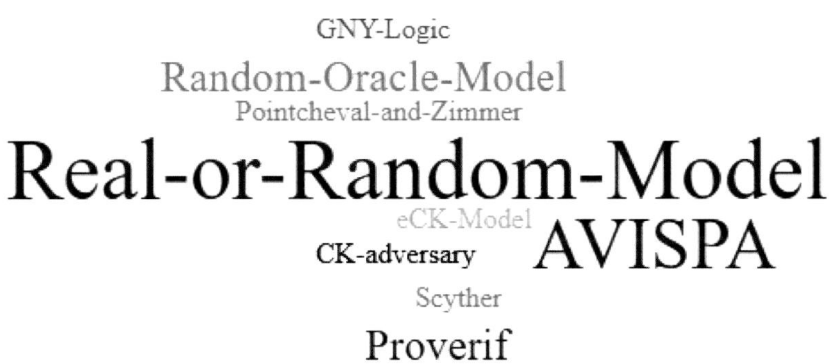

Figure 3: Summary of ECC-based protocols trusted analysis.

Table 2: Summary of ECC-based protocols performance analysis.

Refs.	Performance Analysis		
	Comp (ms)	Comm (bits)	Energy (mJ)
[30]	17.8	1792	–
[26]	–	–	–
[31]	268.4	1376	–
[28]	11912	506	0.3982
[32]	13.34	320	–
[33]	3.988	1538	–
[34]	1.093	864	–
[35]	267.45	1696	–
[36]	32.94	1024	–
[37]	8.9466	-	–
[38]	12.343	1856	–
[24]	200.6	1504	24.07
[23]	61.34	1240	–
[29]	17.833	1152	–
[25]	40.5	1840	–
[27]	–	–	–

4.2 *Physically Unclonable Functions*

PUFs are typically corresponded with human fingerprints as they use the slight differences in integrated circuits to identify one device from another, similar to using fingerprints to identify one human being from another. The circuits can differ in their path delays, how voltage is gained, or their voltage thresholds. PUFs use challenge-response pairs (CRPs) to compare two devices, i.e., the same challenge can be given to two devices, and they will give two different responses. The relationship between the challenge and response can be shown by the following equation [39], C meaning challenge and R meaning response:

Equation 1: PUF Equation

$$R = PUF(C)$$

Majority of the papers that utilized PUFs in their protocols used them for key generation, some used them within the verification message [40, 41], and one paper used them for a one-time shadow identity [42]. Four of the papers also combined their PUF with fuzzy extractors to help with the "noise" from the PUF and generate helper data for use within the protocol.

PUFs for security reasons have two different types, each with their own benefits, strong PUF and weak PUF. The strong PUF allows for many CRPs, while the weak PUF can only provide a small number of CRPs [43]. Five of the PUF papers outlined the types of PUFs that would be implemented with their protocol, three of which outlined weak PUFs, while two outlined strong. Tahavori and Moazami [44] mentioned utilizing a 128-bit arbiter PUF, while Kaveh et al. [45] also discussed a strong PUF, an on-chip-error-correcting PUF. Gope and Sikdar [42] implemented a reconfigurable PUF that used DRAM. They also used an SRAM weak PUF within their protocol. It is assumed that Badar et al. [40] used an SRAM PUF as they outlined that their test bed used an Arduino with SRAM. Liu, Sun [41] also mentioned using an SRAM PUF. Different types of PUFs require different computational and communication costs.

Table 3 shows the performance analysis for the PUF papers. The computational cost for three papers was calculated via another paper's calculation of the execution times for the cryptographic techniques [41, 44, 46]. The rest of the papers created their own test beds to calculate the execution times for the cryptographic techniques, with [42] calculating in a different measurement to the rest of the papers.

Figure 5 presents a summary of these papers, displaying the several different trusted analyses utilized across the articles. As seen by the word cloud, Scyther is used by papers with the other analyses only being used by one paper each. While Figure 4 shows the security analysis for the PUF-based protocols. Similar to the ECC-based protocols there are a few attacks that are only investigated by one paper, for example, key

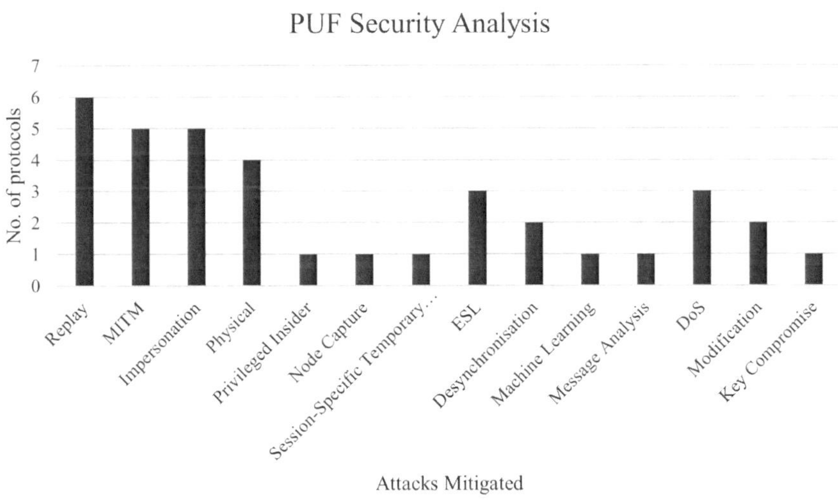

Figure 4: Summary of PUF-based protocols security analysis.

Figure 5: Summary of PUF-based protocols trusted analysis.

compromise attack by Tanveer and Alasmary [47]. Only two papers measured the storage of their protocol, which is important as there are many constrained devices within the smart grid [41, 47].

Once again, the summary table shows the drastic differences between the protocol papers and how there should be universal metrics for identifying the efficiency and effectiveness of authentication protocols [10].

Table 3: Summary of PUF-based protocols performance analysis.

Refs.	Performance Analysis		
	Comp (ms)	Comm (bits)	Storage (bits)
[44]	2.67	1408	–
[42]	94903 clock cycles	–	–
[40]	4.076	1376	–
[45]	1.09	1536	–
[46]	1.511	768	–
[47]	4.34	1206	1065
[41]	43.32	1576	776

4.3 Blockchain

A blockchain keeps a transaction record or ledger that authorized nodes within a system have stored. For a new block to be added to the system all nodes already in the system have to approve the new node. This forms a chain between the blocks. Each new block has a header that includes a hash of the previous block, and the block contains a transaction record. Blockchains allow nodes to trust each other, data tampering is less likely, and is more reliable [48].

Similar to the PUF-based protocols, some of the papers that created blockchain-based protocols calculated their performance analysis via a test bed, while others used previous work. Zhang, Wang [49] calculated their computation time based on an equation, and did calculate a storage cost but no exact number was given, only a variable rate. Badshah, Waqas [20] and Tomar and Tripathi [50] developed test beds that were used to calculate the computation and communication cost of their protocols. While, Wang, Huang [51] used one paper to calculate their performances and Verma, Purohit [52] used the calculations from two papers. Only Li, Zhang [53] calculated a fixed storage cost for their protocol, however they did not calculate a computation cost.

Only two of the papers performed a trusted analysis [20, 50], which leads to an assumption that the other papers may not be as trustworthy. The analyses used were ROR Model, an Adversarial Model, and Scyther. The security analysis, shown by Figure 6, is typically formed by human logic to reason why the protocol mitigates certain attacks, meaning the trusted analysis is important to perform. Eleven of the 16 attacks investigated were only investigated by one paper. This shows that further investigation should have been performed by the papers.

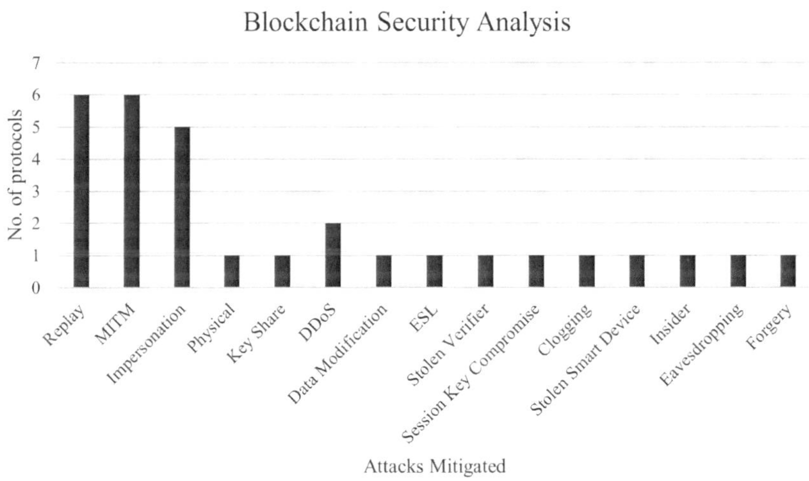

Figure 6: Summary of blockchain-based protocols security analysis.

Table 4: Summary of blockchain-based protocols.

Refs.	Performance Analysis		
	Comp (ms)	Comm (bits)	Storage (bits)
[49]	46.21	–	–
[51]	199.8	–	–
[20]	10.786	1664	–
[50]	7.444	4192	–
[52]	0.0196	1024	–
[53]	–	1169	520

4.4 Biometrics

Biometrics allow a user's identity to be verified, similar to using a password or pin. Biometric keys may be fingerprints, voice recognition, face recognition, or iris recognition. The advantage to biometrics is it cannot be lost, forgotten, guessed easily, and are difficult to forge. Fuzzy extractors are used to allow biometrics to be used in cryptography techniques. They are a pair of functions, one being a generation function to read the biometrics as input and output a secret key and a public reproduction attribute. The other function is to reproduce the biometric key via the biometric data and the public attribute [54].

The majority of the papers that use biometrics in their authentication protocols utilized identifiers, passwords, and biometrics to authenticate a user with a device. Only five papers were reviewed for biometric-based protocols, as biometric protocols only apply to communications including a user. Three of the five papers built their own test bed to find the performance analysis costs [55–57]. Table 5 summarizes the performance analysis from these papers.

Two papers did not use a trusted analysis tool on their protocol, while only one paper investigated the storage cost of their protocol. The trusted analyses were Proverif [58], BAN Logic [56], ROR Model, and AVISPA [57]. Not performing a trusted analysis could mean that the security analyses performed on the protocol were biased or subject to human error. Out of the three papers that did perform a trusted analysis, each of them uses different analyses, making the comparison of the protocols more difficult. Only 11 attacks were investigated by the PUF-based and biometric-based protocols, five of which were only investigated by one paper each, as shown by Figure 7.

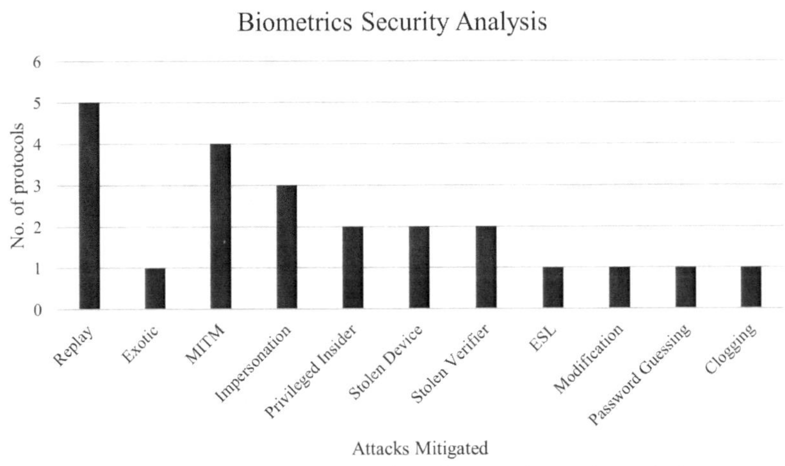

Figure 7: Summary of biometric-based protocols security analysis.

Table 5: Summary of biometric-based protocols.

Refs.	Performance Analysis		
	Comp (ms)	Comm (bits)	Storage (bits)
[55]	56.117	–	–
[59]	8.92	1152	–
[58]	4.117	1536	1107
[56]	7.252	1952	–
[57]	6.226	928	–

5. Future Work

As mentioned above, future work could research and create a universal set of metrics to be utilized by researchers and professionals to evaluate authentication protocols for the smart grid. These metrics could use the breakdown outlined in this paper, namely, security, trusted, and performance analysis, while also including a new metric known as accuracy analysis.

The security analysis could still be a human-based analysis, logically explaining why a protocol mitigates certain attacks. However, the metric could outline the specific attacks that are needed to be reviewed, instead of whichever attacks deemed appropriate by the protocol creator. The benefit of defining this metric is it would be known whether the protocol could not mitigate the attacks, instead of not knowing if the authors have just not investigated that attack.

Performance analysis, similar to security analysis, would not change much, however would have costs that must be found. The benefit of this could be defined execution time for cryptographic techniques or defined ways of measuring the communication cost. This metric could also enforce the calculation of storage cost as smart grid device are typically quite constrained.

The software analysis is harder to define guidelines for due to the numerous applications and types of logic to evaluate the security of authentication protocols. A solution could be having two or three applications/logics to be used to evaluate the protocols that differ in how they evaluate the protocol. The benefit of this is the unbiased evaluation of the protocol and the differences in what the applications are evaluating.

The last analysis that is proposed is an analysis that is not covered by the recent literature which is accuracy analysis. This metric would be evaluating how accurate the protocol is at identifying when an illegitimate entity is attempting to connect to a system device. It would also involve calculating a false alarm rate to identify when a legitimate device is attempting to connect to the system but is recognized as illegitimate. This would add critical information into finding the most effective authentication protocol for the smart grid.

Implementing guidelines for evaluating authentication protocols within the smart grid would be beneficial to this area of research making protocols easier to evaluate, compare, and critique.

6. Conclusion

This paper reviewed recent literature that was proposing authentication protocols for the smart grid and how that affects IoHT; to provide an overview of the evaluation metrics used within the papers. This chapter shows how different the analyses are across the literature and how that makes the protocols hard to compare and critique. Three types of metrics were found to be investigated throughout the literature, namely, security, trusted, and performance analysis. Security analysis explored the attacks that the protocol mitigated. Trusted analysis was performed with analysis tools to outline if the protocol was secure or not. Lastly, performance analysis outlined the computation, communication, and sometimes storage and energy costs of the authentication protocols. All three types had clear differences across the literature, causing difficulties in finding the most efficient protocol, suggesting that there could be future research in this area. Future research proposed could look into guidelines for already utilized evaluation metrics and suggesting new metrics not investigated in recent literature.

References

[1] Dept. of Home Affairs. 2018. *Security of Critical Infrastructure Act 2018*, H. Affairs, Editor.

[2] Kamal, M., A. Aljohani and E. Alanazi. 2020. IoT meets COVID-19: Status, challenges, and opportunities. *arXiv preprint arXiv:2007.12268*.

[3] Ud Din, I., W. Ali, A. Almogren, I. ALRassan and S. Zeadally. 2024. Using smart grid infrastructure for authentication and data management in Internet of Medical Things. *Security and Privacy*, **7**(3).

[4] Nafees, M. N., N. Saxena, A. Cardenas, S. Grijalva and P. Burnap. 2023. Smart grid cyber-physical situational awareness of complex operational technology attacks: A review. *ACM Comput. Surv.*, 55(10): Article 215.

[5] Reda, H. T., A. Anwar, A. N. Mahmood and Z. Tari. 2023. A taxonomy of cyber defence strategies against false data attacks in smart grids. *ACM Comput. Surv.*, 55(14s): Article 331.

[6] Ahmed, M. and A. -S. K. Pathan. 2020. False data injection attack (FDIA): An overview and new metrics for fair evaluation of its countermeasure. *Complex Adaptive Systems Modeling*, 8(4).

[7] Khoei, T., H. Slimane and N. Kaabouch. 2022. Cyber-security of smart grids: Attacks, detection, countermeasure techniques, and future directions. *Communications and Network*, 14: 119–170.

[8] Gunduz, M. Z. and R. Das. 2020. Cyber-security on smart grid: Threats and potential solutions. *Computer Networks*, 169.

[9] Faquir, D., N. Chouliaras, V. Sofia, K. Olga and L. Maglaras. 2021. Cybersecurity in smart grids, challenges and solutions. *AIMS Electronics and Electrical Engineering*, 5(1): 24–37.
[10] Griffiths, T., M. Ahmed and S. Yan. 2024. WIP: Performance metrics of PUF-based authentication protocols for smart grid: A review. In *2024 IEEE 25th International Symposium on a World of Wireless, Mobile and Multimedia Networks (WoWMoM)*.
[11] Gopstein, A., C. Nguyen, C. O'Fallon, N. Hastings and D. Wollman. 2021. NIST framework and roadmap for smart grid interoperability standards, release 4.0, special publication (NIST SP). *2021: National Institute of Standards and Technology*.
[12] Ding, J., A. Qammar, Z. Zhang, A. Karim and H. Ning. 2022. Cyber threats to smart grids: Review, taxonomy, potential solutions, and future directions. *Energies*, 15, DOI: 10.3390/en15186799.
[13] Agarkar, A. and H. Agrawal. 2019. A review and vision on authentication and privacy preservation schemes in smart grid network. *Security and Privacy* 2(2): e62.
[14] Syed Idrus, S. Z., E. Cherrier, C. Rosenberger and J. Schwartzmann. 2013. A review on authentication methods. *Australian Journal of Basic and Applied Sciences*, 7(5): 95–107.
[15] Benmalek, M., Y. Challal and A. Derhab. 2019. Authentication for smart grid AMI systems: Threat models, solutions, and challenges. In *2019 IEEE 28th International Conference on Enabling Technologies: Infrastructure for Collaborative Enterprises (WETICE)*.
[16] Qasaimeh, M., R. Turab and R. Al-Qassas. 2019. Authentication techniques in smart grid: a systematic review. *Telkomnika (Telecommunication Computing Electronics and Control)*, 17: 1584.
[17] Je, S. -M., H. Woo, J. Choi, S. Jung and J. Huh. 2022. A research trend on anonymous signature and authentication methods for privacy invasion preventability on smart grid and power plant environments. *Energies*, 15(12): 4363.
[18] Mall, P., R. Amin, A. Das, M. Leung and K. Choo. 2022. PUF-based authentication and key agreement protocols for IoT, WSNs, and smart grids: A comprehensive survey. *IEEE Internet of Things Journal*, 9(11): 8205–8228.
[19] El Makhtoum, H. and Y. Bentaleb. 2022. Review and evaluation of OTP-based authentication schemes in the metering systems of smart grids. 232–237.
[20] Badshah, A., M. Waqas, G. Abbas, F. Muhammad, Z. Abbas, S. Vimal and M. Bilal. 2022. LAKE-BSG: Lightweight authenticated key exchange scheme for blockchain-enabled smart grids. *Sustainable Energy Technologies and Assessments*, 52: 102248.
[21] Amara, M. and A. Siad. 2011. Elliptic curve cryptography and its applications. In *International Workshop on Systems, Signal Processing and their Applications, WOSSPA*.
[22] Childs, A. and W. van Dam. 2008. Quantum algorithms for algebraic problems. *Review of Modern Physics*, 82.
[23] Egide, N. and F. Li. 2023. HAP-SG: Heterogeneous authentication protocol for smart grid. *Peer-to-Peer Networking and Applications*, 16(3): 1365–1379.
[24] Safkhani, M., S. Kumari, M. Shojafar and S. Kumar. 2022. An authentication and key agreement scheme for smart grid. *Peer-to-Peer Networking and Applications*, 15(3): 1595–1616.
[25] Nkurunziza, E., L. Tandoh, I. Elfadul and F. Li. 2023. ECAAP-SG: Efficient certificate less anonymous authentication protocol for SG. *Security and Privacy*, 6(1): e273.
[26] Goel, H. et al. 2019. Three phase authentication protocol for smart grid communication. In *2019 IEEE Conference on Information and Communication Technology*.
[27] Zhai, F., T. Yang, W. Sun and X. Fang. 2023. Lightweight and dynamic authenticated key agreement and management protocol for smart grid. *Frontiers in Energy Research*, 10.
[28] Garg, S., K. Kaur, G. Kaddoum, J. Rodrigues and M. Guizani. 2020. Secure and lightweight authentication scheme for smart metering infrastructure in smart grid. *IEEE Transactions on Industrial Informatics*, 16(5): 3548–3557.

[29] Hosseinzadeh, M., R. Naqvi, M. Safkhani, L. Tightiz and R. Mehmood. 2023. Secure authentication in the smart grid. *Mathematics*, 11(1): 176.

[30] Abbasinezhad-Mood, D. and M. Nikooghadam. 2018. Design and hardware implementation of a security-enhanced elliptic curve cryptography based lightweight authentication scheme for smart grid communications. *Future Generation Computer Systems*, 84: 47–57.

[31] Kumar, N., G. Aujla, A. Das and M. Conti. 2019. ECCAuth: A secure authentication protocol for demand response management in a smart grid system. *IEEE Transactions on Industrial Informatics*, 15(12): 6572–6582.

[32] Deng, L. and R. Gao. 2021. Certificateless two-party authenticated key agreement scheme for smart grid. *Information Sciences*, 543: 143–156.

[33] Srinivas, J., A. Das, X. Li, M. Khan and M. Jo. 2021. Designing anonymous signature-based authenticated key exchange scheme for internet of things-enabled smart grid systems. *IEEE Transactions on Industrial Informatics*, 17(7): 4425–4436.

[34] Sureshkumar, V., S. Anandhi, R. Amin, N. Selvarajan and R. Madhumathi. 2021. Design of robust mutual authentication and key establishment security protocol for cloud-enabled smart grid communication. *IEEE Systems Journal*, 15(3): 3565–3572.

[35] Baghestani, S. H., F. Moazami and M. Tahavori. 2022. Lightweight authenticated key agreement for smart metering in smart grid. *IEEE Systems Journal*, 16(3): 4983–4991.

[36] Chaudhry, S. A., J. Nebhan, K. Yahya and F. Al-Turjman. 2022. A privacy enhanced authentication scheme for securing smart grid infrastructure. *IEEE Transactions on Industrial Informatics*, 18(7): 5000–5006.

[37] Choudhary, S., A. Kumar and K. Kumar. 2022. An efficient key agreement protocol for smart grid communication. In *2022 2nd International Conference on Emerging Frontiers in Electrical and Electronic Technologies (ICEFEET)*.

[38] Qi, M. 2022. An improved three-factor authentication and key agreement protocol for smart grid. *Journal of Ambient Intelligence and Humanized Computing*.

[39] Kaveh, M. and M. R. Mosavi. 2020. A lightweight mutual authentication for smart grid neighborhood area network communications based on physically unclonable function. *IEEE Systems Journal*, 14(3): 4535–4544.

[40] Badar, H. M. S., K. Mahmood, W. Akram, Z. Ghaffar, M. Umar and A. Das. 2023. Secure authentication protocol for home area network in smart grid-based smart cities. *Computers and Electrical Engineering*, 108: 108721.

[41] Liu, F., Y. Sun, Z. Liu, Y. Yan, H. Li and Y. Han. 2023. Lightweight batch authentication protocol for Bus-NB-IoT hierarchical network in smart grid using physically unclonable function. In *2023 IEEE 9th Intl Conference on Big Data Security on Cloud (BigDataSecurity), IEEE Intl Conference on High Performance and Smart Computing, (HPSC) and IEEE Intl Conference on Intelligent Data and Security (IDS)*.

[42] Gope, P. and B. Sikdar. 2021. A privacy-aware reconfigurable authenticated key exchange scheme for secure communication in smart grids. *IEEE Transactions on Smart Grid*, 12(6): 5335–5348.

[43] Anandakumar, N. N., M. Hashmi and M. Tehranipoor. 2021. FPGA-based physical unclonable functions: A comprehensive overview of theory and architectures. *Integration*, 81.

[44] Tahavori, M. and F. Moazami. 2020. Lightweight and secure PUF-based authenticated key agreement scheme for smart grid. *Peer-to-Peer Networking and Applications*, 13(5): 1616–1628.

[45] Kaveh, M., M. Mosavi, D. Martín and S. Aghapour. 2023. An efficient authentication protocol for smart grid communication based on on-chip-error-correcting physical unclonable function. *Sustainable Energy, Grids and Networks*, 36.

[46] Ma, H., C. Wang, G. Xu, Q. Cao, G. Xu and L. Duan. 2023. Anonymous authentication protocol based on physical unclonable function and elliptic curve cryptography for smart grid. *IEEE Systems Journal*, 1–12.

[47] Tanveer, M. and H. Alasmary. 2023. LACP-SG: Lightweight authentication protocol for smart grids. *Sensors*, 23, DOI: 10.3390/s23042309.

[48] Deng, X., J. Shao, L. Chang and J. Liang. 2021. A blockchain-based authentication protocol using cryptocurrency technology in LEO satellite networks. *Electronics*, 10, DOI: 10.3390/electronics10243151.

[49] Zhang, H., J. Wang and Y. Ding. 2019. Blockchain-based decentralized and secure keyless signature scheme for smart grid. *Energy*, 180: 955–967.

[50] Tomar, A. and S. Tripathi. 2022. Blockchain-assisted authentication and key agreement scheme for fog-based smart grid. *Cluster Computing*, 25(1): 451–468.

[51] Wang, W., H. Huang, L. Zhang, Z. Han, C. Qiu and C. Su. 2020. BlockSLAP: Blockchain-based secure and lightweight authentication protocol for smart grid. In *2020 IEEE 19th International Conference on Trust, Security and Privacy in Computing and Communications (TrustCom)*.

[52] Verma, N., S. Purohit and B. Narwal. 2023. BASB-SG: A biohashing-based authentication scheme for secure blockchain-enabled smart grids. In *2023 5th International Conference on Energy, Power and Environment: Towards Flexible Green Energy Technologies (ICEPE)*.

[53] Li, Y., D. Zhang, Z. Wang and G. Liu. 2023. A blockchain-based cooperative authentication mechanism for smart grid. *Applied Sciences*, 13(11): 6831.

[54] Khan, A. A., V. Kumar, M. Ahmad and S. Rana. 2021. LAKAF: Lightweight authentication and key agreement framework for smart grid network. *Journal of Systems Architecture*, 116: 102053.

[55] Yang, B., G. Xu, X. Zeng, J. Liu and Y. Zhang. 2018. A lightweight anonymous mobile user authentication scheme for smart grid. In *2018 IEEE SmartWorld, Ubiquitous Intelligence & Computing, Advanced & Trusted Computing, Scalable Computing & Communications, Cloud & Big Data Computing, Internet of People and Smart City Innovation (SmartWorld/SCALCOM/UIC/ATC/CBDCom/IOP/SCI)*.

[56] Ma, Z., Y. Yang, X. Liu, Y. Liu, S. Ma and K. Ren. 2020. EmIr-Auth: Eye movement and iris-based portable remote authentication for smart grid. *IEEE Transactions on Industrial Informatics*, 16(10): 6597–6606.

[57] Yu, S. and K. Park. 2022. ISG-SLAS: Secure and lightweight authentication and key agreement scheme for industrial smart grid using fuzzy extractor. *Journal of Systems Architecture*, 131: 102698.

[58] Grover, H. S., Adarsh and D. Kumar. 2020. Cryptanalysis and improvement of a three-factor user authentication scheme for smart grid environment. *Journal of Reliable Intelligent Environments*, 6(4): 249–260.

[59] Khan, A. A., V. Kumar and M. Ahmad. 2019. An elliptic curve cryptography based mutual authentication scheme for smart grid communications using biometric approach. *Journal of King Saud University—Computer and Information Sciences*, 34(3): 698–705.

Chapter 6

Artificial Immune System-Based Framework to Root Out Black Hole Attacks in Internet of Health Things

Mounika Baddula,[1,*] *Biplob Ray,*[1] *Mahmoud El-Khodr,*[1] *Morshed Chowdhury,*[2] *Muna Al-Hawawreh*[2] and *Adnan Anwar*[2]

1. Introduction

The Internet of Health Things (IoHT) is a rapidly rising technology that is revolutionizing healthcare. It allows for early detection of potential health problems, remote monitoring of treatments, and facilitates the preparation of assessments [1]. A recent survey of the Internet of Things reveals that it is a crucial element of digital transformation in healthcare products. IoT wearable devices are especially critical, as they allow for the remote monitoring of patient's health conditions and, in the event of an emergency, can swiftly alert caregivers or physicians about the patient's status [2]. The reliable communication network required by IoHT devices must be as mobile and flexible as the healthcare industry itself. Mobile

[1] School of Engineering and Technology, CQ University, Bundaberg, Australia.
[2] School of Information and Technology, Deakin University, Geelong, Australia.
Emails: b.ray@cqu.edu.au, m.elkhodr@cqu.edu.au, morshed.chowdhury@deakin.edu.au, muna.alhawawreh@deakin.edu.au, adnan.anwar@deakin.edu.au
* Corresponding author: m.baddula@cqu.edu.au

DOI: 10.1201/9781003483267-9

Ad hoc Networks (MANET) complement IoHT systems well, providing the necessary support for these technologies and extending their reach to ensure continuous and effective healthcare communication. However, MANET comes with its own security challenges, one of which is the vulnerability to cyber threats, like black hole attacks, that can compromise the network's integrity and patient safety.

A MANET is a network that consists of mobile nodes without an established setup. A key benefit of such networks is the absence of a necessity for preset and stationary nodes to handle the routing and delivery of packets from sources to destinations [3]. In the MANET environment, mobile nodes are the nodes. When the sending and receiving nodes are within the communication radius, the transmitting node sends the packet directly to the target node. However, when the target node is not within range, the sender node needs to identify the best route for delivering the packet through intermediary nodes [4]. This route will be saved in the memory field, and whenever the same nodes want to communicate with each other, the same route will be used. The destination and source nodes depend on the intermediate node to send and receive packets, and these nodes communicate using a routing protocol. In the process of selecting intermediate nodes, malicious nodes can pretend to be good nodes and attract packets generated from the originating node. This type of activity is called a black hole attack [5].

A black hole attack occurs in MANET when a rogue node exploits the route discovery mechanism of reactive routing protocols by falsely asserting to have the shortest path to the target. This deceitful node announces it possesses the best routes without verifying the route in the routing table. It then intercepts and drops the packets that pass through it [3]. These black hole nodes continuously broadcast their location with the maximum sequence number and the minimum steps. DoS attacks can occur from hazardous network attacks, impacting network and system reliability and availability [5]. As MANET is operating critical-mission applications such as disaster relief, law enforcement, and emergency response, it is essential to have a secure and reliable routing path [6].

Although existing MANET systems employ numerous security mechanisms, the security issues associated with MANET have yet to be fully resolved. This is mainly because many of the existing solutions are threshold-based, which is unsuitable for a dynamic environment such as MANET. Many solutions have relied on detecting and mitigating black hole attacks by overlooking the initial or any following response packets originating from each node. However, these approaches fail to account for several responding packets, which provide a dynamic upper limit for the recipient's sequence number. A new approach has been suggested for identifying black hole attack nodes in MANET, as existing security mechanisms have certain limitations. Our proposed approach is centered around utilizing an AIS. Studies have shown that there are similarities between the tissues in the human body and the systems in MANET [6]. The human immune system's defense system can be metamorphosed into an AIS to shield MANET [5]. One of the advantages of using the AIS algorithm to secure MANET is that it can detect malicious nodes in a distributed and combined manner by not following central management points in the security system. The danger theory is a scientific concept that can enhance the efficiency of the artificial immune system [7]. The existing signals of the nodes, based on the successful transmission of the packets and trust value, can be used to identify black hole attack nodes.

The main contribution of this paper includes:

- This paper proposed an AIS-TSM model based on artificial immune systems, particularly danger theory, to discover the black hole attack nodes in the MANET.
- As part of the detection model, this paper includes a novel trust model to establish trust in the communication between nodes. To avoid disruption to the network, the proposed model prepares each node as a dendritic cell (DC) to detect malicious nodes.
- The proposed detection model and techniques are tested against black hole attacks to evaluate the efficiency of the suggested model in contrast to existing similar solutions.

The paper's structure is briefly outlined as follows. Section 2 discusses the background and related work, while Section 3 presents an overview of the inspiration and proposition of AIS. In Section 4, the proposed black hole attack identification method in the MANET is introduced. Simulations and statistical result analysis are detailed in Section 5. Section 6 contains a discussion, while Section 7 serves as the paper's conclusion.

2. Background and Related Work

This section will cover the background research of IoHT and MANET in 2.1. Then, we will delve into the existing black hole attack in 2.2. Finally, in 2.3, we will review the literature on the proposed solutions for the black hole attack in existing works.

2.1 Background: IoHT and MANET

Smart healthcare has garnered a lot of attention recently due to the improved patient care provided by smart wearable devices and sensors that continuously monitor health and collect data [8]. These smart devices are making homes more intelligent by communicating with each other, thereby improving users' health and supporting their ability to live independently [9]. The IoHT has numerous positive impacts on healthcare, signaling a shift toward models that prioritize patients' needs and preferences, thereby enhancing the overall quality of care [10]. Smart medical devices can facilitate remote health monitoring without human intervention. Diagnosing diseases and monitoring biomedical signals are made possible through smart sensors and advanced communication protocols. The use of IoHT devices enhances healthcare approaches and plays a crucial role in maintaining patient health [11].

MANET (Figure 1) is a group of mobile nodes with a self-configured and self-managed network without any established structure. When the network topology changes, the nodes can move arbitrarily. Each node is considered the router while sending the traffic to other specified nodes, and the network does not have a center. MANET is an open network where the nodes can join and leave the network. MANETs are broadly used in traffic control, military, smart cities, and making in routing protocols [12]. The entire network performance is based on the quality of the routing protocols. The data access is complicated due to the limited storage capacity and resources. The nodes in the network send the packets to the available forward node to reach the destination, improving the communication range [13]. Due to the nodes' random movement, the link between them may disconnect. If the battery of the mobile nodes is drained, the route formed between the nodes will be separated, which affects the network lifetime [14].

In a MANET, the origin and target nodes rely on intermediate nodes to pass messages from one to another through successive hops. Each node located along the journey to the destination will handle the packets. The inherent nature and structure of MANETs open the door to various

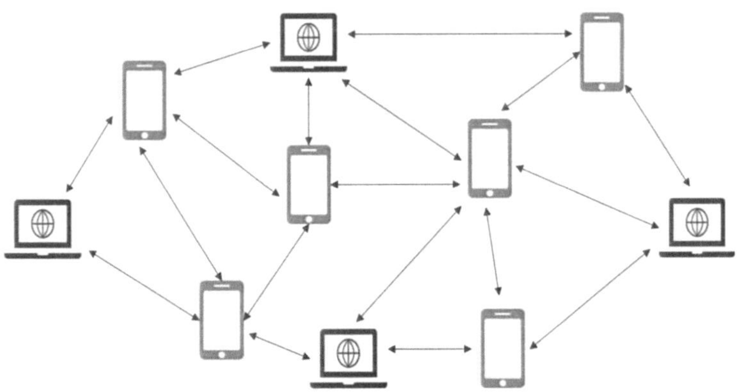

Figure 1: Mobile Ad Hoc Network.

security concerns. Among the prevalent security threats in MANETs are black holes, wormholes, man-in-the-middle, eavesdropping, routing, and traffic analysis attacks. These attacks primarily aim to either halt packet delivery in the network or introduce erroneous data packets. Despite the assumption in MANET that all nodes are reliable, certain rogue nodes can act maliciously, undermining the network's functionality [15]. Black hole attacks, in particular, have a severe impact on network performance. This paper is dedicated to crafting a solution for identifying the nodes responsible for black hole attacks to preserve the integrity of the network.

2.2 Background: Black Hole Attack

A black hole attack is a specific form of a DoS attack targeting MANETs and disrupting the routing service by misusing the AODV routing protocol's route discovery process. In such attacks, a malevolent node falsely claims to have the shortest path to the target node using its routing strategy. As a consequence, this attacker node is always in a position to respond to route queries, which allows it to intercept and discard the data packets. This results in the sent packets failing to reach their intended destination, thereby diminishing the efficiency of the MANET [16]. Numerous studies have investigated the impact of malignant attacks on network efficiency, indicating that black hole attacks are particularly detrimental compared to other kinds of network layer attacks [17].

In the context of AODV protocol within a MANET (Figure 1), the initial action taken by a source node looking to transmit a packet to a destination node involves route discovery. To begin this process, the source node disseminates a Route Request (RREQ) to its adjacent nodes. These nodes, upon receipt of the RREQ, examine their route tables for any preexisting paths to the intended destination. Should a valid route exist, a Route Reply (RREP) is directed back to the source node. Otherwise, the RREQ is propagated further to additional neighboring nodes. A destination sequence number is used by the source node to determine the freshness of the route; a higher sequence number signals a more recent route. During this process, if a malevolent node intercepts the RREQ, it may issue an RREP indicating a highly favorable sequence number to deceive the source node into routing through it. As data packets are routed to this deceitful node, they are then deliberately dropped, resulting in what is known as a black hole attack [18, 19].

To illustrate how this attack works, let's look at an example in Figure 2. Node "A" wants to send a message to node "F." If "A" already knows the way to "F," it just sends the message. But if it doesn't, "A" asks around by sending a message asking for directions, which is called an

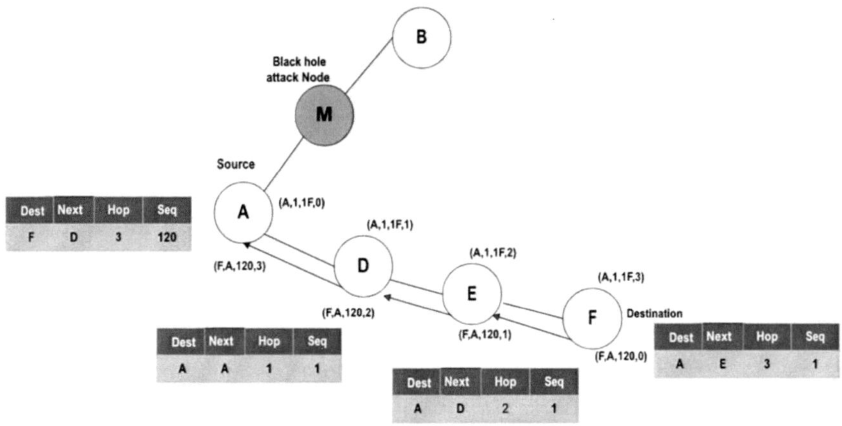

Figure 2: Example of Black Hole Attack process.

RREQ, to the nodes nearby like "D" and "M." Node "D" looks to see if it knows the way to "F." If "D" does, it tells "A" by sending back an RREP. If it doesn't, it asks the next node, and this goes on until "F" gets the RREQ. Then, "F" sends an RREP back to give "A" the route. This tells "A" how many steps, or hops, it takes to reach "F." When "A" sends an RREQ to the bad node "M," "M" pretends it knows a short way to "F" even though it doesn't. It sends a fake RREP to "A." "A" thinks "M" has the best route, so it sends the message to "M." But "M" throws it away.

This is the black hole attack where "M" tricks all the nodes into sending messages its way and then drops them. As this attack affects network efficiency, it is essential to handle this attack and detect it to avoid sending data through its nodes. In this paper, we're focusing on coming up with new solutions for handling and detecting these attacks to maintain network efficiency in MANET.

2.3 *Related Work*

Numerous studies have introduced measures to detect and tackle black hole attacks in MANETs. For instance, research by Shrestha et al. [7] focused on protecting against black hole attacks through an enhancement of the sequence number utilized in the AODV routing protocol. They developed a method that modifies the sequence number within the reply to the RREQ. When a source node encounters a route response with a questionable sequence number, it will issue a new RREQ with an altered sequence number that matches that of the suspicious route reply typically associated with a black hole attack. When the hostile node gets this packet, it will drop the packet and then issue a route response containing an increased sequence number. The source node will learn about the type of suspicious node and stop sending the packets through it, improving the network efficiency. They analyzed the algorithm with 500 nodes using a network simulator 2, which performs better in all the scenarios. In another study, Nitnaware and Thakur [20] developed a mitigation algorithm to identify the harmful nodes and circumvent the genuine node from the attack. They performed the simulation in Qualnet 5.2 simulator with three different scenarios and assessed the performance. In their proposed work, each node has Dynamic MANET On-demand (DYMO), which can estimate the transmission value. If the count of the malicious nodes goes above a set limit, then other nodes in the network will not send packets to them, effectively ignoring them, and they do not send any packets. The algorithm worked well in identifying the black hole attack nodes within the network, leading to better packet delivery rates and more efficient network operation. Vadavi et al. [21] worked to find black hole attacks within the improved AODV protocol. Typically, the standard AODV employs the hop count as a measure to detect such nodes. When packets are dispatched from the source to the destination node, a decoy request is issued to neighboring nodes, which then await responses. Upon receiving these responses, the source node analyses them, identifying any node whose reply doesn't correspond with the actual route owner as a potential threat. Simulations have indicated that by adopting this strategy, black hole attacks can be mitigated, enhancing the overall effectiveness of the network.

The authors in [22] studied real-time surveillance for the detection and prevention of black hole attacks. When nodes in the network want to exchange data packets among themselves, then a provisional network called an ad hoc network will be formed. For this type of network, the resources will be less and the chances for an attack from the malicious node are always high. During a black hole attack, the malicious node falsely claims to have the optimal path to the destination, and upon receiving a packet, it deliberately discards it. Upon receiving an RREQ, the hostile node sends back a route response to the originating node, asserting it possesses a path to the intended destination. In real-time monitoring, the neighboring node of the suspected node listens to all data packets sent by the malicious node. Every node within the network will have discovered (forward packet) and f-count (receive packet). When the f-count of the malicious node reaches the threshold and the r-count to 0 then the node is deemed to be a hostile node. There is a high chance of a false positive for the malicious node when the node status depends on the destination sequence number, but with the help of real-time monitoring, we can reduce the false positives of the attacker nodes.

In a most recent study [23], the authors introduced an approach to enhance the AODV protocol to counter black hole attacks by integrating the Firefly Algorithm alongside an Artificial Neural Network. Some features related to the node's position, latency in data transfer, and power usage within the network are used to train the network and identify the black hole. The experimental outcomes demonstrate that their suggested method surpasses conventional methods in packet delivery rate, throughput, and transmission delay. Along with this direction, we propose a novel approach for identifying black hole attack nodes in MANET and mitigating their impact on the network. We use the Artificial Immune System, specifically the danger theory, which is based on the DC model. This model helps detect black hole attacks, improving the network's performance under attacks.

3. Overview of Artificial Immune System

This section has details about the artificial immune system, danger theory, and DC algorithms. Our proposed detection model primarily utilizes Artificial Immune System (AIS) techniques, which are inspired by the natural Human Immune System (HIS) to detect the greedy or selfish nodes in MANET. AIS is inspired by algorithms in biology and mimics the strategy of the HIS [24]. The capabilities of the human immune system evolve to recognize and eliminate pathogens in foreign objects, as shown in the biological samples. Most importantly, these systems are integrated with the brain-inspired neurotic networks for self-learning and the natural immune system principles to mitigate problems [4, 25]. The fundamental role of the body's immune system is to defend against harmful pathogens and maintain overall well-being [26]. This system is adept at gathering data, adapting through learning and retaining critical information [27]. For instance, it can remember the pathogen that has attacked the body for the first time and generate a system responsible for it so that in future attacks, the system can respond quickly to defend itself from the pathogen. Therefore, inherited from the biological immune system, the AIS is featured in learning, memory, and pattern recognition [6].

The authors in [4] explained three fundamental principles that must be considered when implementing the AIS. First, each individual AIS algorithm should at least be an immune segment like a lymphocyte. The second one is that an idea obtained from experimental or theoretical biology should be used in each AIS algorithm. The third one is that the proposed AIS should be helpful in problem-solving. The AIS has many algorithms [6], in this paper, we focus on using Danger Theory and the Dendritic Cell Algorithm (DCA). As DCA represents the function of the human immune system's dendritic cells, and dendritic cells are the human body's intrusion detection agents in nature, which patrol the tissue and organs for potential pathogen invaders, it will be more helpful in detecting unusual activities of the networks done by selfish nodes in the MANET. Therefore, we build our proposed model using Danger Theory and DCA.

To explain how the DCA works and can help identify the black hole, we will explain how the danger theory and DCs work in nature and then put them in relation to the detection of black hole attacks within MANET. Initially, the danger theory presents that just because a foreign microbe is identified in their system, it will not launch the immune response [25]. The danger signals generated from abnormally exerted cells will trigger the DCs. In other words, the existing foreign microbe in the system should be a threat of any means to trigger the immature DCs to change their state. The role of the Antigen Presenting Cell (APC) is vital within the danger theory to signal the presence of a threat [27]. A danger signal can represent either a positive or negative event, and it is not necessarily a sign of threat. It can represent the presence or a sense of a signal and conceptual ideas for using Danger Theory for anomaly detection. DCs consist of antigen cells that are almost present in all tissues. Immature, semi-mature, and mature are three distinct stages in DCs. The immature DCs mainly contained leukocytes and were present in all tissues. Immature DCs can change their state to semi-mature or mature, relying on the appropriate trigger (set of input signals) to produce a system response by presenting captured antigens to the T-Cells. Immature DCs process four kinds of signals: Pathogen-Associated Molecular Patterns (PAMP), danger signals, safe signals, and inflammation signals. Depending on the potency and combination of these signals, the cells may develop into either semi-mature or fully mature DCs.

PAMP signal can highly detect the presence of virulent pathogens. The safe signal will be released when healthy cells die from a natural cause. If the cell dies abnormally, then the danger signal will be released. These signals will be sent to the T-cell to launch the response by sending the antigens [19]. PAMP signals majorly indicate the existence of infectious antigens in the system. Danger signals are created when body cells are under stress or abnormal death. Safe signals are created when the body cells die naturally. Inflammation signals are created due to increased cell temperature, leading to an unhealthy state or infection. The concentration of the input signals determines the state change for the immature DCs. If immature DCs detect more PAMP and danger signals than safe signals, they will mature and activate T-cells to start an immune response. If PAMP and danger signals are fewer than safe signals, the DCs will become semi-mature and not trigger an immune response [17].

In the MANET network and with existing selfish or greedy nodes, the DCA will help to detect the nodes causing the network's black hole attack. The DCs cannot attack all the foreign molecules that enter the human body, which is good for the human body. Similarly, the network contains many nodes that help send the packet to a destination, but some nodes are selfish in the network. This algorithm helps identify the network attack node by not causing any trouble to other nodes.

4. Proposed Model for Identification of Black Hole Attacks in MANET

This section presents the implementation and design of the AIS-TSM, which aims to identify black hole attack nodes in MANET. To begin the research, a black hole attack scenario was recreated within a MANET, as shown in Figure 3. The AIS-TSM framework was then implemented, with the AODV protocol serving as the backbone for routing. In this setup, a source node transmits data directly to the destination node via an established path, if one exists. If not, the source node emits an RREQ signal to adjacent nodes in search of the most direct route available. Any node that has an established route to the intended destination will reply with an RREP. Nodes keep track of the frequency of RREPs from peers, and this is adjusted within the routing protocol. After analyzing the incoming RREPs, the source node routes the data packet to the end destination and expects an acknowledgment.

If the acknowledgment is not received, the source node reassesses the RREP data and examines the PDR of the nodes. The PDR is determined as the ratio of the number of packets successfully received by the target to the number of packets sent from the originating node [28]. A node with a high count of RREPs but a low PDR triggers a warning, indicating

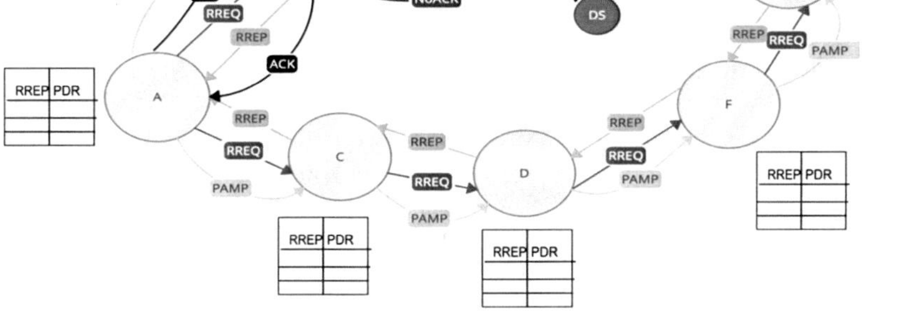

Figure 3: DC active Black Hole Attack model.

potential malicious behavior. Upon detecting such a discrepancy, a "danger signal" is issued to neighboring nodes. This prompts a PAMP signal defensive response aimed at neutralizing the threat posed by the suspected malicious node. Neighboring nodes intensify surveillance of the suspect, gathering more detailed information on its activities. These details are shared with peer nodes in the network to collectively avoid routing packets via harmful nodes, thereby circumventing a potential black hole attack. As monitoring continues, if the suspect node's RREP and PDR metrics improve, indicating reliable behavior, the danger signals are gradually withdrawn, and trust in the node is restored. This dynamic approach allows the network to adapt to threats and ensures data packets are routed through secure and efficient paths based on the above data, mathematical representation of PDR, danger signal, and trust. As we explained, the danger theory algorithm identifies the black hole attack nodes in MANET with the signals and interactions built upon the assumption that each node has a DC's behavior in the AIS-TSM model. Therefore, we use this behavior to establish trust in the selected nodes along the route from source to destination.

The packet delivery ratio (PDR_i) for each node can be calculated using Eq. 1, which incorporates the number of packets successfully delivered to the total number of packets sent, where $N_{delivered,\, i}$ is the number of packets delivered by node (i) and $T_{sent,\, i}$ is total number of packets sent by the node (i).

$$PDR_i = \frac{N_{delivered,i}}{T_{sent,i}} \tag{1}$$

The Eq. 2 determines the danger signal of the node by considering the route replies and the packet delivery ratio of the node

$$D_i = \begin{cases} \dfrac{RREP_i}{PDR_i} - T & if \ \dfrac{RREP_i}{PDR_i} > T \\ 0 & otherwise \end{cases} \tag{2}$$

where D_i is the danger signal of the node I, $RREP_i$ is the number of route reply for node (i), and PDR_i is the packet delivery ratio of the node (i) and T represents the predetermined threshold value derived from the historical network performance data. When the ratio of the RREP and PDR is above a certain threshold value, then the danger signal will be raised. The higher is the value of the danger signal, the more suspicious is the behavior.

$$T_i(t) = \begin{cases} T_i(t-1) \times \delta - \gamma \times P_i(t) & \text{if } D_i(t) = 1 \\ min(T_i(t-1) + \alpha - \gamma \times P_i(t), T_{max}) & \text{if } D_i(t) = 0 \text{ and } PDR_i(t) > PDR_i(t-1) \\ T_i(t-1) - \gamma \times P_i(t) & \text{otherwise} \end{cases} \tag{3}$$

The Eq. 3 determines the trust value of the node. Ti(t) is the trust value of the node (i) at the current time (t), where P_i(t) is the PAMP signal at time t, D_i(t) is the danger signal at time. α represents the decay factor applied to the previous trust level. γ represents the impact of the PAMP signal on the trust level. T_{max} is the maximum possible trust level of the node. D_i(t) represents the danger signal at time t and PDR_i(t) is the packet delivery ratio of node i at time t. $T_i(t-1)$ is the trust value of node i at the previous step.

5. Simulation Results and Statistical Analysis

Section 5 presents the simulation findings of the proposed approach and a comparison of our model and AODV, DSR, AODV-BS OBT-DSR, SAODV, IDS, Sequence number change model [29, 7, 30, 31] with different performance metrics. The efficacy of our new model in detecting black hole incursions within MANETs was assessed through simulations conducted with Network Simulator-3.26. Details of the simulation settings are described in Table 1.

Table 1: Simulation parameters.

Simulation	NS-3.26
Number of nodes	100
Network area	1000m x 1000m
Black hole attack nodes	10
Transmission range	50m
Simulation time	80s

Figure 4 presents a comparative analysis of packet delivery ratios for various routing protocols, including the proposed AIS-TSM, across different network sizes. As a baseline, the traditional AODV protocol shows a strong PDR performance, which remains relatively stable as the number of nodes increases. However, under a black hole attack, the PDR noticeably deteriorates. While the SAODV protocol, incorporating SVM and ANN algorithms, initially demonstrates promising results, its PDR gradually declines with larger network sizes. In contrast, the AIS-TSM model consistently achieves a high PDR, exceeding 93% even with 100 nodes. This highlights the superior performance and robustness of AIS-TSM in maintaining reliable data transmission, even in challenging network conditions.

Figure 5 illustrates the superior performance of the AISTSM model in maintaining high packet delivery ratios, even in the presence of black hole attack nodes. As the number of black hole nodes increases from

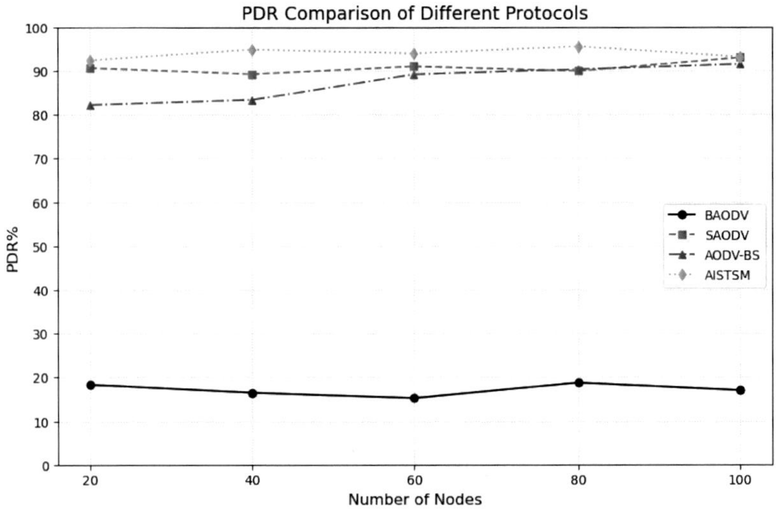

Figure 4: Packet Delivery Ratio (PDR%) compared with the number of malicious nodes in the network.

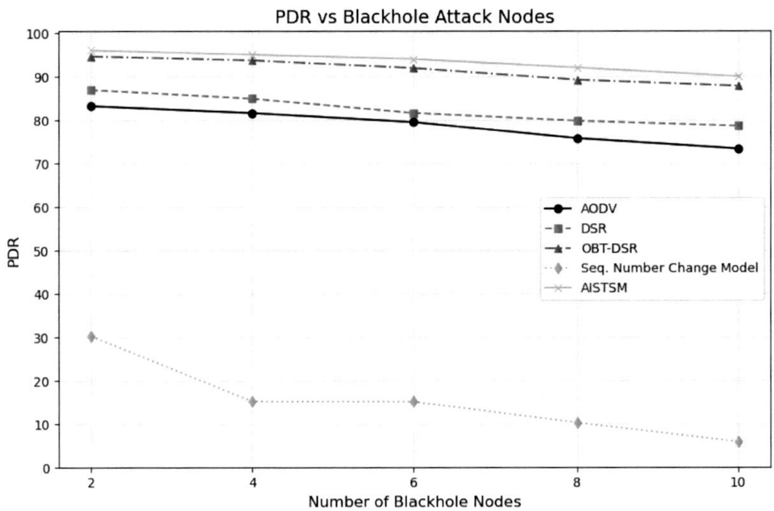

Figure 5: PDR of the different models vs Black Hole Attack node.

2 to 10, AISTSM consistently achieves a high PDR, ranging from 90% to 96%. This resilience stems from the model's ability to select trustworthy nodes and safe routes for packet transmission intelligently. In contrast, standard protocols like AODV and DSR exhibit a significant decline in PDR, with values dropping as low as 73.3% and 78.6%, respectively, with 10 black hole nodes. While OBT-DSR demonstrates some improvement

over the standard protocols, its performance still falls short of AISTSM. The effectiveness of AISTSM lies in its trust-based mechanism. The model proactively identifies and avoids potentially malicious nodes by considering the historical PDR of neighboring nodes. This intelligent route selection, based on trust values derived from past performance, ensures a higher probability of successful packet delivery, even in the face of network attacks.

Figure 6 depicts the throughput of various routing protocols under different black hole node counts, demonstrating the robustness of the proposed AISTSM model. AISTSM achieves a throughput of 100.32 Kbps with two black hole nodes present. While the throughput decreases gradually as the number of malicious nodes increases, AISTSM consistently outperforms other protocols. Even with ten black hole nodes, AISTSM maintains a significantly higher throughput of 94.05 Kbps compared to AODV (74.0 Kbps), DSR (77.0 Kbps), and OBT-DSR (95.6 Kbps). This illustrates the effectiveness of AISTSM's trust-based mechanism in mitigating the impact of black hole nodes and ensuring reliable data transmission.

Figure 7 presents a comparative analysis of routing overhead for various protocols under different malicious node densities. The proposed AISTSM model consistently exhibits lower overhead than AODV, DSR, and OBT-DSR. Specifically, with ten black hole nodes, AISTSM maintains a relatively low routing overhead of 3.9%, while OTB-DSR reaches 4.75%. This efficiency can be attributed to AISTSM's intelligent route selection,

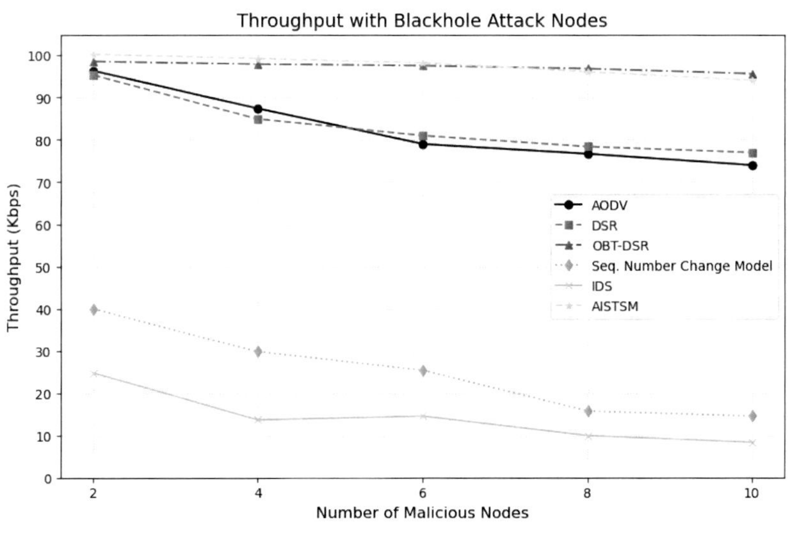

Figure 6: Throughput of the models when the Black Hole nodes present.

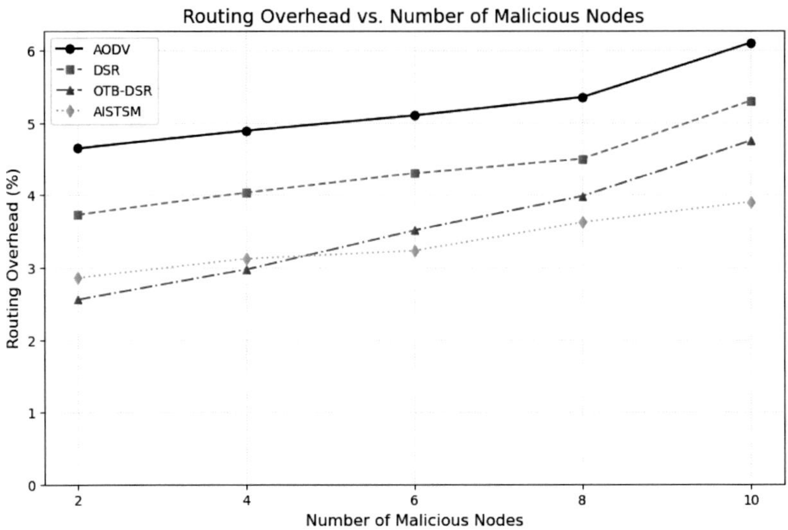

Figure 7: Routing overhead vs malicious nodes.

which minimizes unnecessary network traffic even in the presence of malicious nodes.

6. Discussion

The black hole attack reduces the network performance in MANET. Danger theory and DC algorithms based on AIS are used to identify the black hole attack nodes in the network. Each node in the network is created as a DC to detect the attack nodes. We have redesigned a trust model. The AIS-TSM addresses the persistent issue of black hole attacks in MANETs. Traditionally, such attacks degrade network performance, as malicious nodes falsely lure data packets and then discard them. Our AIS-TSM model introduces a novel approach to detecting black hole attacks by leveraging concepts from the human immune system, specifically danger theory and the behavior of DCs. In this model, each node operates like a DC within the network's immune system, monitoring for anomalies and threats. When a node fails to receive packet acknowledgment, it reviews the RREP and Packet Delivery Ratio metrics in the log table. A significantly lower PDR compared to RREP counts triggers a danger signal. This results in the emission of PAMP signals to alert the entire network, thereby initiating a defensive response.

A key feature of the AIS-TSM is its continuous monitoring and adaptive evaluation of trust levels for each node. Trust is not static; it fluctuates based on behavior indicative of either a threat or benign activity. Nodes that repeatedly exhibit high RREPs but low PDRs receive a reduced trust score. In contrast, nodes demonstrating improved PDR over time will experience a restoration of trust. The network retains flexibility and resilience, mitigating the impact of black hole attacks while optimizing performance by continually reassessing the trustworthiness of its nodes. This approach represents a significant advancement over static methodologies, as it fosters a self-protective network capable of adapting to changing threats and maintaining integrity through collective trust and surveillance mechanisms.

The artificial immune system-based algorithm (AISBA) [5] embodies a broader strategy in identifying malicious nodes through the use of similar DC-inspired mechanisms and PAMP signals. While AISBA excels in general malicious node detection by interpreting the absence of acknowledgment responses as a danger signal, our AIS-TSM approach is distinct in its method of raising the danger signal which is based on PDR and RREP. The usage of PAMP in AISBA is a high-priority signal that expects acknowledgment for the signal. For our model, the PAMP will be used to alert the entire network and neighboring nodes to intensify the whole network. The trust calculation of nodes is different; AISBA is based on a time window-based approach, which takes into account the number of successful and unsuccessful packets within a particular time window. In AIS-TSM, the trust level of each node in the network is dynamically evaluated based on signals that indicate potential danger or safety. When a node exhibits suspicious behavior, such as having a high count of Route Replies yet a low Packet Delivery Ratio, a danger signal is issued, and the PAMP signal will be raised, which negatively affects the node's trust score. Conversely, when a node's PDR improves, indicating reliable behavior, the danger signal dissipates, and the node's trust score is re-calibrated upward. Neighboring nodes take note of these changes and adjust their level of trust accordingly. This adaptive trust management system ensures that no node is permanently excluded from the network based on a single assessment. Instead, nodes can regain trust and be re-integrated into network routing if their performance improves. This not only helps to protect the network from faulty nodes but also enhances overall network performance by considering the most efficient routes, which may include previously suspect nodes that have since proven to be reliable.

In the AODV protocol, the node is considered a black hole attack when the source node does not get the packet acknowledgment. The nodes may not send the acknowledgments due to low power or some other issues. It may not send the packet to another node and reply to the source node, and there is a high chance of identifying the wrong node as the black hole attack node, which reduces the detection rate. Our model continuously monitors the nodes, and the trust value changes based on the danger and

PAMP signals, which is better than other models. Compared with other existing models such as [7, 32], and [33], our model uses a dynamic and intelligent technique to detect black hole attacks in the dynamic MANET environment. More specifically, in their proposed model, Shrestha et al. [7] focused on using the modified sequence number method to identify the black hole attack nodes. When the source node receives a suspicious RREP with a high sequence number, it will resend the RREQ to the nodes equal to the previous suspicious node RREP sequence number. With such a technique, there is a critical limitation when a genuine node sends the RREP with a high sequence. This method will consider the genuine node as a black hole attack node, which will reduce the network performance. Our proposed model handles this issue using a PAMP signal to identify the node's genuineness when the packet acknowledgment is not received. We also do not depend on the sequence number to identify the black hole attack nodes. The AIS-TSM model has high network performance, detection rate, and accuracy compared to the AODV model.

7. Conclusion and Future Work

In conclusion, the AIS-TSM proposed in this paper leverages the danger theory and DC techniques for the detection of black hole attacks in MANET environments, showcasing remarkable efficiency and accuracy. By utilizing PAMP signals for authenticating routes, AIS-TSM achieves an impressive average success rate of 94.5% in identifying malicious nodes, significantly enhancing the security posture of MANETs against such threats. Through comprehensive simulation evaluations, it is evident that AIS-TSM not only outperforms traditional models like AODV in detecting attack nodes but also improves packet delivery ratios and reduces packet loss. This advancement is particularly relevant for the IoHT network, where network reliability and performance are critical. The introduction of AIS-TSM marks a significant step forward in securing remote health systems, ensuring more resilient and sustainable healthcare delivery in the face of evolving cyber threats. In our future work, we would like to protect the MANET network from other attacks and test them in different network conditions.

References

[1] Alshehri, F. and G. Muhammad. 2020. A comprehensive survey of the Internet of Things (IoT) and AI-based smart healthcare. *IEEE Access*, 9: 3660–3678.

[2] Al-Rawashdeh, M., P. Keikhosrokiani, B. Belaton, M. Alawida and A. Zwiri. 2022. IoT adoption and application for smart healthcare: A systematic review. *Sensors*, 22(14): 5377.

[3] Moudni, H., M. Er-rouidi, H. Mouncif and B. El Hadadi. 2019. Black hole attack detection using fuzzy based intrusion detection systems in MANET. *Procedia Computer Science*, 151: 1176–1181.

[4] Behzad, S., R. Fotohi, J. H. Balov and M. J. Rabipour. 2020. An artificial immune based approach for detection and isolation misbehavior attacks in wireless networks. *arXiv preprint arXiv:2003.00870*,.

[5] Jim, L. E., N. Islam and M. A. Gregory. 2022. Enhanced MANET security using artificial immune system based danger theory to detect selfish nodes. *Computers & Security*, 113: 102538.

[6] Abdelhaq, M., R. Alsaqour, A. Algarni, M. Alabdulhafith, M. Alawi, A. Taha and M. Tariq. 2020. Human immune-based model for intrusion detection in mobile ad hoc networks. *Peer-to-Peer Networking and Applications*, 13(3): 1046–1068.

[7] Shrestha, S., R. Baidya, B. Giri and A. Thapa. 2020. Securing blackhole attacks in MANETs using modified sequence number in AODV routing protocol. In *2020 8th International Electrical Engineering Congress (iEECON)*. IEEE.

[8] Qureshi, M. A., K. N. Qureshi, G. Jeon and F. Piccialli. 2021. Deep learning-based ambient assisted living for self-management of cardiovascular conditions. *Neural Computing and Applications*, 1–19.

[9] Muse, E. D., P. M. Barrett, S. R. Steinhubl and E. J. Topol. 2017. Towards a smart medical home. *The Lancet*, 389(10067): 358.

[10] Ida, I. B., A. Jemai and A. Loukil. 2016. A survey on security of IoT in the context of eHealth and clouds. In *2016 11th International Design & Test Symposium (IDT)*. IEEE.

[11] Vishnu, S., S. J. Ramson and R. Jegan. 2020. Internet of medical things (IoMT)-An overview. In *2020 5th International Conference on Devices, Circuits and Systems (ICDCS)*. IEEE.

[12] Zhang, D. -G., P. Z. Zhao, Y. Y. Cui, L. Chen, T. Zhang and H. Wu. 2019. A new method of mobile ad hoc network routing based on greed forwarding improvement strategy. *IEEE Access*, 7: 158514–158524.

[13] Li, Z. and Y. Wu. 2017. Smooth mobility and link reliability-based optimized link state routing scheme for MANETs. *IEEE Communications Letters*, 21(7): 1529–1532.

[14] Dorri, A., S. R. Kamel and E. Kheirkhah. 2015. Security challenges in mobile ad hoc networks: A survey. *arXiv preprint arXiv:1503.03233*.

[15] Al-Shareeda, M. A. and S. Manickam. 2022. Man-in-the-middle attacks in mobile ad hoc networks (MANETs): Analysis and evaluation. *Symmetry*, 14(8): 1543.

[16] Shahabi, S., M. Ghazvini and M. Bakhtiarian. 2016. A modified algorithm to improve security and performance of AODV protocol against black hole attack. *Wireless Networks*, 22(5): 1505–1511.

[17] Hamamreh, R. A. 2018. Protocol for multiple black hole attack avoidance in mobile ad hoc networks. In *Recent Advances in Cryptography and Network Security*. IntechOpen.

[18] Yasin, A. and M. Abu Zant. 2018. Detecting and isolating black-hole attacks in MANET using timer based baited technique. *Wireless Communications and Mobile Computing*, 2018(1): 9812135.

[19] Jaisankar, N., R. Saravanan and K. D. Swamy. 2010. A novel security approach for detecting black hole attack in MANET. In *International Conference on Business Administration and Information Processing*. Springer.

[20] Nitnaware, D. and A. Thakur. 2016. Black hole attack detection and prevention strategy in DYMO for MANET. In 2016 *3rd International Conference on Signal Processing and Integrated Networks (SPIN)*. IEEE.

[21] Vadavi, J. and A. G. Sugavi. 2017. Detection of black hole attack in enhanced AODV protocol. In *2017 International Conference on Computing and Communication Technologies for Smart Nation (IC3TSN)*. IEEE.

[22] Kshirsagar, D. and A. Patil. 2013. Blackhole attack detection and prevention by real time monitoring. In *2013 Fourth International Conference on Computing, Communications and Networking Technologies (ICCCNT)*. IEEE.

[23] Rani, P., S. Kavita, Verma, D. B. Rawat and S. Dash. 2022. Mitigation of black hole attacks using firefly and artificial neural network. *Neural Computing and Applications*, 34(18): 15101–15111.

[24] Mazhar, N. and M. Farooq. 2008. A sense of danger: dendritic cells inspired artificial immune system for manet security. In *Proceedings of the 10th Annual Conference on Genetic and Evolutionary Computation*.

[25] Jim, L. E. and M. A. Gregory. 2019. Improvised MANET selfish node detection using artificial Immune system based decision tree. In *2019 29th International Telecommunication Networks and Applications Conference (ITNAC)*. IEEE.

[26] Jim, L. E. and M. A. Gregory. 2018. AIS reputation mechanism in MANET. In *2018 28th International Telecommunication Networks and Applications Conference (ITNAC)*. IEEE.

[27] Shahabi, S., M. Ghazvini and M. Bakhtiarian. 2016. A modified algorithm to improve security and performance of AODV protocol against black hole attack. *Wireless Networks*, 22: 1505–1511.

[28] Draz, U., T. Ali, S. Yasin and A. Shaf. 2018. Evaluation based analysis of packet delivery ratio for AODV and DSR under UDP and TCP environment. In *2018 International Conference on Computing, Mathematics and Engineering Technologies (iCoMET)*. IEEE.

[29] Pandey, S. and V. Singh. 2020. Blackhole attack detection using machine learning approach on MANET. In *2020 International Conference on Electronics and Sustainable Communication Systems (ICESC)*. IEEE.

[30] Mwangi, E. G., G. M. Muketha and G. N. Kamau. 2020. Optimized Trust-Based DSR Protocol to Curb Cooperative Blackhole Attacks in MANETs Using NS-3..

[31] Reddy, B. and B. Dhananjaya. 2022. The AODV routing protocol with built-in security to counter blackhole attack in MANET. *Materials Today: Proceedings*, 50: 1152–1158.

[32] Yassein, M. B., I. Hmeidi, Y. Khamayseh, M. Al-Rousan and D. Arrabi. 2018. Black Hole Attack security issues, challenges & solution in MANET. In *CS & IT Conference Proceedings*. CS & IT Conference Proceedings.

[33] Dhende, S., S. Musale, S. Shirbahadurkar and A. Najan. 2017. SAODV: Black hole and gray hole attack detection protocol in MANETs. In *2017 International Conference on Wireless Communications, Signal Processing and Networking (WiSPNET)*. IEEE.

Chapter 7

Sustainable Healthcare Cybersecurity Solutions for the Internet of Health Things

Maheen Islam, Mohammad Rifat Ahmmad Rashid, Rashedul Amin Tuhin, Md. Mostofa Kamal Rasel, Sofia Noor Rafa, Md. Sawkat Ali, Taskeed Jabid, Mohammad Manzurul Islam and *Md. Hasanul Ferdaus**

1. Introduction

The widespread availability of internet access has spurred the creation of an interconnected ecosystem of medical devices, known as the Internet of Health Things (IoHT). This network enhances healthcare delivery but also exposes sensitive patient information and system operations to cyberattacks.

1.1 Overview of IoHT and its Impact on Healthcare

The IoHT refers to an interconnected network of internet-enabled medical devices designed to manage continuous data streams through sensor-based, cloud-supported systems. These devices collectively impact

Department of Computer Science and Engineering, East West University, Dhaka, Bangladesh.
Emails: maheen@ewubd.edu, rifat.rashid@ewubd.edu, mcctuhin@ewubd.edu, mostofa.kamal@ewubd.edu, sofiautilitarian@gmail.com, alim@ewubd.edu, taskeed@ewubd.edu, mohammad.islam@ewubd.edu
* Corresponding author: hasanul.ferdaus@ewubd.edu

DOI: 10.1201/9781003483267-10

healthcare by enhancing information management, supporting patient care, and simplifying clinical workflows.

Remote Patient Monitoring (RPM) stands out as one of the primary uses of IoHT. RPM facilitates continuous tracking of key health indicators such as blood pressure, glucose levels, heart rate, and hemoglobin content, reducing the need for in-person hospital visits. This function allows for early intervention, improving patient outcomes while lowering healthcare costs [1, 2]. RPM is especially beneficial for managing chronic illnesses, such as cardiovascular conditions and diabetes, that require constant observation [3, 4].

Additionally, IoHT devices play an essential role in data management by transforming traditional medical equipment into intelligent systems capable of processing large volumes of real-time data [5]. These devices connect to cloud platforms, where data can be stored and analyzed to support advanced analytics and machine learning (ML), providing predictive insights that aid clinical decision-making [6, 7]. This integration enables healthcare providers to access accurate, timely information, thereby improving patient management and the quality of care delivered.

The autonomy of these devices in data gathering and analysis also enhances operational efficiency for healthcare facilities, significantly cutting down data management costs [8–10]. Their flexibility allows for rapid adaptation to changing healthcare needs, making them a valuable asset for any healthcare facility focused on enhancing service quality and patient care [11]. Overall, IoHT fosters a robust and adaptive ecosystem that supports a wide range of healthcare functions, facilitating patient-centered care while increasing the operational efficiency of healthcare systems [12].

1.2 Cybersecurity Challenges in IoHT

The IoHT offers numerous advantages by integrating medical devices and connecting them to intelligent cloud services, facilitating seamless healthcare operations. Yet, this connectivity introduces significant cybersecurity risks, including data breaches and ransomware attacks. As healthcare increasingly depends on IoHT, it expands the potential attack surface, making these systems vulnerable to a wide range of cyber threats [13].

IoHT devices, inherently susceptible due to their network connections, are attractive targets for cybercriminals. The sensitive Patient Health Information (PHI) they gather, if compromised, risks patient privacy and can impair the accuracy of diagnostics and treatments, underscoring the necessity of stringent cybersecurity practices [13]. Ransomware poses a particularly serious risk, as attackers can encrypt critical medical data, demanding ransom payments for access. Such incidents can disrupt patient care and impose severe financial burdens on healthcare institutions, highlighting the urgent need for robust defenses against the rising wave of ransomware [14].

Many IoHT devices also lack essential security measures like secure boot processes, access controls, and strong encryption. Often, these vulnerabilities result from cost-saving or regulatory gaps, leaving devices prone to tampering or remote cyberattacks. Specialized malware that exploits these vulnerabilities is an additional threat, as it can infiltrate systems undetected, interfere with device communication, and alter diagnostic data, jeopardizing patient outcomes. Up-to-date security features are essential to counter these risks and detect potential breaches early [15, 16]. Furthermore, Denial of Service (DoS) and Distributed Denial of Service (DDoS) attacks are concerning as they overwhelm networks, potentially halting critical procedures and affecting the reliability of connected medical devices [18].

Compounding these issues, many IoHT devices run on outdated or unpatched software, exposing them to known vulnerabilities. Healthcare organizations often find it challenging to keep pace with necessary updates, particularly on older devices with recognized security flaws [8, 19]. The dependence on cloud-based services for managing medical data introduces further cybersecurity complexities. Securing data transmission to and from IoHT devices requires multi-layered protection to prevent unauthorized access and ensure the integrity of patient information [20]. Additionally, authorization protocols are frequently insufficient, making it easier for unauthorized users to gain access. Implementing stronger authentication measures, such as multi-factor and biometric verification, is essential for maintaining the security of IoHT devices [21].

1.3 Need for Sustainable Cybersecurity Solutions

To guard against evolving cyber threats, healthcare systems must adopt sustainable cybersecurity solutions. This section examines the effectiveness of various technologies and strategic approaches to cybersecurity, recognizing the critical roles of firewalls, authorization processes, and encryption in mitigating risks. Yet, as cyber threats grow in complexity, there is a pressing need for a more adaptive and robust cybersecurity framework.

With the integration of the IoHT, healthcare faces considerable risks, including data breaches, ransomware, and malware attacks. The complexity of securing IoHT devices demands not only immediate protection but also strategies that evolve with new technologies and threats [13, 14]. Advanced technologies, such as artificial intelligence (AI), are invaluable in identifying vulnerabilities. AI systems can analyze massive datasets to detect cyber threats and patterns beyond human capability, which is critical as IoHT data continue to grow [13, 14].

Zero Trust Architecture (ZTA) is essential for ensuring that every user and device is verified before accessing healthcare systems. ZTA is particularly effective against risks posed by outdated software and weak encryption, applying a "never trust, always verify" model and using micro-segmentation to limit an attacker's network access after a breach [15, 16]. Blockchain technology offers another layer of security for IoHT by enabling secure, decentralized data management. With blockchain, data transactions are protected against unauthorized changes, reducing risks associated with single points of failure—a key factor in safeguarding IoHT data integrity [17, 18].

To counter DDoS attacks and the risks from unpatched devices, healthcare providers must implement resilient network designs with redundancy and failover mechanisms, ensuring the continuity of critical services and protecting sensitive information [8, 19].

Maintaining IoHT security also requires regular software updates, regulatory compliance, and continuous monitoring. Conducting audits, risk assessments, and adhering to standards like HIPAA are vital to establish consistent security practices across healthcare organizations [4, 6, 10]. A security-conscious culture within healthcare, supported by strong governance and staff training, is crucial. By integrating AI-driven threat detection, ZTA, blockchain, resilient network designs, and advanced encryption, healthcare providers can proactively build defenses against cyber threats, ensuring patient data protection and operational integrity [20–22].

1.4 Main Contributions

This paper presents a comprehensive exploration of sustainable cybersecurity solutions for the IoHT. The key contributions are as follows:

- **In-Depth Analysis of Cybersecurity Challenges in IoHT:** Identifies and categorizes the cybersecurity risks inherent in IoHT systems, including vulnerabilities in device software, network layers, and human factors.
- **Review of Existing Cybersecurity Measures:** Provides a detailed assessment of current cybersecurity techniques, such as encryption, intrusion detection systems (IDS), and access control, highlighting their strengths and limitations.
- **Proposal of Sustainable Cybersecurity Solutions:** Introduces advanced techniques like ZTA, AI-driven threat detection, blockchain technology, and lightweight encryption tailored for resource-constrained IoHT devices.

- **Creation of a Security-Aware Culture Framework:** Emphasizes the role of cybersecurity training and best practice dissemination to mitigate human errors and insider threats.
- **Governance and Policy Frameworks:** Discusses policy recommendations for ensuring compliance with global cybersecurity standards, including the integration of ethical considerations and patient consent in IoHT systems.
- **Future Directions in IoHT Cybersecurity:** Maps out emerging trends and technologies, such as post-quantum cryptography, edge computing, and big data analytics, for enhancing healthcare security.
- **Actionable Recommendations:** Provides actionable insights for ongoing research in areas like human-centered cybersecurity, real-time threat detection, and IoHT-specific encryption methods.
- **Holistic Perspective:** Proposes an integrated approach combining state-of-the-art technologies, robust governance, and strategic human intervention to build resilient and adaptive cybersecurity infrastructures.

1.5 Chapter Road Map

This paper is organized as follows: The **Introduction** provides an overview of the IoHT, highlighting its transformative impact on healthcare and the associated cybersecurity challenges, along with the need for sustainable solutions. The next section, **The Current State of Healthcare Cybersecurity**, explores existing measures such as encryption techniques, IDS, and access controls, while identifying critical gaps and vulnerabilities. **Sustainable Cybersecurity Solutions** proposes innovative approaches, including advanced encryption methods, AI-driven threat detection, ZTA, and resilient network design tailored for IoHT systems. The section on **Creating a Security-Aware Culture** emphasizes the human factor, focusing on training, dissemination of best practices, and fostering awareness among healthcare professionals. **Governance and Policy Frameworks** discusses regulatory compliance, ethical considerations, and governance mechanisms to secure IoHT operations, along with strategies for real-time monitoring and collaboration among stakeholders. **Future Directions** highlights emerging trends such as post-quantum cryptography, blockchain, edge computing, and big data analytics, while offering actionable recommendations for ongoing research and development. Finally, the **Conclusion** summarizes the findings, stressing the need for a balanced approach that integrates technological innovations, robust governance, and human oversight to address cybersecurity challenges in IoHT.

2. The Current State of Healthcare Cybersecurity

Healthcare systems are increasingly adopting comprehensive cybersecurity measures to safeguard sensitive patient data and medical devices against cyber threats. This section provides an overview of these security protocols within the context of the IoHT and evaluates their effectiveness.

2.1 *Assessment of Existing Cybersecurity Measures*

As IoHT networks become integral to healthcare systems, robust cybersecurity is essential to protect both patient data and medical devices. This section reviews commonly used security methods, including encryption, IDS, and access controls, noting both their strengths and areas needing improvement.

2.1.1 Encryption Techniques

Encryption is a cornerstone of healthcare cybersecurity, securing data confidentiality and integrity during both transmission and storage. Techniques like SSL/TLS are critical for securing communications between devices and healthcare systems, providing effective defense against eavesdropping and unauthorized access. End-to-end encryption further ensures that data remain private from origin to destination, accessible only to the intended recipient [23].

However, with the advent of quantum computing, traditional encryption methods such as ECC and RSA may face vulnerabilities. This potential threat has accelerated research into quantum-safe cryptography, which aims to ensure encryption remains a reliable defense in the face of future advancements in quantum technology [13].

2.1.2 Intrusion Detection Systems (IDS)

IDS are essential for monitoring network traffic and identifying possible cyber threats. These systems use advanced ML and DL algorithms—such as LSTM and random forests—to analyze data flow, detecting anomalies that may indicate cyberattacks or system weaknesses. Such proactive monitoring is crucial for maintaining healthcare network security [24, 25]. The use of IDS integrated with hybrid cloud-based systems is becoming more common, enhancing the monitoring of distributed healthcare networks and providing scalable, flexible solutions that adapt to complex healthcare environments [16].

2.1.3 Access Controls and Authentication

Table 1 provides a comparison of cybersecurity measures in healthcare's connected systems. Access control mechanisms, including multi-factor

Table 1: Comparison of cybersecurity measures in healthcare internet-connected interconnecting electronics systems.

Security Measure	Techniques Used	Benefits	Limitations
Encryption	SSL/TLS, End-to-End, Quantum-Safe	Protects data in transit and at rest	Vulnerable to quantum computing attacks
IDS	ML-based (LSTM, Random Forests)	Real-time detection of security threats	High computational requirements
Access Controls	MFA, RBAC, Biometric Authentication	Prevents unauthorized access	Poor implementation in some systems

authentication (MFA) and role-based access control (RBAC), are vital for verifying user identities and controlling access to sensitive data. These controls prevent unauthorized access, ensuring only authenticated users can access healthcare resources. However, implementation challenges remain, as configuration errors or management lapses can create vulnerabilities that attackers may exploit. Continuous review and meticulous attention to access control protocols are essential [21]. New technologies, such as biometric authentication and blockchain-based identity management, offer enhanced security, providing more secure and tamper-resistant identity and access management compared to traditional methods [26].

2.2 Gaps and Vulnerabilities in the Existing Framework

Figure 1 presents a risk matrix that categorizes and prioritizes gaps and vulnerabilities within cyber-connected medical systems. This matrix is a valuable tool for identifying critical weaknesses by organizing risks according to their likelihood and potential impact. By visualizing these factors, the matrix helps healthcare providers target areas needing immediate action. High-risk vulnerabilities—such as network-level deficiencies, device security gaps, and emerging ransomware threats—are located in the matrix's bottom-right corner, signifying both a high probability of occurrence and severe consequences.

2.2.1 Vulnerabilities in Cyber-Connected Interconnecting Electronics Devices

Internet-enabled medical devices, essential in healthcare for their data-driven insights, often lack adequate security features, making them vulnerable to recurring cyberattacks. This section outlines the primary exploitable areas in these devices and the critical need to address their internet-related vulnerabilities.

- **Device-Level Vulnerabilities:** A significant factor in the security challenges of internet-connected medical devices is outdated or

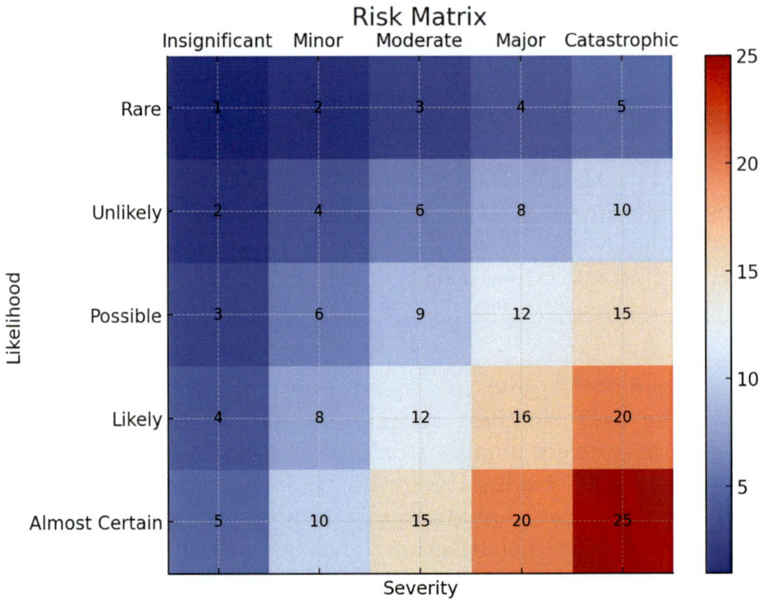

Figure 1: Risk matrix based on the gaps and vulnerabilities in the existing framework.

insufficient software. Commonly used devices like ventilators, infusion pumps, and patient monitors often lack the necessary security protocols. Studies have revealed that 73% of IV pumps, for instance, contain vulnerabilities that pose threats to patient safety and healthcare service continuity [27]. Moreover, many devices use weak or easily accessible credentials, such as simple passwords, making unauthorized access straightforward [28]. Additionally, some devices transmit sensitive medical data without adequate encryption, leaving it exposed to potential interception, which could result in serious privacy breaches [29].

- **Network-Level Vulnerabilities:** The network layer, responsible for data routing, can be vulnerable due to insufficient segmentation, which leaves the entire network exposed if one segment is compromised. Segmentation into smaller subnetworks can limit unauthorized access, enhancing network security. However, outdated communication protocols continue to persist in healthcare systems, increasing susceptibility to modern cyber threats like Ripple20, which exploits vulnerabilities in common TCP/IP stacks [18].
- **Management and Operational Challenges:** Effectively managing the numerous devices within healthcare networks is a substantial undertaking, as it requires accurate tracking of connected devices, their activities, and their maintenance status. A lack of precise

inventory can lead to delayed patching of vulnerabilities, increasing attack risks [30]. The vast number of devices often means patches may be missed, leaving devices unprotected against emerging threats [29].

- **Emerging Threats and Mitigation Strategies:** The rise of sophisticated malware, such as ransomware, has made IoHT systems particularly vulnerable. Ransomware restricts access to devices or networks, demanding payment for restoration, which disrupts healthcare services and can lead to illegal financial transactions [31]. Advanced persistent threats (APTs) also pose significant challenges, as they allow attackers to maintain prolonged, often undetected, access to medical networks. Mitigation strategies include implementing advanced IDS that leverage ML and DL to identify and counter potential threats. IDS integrated with models like Artificial Neural Networks (ANN) and Bidirectional Long Short-Term Memory (BLSTM) have shown promising results in detecting anomalies in IoHT devices [9]. Additional measures, such as network segmentation and virtual patching, are crucial for containing vulnerabilities, especially when real-time patching is not feasible [4].

2.2.2 Insider Threats and Human Factors

Human error and insider threats are significant cybersecurity risks in healthcare, particularly within the IoHT. This section examines how these human factors contribute to security breaches and explores ways to mitigate these risks, recognizing that these challenges persist despite technological advances.

- **Human Error in Cybersecurity:** Research indicates that around 90% of cybersecurity vulnerabilities are linked to human error, underlining the impact of individual mistakes on data security. In healthcare, employees across various departments are often responsible for common security lapses, which cybercriminals exploit. Medical professionals, under high-pressure conditions, may inadvertently bypass security measures—clicking on phishing emails or mishandling sensitive information, for example—which can lead to unauthorized access. Limited cybersecurity training further heightens susceptibility to social engineering attacks, an increasing threat in healthcare settings [1, 2].
- **Insider Threats:** Insider threats come from within the organization, either through intentional misuse of access or unintentional errors. These threats can be driven by various motives—personal, financial, or political—or simply by employees misusing their access. Whether malicious or accidental, insider threats pose serious risks, especially in handling sensitive patient data. Additionally, third-party vendors

and contractors often require access to healthcare systems, adding another layer of potential vulnerabilities [3, 4].

- **Mitigation Strategies:** Mitigating these risks requires robust access controls that limit IoHT device access based on role-specific needs. Regular cybersecurity training helps staff recognize and respond to phishing and social engineering tactics. A comprehensive insider threat strategy should involve coordination between IT, security, HR, and legal teams to set up policies and response plans that align with regulatory standards. Prioritizing awareness and clear monitoring protocols is essential for securing medical data while maintaining operational efficiency [5, 6].

3. Sustainable Cybersecurity Solutions

Table 2 provides a comprehensive summary of the sustainable cybersecurity solutions and advanced techniques discussed in the paper, specifically in the context of the IoHT systems. Each subsection is outlined with a brief description and the corresponding reference numbers. The table covers various aspects, including advanced encryption methods (e.g., symmetric, asymmetric, homomorphic, and post-quantum cryptography), AI-driven threat detection mechanisms, ZTA implementation, and resilient network design strategies.

3.1 *Advanced Encryption Techniques*

The grounds of security measurements are confidentiality, availability, and integrity. Encryption algorithms used to date are typically techniques serving as the security provider of the transmitted data to deploy the security measurements and play a significant role in ensuring the ground elements of security. In terms of internet-enabled electronics, the devices need to make sure that they are seamlessly operable without sacrificing the security measurements adopted. Advanced encryption techniques need to fulfill that goal. This section explores the latest developments in encryption technologies and their application in securing IoHT-oriented devices and sensitive prophylactic information.

3.1.1 Symmetric and Asymmetric Cryptography

Encryption is the technique for hiding and unhiding data and ensuring access to only the authorized end of the data. Encrypting and decrypting data can be as simple as locking the data's unhidden appearance with a solitary key or symmetric encryption. On the other hand, using two keys, one for locking the data as encrypted and another for unlocking the encrypted data for data disguising and unpacking, is known as asymmetric encryption. Asymmetric encryption is a two-key procedure,

Table 2: Summary of sustainable cybersecurity solutions and advanced techniques for IoHT systems with reference citations.

Subsection	Description	References
	Advanced Encryption Techniques	
Symmetric and Asymmetric Cryptography	Discusses symmetric (single-key) and asymmetric (two-key) encryption techniques, highlighting the efficiency of ECC (Elliptic Curve Cryptography) for IoHT devices.	[38–40]
Homomorphic Encryption	Explores encryption allowing computation on encrypted data without decryption, suitable for maintaining data privacy in IoHT but computationally intensive.	[41, 42]
Post-Quantum Cryptography	Addresses the development of encryption techniques resistant to quantum computing capabilities, focusing on lattice-based cryptographic procedures.	[43]
Lightweight Encryption for IoHT Devices	Highlights lightweight algorithms (e.g., PRESENT, SPECK) designed for resource-constrained IoHT devices, ensuring robust security without heavy computational demands.	[44]
	AI-Driven Threat Detection	
Anomaly Detection Using ML Techniques	Discusses using ML (e.g., SVM, Random Forests) and DL (e.g., CNN, LSTM) models to detect cybersecurity threats like DDoS attacks, unauthorized access, and data tampering.	[45–49]
Threat Prevention Using Predictive Analytics	Explains using historical data and AI models (e.g., ARIMA) for predicting cybersecurity threats, enabling proactive security measures.	[50–53]
	Zero Trust Architecture (ZTA)	
Micro-segmentation and Access Controls	Describes fragmenting networks into smaller segments that require security authorization, crucial for protecting sensitive data and medical devices.	[54–56]
Identity and Access Management (IAM) in Healthcare	Emphasizes the role of IAM in ensuring that only authorized users access critical therapeutic systems, incorporating MFA and RBAC for added security.	[57]
Continuous Authentication and Monitoring	Focuses on continuous re-verification of authenticated users and real-time monitoring to detect anomalies or unauthorized activities in therapeutic systems.	[55, 57]

Table 2 contd. ...

...Table 2 contd.

Subsection	Description	References
	Resilient Network Design	
Redundancy and Failover Mechanisms	Highlights the importance of backups and failover systems for maintaining availability and reliability, particularly in critical therapeutic environments.	[58–60]
Segment and Isolate the Network	Details network segmentation to prevent malware spread and the use of VLANs and ACLs for added security in medical networks.	[61–63]
Incident Response and Recovery Planning	Outlines the key components of an incident response plan including detection, containment, eradication, and recovery, supported by AI-driven monitoring for real-time threat detection.	[64–66]

and for security purposes, a network needs to be capable of delivering keys as per requirements. Management of keys required for performing Asymmetric Encryption leading to decryption in the procedure is a complex task in a network consisting of many internet-enabled electronic devices due to the complexity of locker and unlocked assignment as per device demands [38, 39].

Encryption algorithms like ECC or Elliptic Curve Cryptography and RSA are cryptosystems that have more than one key for locking and unlocking raw and encrypted data. The ECC cryptosystem can solve the key-assignment difficulty as it is more efficient than the latter and offers keys by maintaining a comparatively smaller size. The cryptosystems following the asymmetric manner to provide data security need to become part of the devices forming an IoHT-dependent network in the medical sector as they can make data more secure. For example, ECC is suitable for resource-constrained IoHT devices such as wearable health monitors as the algorithm is memory-efficient [40].

3.1.2 Homomorphic Encryption

Homomorphic cryptosystems do not involve retrieving the original orientation of the data from the encrypted data to proceed with computational actions on the data. The idea of such a cryptosystem is a recent technology and is on its way to receiving adoption more widely in the cybersecurity scenario. This encryption method can notably be beneficial in prophylactic organizations concerning IoHT, as data privacy is paramount in such scenarios. By allowing computations on encrypted health data, healthcare providers can generate insights while keeping patient data secure or encrypted. However, homomorphic encryption is still computationally intensive, and ongoing research focuses on optimizing its efficiency for real-time applications in internet-enabled electronic healthcare devices as IoHT-dependent sectors need to address network capability and network security simultaneously [41, 42].

3.1.3 Post-Quantum Cryptography

Quantum computing can break the encryption strength of concurrent stalwart cryptosystems such as RSA and ECC. The algorithms emerging in the post-quantum era are expected to provide better encrypting procedures and ensure the resistance to quantum computing capabilities of breaking encryption. Lattice-based cryptographic procedures address the cybersecurity risks lying with quantum computers. Such cryptography expected in the post-quantum era will be crucial in ensuring the long-term security of IoHT systems, where the protection of sensitive patient data is of the highest priority [43].

3.1.4 Lightweight Encryption for IoHT Devices

Many IoHT devices can process limited power and memory, making traditional encryption methods impractical. Lightweight encryption algorithms like PRESENT and SPECK can provide security while minimizing computational overhead. These algorithms are crucial for securing wearable devices, sensors, and other IoHT components with limited resources. Lightweight encryption ensures that even resource-constrained IoHT devices can maintain robust data protection without sacrificing performance [44].

3.2 AI-Driven Threat Detection

Any threat to the internet-connected system can be detected in advance with the help of modern AI tools that consider the anomaly in the system.

3.2.1 Anomaly Detection Using Machine Learning Techniques

ML and DL techniques are essential for detecting cybersecurity risks in healthcare systems. Timely identification of these risks is critical, and ML and DL algorithms can classify, detect, and identify anomalies within extensive datasets, distinguishing actual threats from harmless irregularities in the data. DL methods, such as Convolutional Neural Networks (CNNs) and Long Short-Term Memory (LSTM) networks, have shown substantial effectiveness in detecting anomalies within IoHT network traffic. These techniques are particularly useful for identifying complex cybersecurity threats, including DDoS attacks, data tampering, and unauthorized access. Hybrid models that combine CNN and LSTM have demonstrated high detection accuracy, yielding improved false positive and false negative rates, thereby enhancing threat detection performance [45, 46].

Supervised learning classifiers, like Support Vector Machines (SVMs) and Random Forests, excel when working with labeled data. They can effectively classify network activity as either benign or malicious, enabling real-time threat identification. Random Forest models, in particular, have proven effective in detecting botnet attacks, making them valuable for securing IoHT networks [47, 48]. Unsupervised learning approaches, such as clustering and autoencoders, are equally effective in identifying cybersecurity threats without needing labeled data. These methods are adept at recognizing patterns that deviate from typical network behavior, identifying non-documented or emerging risks. In healthcare environments, where new and undocumented cyber threats frequently arise, unsupervised techniques provide a robust means of anomaly detection [49].

3.2.2 Threat Prevention Using Predictive Analytics

Analyzing data from the past can be effective for safeguarding networks consisting of internet. In medical sectors, where electronic systems are increasingly interconnected, predictive analytics offers a proactive approach to cybersecurity by analyzing historical data to foresee potential threats. This analysis enables medical organizations to address cybersecurity issues before they escalate, adopting a preventive stance in managing cyber risks.

Cyber risks come in various forms, including malware infections, ransomware attacks, and system intrusions. Predictive models powered by AI can identify early indicators of these threats, allowing healthcare organizations to take preventive action. For instance, AI-driven models like the Autoregressive Integrated Moving Average (ARIMA) model can forecast potential disruptions by analyzing historical network behavior, giving healthcare systems a way to anticipate and address risks before they impact operations [50].

Insight-generating analytics also play a crucial role in managing vast networks of interconnected medical devices. These analytics can detect the probability of specific types of attacks, such as botnets and man-in-the-middle attacks, by analyzing traffic patterns and identifying early signs of malicious activity. For example, predictive models combined with anomaly detection techniques can help foresee botnet attacks, enabling prompt intervention [52]. Furthermore, the integration of predictive analytics with blockchain technology has been proposed to prevent data tampering and ensure the integrity of IoHT systems, adding a layer of security to data handling within healthcare networks [53].

3.3 Zero Trust Architecture

The cybersecurity consolidation of ZTA brought a fresh perspective to the data, device, and network security paradigm. Such approaches never accept a data transmission request before verifying the ends appropriately. Medical sectors consisting of internet-enabled medical electronics and versatile medical, organizational, and executive information need such cybersecurity frameworks to ensure data, device, and network security are inherently connected with the flow of operation. The adoption of ZTA in therapeutic systems aims to enhance security and mitigate the risk of data breaches and unauthorized access by implementing strict verification and monitoring of all users and devices [54].

3.3.1 Micro-Segmentation and Access Controls

The framework ZTA relies on the micro-segmentation policy where the network gets fragmented into small-scale divisions, and every network fragment requires security authorization to grant access. Such a policy is crucial in therapeutic networks where sensitive data, such as patient records, need strong protection. Parallel access from various ends to a network is efficaciously prevented by the micro-segmentation policy of the ZTA approach as it separates the functionally discrepant network subdivisions. ZTA's policy is effective in providing security to medical devices such as wearable monitors and imaging systems [55, 56].

3.3.2 Identity and Access Management (IAM) in Healthcare

IAM is the centerpiece of ZTA because it allows access to the most valuable therapeutic assets to those users who have permission to use them. Most IAM installations in therapeutic environments come installed with MFA and RBAC for added security. Through IAM installations in place, organizations can thus enforce strict access policies whose contexts keep dynamic with every new instance of user behavior, device status, and location in real time. With this level of access control, therapeutic providers observe regulatory compliances like HIPAA and reduce any form of information breach to a minimal state [57].

3.3.3 Continuous Authentication and Monitoring

Continuous authentication forms a major part of the ZTA phenomena and holds a very crucial place in the security of a ZTA environment for therapeutic considerations. As opposed to traditional authentication, continuous authentication will need authenticated users to repeatedly re-verify themselves throughout all of their sessions, while traditional authentication allows users to validate once at login. No solitary and smallest or quickest possible data transmission can occur without verifying the authority of the ends requesting access in the scenario. Regular monitoring of network activity provides the added capacity for real-time anomaly detection of unauthorized attempts, activities, or even anomalies in behavior patterns that could detect any breach before they can scale. The philosophy promises immense scope for therapeutic systems to benefit from it: for example, in general, assurance of protection for both IoHT devices and patient data adds an extra security layer according to [55, 57].

3.4 Resilient Network Design

The contribution of resilient network design is very important in terms of maintaining reliability and safety in therapeutic systems integrated with IoHT. This section identifies how robust, fault-tolerant networks can be built to withstand most cyberattacks and ensure easier recovery in case of disruption. In particular, attention should be paid to redundancy, segmentation, and incident response planning, because all these are indispensable in protecting therapeutic infrastructure.

3.4.1 Redundancy and Failover Mechanisms

One aspect is the redundancy feature, based on the backup systems that automatically take immediate responsibility in the event of the failure of the primary systems. The backups ensure that the critical therapeutic systems are accessible at all times in the case of cyberattacks or malfunctioning, such as patient records and life-supporting devices. Such failovers are very critical in the intensive care environment, automating the process of transferring tasks to standby servers in case of server failure. These systems possess qualities that ensure continued therapeutic service with minimal disruption due to cyberattacks on life-critical systems [58, 59].

Failover mechanisms add redundancy to the network classically used for immediate switching between primary and backup systems in case of failures either in the network or system. Multi-layer redundancy is frequent in therapeutic networks, where local and cloud backups exist for operations, thus allowing faster recovery from each range of disruptions, from DDoS attacks up to ransomware incidents [60].

3.4.2 Segment and Isolate the Network

Segmentation plays a very important role in a prophylactic system to help prevent proliferation once an attack has taken place over the network. Segmentation segregates the network into small segments which, once breached due to malware or unauthorized access, cannot laterally move. Medical devices, EHR, and administrative networks are indispensable systems that need to be kept segmented so that any potential breach does not escalate. It will be suitable for the IoHT environment since, if not, one compromised device could otherwise lead to exposure on the network altogether [61].

Micro-segmentation can further enforce finer controls on the communications of network segments, thus raising their protection to even higher levels. This will be necessary in case of breaches, so that the compromised devices can be isolated in time, reducing the attack surface. Application of technologies such as Virtual Local Area Networks (VLANs) and using strict Access Control Lists ACLs for protection against outside attacks on sensitive patient data and medical devices themselves is also possible [62, 63].

3.4.3 Incident Response and Recovery Planning

A comprehensive Incident Response Plan (IRP) is essential for developing a resilient network design that can effectively respond to cyberattacks.

Upon detecting a cyber threat, a well-structured IRP enables containment and rapid restoration of operations, ensuring minimal disruption to healthcare services. Key components of an effective IRP include:

- **Detection and Analysis:** Continuous monitoring solutions, driven by advanced detection technologies, identify abnormalities or unauthorized activities, promptly triggering real-time alerts for any potential cyber threats [64].
- **Containment and Eradication:** Following detection, containment protocols should isolate affected systems to prevent the spread of infection. Eradication measures then follow, removing any malware and restoring security to compromised systems [65].
- **Recovery:** To ensure swift restoration of critical services such as patient monitoring and medical record-keeping, healthcare providers rely on backup and failover mechanisms. Maintaining system integrity and security is vital to minimizing the impact of a cyber incident on healthcare operations [66]. Regular testing and updates of IRP are crucial to counter emerging threats and maintain the resilience of healthcare networks [67].

4. Creating a Security-Aware Culture

Internet-connected devices can become vulnerable to unauthorized access due to the lack of awareness among the stakeholders. However, most of these risks can be mitigated by raising awareness about the risks and by following carefully designed practices.

4.1 Importance of Cybersecurity Training in Healthcare

Human factors play a significant role in healthcare cybersecurity, with over 90% of data breaches attributed to human error. Staff training, therefore, is one of the most effective measures to prevent security incidents [32]. In many cases, healthcare professionals under stress may unintentionally bypass security protocols or fall victim to phishing attacks, which can lead to the leakage of sensitive patient information [33]. Both malicious and accidental insider threats are prominent issues in healthcare cybersecurity. Non-malicious employees may unintentionally misuse their access privileges, creating serious vulnerabilities within the system [34]. Recognizing this, the U.S. Department of Health and Human Services has highlighted the need for ongoing cybersecurity training to mitigate insider threats and keep healthcare workers informed about new and emerging risks [35].

Regular training helps staff recognize and respond to risks such as phishing, social engineering, and the security challenges posed by advancing technologies. Effective training programs should be routinely updated to reflect the latest best practices, particularly regarding IoHT device security and measures to protect patient data [21]. Training should cover essential topics like password management, device security, and identifying suspicious communications, equipping healthcare personnel with the knowledge to maintain a secure environment for patient information.

4.2 Dissemination of Best Practices among Providers

Healthcare providers play a crucial role in securing healthcare systems. One of the most essential cybersecurity practices is MFA, which involves verifying at least two factors before granting access to systems or data. MFA is particularly significant in healthcare, where it adds a layer of protection against unauthorized access in cases of compromised credentials [36]. By combining forms of identification, such as a password with a biometric factor, MFA significantly reduces the risk of data breaches.

Another important practice is RBAC, which restricts access to sensitive data based on a healthcare employee's job function. RBAC ensures that only authorized personnel can access certain information, thus reducing the likelihood of data misuse or insider threats [15]. For example, administrative staff may access appointment schedules, while medical professionals have access to patient health records, but not financial data.

Regular security audits are also essential to identify potential vulnerabilities. These audits evaluate a healthcare organization's adherence to security protocols and compliance requirements, ensuring that policies and technologies are up-to-date and effective against evolving cyber threats [36]. Audits and compliance reviews help organizations minimize risks and regulatory penalties.

Another security concern is the rapid increase in IoHT devices, which connect through wearable health monitors and networked diagnostic equipment. These interconnected devices create potential entry points for cyberattacks. Healthcare providers must ensure that IoHT devices receive timely updates, use encrypted data transfers, and are continuously monitored for suspicious activity [29]. Such practices help protect sensitive patient information from threats associated with IoHT devices.

Regular cybersecurity training for healthcare staff is also critical. As cyber threats become more sophisticated, periodic training sessions keep personnel informed about the latest threats and security practices. Role-based training programs tailored for clinicians and IT staff ensure that all employees understand their responsibilities in protecting patient data [14]. An incident reporting culture is equally important. Healthcare staff should feel empowered to report any suspicious activity without fear of repercussions. Early reporting can help contain security threats and prevent escalation [15]. Leadership should support cybersecurity initiatives by allocating the necessary resources to ensure that systems are secure [35].

By implementing best practices like MFA, RBAC, regular audits, IoHT device security, continuous training, and a supportive incident reporting culture, healthcare organizations can minimize cyber threats and protect sensitive patient data.

5. Governance and Policy Frameworks

IoT further enhances real-time data collection in healthcare, hence improving device-to-device, device-to-patient, and device-to-healthcare-provider communication. On the other hand, rapid digitalization has taken the sector outside to a completely new series of cybersecurity attacks which were previously unknown. This therefore calls for strong governance frameworks and policies that can assure data integrity, adherence to healthcare standards, and protection against cyber threats. It is, therefore, within the scope of this section to discuss the development of such a framework, considering global regulations, taking into account policies on continuous monitoring and updates, collaboration, ethics, incident response, and supply chain security.

5.1 *Development of Cyberspace Security Policy*

Security convention of IoTs: Advanced technology requires complication that is met with IoHT system governance framework. Advanced technologies, such as blockchain and AI, are one of the strong ways to enforce data security. Blockchain, in healthcare, makes all transactions of data more transparent and non-vulnerable in nature; hence, the risks related to tampering are reduced. The integration of smart contracts into blockchain systems means that some predefined security policies can automatically be enforced. It is also effective in real time for the governance framework [1, 2].

AI in governance frameworks will also provide healthcare organizations with the capability to activate updates of their policy resources about newly emerging threats. Such AI-driven systems will monitor network activities at regular periodic intervals and segregate the anomalies to refurbish the security measures without human interference or any other intervention. In this manner, IoHT environments will remain in a state of protection against the ever-evolving cyber threats [3].

5.2 *Compliance with Healthcare Cybersecurity Standards*

Healthcare providers are, therefore, strictly regulated in terms of data protection and security of the systems. Certain regulations, like the U.S.'s HIPAA and the EU's GDPR, imposed a special regime of security with respect to the handling of patient data. New regulations, like the EU's Cyber Resilience Act and the IoT Cybersecurity Improvement Act, require increasingly progressive security from connected devices in service, driven by IoHT systems that are becoming increasingly complex [4, 5].

5.2.1 HIPAA and International Data Protection Laws

Healthcare, being what it is, is the most scrutinized sector on the face of this earth. Highly regulated per se, IoHT systems fall within various national and international data protection laws to which they must adhere. It sets a baseline for confidentiality, integrity, and availability of patient information, which could be found in the United States, whereas the EU under the General Data Protection Regulation puts rigid requirements on any organization dealing with personal health data with very heavy fines in case of violations. Recently, the NIS Directive 2 and the Cyber Resilience Act are already being promulgated within the EU about IoT devices for that challenge and will create a compulsion toward higher-grade encryption standards and continuous monitoring practices for healthcare organizations [4].

5.2.2 Operative Monitoring and Policy Elaboration

Other key components of the sustainable governance framework involve real-time monitoring and updating of policies. In an IoHT environment, AI-driven systems have the ability to make organizations monitor emergent threats and take action against them in real time. To this effect, within the system, a great chunk of data emanating from IoT devices is analyzed for patterns indicative of the appearance of security vulnerabilities. The changes required to mitigate the risks of the detected threats can thus be automatically updated in policies without human interference.

With blockchain, there is more transparency and traceability for each and every transaction of healthcare data because automation of policy enforcement is necessary to maintain regulations set by healthcare organizations such as HIPAA and GDPR. Once automation is involved, then human error is reduced; hence, there will be resilience in terms of the security of the system [1, 7].

5.3 Cooperation between Stakeholders

The security governance frameworks for healthcare IoT should not be given to the discretion of a single health service provider. Interoperable security policies will ensure that the device makers are compelled to manufacture on well-defined frameworks with regulators and government bodies. While the manufacturers will go all the way to ensure IoHT devices are designed to be inherently secure, with innate capabilities for encryption and secure boot mechanisms, due compliance ought to be sought to be imposed by the regulators through legislation and laws, as under the California IoT Security Law 5. Thus, the governance mechanisms are viewed in a holistic light with a multi-stakeholder approach, which very well can answer various challenges thrown at large by IoHT systems.

5.4 *Incident Response and Disaster Recovery Policies*

The governance arrangements are expected to identify incident response as well as disaster recovery plans due to recent trends for various types of cyberattacks. It defines the roles and different processes regarding detection, containment as well as recovery from cyberattacks. Newer regulations provided by NIST put more power in incident response through continuous monitoring, data backup as well as rapid recovery processes [8]. These elements included within the governance framework will definitely help the possibility of enabling healthcare organizations to reduce the outcomes of the attack so that they could retain the operation at a much faster speed.

5.5 *Ethical Issues and Patient Consent*

Governance frameworks will have to be applied with increasing awareness of ethical implications. Such practice is a functional requirement of the increasingly prevalent use of IoHT devices within healthcare concerning patient or the involved person's consent and data privacy. Both AI and IoT devices, given their very nature, have a tendency to collect sensitive data in voluminous amounts; most of the data are collected from instances that have never directly interacted with a patient. Any governance frameworks are required to ensure that patients receive full information about intended use and explicit consent from them. A framework designed from data could use policies related to data management and consent management systems in a much articulate manner so that this requirement is built into it hence allowing the health organizations to uphold the ethical standards while autonomy is assured to the patients [9].

5.6 *Security of Supplies*

The international nature of manufacturing IoHT devices brings a number of other vulnerabilities in the supply chain. Devices can even be compromised long before they actually reach the healthcare provider. Therefore, it is very important that the governance frameworks must also include mechanisms for comprehensive supply chain security protocols. Third-party audits will deter the attack in the supply chain, and device certification processes enable due diligence in order for the manufacturers to go through various global cybersecurity standards [10, 11].

6. Future Directions

This section discusses the future direction of IoHT considering the trends of using digital technologies in the healthcare system and the recommendations for research and development. Figure 2 illustrates a

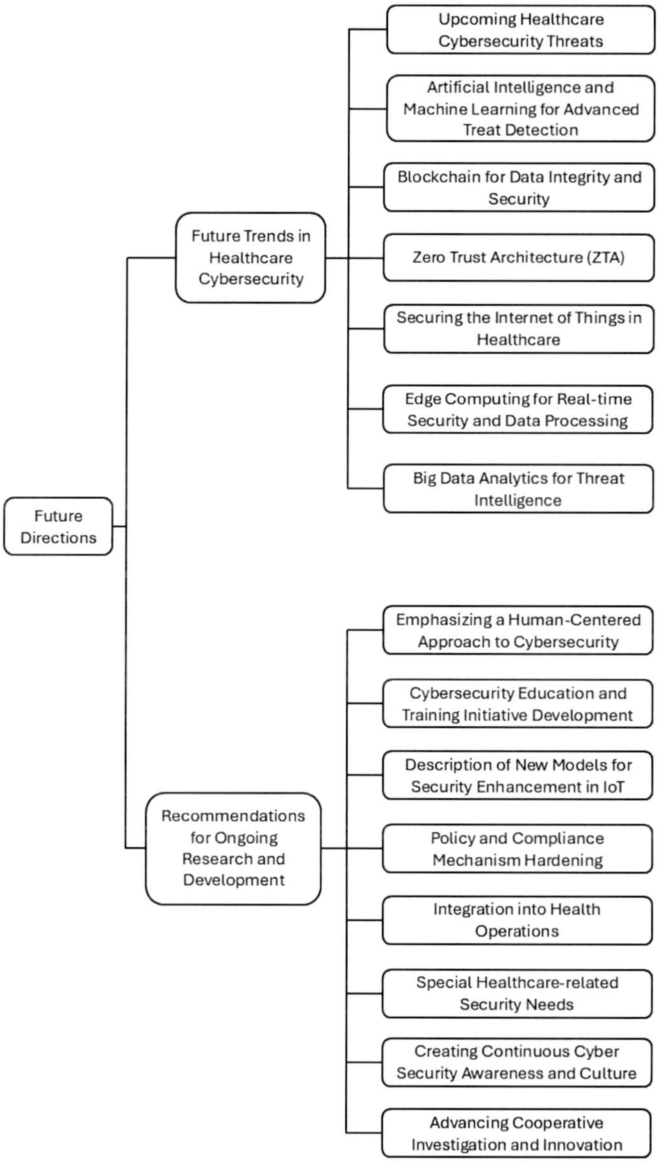

Figure 2: Mind map of future directions in healthcare cybersecurity.

comprehensive mind map outlining the future directions in healthcare cybersecurity.

6.1 Future Trends in Healthcare Cybersecurity

The future of health cybersecurity will take not only from the emergent technologies but also from the ever-changing dimensions of threats. Below, the trends and developments have been described that may shape the landscape for health cybersecurity.

6.1.1 Upcoming Healthcare Cybersecurity Trends

Novel technologies and the dynamically changing character of cyber threats create volatile intersections that will shape the future course of healthcare cybersecurity. As more health organizations depend on their digital systems, connected devices, and sensitive data volume, the dangers keep on growing. In this respect, novel strategies in cybersecurity are highly relevant for the protection of critical patient information and safeguarding the free flow of healthcare systems. The following are some key trends and innovations that will deeply characterize the future of healthcare cybersecurity.

6.1.2 Artificial Intelligence and Machine Learning for Advanced Threat Detection

AI and ML are the new technologies considered to herald a new revolution in the cybersecurity landscape of healthcare, making for far better and near real-time mechanisms for threat detection. Whereas health systems can generate terabytes of data from patient records, connected medical devices, and operational systems, the AI-driven platforms analyze it all at speeds no human could keep up with and detect patterns that indicate a security breach is on its way. AI-driven systems do very well in picking up minute abnormal patterns in network traffic, device behavior, or data access patterns, which hold the key to blocking ransomware attacks, phishing, and other types of cybersecurity threats. AI in the cybersecurity domain is, however, a two-edged sword. Much as it may improve the mechanisms of defense, it is being used by cybercriminals to mount sophisticated kinds of attacks. Advanced algorithms of AI may run such phishing scams, or the data may be manipulated in such a way that it cannot be found by traditional security. Healthcare organizations need to find a middle path between their policy of constantly upgrading the security systems via AI and deploying human intervention against such intelligent threats [68].

6.1.3 Blockchain for Data Integrity and Security

Among the newer promising solutions to improve data security and integrity in healthcare, blockchain technology is getting fast recognition.

This is where blockchain replaces the health data of patients' records, their medical history, and pharmaceutical supply chains, making them tamper-proof and fully transparent through an immutable, decentralized ledger. Decentralization altogether cancels out the disadvantages of centralized storage of data, wherein one breach would mean the compromise of vast extents of information. This also means that blockchain in healthcare can store and disseminate information on patients without data tampering or unauthorized access. This will also help a great deal in the verification of the authenticity of medical devices and drugs in the supply chain to ensure only genuine verified products come into use. This technology allows data management of the patients. This may enable them to control who accesses their records for the purpose of permitting or disallowing services to themselves, hence making compliance with privacy regulations easier. Blockchain in health brings strong security that reduces the chances of cyberattacks and data breaches [69].

6.1.4 Zero Trust Architecture (ZTA)

ZTA represents a fundamentally new paradigm in cybersecurity in general and within the health system, since the earlier used perimeter-based model of security just cannot operate anymore. This, in turn, has created a larger attack surface area, with the pervasive adoption of connected medical devices, cloud services, and remote access to healthcare networks—in essence, clear boundaries around a security perimeter have almost become impossible to define. ZTA addresses this with the principle of not trusting any user, device, or system by default, even while remaining within the network. ZTA within health settings will keep permitting user, device, and application verification with respect to identity and access rights before access to resources is granted. That is quite important in the IoHT context, where multiple devices interlink and share sensitive data regarding patients. Again, ZTA shall help in blocking insider threats and unauthorized lateral movements across a network by reducing the probabilities of threats to breach data. This is done by ZTA increasing the possibility for isolation upon the occurrence of any device compromise, which prevents an entire set of damages due to the possibility of a cyberattack [70].

6.1.5 Securing the Internet of Things in Healthcare

The proliferation of the IoT devices in healthcare–from wearables and patient monitors to MRI machines and smart insulin pumps–has exponentially increased the cybersecurity challenges facing healthcare providers. Most IoT devices are built with no enhanced security features, running on very outdated operating systems or perhaps missing proper encryption protocols. These easily make them target points for cyber thieves to manipulate and execute almost all kinds of attacks, including ransomware or data breach. Thus, healthcare organizations need to make IoT security a major priority in connected device growth. Other future trends involve embedding advanced security into devices right at the beginning, including encryption, MFA, and secure communication protocols. This will not only let network segmentation segregate vulnerable devices from critical systems to reduce the wide attack surface but also segregate the critical resources. Continuous monitoring for compromise in IoT devices is going to be equally indispensable while performing real-time threat detection to keep IoT devices secure.

6.1.6 Edge Computing for Real-Time Security and Data Processing

Another important finding of the trend, that is being adopted in healthcare and which has defined the future of cybersecurity, is edge computing. Instead of this, edge computing allows for processing closer to its source, that is, IoT devices or health facilities of cloud servers that are more central, thereby attaining a critical feat in reducing latency across real-time healthcare applications from patient monitoring up to emergency response systems. From the point of view of cybersecurity, a couple of advantages come about with edge computing. This reduces exposure to sensitive patient information during the transmission of data. In a similar vein, edge computing increases security through the speed at which the threat detection and response are affected, given that all forms of possible cyberattacks can be detected and contained in real time. While edge computing integrated with AI and ML models enhances security even further, predictive analytics can actually prevent an attack before its very occurrence [71].

6.1.7 Big Data Analytics for Threat Intelligence

While big data analytics is becoming pervasive in the healthcare industry for value-based care, it is also emerging as an important technology in cybersecurity. Analytics on large data sets from EHRs, IoT devices, and network activities will also continue to provide health organizations with an important insight into potential vulnerability within a sea of threats. Big data analytics enable security teams to recognize patterns and trends in cyberattacks where real-time intelligence would have been applicable to the various defense mechanisms. The threat modeling and simulation analysis techniques of big data analytics will, in turn, help healthcare providers predict and prevent cyberattacks in the near future. This proactive security allows less possibility of a successful attack and decreases the impact on patient care and organizational operations [72].

6.2 Recommendations for Ongoing Research and Development

Consequently, these challenges call for continued research concerning issues related to cybersecurity in the future. This section identifies some suggestions related to some promising areas of research and development concerning novel cybersecurity solutions to be employed in healthcare. In summary, given the ongoing swift advancements in technology, the growing intricacy of healthcare systems, and the persistent emergence of cyber threats, it is imperative to complement solely technical methods by placing greater emphasis on a human factors-oriented approach to safeguarding sensitive data security and privacy within the healthcare sector.

6.2.1 *Emphasizing a Human-Centered Approach to Cybersecurity*

Human error is still one of the major vulnerabilities concerning cyber threats in healthcare, even with the implementation of technical methodologies. In [68], the authors focus on good cyber hygiene among healthcare professionals; good cyber hygiene acts as a form of protection against cybercrime. Human behavior is the most crucial element in data breach prevention, and future studies should involve human-centered approaches together with cybersecurity approaches. The nature of the training programs is dynamic and customized, linking directly with the specific roles of the healthcare professionals. Interestingly, [69] mentions that with a focus on human awareness and changing behavior, the insider threat can be minimized as well as the need for organizational security. These considerations should, therefore, be incorporated into the daily regimen of healthcare practitioners so that they are constantly up-to-date on existing threats and best practices in cybersecurity.

6.2.2 *Cybersecurity Education and Training Initiative Development*

The extent of cybersecurity education and training must evolve to align more closely with the specific requirements of various roles within the healthcare sector. The authors assert that breaches related to human factors can be minimized by implementing training initiatives focused on practical, real-world situations. This study emphasizes the necessity of integrating cybersecurity education into the everyday practices of healthcare practitioners to facilitate ongoing learning. Also, lucid and practically applicable are the requirements under conditions involving electronic internet connectivity that can be maintained through a sustainable cybersecurity practice according to [68]. The research in the future hence should take a path to identify new ways of making cybersecurity education more accessible and interesting in adequately empowering staff that routinely use IoHT devices and are capable of responding to cyberattacks.

6.2.3 Description of New Models for Security Enhancement in IoT

The proliferation of IoT devices in healthcare gives rise to many cybersecurity issues. The authors then mention that good-quality research production should focus on developing scalable frameworks for securing IoT systems [4]. These include digital twin usage: simulated versions of the real-world systems to find vulnerabilities before they occur. This also motivated the authors to call for further research in real-time monitoring and encryption methods to safeguard patient information across the connected devices. IoT security consolidates the hub of these healthcare systems and ensures growth in the number of connected devices in no way compromises patient safety.

6.2.4 Policy and Compliance Mechanism Hardening

Besides the technical solution, the policy and compliance framework enhancement significantly supports the advancement of cybersecurity in the health sector. Thus, cybersecurity must be inculcated at each level within an organization. In fact, the collaboration of functions of IT, clinical, and administrative must be effective. On the other hand, it is expected that research will be carried out with the view of developing tools that will enable healthcare organizations to monitor and record compliance with a minimum level of risks involved in non-conformity. Indeed, in [7], the authors highlighted the need to make the security features part of the operational procedures in healthcare organizations. These therefore are integrated into the patient's care and do not get in the way of this work.

6.2.5 Integration into Health Operations

In addition, linkage of cybersecurity with daily activities is also essential in order to reduce the impact of the cyber threat. According to [7], the researchers are of the view that recognition of automation and AI-based solutions will enhance the capability of real-time threat detection with minimum disturbance in operation significantly. Up until now, significant studies are still required in the area of developing systems-thinking approaches connecting cybersecurity efforts with operational healthcare strategies. Moreover, [5] identifies the need to strike a balance between security measures and operational efficiency to ensure that the security mechanisms do not inhibit healthcare services delivery.

6.2.6 Special Healthcare-Related Security Needs

Cybersecurity challenges in the healthcare domain have to do with security regarding EHRs or cloud-based applications. Such solutions should correspond to the criteria of suitable solutions. Advanced encryption technologies and blockchain also need serious research efforts in the future for the security of EHR, as noted in the paper [5]. These solutions can secure sensitive healthcare data while still keeping it accessible to authorized personnel. Moreover, there are some IoT-specific encryption protocols proposed in the case of [4], which may be useful protection for large volumes of data generated by connected medical devices. In this respect, future research will have to be channeled into the development of technologies that would respond to the needs of cybersecurity in healthcare systems.

6.2.7 Creating Continuous Cyber Security Awareness and Culture

Continuous awareness of insider threat levels and a well-managed healthcare environment can only be ensured through continuous training in cybersecurity. In this line, the authors of [2] affirm that awareness of cybersecurity needs to have a culture in which cybersecurity implications are understood and valued at every level of an organization. This would involve incorporating new information on novel threats and best practices for dealing with emerging risks into the performance metrics of healthcare personnel. In addition, offering incentives for security compliance and awareness would foster a cybersecurity culture within the healthcare facilities.

6.2.8 Advancing Cooperative Investigation and Innovation

There is, therefore, an urgent need for focused research in the cybersecurity of the health sector by health providers, academia, and government institutions. The authors in [8] highlighted the need to conduct research in laying a foundation for smoothly integrating such secure technologies as telemedicine and cloud-based services into treatment methods. Further research undertakings should encourage interdisciplinarity for holistic solutions in the healthcare domain, integrating novel practices into sound policy frameworks.

7. Conclusions

Although IoHT is one promising domain of interest for the medical field, it inherits essential cybersecurity issues and their respective precautions matching the criteria to address an extensive array of problems based on security. These preventions need to be long term and apt for two or more disparate cybersecurity-related issues.

Some of the IoHT security strengthening to be insisted on within this chapter are AI-driven threat detection, ZTA, and blockchain technology. Likewise, AI-based systems have the potential to drive real-time identification and mitigation of emerging threats for persistent protection in dynamic threat landscapes. On the other side, ZTA performs rigid access by giving access to only those users and devices that are trusted, thus reducing the intensity factor of unauthorized access to sensitive healthcare data. Therefore, the decentralization and immutability of blockchain develop very good security protocols, which eventually serve ideally to ensure the safety of the data of patients concerning preservation.

This chapter really tightens the premise of human-centered methodologies as representing the most important elements of the pursuit of cybersecurity sustainability. Also, several strategies are considered regarding cyber vulnerabilities relevant to the contemporary technological environment. Strong governance structures, further cybersecurity training, and relentless focus on compliance with regulations help to enhance the security mindset of healthcare organizations. Of course, human factors are arguably the most pernicious form of systemic vulnerability in cybersecurity, but if recognized and properly managed, they can empower health systems to minimize the threat of human failure.

In other words, IoHT systems could only strive toward ideal sustainable security if an integrated approach pursued state-of-the-art technologies under strong governance and with a push of human oversight. When health organizations strike a balance between technological advancements and strategic human intervention, they get closer to constructing robust cybersecurity infrastructures that can adapt to newer threats and protect the integrity of patient data in the long run.

References

[1] Nikam, P., M. Sathe and G. P. Khapre. 2023. Internet of Things in Healthcare. *Int. J. Res. Appl. Sci. Eng. Technol.*, 11(V): 4322–4327. https://doi.org/10.22214/ijraset.2023.52488.

[2] Islam, S. M. N. 2023. The role of the Internet of Things in Healthcare transformation. *Int. Trans. Artif. Intell.*, 2(1): 1–6. https://doi.org/10.33050/italic.v2i1.380.

[3] Goyal, R. and R. Sharma. 2024. Internet of Things in Healthcare. *Int. J. Sci. Res. Eng. Manag.*, 8(4): 1–5. https://doi.org/10.55041/IJSREM30610.

[4] Suresh, P. and S. Manju Bargavi. 2024. IoT for Healthcare Data Analytics. *Int. J. Res. Pub. Rev.*, 5(5): 6365–6369. https://doi.org/10.55248/gengpi.5.0524.1421.

[5] Lakra, P. 2024. The role of Internet of Things in Healthcare. *Futuristic Trends in IoT*, 3(9): 71–74. https://doi.org/10.58532/v3bbio9p2ch4.

[6] Lalitha. 2024. Chapter 17: IoT in Healthcare Applications. In *IoT and AI Applications in Healthcare*. CRC Press. https://doi.org/10.1201/9780429352898-17.

[7] Omar Ibrahim Obaid and Saba Abdul-Baqi Salman. 2022. Security and privacy in IoT-based healthcare systems: A review. *Mesopotamian Journal of Computer Science*, 29–39. https://doi.org/10.58496/MJCSC/2022/007.

[8] Suliman Abdulmalek, Abdul Nasir, Waheb A. Jabbar, Mukarram A. M. Almuhaya, Anupam Kumar Bairagi, Md. Al-Masrur Khan and Seong-Hoon Kee. 2024. IoT-based healthcare-monitoring system towards improving quality of life: A review. *Healthcare*, 10(10): 1993. https://doi.org/10.3390/healthcare10101993.

[9] Vippalapalli, V. and S. Ananthula. 2016. Internet of things (IoT) based smart health care system. *International Conference on Signal Processing, Communication, Power and Embedded System (SCOPES)*, Paralakhemundi, India, pp. 1229–1233.

[10] Darshan, K. R. and K. R. Anandakumar. 2015. A comprehensive review on usage of Internet of Things (IoT) in healthcare system. In *2015 International Conference on Emerging Research in Electronics, Computer Science and Technology (ICERECT),* 132–136. Mandya, India, 2015. https://doi.org/10.1109/ERECT.2015.7499001.

[11] Chataut, R., A. Phoummalayvane and R. Akl. 2023. Unleashing the power of IoT: A comprehensive review of IoT applications and future prospects in Healthcare, Agriculture, Smart Homes, Smart Cities, and Industry 4.0. *Sensors,* 23(16): 7194. https://doi.org/10.3390/s23167194.

[12] Tarish, H. A., R. Hassan, K. A. Zainol Ariffin and M. M. Jaber. 2024. Network security framework for Internet of Medical Things applications: A survey. *Journal of Intelligent Systems,* 1–18. https://doi.org/10.1515/jisys-2023-0220.

[13] Das, S., T. K. Samal, B. K. Mohanta and A. Nayak. 2023. Emerging cyber threats in Healthcare: A study of attacks in IoMT ecosystems. *IEEE Proceedings.* https://doi.org/10.1109/i-smac58438.2023.10290147.

[14] Iyanda, C., T. Ogunwola and Z. Olalekan. 2023. Cybersecurity challenges in the age of IoT: Safeguarding quality and compliance in connected medical devices. *IARJSET,* 10(1): 55–61. https://doi.org/10.17148/iarjset.2023.101003.

[15] Longras, C. M., T. Pereira and A. Amaral. 2023. Cybersecurity challenges in healthcare medical devices. I*n Lecture Notes in Computer Science,* 10: 124–135. https://doi.org/10.1007/978-3-031-25222-8_6.

[16] Somnathea, A. T., N. Gopinath, G. Deena, R. Anandh, S. kumar and K. S. Tiwari. 2024. Cyber security challenges and effective security measures for IOT-based intelligent healthcare systems. *Recent Advances in Electrical & Electronic Engineering,* 17. https://doi.org/10.2174/0123520965276302240115075612.

[17] Somasundaram, R. and M. Thirugnanam. 2021. Review of security challenges in healthcare Internet of Things. *Wireless Networks,* 28(3): 145–162. https://doi.org/10.1007/S11276-020-02340-0.

[18] Obaid. 2022. Cybersecurity in healthcare IoT: Threats and solutions. *Middle East Journal of Computer Science and Communication.* https://doi.org/10.58496/MJCSC/2022/007.

[19] Kumar. 2023. Healthcare IoT: A comprehensive study on cybersecurity. *Electronics,* 12(9). https://doi.org/10.3390/electronics12092050.

[20] Nusairat, T., M. M. Saudi and A. Ahmad. 2023. A recent assessment for the ransomware attacks against the Internet of Medical Things (IoMT): A review. *IEEE Proceedings.* https://doi.org/10.1109/iccsce58721.2023.10237161.

[21] Jackson, G. W. and S. Rahman. 2019. Exploring challenges and opportunities in cybersecurity risk and threat communications related to the medical Internet of Things (MIoT). *International Journal of Network Security & Its Applications,* 11(4): 51–62. https://doi.org/10.5121/IJNSA.2019.11405.

[22] Suresh, P., V C. and S. M. Bargavi. 2024. IoT for healthcare data analytics. *International Journal of Research Publication and Reviews,* 5(5): 6365–6369. https://doi.org/10.55248/gengpi.5.0524.1421.

[23] McGee, Z. and others. 2023. Security vulnerabilities in medical: An analysis of medical devices and software. *Medical & Biological Engineering & Computing,* 61(2): 35–48. https://doi.org/10.1007/s11517-023-02729-6.

[24] Algethami, S. A. and S. S. Alshamrani. 2024. A deep learning-based framework for strengthening cybersecurity in Internet of Health Things (IoHT) environments. *Applied Sciences,* 14(11). https://doi.org/10.3390/app14114729.

[25] Brodie, D. (2023). Improving medical iot security through network segmentation. *Cynerio White Paper.* [Online]. Available: Cynerio White Paper. [Accessed: 12-Sep-2024].

[26] Somasundaram, R. and M. Thirugnanam. 2021. Review of security challenges in healthcare Internet of Things. *Wireless Networks,* 27: 5503–5509. https://doi.org/10.1007/s11276-020-02340-0.

[27] Smith. 2023. IoHT device management: Overcoming the visibility challenge. *HealthTech Insider*. [Online]. Available: HealthTech Insider. [Accessed: 12-Sep-2024].

[28] Stevens. R. 2022. Ransomware attacks on IoT devices in medical systems. *Cybersecurity Today*. [Online]. Available: Cybersecurity Today. [Accessed: 12-Sep-2024].

[29] Tervoort, T. and others. (2022). Scoping review on cybersecurity dangers in medical equipment due to outdated software. *International Journal of Medical Informatics*, 164: 120–136. https://doi.org/10.1016/j.ijmedinf.2022.104758.

[30] Algethami, S. 2023. Advanced AI methods for detecting IoHT vulnerabilities. *Journal of Applied AI in Medical*, 4(2): 85–96. https://doi.org/10.1016/j.jaihc.2023.0014. More than 90% of Cyberattacks are Made Possible by Human Error. TechXplore (2023). [Online]. Available: TechXplore Article. [Accessed: 14-Sep-2024].

[31] Nifakos, S., K. Chandramouli, C. K. Nikolaou, P. Papachristou, S. Koch, E. Panaousis and S. Bonacina. 2021. Influence of human factors on cyber security within healthcare organisations: A systematic review. *Sensors*, 21(15): 5119. https://doi.org/10.3390/s21155119.

[32] Duckworth. 2024. The human factor: addressing insider threats in healthcare cybersecurity. *Blackwell Security*. [Online]. Available: Blackwell Security Blog. [Accessed: 14-Sep-2024].

[33] HHS Warns HPH Sector About Insider Threats in Healthcare. 2024. *HIPAA Journal*. [Online]. Available: HIPAA Journal Article. [Accessed: 14-Sep-2024].

[34] Understanding Human Factors of Cybersecurity: Drivers of Insider Threats. 2023. *IEEE Xplore*. https://doi.org/10.1109/HICSS.2023.478.

[35] Navigating Insider Threats in Healthcare. 2023. *Cureus*. [Online]. Available: Cureus Article. [Accessed: 14-Sep-2024].

[36] Mahajan, R. and R. Arora. 2024. Data analysis using IoT technologies for enhanced healthcare decision-making. pp. 100–110. *In*: Whig, P., S. Sharma, S. Sharma, A. Jain and N. Yathiraju (eds.). *Practical Applications of Data Processing, Algorithms, and Modeling*. IGI Global. https://doi.org/10.4018/979-8-3693-2909-2.ch008.

[37] Papachristou, P. and others. 2021. Influence of human factors on cyber security within healthcare organisations: A systematic review. Sensors, 21(15). https://doi.org/10.3390/s21155119.

[38] Wazzan, M. and others. 2021. Internet of Things botnet detection approaches: Analysis and recommendations for future research. *Applied Sciences*, 11(12). https://doi.org/10.3390/app11125713.

[39] Yaacoub, J. P. and others. 2022. Advanced digital forensics and anti-digital forensics for IoT systems: Techniques, limitations, and recommendations. *Internet of Things*, 19. https://doi.org/10.1016/j.iot.2022.100544.

[40] Yulianto, S. and others. 2016. Information security maturity model: A best practice driven approach to PCI DSS compliance. In *2016 IEEE Region 10 Symposium (TENSYMP)*. https://doi.org/10.1109/TENCONSpring.2016.7519379.

[41] Zahedi and others. 2020. Systemic risk management plan for Electronic Medical Records (EMR): Why and How? *HTI Open Access Collection*. https://doi.org/10.3233/SHTI200016.

[42] Zhao and others. 2020. A large-scale empirical study on the vulnerability of deployed IoT devices. *IEEE Transactions on Dependable and Secure Computing*, 19(3). https://doi.org/10.1109/TDSC.2020.3037908.

[43] Wazzan, M. and others. 2021. Internet of Things botnet detection approaches: Analysis and recommendations for future research. *Applied Sciences*, 11(12). https://doi.org/10.3390/app11125713.

[44] Olawale, O. P. and others. 2023. The detection of abnormal behavior in healthcare IoT using IDS, CNN, and SVM. In *Mobile Computing and Sustainable Informatics*, 375–394. Springer. https://doi.org/10.1007/978-3-030-86760-1_20.

[45] Zoppi, T. and others. 2023. Which algorithm can detect unknown attacks? Comparison of supervised, unsupervised and meta-learning algorithms for intrusion detection. *Computer & Security*, 127. https://doi.org/10.1016/j.cose.2023.103107.

[46] Houda and others. 2022. Explainable Deep Learning framework for intrusion detection in IoT networks. *IEEE Open Journal of Communications Society*, 3: 1164–1176. https://doi.org/10.1109/OJCOMS.2022.3184815.

[47] Zhang and others. 2022. Deep Learning-based double-contention random access for massive machine-type communications. *IEEE Transactions on Wireless Communications*, 22: 1794–1807. https://doi.org/10.1109/TWC.2021.3072116.

[48] Yadav, N. and others. 2023. Intrusion detection system on IoT with 5G network using Deep Learning. *Wireless Personal Communications*, 123. https://doi.org/10.1007/s11277-023-10175-2.

[49] Mohammad. 2020. Forecasting cybersecurity threats using time-series data. *IEEE Transactions on Information Forensics and Security*, 15: 1246–1257. https://doi.org/10.1109/TIFS.2020.2969841.

[50] Papachristou, P. and others. 2021. Predictive analytics for healthcare IoT security. *Sensors*, 21(10): 1–10. https://doi.org/10.3390/s21155119.

[51] Mittal, R. and P. Verma. 2021. Blockchain-based security framework for healthcare IoT. *IEEE Transactions on Engineering Management*, 68(3): 789–803. https://doi.org/10.1109/TEM.2020.2991234.

[52] Wu, Z., X. Yuan, P. Xu, Y. Qin and L. Jin. 2023. Research on medical security system based on zero trust. *Sensors*, 23(5). Available: MDPI.

[53] Xie, L. J., F. L. Hang, W. Guo, Y. Lv and H. Chen. 2021. A micro-segmentation protection scheme based on zero trust architecture. In *6th International Conference on Information Science, Computer Technology and Transportation* (ISCTT 2021), Xishuangbanna, China, Nov. 26–28. https://doi.org/10.1109/ISCTT.2021.9605084.

[54] SailPoint. 2022. Zero Trust & Micro-Segmentation Explained. SailPoint. Available: SailPoint.

[55] Zhang, P. F., C. Tian, T. Shang, L. Liu, L. Li, W. Wang and Y. Zhao. 2021. Dynamic access control technology Internet of Things in healthcare based on zero-trust light verification network model. In *2021 International Conference on Communications, Information System and Computer Engineering (CISCE)*, Beijing, China, May 14–16. https://doi.org/10.1109/CISCE52179.2021.9445924.

[56] Vallathan, G., V. Rajamani and M. P. Harinee. 2020. Enhanced medical data security and perceptual quality for healthcare services. In *2020 International Conference on System, Computation, Automation and Networking (ICSCAN)*, Pondicherry, India, Jul. 3–4. https://doi.org/10.1109/ICSCAN49426.2020.9262309.

[57] Mamdouh, M., A. Awad, H. Hamed and A. Khalaf. 2020. Outlook on security and privacy in IoHT: Key challenges and future vision. In *Internet of Things*. Springer. https://doi.org/10.1007/978-3-030-44289-7_67.

[58] Sharma, P., S. Namasudra, N. Chilamkurti, B. G. Kim and R. González Crespo. 2022. Blockchain-based privacy preservation for IoT-enabled healthcare system. *ACM Transactions on Sensor Networks*. https://doi.org/10.1145/3577926.

[59] Upreti, K., P. Vats, G. Borkhade, R. Raut, S. N. Hundekari and J. Parashar. 2023. An IoHT system utilizing smart contracts for machine learning-based authentication. In *2023 International Conference on Emerging Trends in Networks and Computer Communications (ETNCC)*. https://doi.org/10.1109/ETNCC59188.2023.10284960.

[60] Vinnarasi, P. A., R. Dayana and K. Vadivukkarasi. 2023. Healthcare data security using blockchain technology. In *2023 International Conference on Intelligent Systems for Communication, IoT and Security (ICISCoIS)*. https://doi.org/10.1109/ICISCoIS56541.2023.10100572.

[61] Ali, M. Almaiah, F. Hajjej, M. Pasha, O. H. Fang, R. Khan and J. Teo. 2022. An industrial IoT-based blockchain-enabled secure searchable encryption approach for healthcare systems using neural network. Sensors (Basel, Switzerland). https://doi.org/10.3390/s22020572.

[62] Rahman, M. A., M. S. Hossain, M. S. Islam, N. Alrajeh and G. Muhammad. 2020. Secure and provenance enhanced Internet of Health Things framework: A blockchain managed federated learning approach. *IEEE Access*. https://doi.org/10.1109/ACCESS.2020.3037474.

[63] Alkatheiri, M. S. and A. Alghamdi. 2023. Blockchain-assisted cybersecurity for the internet of medical things in the healthcare industry. *Electronics*. https://doi.org/10.3390/electronics12081801.

[64] Zhang, R., R. Xue and L. Liu. 2021. Security and privacy for Healthcare blockchains. *IEEE Transactions on Services Computing*. https://doi.org/10.1109/TSC.2021.3085913.

[65] Ali, B. Al-rimy, F. S. Alsubaei and A. A. Almazroi. 2023. HealthLock: Blockchain-based privacy preservation using homomorphic encryption in Internet of Things Healthcare applications. *Sensors (Basel, Switzerland)*. https://doi.org/10.3390/s23156762.

[66] Abbas, R. Alroobaea, M. Krichen, S. Rubaiee, S. Vimal and F. M. Almansour. 2021. Blockchain-assisted secured data management framework for health information analysis based on Internet of Medical Things. *Personal and Ubiquitous Computing*. https://doi.org/10.1007/s00779-021-01583-8.

[67] Kumar, S. and R. R. Mallipeddi. 2022. Impact of cybersecurity on operations and supply chain management: Emerging trends and future research directions. *Production and Operations Management*, 31(10): 4488–4500. https://doi.org/10.1111/poms.13859.

[68] Bhuyan, S. and others. 2020. Transforming healthcare cybersecurity from reactive to proactive: Current status and future recommendations. *Journal of Medical Systems*, 44(1): 1–9. https://doi.org/10.1007/s10916-019-1507-y.

[69] Jerbi, D. 2023. Beyond firewalls: Navigating the jungle of emerging cybersecurity trends. *Journal of Current Trends in Computer Science Research*. https://doi.org/10.33140/jctcsr.02.02.14.

[70] Salvi, H. U. and S. S. Surve. 2023. Emerging trends and future prospects of cybersecurity technologies: addressing challenges and opportunities. *International Journal of Scientific Research in Science and Technology*. https://doi.org/10.32628/ijsrst52310432.

[71] Alagheband, M. R., A. Mashatan and M. Zihayat. 2020. Time-based gap analysis of cybersecurity trends in academic and digital media. *ACM Transactions on Management Information Systems (TMIS)*, 11(1): 1–20. https://doi.org/10.1145/3389684.

[72] Alani, M. 2021. Big data in cybersecurity: A survey of applications and future trends. *Journal of Reliable Intelligent Environments*, 7(1): 1–30. https://doi.org/10.1007/s40860-020-00120-3.

Chapter 8

Contemporary Defense Mechanisms against Human Hacking in IoHT

*Alexander Pamenter** and *Nazim Choudhury*

1. Introduction

The Internet of Health Things (IoHT) refers to the network of connected devices and technologies used in healthcare to monitor, diagnose, and treat patients. The rapid integration of the IoHT into modern healthcare systems has revolutionized how patient care is delivered, monitored, and managed [34]. IoHT devices, ranging from wearable health monitors to connected surgical instruments, provide unprecedented opportunities for real-time data collection, remote diagnostics, and personalized treatment [36]. However, as healthcare becomes increasingly reliant on these interconnected technologies, it also becomes a prime target for sophisticated cyber threats [33]. Among these threats, social engineering poses significant risks to patient safety, data integrity, and operational continuity [13].

Cybersecurity matures as vulnerabilities in software evolve. In the current digital age, the most vulnerable part has become the human element since people have become more interconnected than ever [37].

University of Wisconsin, Green Bay, WI, 54311.
* Corresponding author: alexander.pamenter@gmail.com

DOI: 10.1201/9781003483267-11

This leads the social engineering to be the most predominant threat in the sophisticated IoHT environment [3]. It has the capability of challenging all networks irrespective of their robust firewalls, complex cryptography, contemporary intrusion detection systems (IDS), and anti-virus software [38]. Cyberattacks via social engineering are especially critical and dangerous for the internet of the healthcare industry where the privacy of information is critical [22].

Social engineering falls broadly into two categories: (i) *hunting* and (ii) *farming* [3]. Hunting is where the attacker attempts to achieve a security breach in a single encounter. Whereas in farming, a less common approach, the attacker attempts to create a relationship with the victim [3]. The specific type of social engineering that this paper will be focusing on is ***phishing***. This is where an attacker attempts to acquire parasocial information [35] through methods such as fake emails or a counterfeit website [3]. Normally to find a victim, the attacker has to send out large quantities of attempts, as only a small percentage of targets may fall for the scam [27]. However, in another form of phishing, known as spear-phishing, the attacker researches a specific victim and uses that information to gain more trust than a generic phishing attack would have [23].

The digitized version of health-related records, also known as electronic health records, belonging to the patients not only allows simultaneous accesses by multiple stakeholders involved in efficient delivery of medical services but also an integral part of IoHT. These records contain both patients' personal information and legal records generated in the hospital environment. The increased number of accesses and the usages of diverse interconnected IoHT devices pose threats to security and privacy [40]. Besides, these records must conform to three fundamental security tenets: (i) confidentiality, (ii) integrity, and (iii) availability (CIA) [39]. Therefore, like other cyber systems, IoHT is prone to social engineering-based cyberattacks where data privacy is critical [28]. Besides, IoHT refers to the growing number of medical devices that are interconnected and often connected to the World Wide Web [13]. These devices have greatly improved patient care [13]; however, they are very susceptible to any data breaches or interruption in care which could harm patients [6]. Therefore, to prevent this there are several methods that can be taken to help mitigate the effects like multi-factor authentication (MFA) [23], network segmentation, or system monitoring [9]. MFA is split into three main categories: knowledge based, such as passwords, control based, such as smart cards or wrist bands, and inheritance based, such as fingerprints and retinal scans [23]. Network segmentation is split into two main parts: compartmentalization and layering [15]. In compartmentalization, the network resources with varying security levels and requirements should be organized into distinct zones, each safeguarded by firewalls [15] and in layering protection emphasizes that network security should involve multiple complementary access control layers rather than relying on a single point [15].

2. Social Engineering, Ransomware, and Phishing Attacks

2.1 *Social Engineering*

A social engineering attack is where an individual attempts to exploit human psychology to gain access to sensitive information [25]. A social engineering attack can be split into 4 main parts: research, hook, play, out [20]. In the research phase, the attacker attempts to get as much information about a target as possible [3]. In the hook phase, the attacker will attempt to gain the trust of the victim before then moving onto the third phase play. In this phase, the attacker attempts to extract the sensitive information from the victim using the information that was gathered during the research phase. Finally, the out phase this is where the attacker attempts to cover his tracks and intending to leave the victim none the wiser [20].

Today social engineering attacks make up one of the biggest threats in cybersecurity [20] and is used as an umbrella term to house several different forms of attacks [25]. These attacks can broadly be categorized into 3 categories based on how the attack is performed: technical, social, and physical [20]. The social approach involves preying on the victim's emotions and psychology. The technical approach involves using social networks to collect the sensitive information. Finally, the physical approach involves any method of physical reconnaissance on a target [20].

These social engineering attacks are a threat to the healthcare sector as seen in the 2016 ransomware attack on "Lukaskrankenhaus Neuss," a hospital in Germany [2]. In this attack, social engineering was used to infiltrate the hospital and install ransomware. This caused critical systems within the hospital to be out for days [14]. A common form of social engineering attack is a phishing attack.

2.2 *Phishing*

The term "phishing" began to be used around 1996 to refer to the fraudulent emails that attackers would send out [21]. It is believed that the word originated from the fact that the fake emails were analogously referred to as "hooks" hence the reference to fishing. The "ph" was either added simply to distinguish the term or in reference to phreaking [21]. Phreaking or phone-freak was an early form of hacking where whistles and other devices known as blue boxes were used to mimic calling tones to activate automatic switches at telecommunication companies [11]. One of the first known phishing attacks attempted to steal the login information for AOL (American Online) accounts [21]. However, these attackers soon realized that they could employ this tactic to attempt to steal banking information leading to PayPal becoming the biggest target for phishing attempts by 2008 [21]. Around this time other forms of phishing were being developed including creating fake websites or high jacking real websites to steal login credentials [21]. As people grew aware of these older phishing attacks, new forms of phishing attacks arose: pharming and spear-phishing. Pharming is where a legitimate website's traffic is diverted to a fake website in order to collect personal information [20], whereas spear-phishing is where an attacker researches a specific victim and uses that information in an attempt to gain more trust than a generic phishing attack would have [23]. Today there are several more types of phishing attacks including whaling phishing and vishing. In whaling phishing a spear-phishing attack that is performed on an important individual is a business [20]. Vishing is where the attacker uses voice technologies in an attempt to extract sensitive information from the victim [4].

Phishing attacks are a major problem in the U.S. [8]. Several attacks on hospitals have occurred using phishing attacks [2]. Two prominent examples are the 2014 Boston Children's Hospital attack where phishing emails along with other cyberattacks were used to disrupt hospital operations and shut down its donations website and the 2016 Hollywood Presbyterian Medical Center attack where attackers, also using phishing emails, inserted ransomware into the hospitals systems. This ended up costing the hospital $17,000 in bitcoin [14].

2.3 *Ransomware*

Ransomware is a type of malware that prevents access to a computer system until a payment is made [10]. It comes in two main categories cryptographic and locker. In a cryptographic ransomware the victim's files are encrypted and the original files are destroyed. In comparison, a locker ransomware simply locks the victim out of their system while leaving the files intact [17]. Ransomware has four generalized phases but do note some ransomware may not have all four. The four phases are infection, communication with Command & Control, destruction, and extortion [17]. In the infection stage, the machines are infected with the virus. In the communication with C&C phase, the ransomware communicates back with its command and control server. In the destruction phase, the malicious acts of the ransomware are committed such as encryption of files and blocking access to systems. Finally in the extortion phase the attacker attempts to extract money from the victim usually using a note with payment instructions [17].

While first ransomware was made in 1984 with the AIDS Trojan virus little was done with ransomware until 2005 due mainly to a lack of targets [17]. During 2005 the first modern malware comes out called trojan.gpcode or simply as gpcode [19]. Up until this point all ransomware was cryptographic as the first locker ransomware did not come out until 2007 [19]. Before around 2009 many of these ransomware attackers had difficulty collecting the ransom payments. This was until the advent of crypto currencies like bitcoin. While it is possible to track transactions it gives the ransomware attackers a way to pseudo-anonymously transfer large sums of money anywhere in the world [17]. Due to this ransomware spread rapidly and in 2011 around 60,000 different families of new ransomware were found [17]. Then in 2012 a new threat emerged: toolkits. These toolkits were sold from criminals to criminals to allow less sophisticated attackers to create their own ransomware [17]. With its ease of access with toolkits and ease of payment with cryptocurrencies, ransomware attacks have become the biggest cyber threat [17].

With ransomware attacks being relatively easy to pull off and lack of adequate defense, hospitals are a prime target with 14 being the target of a ransomware attack by 2018 [30]. Two examples of ransomware attacks on hospitals are the 2020 Brno University Hospital attack where the ransomware attack shut down the entire network causing doctors to be unable to access patient information and forcing them to make handwritten notes [14]. In the second example, the Champaign-Urbana Public Health District was targeted in 2020 causing them to be unable to use their communication system until they paid the attackers $37,000 [14].

3. Modern Countermeasures to Phishing and Social Engineering Attacks

a. Improved MFA

Due to the increasing threats that are posed by social engineering attacks it is important that companies move away from single factor authentication and toward MFA methods [18]. MFA can be split into three main categories: knowledge (what you know), possession (what you have), and inheritance (what you are) [29]. Knowledge-based authentication includes passwords, pin, and security questions. The most common being passwords [18], they are not inherently a weak form of security and are often used in MFA; however, their widespread adoption has led to several problems, such as users reusing passwords over multiple sites which causes the secret passwords to be not-so-secret [18]. The next part of MFA is possession. This includes things like smart cards or one time passwords (OTPs) [29]. OTPs are single use codes that can be sent to the user via their mobile device making them a common choice for two-factor authentication (2FA). Another choice are smart cards. These cards can either be inputted into a connected USB device or using radio-frequency identification frequency (RFID) the cards can be quickly identified by RFID receivers [29]. The final part to MFA is inheritance. This mainly revolves around biometric data such as fingerprints, retinal scans, and voice recognition [18]. Though the most secure part of MFA unlike other forms of authentication, these biometric authenticators can sometimes have problems with correctly identifying legitimate users [18].

Although MFA is much more secure than single factor authentication (SFA), it has been slow to be implemented due to human-centered issues [5]. These issues usually revolve around lack of experience with the systems and understanding of their importance [5]. The weaknesses in SFA are even clearer in the IoHTs where attackers gaining access to critical systems could negatively affect patient care [32].

b. AI-Powered Intrusion Detection Systems

Another form of defense against social engineering attacks are AI-powered IDS [24]. IDS can be split into 3 main categories that being signature-based detections (SD), anomaly-based detection (AD), and stateful protocol analysis (SPA) [12]. SD also known as knowledge-based detection relies on detecting known threats through patterns or strings. Because of SD's limitations it is vulnerable to new attacks that it is not aware of [12]. AD is where the system has previous user behaviors and sometimes sets of rules and watches to see if there are any activities which it views as anomalous [24]. AD using ML/AI can be split into 3 categories based on how the AI detection model was trained: supervised, semi-supervised, and unsupervised [31]. In supervised learning, the AI is given a training dataset that has been labeled either normal or anomalous. In an unsupervised learning, the model is given the data with the assumption that most of the data are normal. Finally in semi-supervised learning, parts of both supervised and unsupervised are used. The model is established with a small amount of annotated data but is then given a larger set of unannotated data to train on [31]. Finally SPA is based on predetermined profiles of allowable use of protocols made by international standards organizations [12, 26]. These categories of IDS are not mutually exclusive and can and should be used in tandem with each other for a more secure network [12].

4. Comparisons of Attacks and Countermeasures

In the social engineering, ransomware and phishing attacks on the healthcare sector were presented. This section will go over each of them and compare them to the defense presented in the previous section to see if they would have helped stop or mitigate the effects of attacks.

In 2014, the Boston Children's Hospital was the subject of a DDoS attack and a phishing attack [14]. The DDoS attack could have been mitigated with a proper IDS system that could detect the attacker's packets [7]. The phishing side of the attack could be prevented with an increased use of MFA [1]. Even if the attacker was able to gain the password of the victim through the phishing attack the other MFA methods would prevent unauthorized access such as having a fingerprint scanner in place or a RFID card which the attacker would not have been able to get past.

In 2016, the Lukas Hospital was the subject of a ransomware attack which caused the hospital's system to go offline and forcing them to use pen and paper until the system was back online. Overall, it took them over a month to return to normal but due to the hospital's IT team they did not have to pay the attacker and could instead restore to a backup [2]. While their IT team did well to have a backup system in place using an improved IDS such as [16]'s L-IDS may have prevented the ransomware from even causing any damage in the system [16].

Also in 2016 the Hollywood Presbyterian Medical Center was hit with a phishing attack which turned into a ransomware attack, but unlike the Lukas Hospital the Hollywood Presbyterian Medical Center did not have a backup in place and indeed ended up paying the attackers $17,000 [14]. Similar to the Lukas Hospital incident, implementing an IDS could have helped prevent or mitigate the effects of the ransomware attack.

In 2020, during the COVID-19 pandemic the Brno University Hospital was hit with a ransomware attack which caused a shutdown of its entire IT systems [14]. The possible spear-phishing attack that led to this could possibly have been stopped if the hospital had implemented an MFA system which would have made it harder for the attackers to gain access even after gaining information from the victim. Along with this, an improved IDS could have possibly prevented or mitigated the attack by detecting the ransomware before it did any damage.

Also in 2020, the Champaign-Urbana Public Health District fell victim to a ransomware attack. The attackers took over their website and forced them to pay $350,000 for its return [14]. The lax security measures of the health district could have been greatly improved with an IDS that may have been able to detect the ransomware before it did any damage.

5. Conclusion

While the threats of cyberattacks through social engineering to ransomware are increasing especially in the healthcare sector, there are several methods that can mitigate the effects that these cyberattacks can have. Several of the examples in the previous section could have first mitigated their losses if they had regular backups like the Lukas Hospital. Also having IDS that could have detected the ransomware before it did damage like the one presented in [16] could have prevented them all. Other than that, simply adding MFA steps to login to critical systems could have prevented some of the attackers from being able to deploy the ransomware in the first place. Overall based on the examples adding MFA and IDS to a health system could have proven beneficial in at least mitigating the effects of social engineering, phishing, and ransomware.

References

[1] Elhoseny, M., N. N. Thilakarathne, M. I. Alghamdi, R. K. Mahendran, A. A. Gardezi, H. Weerasinghe and A. Welhenge. 2021. Security and privacy issues in medical internet of things: Overview, countermeasures, challenges and future directions. *Sustainability,* 13(21): 11645.

[2] Jayaprakash, V. and A. K. Tyagi. 2021. Security optimization of resource-constrained Internet of Healthcare Things (IoHT) devices using asymmetric cryptography for blockchain network. In *International Conference on Network Security and Blockchain Technology* (pp. 225–236).

[3] Rundle, J. 2024. Healthcare providers face stiffer cyber rules even as they cry for help. WSJ. Retrieved from https://www.wsj.com/articles/healthcare-providers-face-stiffer-cyber-rules-even-as-they-cry-for-help-b466197a, accessed on 26 Dec 2024.

[4] Mamdouh, Moustafa, Ali Ismail Awad, Ashraf A. M. Khalaf and Hesham F. A. Hamed. 2021. Authentication and identity management of IoHT devices: Achievements, challenges, and future directions. *Computers & Security,* 111: 102491.

[5] Ani, U. D., H. He and A. Tiwari. 2019. Human factor security: Evaluating the cybersecurity capacity of the industrial workforce. *Journal of Systems and Information Technology,* 21(1): 2–35.

[6] Breda, Filipe, Hugo Barbosa and Telmo Morais. 2017. Social engineering and cyber security. *INTED2017 Proceedings*. IATED.

[7] Salahdine, F. and N. Kaabouch. 2019. Social engineering attacks: A survey. *Future Internet,* 11(4): 89.

[8] Shahid, Jahanzeb, Rizwan Ahmad, Adnan K. Kiani, Tahir Ahmad, Saqib Saeed and Abdullah M. Almuhaideb. 2022. Data protection and privacy of the Internet of Healthcare Things (IoHTs). *Applied Sciences,* 12(4): 1927. https://doi.org/10.3390/app12041927.

[9] Kikerpill, K. 2023. (M)asking for a return: Social hypocrisy and social engineering. In *Masks and Human Connections: Disruptive Meanings and Cultural Challenges* (pp. 47–59). Springer.

[10] Blythe, Mark, Helen Petrie and John A. Clark. 2011. F for fake: Four studies on how we fall for phish. In *Proceedings of the SIGCHI Conference on Human Factors in Computing Systems,* pp. 3469–3478.

[11] Suleski, Tance, Mohiuddin Ahmed, Wencheng Yang and Eugene Wang. 2023. A review of multi-factor authentication in the Internet of Healthcare Things. *Digital Health,* 9.

[12] Harman, L. B., C. A. Flite and K. Bond. 2012. Electronic health records: Privacy, confidentiality, and security. *AMA Journal of Ethics,* 14(9): 712–719.

[13] Haas, S., S. Wohlgemuth, I. Echizen, N. Sonehara and G. Müller. 2011. Aspects of privacy for electronic health records. *International Journal of Medical Informatics,* 80(2): e26–e31.

[14] Shahid, Jahanzeb, Rizwan Ahmad, Adnan K. Kiani, Tahir Ahmad, Saqib Saeed and Abdullah M. Almuhaideb. 2020. Data protection and privacy of the Internet of Healthcare Things (IoHTs). *Applied Sciences*, 2.

[15] Farringer, Deborah R. 2016. Send us the bitcoin or patients will die: Addressing the risks of ransomware attacks on hospitals. *Seattle UL Rev.*, 40: 941.

[16] Kaur, Kawalpreet, Amanpreet Kaur, Yonis Gulzar and Vidhyotma Gandhi. 2024. Unveiling the core of IoT: Comprehensive review on data security challenges and mitigation strategies. *Frontiers in Computer Science*, 8.

[17] Mhaskar, Neerja, Mohammed Alabbad and Ridha Khedri. 2021. A formal approach to network segmentation. *Computers & Security*, 103: 102162.

[18] Wang, Zuoguang, Limin Sun and Hongsong Zhu. 2020. Defining social engineering in cybersecurity. *IEEE Access*, 8: 85094–85115.

[19] Salahdine, Fatima and Naima Kaabouch. 2019. Social engineering attacks: A survey. *Future Internet*, 11.4: 89.

[20] Salem T. Argaw, Juan R. Troncoso-Pastoriza, Darren Lacey, Marie-Valentine Florin, Franck Calcavecchia, Denise Anderson, Wayne Burleson, Jan-Michael Vogel, Chana O'Leary, Bruce Eshaya-Chauvin and Antoine Flahault. 2020. Cybersecurity of Hospitals: Discussing the challenges and working towards mitigating the risks. *BMC Medical Informatics and Decision Making*, 20: 1–10.

[21] Mahjabeen, Farhana and Md. Aminul Islam. 2024. Mitigating the impact of ransomware on critical healthcare systems: Insights from case studies and proposed mitigation strategies. *Journal of Multidisciplinary Research*, 10.02.

[22] San Martino, Antonio and Xavier Perramon. 2010. Phishing secrets: History, effects, countermeasures. *Int. J. Netw. Secur.*, 11(3): 163–171.

[23] Kumar, Sanjeev. An Analysis of Phreaking as a Sight of Cybercrime, 4: 2472.

[24] Chinta, Mukesh, Jitendra Alaparthi and E. Koda. 2016. A study on social engineering attacks and defence mechanisms. *Int. J. Comput. Sci. Inf. Secur. IJCSIS*, 14: 225–231.

[25] Issac, Biju, Raymond Chiong and Seibu Mary Jacob. 2014. Analysis of phishing attacks and countermeasures. *arXiv preprint arXiv:1410.4672*.

[26] Kiser, Susan and Balasundram Maniam. 2021. Ransomware: Healthcare industry at risk. *Journal of Business and Accounting*, 14.1: 64–81.

[27] Harun Oz, Ahmet Aris, Albert Levi and A. Selcuk Uluagac. 2022. A survey on ransomware: Evolution, taxonomy, and defense solutions. *ACM Computing Surveys (CSUR)*, 54.11s: 1–37.

[28] Richardson, Ronny and Max M. North. 2017. Ransomware: Evolution, mitigation and prevention. *International Management Review*, 13.1: 10.

[29] Spence, Nikki, M. B. B. S. Niharika Bhardwaj and David P. Paul III. 2018. Ransomware in healthcare facilities: A harbinger of the future? *Perspectives in Health Information Management*, 1–22.

[30] Reno, Jim. 2013. Multifactor authentication: Its time has come. *Technology Innovation Management Review*, 3.8: 51.

[31] Tance Suleski, Mohiuddin Ahmed, Wencheng Yang and Eugene Wang. 2023. A review of multi-factor authentication in the Internet of Healthcare Things. *Digital Health*, 9: 20552076231177144.

[32] Das, Sanchari, Bingxing Wang and L. Jean Camp. 2019. Mfa is a waste of time! Understanding negative connotation towards MFA applications via user generated content. *arXiv preprint arXiv:1908.05902*.

[33] Suleski, Tance and Mohiuddin Ahmed. 2023. A data taxonomy for adaptive multifactor authentication in the internet of health care things. *Journal of Medical Internet Research*, 25: e44114.

[34] Kedalu Poornachary Vijayakumar, Krishnadoss Pradeep, Ananthakrishnan Balasundaram and Manas Ranjan Prusty. 2023. Enhanced cyber attack detection

process for Internet of Health Things (IoHT) devices using deep neural network. *Processes,* 11.4: 1072.

[35] Hung-Jen Liao, Chun-Hung Richard Lin, Ying-Chih Lin and Kuang-Yuan Tung. 2013. Intrusion detection system: A comprehensive review. *Journal of Network and Computer Applications,* 36.1: 16–24.

[36] Makani, Ruchi and B. V. R. Reddy. 2018. Taxonomy of machine leaning based anomaly detection and its suitability. *Procedia Computer Science,* 132: 1842–1849.

[37] Yang, Y., K. McLaughlin, S. Sezer, Y. B. Yuan and W. Huang. 2014. Stateful intrusion detection for IEC 60870-5-104 SCADA security. *2014 IEEE PES General Meeting| Conference & Exposition*. IEEE.

[38] Guangsen, Zhang and Manish Parashar. 2006. Cooperative defence against DDoS attacks. *Journal of Research and Practice in Information Technology,* 38.1: 69–84.

[39] Afridi, Sheeba. 2024. Revolutionizing Phishing Defense: A Comprehensive Overview of Defense Mechanisms and Measurement Strategies.

[40] Mofidi, Farhad, Sena G. Hounsinou and Gedare Bloom. 2024. L-IDS: A multi-layered approach to ransomware detection in IoT. *2024 IEEE 14th Annual Computing and Communication Workshop and Conference (CCWC)*. IEEE.

Chapter 9

Advancements in IoHT

Transforming Healthcare through Technology

Shravan Somashekara Rai

1. Introduction

The Internet of Health Things (IoHT) is revolutionizing modern healthcare by seamlessly integrating smart, connected devices with digital networks to create an ecosystem that monitors, analyzes, and improves patient outcomes. At its core, IoHT extends the capabilities of the Internet of Things (IoT) into healthcare, combining non-invasive sensors, wearable technologies, machine learning, and artificial intelligence (AI) analytics. Picture tiny, smart sensors and wearable devices working tirelessly behind the scenes, collecting a wealth of health data that was once invisible to us. This networked framework gathers real-time health data such as heart rate, oxygen saturation, blood glucose, and more, turning it into actionable insights that enable personalized and proactive care. By bridging the physical and digital realms, IoHT empowers patients and clinicians with unparalleled tools for managing health and addressing medical challenges with precision.

Teladoc Health Inc.
Email: shravansomashekara.rai@gmail.com

DOI: 10.1201/9781003483267-12

The journey of IoHT is a fascinating tale of technological evolution. It wasn't so long ago that medical monitoring meant bulky machines and infrequent measurements. The roots of IoHT lie in the early advancements of telemedicine and the adoption of wireless sensor networks, where standalone devices began capturing vital signs for clinical use. These initial efforts, while transformative at the time, were limited in scope. Over the years, IoHT has evolved from rudimentary data collection tools into sophisticated systems that provide continuous monitoring, predictive analytics, and actionable recommendations. The integration of edge computing has further refined this process. By processing data closer to its source, these systems have dramatically reduced delays, turning what once might have been an hour-long analysis into near-instantaneous insights. It's like having a team of medical experts constantly monitoring your health, ready to provide guidance at a moment's notice. This shift has propelled IoHT from being a mere extension of traditional healthcare into a dynamic enabler of personalized, preventive, and scalable care solutions.

As IoHT has matured, it has become a pivotal response to some of the most pressing global healthcare challenges, particularly those posed by aging populations and the increasing prevalence of chronic diseases. By 2050, the United Nations predicts that the global population aged 60 and above will double to over two billion. Such demographic shifts place enormous stress on healthcare systems already stretched thin [10]. IoHT steps in to address this by enabling remote health monitoring, empowering seniors to live independently while maintaining access to quality care. This minimizes the need for frequent hospital visits and institutional care, fostering a sense of autonomy among older individuals.

The prevalence of chronic diseases such as diabetes, cardiovascular conditions, and respiratory disorders further underscores the urgency of IoHT adoption. These conditions, which often require continuous monitoring and timely interventions, benefit immensely from IoHT's ability to deliver real-time insights. Wearable devices can alert patients and healthcare providers to irregularities, allowing for swift action to prevent complications. For instance, glucose monitoring systems connected to IoHT networks can provide alerts for insulin adjustments, while heart monitoring devices can flag arrhythmias and trigger emergency responses. This fusion of technology and care not only improves patient outcomes but also significantly reduces healthcare costs.

The IoHT has proven particularly vital during public health crises, such as the COVID-19 pandemic. With physical distancing measures in place, telemedicine surged to the forefront of healthcare delivery, relying heavily on IoHT infrastructure to facilitate remote consultations and continuous patient monitoring. Patients could remain connected to their healthcare providers without exposing themselves to potential risks, while clinicians gained access to critical health data for decision-making [16]. This crisis underscored the resilience of IoHT systems, proving their indispensability in maintaining continuity of care even in the most challenging circumstances.

The integration of AI within IoHT networks takes its capabilities to unparalleled heights, enabling advanced predictive analytics that anticipate health risks before they manifest into critical conditions. Machine learning algorithms analyze vast amounts of health data, identifying patterns that human observation might miss. For instance, IoHT platforms combined with AI can predict the likelihood of a diabetic patient experiencing hypoglycemia based on glucose trends and other biomarkers. This anticipatory approach transforms healthcare from a reactive model to one that is proactive and preventative, ultimately saving lives and improving quality of care.

The evolution of IoHT represents a paradigm shift in how healthcare is conceptualized, delivered, and experienced. By converging cutting-edge technologies with an acute understanding of human health needs, IoHT creates an ecosystem where data and insights drive better outcomes for individuals and communities alike. The story of IoHT is not just about technological progress—it is about its transformative potential to address humanity's most profound healthcare challenges, promising a future where care is accessible, efficient, and deeply personal. The road ahead for IoHT is filled with opportunities to redefine what is possible in health and well-being, making it an inspiring frontier for innovation and hope.

2. Key Advancements in IoHT

- **Wearable Health Devices**

Wearable technology has emerged as a cornerstone of modern health monitoring, leveraging advancements in sensors and IoT systems to provide continuous and real-time data on critical health metrics. Devices such as ECG monitors, blood pressure cuffs, and SpO2 sensors are now integrated into wearable systems like smartwatches, wristbands, and chest straps. These technologies allow users and healthcare providers to track vital signs with remarkable precision. For instance, wearable ECG devices monitor cardiac activity and can detect arrhythmias, significantly reducing the risk of life-threatening conditions [12]. Similarly, SpO2 sensors are widely used to measure oxygen saturation levels, crucial for managing respiratory diseases and conditions like COVID-19. Blood pressure monitors in wearables, such as those employing cuffless methods, offer non-invasive and regular monitoring, enabling proactive hypertension management [12].

The realm of wearable technology has expanded further with innovative sensor designs, including skin-based, textile-based, and implantable options. Skin-based wearables, often referred to as electronic skin (e-skin), adhere directly to the body and monitor parameters like hydration, sweat composition, and muscle activity. Textile-based wearables integrate sensors into fabrics, transforming clothing into intelligent monitoring tools. These garments, such as smart shirts embedded with ECG sensors, provide comfort and functionality, allowing for seamless monitoring during daily activities. Implantable devices, although less common, provide continuous and highly accurate data directly from within the body. For instance, implantable glucose monitors for diabetes patients deliver real-time glucose readings, reducing the need for frequent invasive tests [14].

Fitness tracking is one of the most ubiquitous applications of wearable health technology, catering to both general wellness and athletic performance. Devices like Fitbit and Apple Watch track steps, calories burned, and heart rate, helping individuals achieve fitness goals. However, the capabilities of these devices extend beyond fitness. For instance, smartwatches now incorporate fall detection features and ECG functionality to provide users with health insights and alerts during emergencies [14]. Disease management has also benefited immensely from wearables. For diabetes patients, continuous glucose monitors (CGMs) are a game-changer, enabling real-time glucose monitoring and personalized insulin management plans. Similarly, wearable ECG devices allow cardiac patients to track heart health continuously, improving early detection and management of cardiac events [12].

The versatility of wearable sensors has also driven their adoption in managing chronic diseases. For example, wearable systems for hypertension combine continuous blood pressure monitoring with cloud-connected analytics, enabling doctors to adjust treatments based on comprehensive data trends. In cardiac care, wearable ECG monitors have transitioned from clinical tools to consumer devices, helping identify irregular heart rhythms like atrial fibrillation before symptoms escalate. Beyond disease management, wearable technologies are increasingly used for mental health monitoring, capturing metrics like sleep patterns and stress levels to provide holistic insights into overall well-being.

These advancements in wearable health technologies signify a transformative shift in how healthcare is delivered and experienced. By providing real-time, personalized data, wearable devices empower individuals to take proactive control of their health while enabling clinicians to offer more precise and timely interventions. With continuous innovation in sensor design and integration, the potential applications of wearable health technologies are bound to expand further, bringing a future of more connected and informed healthcare within reach.

- **Telemedicine and Remote Patient Monitoring**

Telemedicine emerged as a cornerstone of healthcare delivery during the COVID-19 pandemic, demonstrating its potential to transform care during crises and beyond. As the pandemic disrupted traditional healthcare models, telemedicine offered a lifeline, ensuring continued access to care while adhering to social distancing measures. Enabled by advancements in Internet of Things (IoT) technologies and real-time monitoring systems, telehealth expanded its reach, providing remote consultations, diagnostics, and patient monitoring that redefined the boundaries of modern healthcare.

During the pandemic, telemedicine bridged the gap between patients and providers, mitigating the risks of in-person visits. The Centers for Medicare & Medicaid Services (CMS) expanded telehealth access, allowing patients to receive care from their homes under temporary waivers [16]. This policy shift, coupled with the rapid adoption of smartphones, video conferencing platforms, and IoT devices, made remote consultations widely feasible. The scalability of telemedicine was critical in managing the surge of patients while reducing the strain on healthcare systems. Studies revealed that telemedicine facilitated effective management of chronic diseases, mental health issues, and post-COVID care, showcasing its versatility and resilience [16, 14].

Real-time monitoring systems, integrated with IoT sensors, revolutionized telehealth by enabling continuous, remote patient tracking. These systems leveraged wearable devices and non-invasive sensors to capture vital health data, such as heart rate, blood pressure, and oxygen saturation. These data were transmitted securely to cloud-based platforms for analysis, providing clinicians with actionable insights in real time [4, 14]. For instance, IoT-enabled remote monitoring allowed healthcare providers to track the health of high-risk patients during isolation, enabling early interventions that reduced hospital admissions.

Beyond the pandemic, the integration of IoT sensors in telehealth is paving the way for more proactive and personalized care models. IoT sensors, when paired with edge and cloud computing, provide real-time analysis of patient data, allowing for predictive analytics and timely alerts for both patients and providers. These systems are particularly beneficial for managing chronic conditions such as diabetes and heart disease, where consistent monitoring is crucial [4, 15]. By creating a seamless flow of health information, IoT technologies enhance the precision and efficiency of telemedicine services, reducing diagnostic delays and improving patient outcomes.

The pandemic underscored the importance of telemedicine in delivering healthcare during emergencies, but its applications extend well beyond crisis management. Telehealth systems integrated with IoT are now transforming rural healthcare by connecting patients in remote locations to specialists in urban centers. The ability to provide decentralized care has not only improved accessibility but also reduced healthcare disparities [14, 16]. These systems have also enabled home-based monitoring for aging populations, enhancing their independence while ensuring timely medical support.

While telemedicine has shown remarkable promise, challenges remain in areas such as data security, regulatory compliance, and digital literacy. The reliance on connected devices raises concerns about cybersecurity and the privacy of patient information. Addressing these challenges will require robust frameworks and advancements in encryption technologies to safeguard sensitive health data [14]. Moreover, the success of telemedicine hinges on equitable access to digital infrastructure, emphasizing the need for initiatives to bridge the digital divide in underserved communities.

The fusion of telemedicine, IoT, and real-time monitoring is shaping the future of healthcare, driving it toward a more connected, patient-centric model. As we transition to a post-pandemic world, telehealth stands as a testament to the resilience and adaptability of healthcare systems, offering a blueprint for addressing future challenges while continuing to enhance the quality of care.

- **AI-Driven Analytics**

The integration of Artificial Intelligence (AI) and Machine Learning (ML) within the Internet of Health Things (IoHT) ecosystem is revolutionizing healthcare. This transformative alliance enables sophisticated disease prediction, personalized medicine, and real-time monitoring, advancing the quality and accessibility of healthcare services.

AI-ML systems are critical in managing chronic diseases such as diabetes and hypertension. IoT-enabled devices continuously monitor physiological metrics like glucose levels and blood pressure, transmitting these data to cloud-based systems for analysis [15]. By leveraging predictive algorithms, these systems track disease progression and facilitate timely interventions, reducing complications. For acute conditions like strokes and heart attacks, wearable devices integrated with advanced machine learning models, such as Fuzzy-LSTM, play a crucial role [8]. These wearables analyze real-time data from sensors, including electrocardiogram (ECG) readings and blood oxygen levels, to detect abnormalities early and enable rapid medical response.

Personalized medicine has seen significant advancements through the fusion of AI-ML and IoHT. Patient-specific data from wearable biosensors and electronic health records (EHRs) are analyzed to develop tailored treatment plans. These insights help clinicians optimize drug dosages, ensuring efficacy while minimizing adverse effects [15]. Wearable devices further enhance this process by providing real-time feedback on drug performance, allowing for dynamic dosage adjustments based on individual responses.

Remote monitoring has become a cornerstone of modern healthcare, supported by IoHT-enabled wearables and edge-cloud architectures. These systems continuously track vital parameters such as heart rate, oxygen saturation (SpO2), and body temperature. Predictive analytics derived from these data forecast potential health deterioration, enabling preemptive alerts and interventions. By facilitating at-home care, these technologies not only enhance patient outcomes but also alleviate the burden on healthcare infrastructure [4].

Diagnostics and medical imaging have also been significantly improved by AI-powered systems. Deep learning algorithms analyze complex medical images, such as X-rays and MRIs, to detect pathologies like tumors and fractures with remarkable accuracy. The advent of explainable AI has further strengthened trust in these systems, offering transparency in decision-making and empowering clinicians with actionable insights [13].

Behavioral analytics supported by IoHT wearables have revolutionized patient compliance tracking and lifestyle management. These systems monitor adherence to prescribed treatments, such as medication schedules or rehabilitation exercises, and provide personalized recommendations to encourage healthier habits. By analyzing real-time data, they empower patients to make informed decisions about their health, reducing risks associated with chronic conditions [5].

On a broader scale, IoHT networks are instrumental in epidemic tracking and prevention. By collecting and analyzing population-level health data, predictive models identify emerging disease outbreaks in real time. This capability proved invaluable during the COVID-19 pandemic, where IoHT systems enabled rapid response planning and resource allocation to manage case surges effectively [16].

Despite these advancements, challenges remain. Issues such as data privacy, device energy efficiency, and platform interoperability must be addressed to fully realize the potential of AI and IoHT in healthcare. Future innovations are expected to focus on enhancing system transparency and trust through explainable AI, alongside developing robust frameworks for secure and efficient data management.

As IoHT continues to evolve, its synergy with AI and ML promises a future where healthcare is not only proactive and personalized but also universally accessible. These technologies are redefining the boundaries of medical care, fostering a more resilient and efficient healthcare ecosystem.

3. Enhancing Healthcare through IoHT

- **Edge and Cloud Computing Integration**

The integration of edge and cloud computing has transformed healthcare systems by enabling real-time data processing and scalable analytics. Edge computing, which brings computation closer to the data source, provides significant benefits for healthcare applications where immediacy is critical. This approach reduces latency, enhances data privacy, and optimizes bandwidth usage, making it an ideal solution for real-time patient monitoring and diagnostics. When combined with cloud computing, which offers robust storage and extensive computational power, edge-cloud hybrid models emerge as a powerful framework for modern healthcare delivery [5, 11].

Edge computing excels in scenarios requiring immediate data processing. For instance, wearable devices and IoT sensors deployed in patient monitoring systems capture critical parameters such as ECG signals, oxygen levels, and heart rates. Edge devices process these signals locally, enabling real-time decision-making in scenarios like detecting arrhythmias or issuing alerts for abnormal vitals [11]. This capability is particularly valuable in emergency settings or for patients in remote locations where reliable network access may be limited. By handling initial data analysis at the edge, these systems reduce the dependency on constant cloud connectivity, ensuring timely and effective responses [5].

The hybrid edge-cloud model further amplifies these benefits by leveraging the complementary strengths of both architectures. A notable example is the two-stage ECG analysis system, which demonstrates edge-cloud collaboration in decentralized healthcare settings. In this case study, an edge device performs a preliminary binary classification of ECG data using a lightweight machine learning model optimized for sensitivity. Abnormal signals are then transmitted to the cloud for more detailed multiclass classification using resource-intensive deep learning algorithms [11]. This approach not only minimizes network bandwidth usage by filtering normal signals locally but also ensures high accuracy in detecting complex conditions such as arrhythmias.

Such hybrid models are transformative for healthcare in underserved and resource-constrained regions. For example, patients in rural clinics equipped with edge devices can receive immediate assessments, while the cloud infrastructure supports deeper analysis and long-term data storage. This model bridges the gap between localized healthcare delivery and centralized expertise, enabling timely interventions and enhanced diagnostic capabilities. In one use case, the integration of edge and cloud computing reduced latency by 60% and cut energy consumption threefold, highlighting its efficiency and sustainability.

Edge-cloud systems are also pivotal in advancing personalized medicine and chronic disease management. For instance, diabetes and hypertension monitoring solutions use edge devices to track patient vitals continuously, while the cloud aggregates historical data for trend analysis and predictive insights. These insights inform clinicians about potential health deteriorations, enabling proactive care [11, 5]. This dynamic interplay between edge immediacy and cloud scalability sets the stage for healthcare systems that are both responsive and deeply analytical.

The synergy of edge and cloud computing redefines healthcare delivery, offering scalable, reliable, and real-time solutions. By combining the speed of edge processing with the computational depth of cloud infrastructure, this integration addresses critical challenges in decentralized healthcare, paving the way for more efficient, equitable, and patient-centered systems.

• Applications in Hospitals and Clinics

The advent of the IoHT has revolutionized operations in hospitals and clinics, particularly through the development of intelligent hospital wards. These wards leverage IoHT systems for early warning mechanisms, optimizing resource utilization, and minimizing health deterioration among patients. By integrating IoHT-enabled devices with advanced analytics, healthcare facilities are better equipped to provide proactive, patient-centric care while enhancing operational efficiency.

Smart Rooms

Intelligent hospital wards are increasingly relying on IoHT systems to implement early warning systems that monitor patients continuously. These systems integrate non-invasive sensors, wearable devices, and real-time analytics to track vital signs such as heart rate, blood pressure, and oxygen levels. For example, a hospital ward might deploy wearable ECG monitors that transmit data to a centralized IoHT platform, which uses predictive algorithms to detect early signs of cardiac events [5, 14].

When an anomaly is detected, alerts are automatically sent to healthcare providers, enabling timely interventions that prevent complications. This capability has been shown to significantly reduce critical incidents, particularly in high-risk wards such as intensive care units [6].

Resource Management

IoHT also plays a pivotal role in optimizing hospital resources. Through real-time monitoring and data aggregation, IoHT systems provide actionable insights that assist in resource allocation, staff scheduling, and bed management. For instance, sensors embedded in patient rooms can track occupancy and environmental conditions, ensuring optimal patient comfort while reducing energy consumption [14]. Furthermore, IoHT-enabled dashboards allow administrators to visualize patient flow, making it easier to allocate resources efficiently during peak demand. One use case demonstrated how IoHT integration reduced patient wait times and improved bed turnover rates in a multi-specialty hospital, leading to better patient outcomes [5].

Beyond resource optimization, IoHT helps minimize patient health deterioration by enabling continuous, personalized monitoring. For chronic disease patients or those recovering from surgery, wearable devices transmit critical health metrics to IoHT platforms, which analyze trends and predict potential health declines. For instance, in a ward managing post-operative cardiac patients, IoHT systems flagged deviations in vital signs that correlated with early signs of sepsis. Clinicians were alerted promptly, leading to immediate interventions that prevented further complications [14]. These proactive measures reduce the likelihood of rehospitalizations, enhance recovery times, and improve overall patient satisfaction.

The integration of IoHT in hospitals and clinics extends beyond patient monitoring to encompass predictive maintenance of medical equipment. IoHT systems monitor devices such as ventilators and infusion pumps, identifying potential failures before they occur. This not only ensures the reliability of life-saving equipment but also reduces maintenance costs and unplanned downtime [5].

In essence, IoHT has transformed hospitals and clinics into intelligent ecosystems where data-driven insights guide both clinical and operational decisions. By enabling early warning systems, optimizing resources, and reducing health deterioration, IoHT empowers healthcare providers to deliver safer, more efficient, and patient-focused care. The future of healthcare lies in such interconnected systems, where technology and human expertise converge to redefine patient outcomes.

4. Case Studies and Emerging Trends

- **Senior-Centric IoHT Solutions**

The integration of the IoHT into senior care is transforming how aging populations are monitored and supported. By combining wearable sensors, IoT devices, and real-time analytics, IoHT solutions cater to the unique needs of older adults, ensuring their safety, enhancing their quality of life, and reducing the burden on caregivers. A case study on monitoring applications for aging populations demonstrates how IoHT systems empower seniors to live independently while providing healthcare providers with critical insights for timely interventions [5].

One notable example of IoHT in senior care is the deployment of remote monitoring systems that continuously track physiological and environmental parameters. Wearable devices equipped with sensors for heart rate, SpO2 levels, and motion detection collect real-time data and transmit it to IoHT platforms for analysis. In a recent implementation, a system designed for geriatric care used wearable devices in combination with edge computing to identify health anomalies such as arrhythmias or falls [5]. The edge layer processed data locally, triggering immediate alerts to caregivers, while the cloud layer stored historical data for long-term trend analysis. This hybrid model not only improved response times but also enabled predictive analytics, allowing clinicians to preemptively address potential health issues [10].

Chronic Care

Another case study highlighted the use of IoHT for seniors managing chronic conditions such as diabetes and hypertension. A hybrid IoHT model integrated home-based sensors with centralized health monitoring systems, providing continuous feedback on vital signs [10]. For example, a diabetic senior's glucose levels were monitored in real time, with deviations from normal ranges triggering automated recommendations for dietary adjustments or medication reminders. This setup empowered seniors to actively participate in their health management while significantly reducing hospital visits and complications.

These senior-centric IoHT solutions are more than technological innovations—they are lifelines that bridge the gap between independence and safety for aging individuals. By seamlessly integrating real-time monitoring, predictive analytics, and caregiver support, IoHT systems ensure that seniors receive the care they need, exactly when they need it. This approach not only improves the well-being of older adults but also redefines the possibilities for aging with dignity in a connected world.

- **Integration of IoHT with AI and Machine Learning**

The integration of predictive analytics and explainable AI (XAI) within the Internet of Medical Things (IoMT) is revolutionizing chronic disease management. By leveraging real-time data from IoMT devices, predictive models offer actionable insights into disease progression, enabling early interventions and personalized care plans. Meanwhile, XAI ensures that these decisions are transparent and interpretable, fostering trust among patients and clinicians while driving more informed healthcare delivery.

Machine Learning and Predictive Analytics

Predictive analytics has proven to be a game changer in managing chronic conditions such as diabetes, hypertension, and cardiovascular diseases. IoMT systems equipped with machine learning algorithms process vast amounts of data from wearable sensors, EHRs, and patient history to predict potential health deteriorations [7, 15]. For instance, an IoMT-enabled hybrid model utilized predictive algorithms to monitor patients with diabetes by analyzing glucose levels, dietary patterns, and physical activity. The system flagged anomalies in glucose trends, prompting early medical interventions that prevented severe complications [10].

These predictive systems are further enhanced by cloud-based platforms that aggregate historical data for longitudinal analysis. A case study involving patients with hypertension demonstrated the utility of predictive analytics in identifying individuals at risk of sudden blood pressure spikes. IoMT devices transmitted real-time readings to a centralized system, where predictive models alerted clinicians to potential crises hours before they occurred. This proactive approach not only reduced emergency hospital visits but also improved patient outcomes through timely medication adjustments [7, 15].

Explainable AI

Explainable AI plays a pivotal role in ensuring that predictive analytics in IoMT is both effective and transparent. Traditional black-box AI models often struggle to gain acceptance in healthcare due to their lack of interpretability. XAI addresses this challenge by providing clear and understandable explanations for AI-driven decisions [13]. For example, a machine learning model predicting early signs of heart failure was integrated with XAI techniques to highlight the key parameters influencing its predictions, such as variations in ECG patterns or oxygen saturation levels. Clinicians could review these explanations, ensuring alignment with clinical knowledge and fostering trust in the system.

The fusion of XAI and IoMT also empowers patients to take an active role in managing their health. For instance, a system designed for chronic disease patients used explainable models to deliver insights into daily habits impacting their condition. A patient managing hypertension received visual explanations linking poor sleep patterns to elevated blood pressure, encouraging behavioral changes that improved overall health [13, 15]. This transparency not only enhances patient engagement but also strengthens adherence to treatment plans.

The integration of predictive analytics and XAI within IoMT represents a paradigm shift in chronic disease management. By combining the foresight of predictive models with the clarity of explainable AI, these systems offer a balanced approach to proactive healthcare. Patients and clinicians benefit from timely, transparent, and actionable insights, paving the way for more personalized and effective interventions. In an era where trust and efficiency are paramount, this synergy exemplifies the future of connected and intelligent healthcare.

5. Challenges and Future Directions

- **Challenges**

The IoHT holds immense potential to revolutionize healthcare through interconnected devices and real-time data exchange. However, achieving seamless integration is often hindered by interoperability and standardization challenges. Coupled with concerns about privacy and data security, these issues present significant barriers to widespread adoption. Addressing these challenges is critical to unlocking the full potential of IoHT in delivering efficient, safe, and patient-centric healthcare.

Interoperability

Interoperability among IoHT devices is a persistent issue, stemming from the lack of universal communication standards. IoHT devices, developed by different manufacturers, often use proprietary protocols, making it difficult for systems to exchange data seamlessly [9]. For example, a hospital deploying wearable devices for monitoring vital signs may encounter integration issues when attempting to combine data with EHRs from a different vendor. This fragmentation not only limits the scope of IoHT applications but also complicates efforts to create unified patient records. The absence of standardization undermines data consistency and delays the realization of connected healthcare ecosystems.

Standardization

Efforts to address interoperability have focused on adopting standard frameworks such as Fast Healthcare Interoperability Resources (FHIR) and Health Level Seven (HL7). These frameworks provide guidelines for data exchange across diverse IoHT devices, fostering compatibility and coherence [9]. For instance, implementing FHIR in a multi-device hospital environment allows data from IoMT wearables, remote patient monitoring systems, and cloud platforms to integrate seamlessly into centralized dashboards. Such solutions enable clinicians to access comprehensive patient profiles in real time, enhancing diagnostic accuracy and care coordination.

Data Security

Equally pressing are concerns around privacy and data security, exacerbated by the sensitive nature of health information. IoHT systems continuously generate and transmit data, increasing exposure to cyber threats. Without robust security measures, these systems are vulnerable to breaches that could compromise patient confidentiality and trust. A recent case highlighted how inadequate encryption in a wearable glucose monitoring system allowed unauthorized access to patient data, raising alarms about privacy risks [7].

Addressing these risks requires a multi-layered approach to data security. Encryption, secure communication protocols, and regular software updates are foundational measures to safeguard IoHT systems [7]. Additionally, privacy-enhancing technologies, such as differential privacy and blockchain, have emerged as effective tools for protecting patient data while enabling secure data sharing. For example, a blockchain-based IoHT platform for chronic disease management used smart contracts to enforce strict access controls, ensuring that only authorized stakeholders could access sensitive data [7]. This approach not only enhances security but also builds patient confidence in IoHT systems.

In tackling both interoperability and security challenges, collaboration among stakeholders is paramount. Policymakers, manufacturers, and healthcare providers must work together to establish universal standards and robust security frameworks. Initiatives like the Global Consortium for eHealth Interoperability exemplify the collaborative effort needed to harmonize IoHT development and deployment [9]. By addressing these foundational challenges, the healthcare industry can pave the way for an IoHT ecosystem that is secure, interoperable, and poised to deliver transformative benefits to patients and providers alike.

- **Future Potential**

The IoHT is driving a paradigm shift in personalized medicine, enabling proactive care and tailored treatments. By integrating real-time data from wearable sensors, cloud platforms, and advanced analytics, IoHT offers an unprecedented level of customization in healthcare. However, as the volume and sensitivity of health data grow, the need for robust security measures becomes paramount. Emerging technologies like blockchain and quantum computing are now being integrated into IoHT to ensure data integrity and privacy, fostering greater trust and adoption.

Personalized Medicine

IoHT systems have significantly advanced personalized medicine by providing continuous monitoring and real-time insights tailored to individual needs. For example, wearable devices equipped with IoHT sensors track vitals such as heart rate, glucose levels, and physical activity. These data are analyzed to create dynamic health profiles, which inform customized treatment plans and interventions [10, 14]. In one case, an IoHT-enabled hybrid model monitored diabetes patients, adjusting insulin dosages based on real-time glucose readings and dietary habits. This proactive approach not only minimized complications but also empowered patients to take control of their health [10].

Proactive Care

Proactive care through IoHT extends beyond chronic disease management to include predictive analytics for early detection of potential health issues. By analyzing historical and real-time data, IoHT systems can identify patterns indicative of emerging conditions. For instance, a wearable device designed for cardiac monitoring flagged early signs of arrhythmias in patients, prompting timely medical interventions [14]. Such capabilities are particularly valuable in elderly care, where early detection of deteriorations can prevent hospitalizations and improve quality of life.

Security

However, the integration of IoHT into personalized medicine brings with it challenges related to data security and privacy. Health data, being highly sensitive, are a prime target for cyberattacks. Traditional security measures, while effective to some extent, often fall short in addressing the complex, decentralized nature of IoHT ecosystems. Blockchain technology offers a promising solution by creating secure, immutable ledgers for storing and sharing IoHT data [9]. For example, a blockchain-based IoHT platform for remote patient monitoring used smart contracts to enforce strict access controls, ensuring that only authorized stakeholders could view or modify patient data. This approach not only enhanced data integrity but also streamlined regulatory compliance.

Quantum Computing

Quantum computing is emerging as another frontier in enhancing IoHT security. While still in its infancy, quantum cryptography promises unbreakable encryption, making it virtually impossible for attackers to intercept sensitive health information. By integrating quantum-resistant algorithms into IoHT frameworks, healthcare providers can future-proof their systems against potential threats posed by quantum-enabled cyberattacks [9]. For example, a pilot project utilized quantum key distribution (QKD) to secure data transfers between IoHT devices and cloud platforms, demonstrating the potential of this technology to revolutionize healthcare security.

The synergy between IoHT, blockchain, and quantum computing also fosters new opportunities in data sharing and interoperability. Blockchain's decentralized architecture enables secure, cross-platform data exchange, breaking down silos between healthcare providers. In combination with quantum encryption, this creates a robust framework for sharing patient data across institutions while maintaining privacy. Such integrations pave the way for global health networks, where insights from diverse populations contribute to more accurate predictive models and personalized treatments [9, 10].

In this new era of connected healthcare, the convergence of IoHT with cutting-edge technologies like blockchain and quantum computing ensures that the promise of personalized medicine is realized without compromising security. By addressing the twin goals of customization and trust, these innovations are setting the stage for a healthcare system that is not only more effective but also deeply secure and patient centric. This transformative approach exemplifies the future of proactive, personalized care in a connected world.

6. Conclusion

The IoHT has emerged as a transformative force in healthcare, revolutionizing how medical services are delivered and consumed. From personalized medicine to real-time monitoring, IoHT systems have redefined patient care by leveraging connected devices, advanced analytics, and seamless data exchange. In intelligent hospital wards, IoHT has enabled early warning systems that continuously track patient vitals and predict potential health deteriorations, leading to timely interventions and improved outcomes [5, 14]. Wearable devices integrated with IoHT have empowered patients to manage chronic diseases, offering real-time feedback on their health while reducing the burden on healthcare systems.

The integration of IoHT into healthcare has also enhanced resource optimization and operational efficiency. Intelligent dashboards fueled by IoHT data have streamlined hospital operations, enabling better allocation of staff, equipment, and beds during peak demand. Meanwhile, hybrid edge-cloud architectures have brought real-time data processing closer to the source, improving the speed and accuracy of diagnostics. For instance, a two-stage ECG analysis system using edge-cloud collaboration significantly reduced latency and enhanced diagnostic precision for cardiac patients [11, 10]. These advancements highlight the potential of IoHT to bridge gaps in accessibility and deliver care more equitably across diverse populations.

Yet, the growing reliance on IoHT underscores the need to address its inherent challenges, particularly in cybersecurity and data privacy. As IoHT devices generate and transmit sensitive health information, they become prime targets for cyberattacks. Ensuring the integrity and security of these systems is paramount for fostering trust and safeguarding patient data. This transition leads us to the next chapter, where we will explore the multifaceted cybersecurity and data privacy challenges in IoHT. From tackling interoperability issues to implementing advanced encryption techniques, the next chapter will delve into the strategies and technologies shaping the secure future of IoHT.

References

[1] Ianculescu, M., A. Alexandru, N. -D. Nicolau, G. Neagu and O. Bica. 2019. IoHT and edge computing, warrants of optimal responsiveness of monitoring applications for seniors: A case study. *2019 22nd International Conference on Control Systems and Computer Science (CSCS)*, Bucharest, Romania, pp. 655. doi: 10.1109/CSCS.2019.00118.

[2] da Costa, C. A., C. F. Pasluosta, B. Eskofier, D. B. da Silva and R. da Rosa Righi. 2018. Internet of Health Things: Toward intelligent vital signs monitoring in hospital wards. *Artificial Intelligence in Medicine*, 89: 61–69. doi: 10.1016/j.artmed.2018.05.005.

[3] Alfian, G., M. Syafrudin, N. L. Fitriyani, M. A. Syaekhoni and J. Rhee. 2021. Utilizing IoT-based sensors and prediction model for health-care monitoring system. In *Artificial Intelligence and Big Data Analytics for Smart Healthcare*, Elsevier, pp. 63–75. doi: 10.1016/B978-0-12-822060-3.00009-7.

[4] Nauman, A., Y. A. Qadri, R. Ali and S. W. Kim. 2021. Machine learning-enabled Internet of Things for medical informatics. In *Machine Learning, Big Data, and IoT for Medical Informatics*, Elsevier, pp. 111–125. doi: 10.1016/B978-0-12-821777-1.00016-1.

[5] Krishnamoorthy, R., Meenakshi Gupta, Gundala Swathi, Kazuaki Tanaka, Ch Raja and Janjhyam Venkata Naga Ramesh. 2023. An intelligent IoT-based smart healthcare monitoring system using machine learning. In *Artificial Intelligence and Internet of Things*, Taylor and Francis. doi: 10.1201/9781003403678-16.

[6] Abubeker, K. M., A. Joshy, A. T. George and G. Gopika. Oct. 2022. Internet of Healthcare Things (IoHT) enabled incessant real time patient monitoring system using non-invasive sensors. *2022 10th International Conference on Reliability, Infocom Technologies and Optimization (Trends and Future Directions) (ICRITO)*, Noida, India, pp. 1–6. doi: 10.1109/ICRITO56286.2022.9964893.

[7] Mercati, P. and G. Bhat. 2024. Self-sustainable wearable and Internet of Things (IoT) devices for health monitoring: Opportunities and challenges. *IEEE Design & Test*, 41(1): 1–15. doi: 10.1109/MDAT.2024.3432862.

[8] Munagala, N. K., L. R. R. Langoju, A. D. Rani and D. R. K. Reddy. 2022. A smart IoT-enabled heart disease monitoring system using meta-heuristic-based Fuzzy-LSTM model. *Biocybernetics and Biomedical Engineering*, 42(4): 1183–1204. doi: 10.1016/j.bbe.2022.10.001.

[9] Bhuiyan, M. N., M. M. Rahman, M. M. Billah and D. Saha. 2021. Internet of Things (IoT): A review of its enabling technologies in healthcare applications, standards protocols, security, and market opportunities. *IEEE Internet of Things Journal*, 8(13): 10474–10489. doi: 10.1109/JIOT.2021.3062630.

[10] Singh, N., S. P. Sasirekha, A. Dhakne, B. S. Thrinath, D. Ramya and R. Thiagarajan. 2022. IoT-enabled hybrid model with learning ability for E-health care systems. *Measurement: Sensors*, 24, doi: 10.1016/j.measen.2022.100567.

[11] Xiaolin, L., B. Cardiff and D. John. 2024. A two-stage ECG classifier for decentralized inferencing across edge-cloud continuum. *IEEE Sensors Journal*, 24(14): 23324–23332. doi: 10.1109/JSEN.2024.3406780.

[12] Iqbal, S. M. A., I. Mahgoub, E. Du, M. A. Leavitt and W. Asghar. 2021. Advances in healthcare wearable devices. *NPJ Flexible Electronics*, 5(9): 1–12. doi: 10.1038/s41528-021-00107-x.

[13] Wani, N. A., R. Kumar, J. Bedi and I. Rida. 2024. Explainable AI-driven IoMT fusion: Unravelling techniques, opportunities, and challenges with Explainable AI in healthcare. *Information Fusion*, 110: 102472. doi: 10.1016/j.inffus.2024.102472.

[14] Mamdiwar, S. D., Z. Shakruwala, U. Chadha, K. Srinivasan and C. Y. Chang. 2021. Recent advances on IoT-assisted wearable sensor systems for healthcare monitoring. *Biosensors*, 11(10): 372. doi: 10.3390/bios11100372.

[15] Siddiqui, S. A., A. Ahmad and N. Fatima. 2023. IoT-based disease prediction using machine learning. *Computers and Electrical Engineering*, 108: 108675. doi: 10.1016/j.compeleceng.2023.108675.

[16] Wahezi, S. E., L. R. Kohan, B. Spektor, S. Brancolini, T. Emerick, J. M. Fronterhouse and A. D. Kaye. 2021. Telemedicine and current clinical practice trends in the COVID-19 pandemic. *Best Practice & Research Clinical Anaesthesiology*, 35(3): 307–319. doi: 10.1016/j.bpa.2020.11.005.

Section IV

Emerging Trends and Futuristic Challenges

DOI: 10.1201/9781003483267-13

Chapter 10

Emerging Trends in IoHT

Khudeija Kassam

1. Introduction

Conventional healthcare systems cannot meet the needs of a large population. Medical services are still out of reach and too expensive for many people, despite a strong infrastructure. The advent of Internet of Things (IoT) in the healthcare sector has significantly advanced the efficiency and effectiveness of healthcare delivery leading to improved quality of life, reducing hospitalization and expenses by providing real-time monitoring, data collection, and communication between devices.

The security and privacy of these Internet of Healthcare Things (IoHT)-based healthcare systems frequently receive insufficient attention as a result of the rapid development. Serious repercussions can arise from inadequate security measures in IoHT healthcare systems, including compromised patient privacy from eavesdropping and delayed detection of life-threatening situations due to Denial of Service (DoS) attacks that disrupt IoHT devices' regular operations.

1.1 Chapter Roadmap

The chapter is organized as follows: Section 2 Fundamentals of IoHT, Section 3 Services and Applications of IoHT by the Medical Industry, Section 4 Ongoing Trends of IoHT, Section 5 Challenges with IoHT, and Section 6 Conclusion.

London South Bank University, London, UK.
Email: kkhudeija@gmail.com

DOI: 10.1201/9781003483267-14

2. Fundamentals of IoHT

A subset of the IoT and the IoHT combines intelligent medical devices and applications to enhance medical procedures, patient care, and healthcare delivery. IoHT describes a wide range of networked wearables, medical equipment, sensors, and applications that collect, share, and analyze health-related data in real time.

2.1 *IoHT Architecture*

Figure 1 illustrates the three layers that make up the IoHT architecture: sensor layer, personal server layer, and medical server layer. Every layer plays a unique role in the IoHT system's overall operation.

The sensor layer serves as a foundational layer. Vital physiological data from patients are gathered by a variety of biomedical sensors such as body temperature sensors, respiratory rate sensors, blood pressure sensors, and pulse oximetry sensors. With the use of pulse sensors, life-threatening illnesses such pulmonary embolisms, cardiac arrest, and vasovagal syncope can be monitored. The pulse can be detected by the fingertips, wrist, earlobe, chest, and more [11]. Respiratory rate sensors measure a patient's respiratory rate or number of breaths taken per minute. This can be used to diagnose illnesses such as lung cancer, apnea episodes, asthma attacks, tuberculosis, hyperventilation, and more. Utilizing body temperature sensors can measure a person's body temperature and identify fevers, heatstroke, hypothermia, and other conditions. Blood pressure (BP), a key health indicator that is routinely and widely monitored, can be checked using blood pressure monitors. Blood pressure monitoring can help identify hypertension, a condition

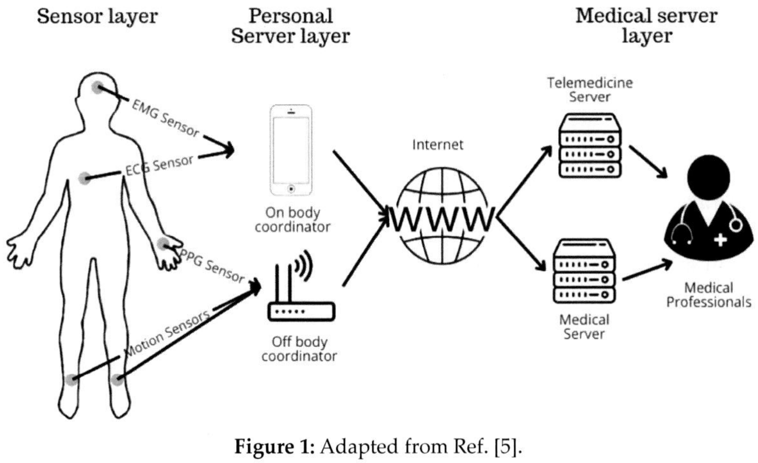

Figure 1: Adapted from Ref. [5].

that increases the risk of heart attacks and other cardiovascular illnesses. Pulse oximetry sensors measure the blood's oxygen content, a vital indicator that can aid in the diagnosis of diseases like hypoxia. These sensors collect data, which are then sent to the following layer for processing. This layer serves as the first input for the healthcare system and is essential for real-time health monitoring.

Personal server layer is a bridge between the medical servers and the sensors. Health data gathered from several sensors are processed, managed, and transmitted by this layer. The purposes of personal servers are to process and store patients' data locally before sending to the centralized medical servers. A personal server is required to be able to operate normally when the network connection to the medical server is lost [1]. On-body devices that are worn or carried by the patient, such as smartwatches, fitness trackers, smartphones, continuously collect data from the sensors and store them locally. Off-body devices are external, network infrastructure-related devices, like routers and gateways, serve as a communication link between the devices and medical server.

Medical server layer is an intricate component that is vital to the management of healthcare data, communication, and clinical decision support. The medical server, telemedicine server, and medical professionals are the three primary components that form this layer.

i. The Medical Server functions as the primary hub for managing, processing, and storing data in the healthcare system. Its functions are: Data Storage: The medical server holds a massive amount of health-related data, such as electronic health records (EHRs), test results, medical history, and data from wearables and other medical devices that are monitored in real time. Data management: Oversees the availability, security, and integrity of patient data to guard sensitive data against loss and unauthorized access. This involves putting access controls, encryption, and backup solutions in place. Data processing: Advanced analytics and machine learning algorithms are used to process incoming data. In addition to supporting clinical decision-making, this processing can be used to identify trends and forecast medical implications. Interoperability: The medical server ensures that other healthcare systems, such as pharmacy management systems and laboratory information systems, integrate seamlessly, providing comprehensive patient care.

ii. Telemedicine Server is a specialized component that supports remote healthcare services and virtual consultations. Its main responsibilities are: Enabling virtual visits for healthcare professionals: The Telemedicine Server makes it possible for medical professionals to visit patients virtually and communicate with them in real time via chat, video conferencing, or messaging apps. Data transmission: During telehealth sessions, patient data are securely transferred between patients and healthcare professionals such as medical history and information from real-time health monitoring. Integration with medical devices: The telemedicine server may establish connections with a range of wearables and medical devices in order to collect and transmit health data, allowing for the remote monitoring of patients conditions. Patient engagement: It improves patient engagement and adherence to treatment programs by giving patients access to their health information, making appointments easier, and sending reminders for follow-up care or medication.

iii. Healthcare Practitioners including physicians, nurses, and other healthcare workers. They interact with the medical server. Access patient data: In order to make well-informed decisions about diagnosis and treatment, medical practitioners use the medical server to access comprehensive patient records. Clinical decision support: The medical server's analytics and insights are useful to medical practitioners as they help with condition diagnosis, treatment planning, and adverse event prevention. Collaboration and communication: By enabling information sharing, case discussions, and patient care coordination, the medical server layer promotes cooperation and communication between healthcare professionals.

2.2 *IoHT Networks*

The IoHT is a term used to describe networks intended for the safe and effective exchange of data and information related to healthcare [9]. By connecting various medical systems, sensors, and devices, these networks enable better healthcare services, real-time data analysis, and remote patient monitoring. An outline of IoHT networks can be found below [9]:

Wireless Sensor Networks (WSNs): WSNs are networks of connected sensors and devices that can monitor various aspects of an individual's health. Examples include environmental sensors used in medical settings, wearable technology, and sensors that are implanted.

IoHT Gateways: IoHT networks usually have gateways or hubs that help IoHT devices and local or remote healthcare IT infrastructure to communicate with each other. The gateways act as intermediaries, compiling information and carrying out simple operations and securely sending data—often all at the same time.

Cloud Integration: IoHT networks often use cloud computing to manage the enormous volumes of data produced by healthcare devices. Healthcare practitioners can access patient records remotely, perform real-time patient monitoring, and analyze data.

Edge Computing: IoHT networks leverage edge devices for decentralized data processing. In critical healthcare situations, this lowers latency and facilitates faster decision-making.

5G Technology: The rapid development of IoHT networks are mainly due to the significant increase in connection speeds and data transmission capacities made possible by 5G technology. Stable, low latency connections are essential for telemedicine and real-time patient monitoring applications.

IoT Protocols: To guarantee accurate and timely data transfer, IoHT networks use a variety of communication protocols created specifically for the IoT. MQTT, CoAP, and HTTP are frequently used.

Security: Preserving security in IoHT networks is critical due to the sensitivity of healthcare data. Strong authentication, encryption, and access control procedures are put in place.

Scalability: In order to handle the increasing number of sensors and devices, IoHT networks need to be scalable. In healthcare settings where a rapid increase in the number of connected devices is anticipated, scalability is essential.

Interoperability: A variety of devices developed by different manufacturers that use different communication protocols must all function effectively. For seamless healthcare data transmission, interoperability must be considered during the design of IoHT networks.

Energy Efficiency: Since many IoHT devices run on batteries, they must have a high level of energy efficiency in order to provide constant real-time monitoring without the need for frequent recharging. It is critical to develop energy saving methods and low power communication protocols.

Compliance: In order to preserve patient privacy and fulfill legal requirements, IoHT networks must abide by healthcare laws, such as the Health Insurance Portability and Accountability Act (HIPAA) in the United States.

Data Analytics: To extract useful insights and improve the quality of patient care, the volumes of data produced by IoHT networks commonly include data analytics and machine learning components.

Telemedicine Integration: Designed to work seamlessly with telemedicine systems, IoHT networks enable online health consultations and services.

Patient Portals: As part of their effort to give patients more control over their treatment, some IoHT networks include patient portals that let users interact with healthcare providers and view their personal health information.

Research and Clinical Trials: IoHT networks facilitate ongoing data collection from clinical trial participants, guaranteeing that data are up to date and supporting medical research.

Healthcare Management: By enhancing hospital operations and maximizing resource allocation, IoHT networks significantly contribute to healthcare management.

IoHT networks have a considerable impact on patient care, medical research, and remote monitoring, making them essential to the modern healthcare environment. As technology advances and the need for easily accessible healthcare solutions grows, they evolve.

3. Services and Applications of IoHT by the Medical Industry

The IoHT-based system can be used in a number of instances such as personal healthcare, chronic illness management, child care, elderly care, and fitness tracking. To give a thorough understanding, this section concentrates on services and applications. Services are used to build applications whereas applications are utilized directly by users and patients. Consequently, services are developer-centric whereas applications are user-centric [10].

3.1 IoHT Services

IoT is expected to facilitate a wide range of healthcare services to bring together hospitals, patients, doctors, medical equipment, biosensors, and other healthcare personnel under a unified framework, offering specific healthcare solutions. While there is no universally accepted definition of IoT services within the healthcare context, there are instances where a service may not be distinctly separated from a specific solution or application. This suggests that a service is inherently generic and can serve as a foundational element for a variety of solutions or applications [10].

Assisted Aided Living Services

One of the key services provided by the IoHT-based system is Ambient Assisted Living (AAL), which is particularly beneficial for elderly individuals, those with physical disabilities and patients suffering from acute illnesses. The aim of AAL is to enable them to remain independent in a convenient and secure way. AAL services' solutions can help them by feeling more confident by guaranteeing increased autonomy and offering support in times of need.

A variety of devices and sensors are utilized across different applications to support these services. Biosensors are used to monitor and record patient data. These biosensors can be integrated into various smart devices, enabling the collection of real-time health information. The data are then transmitted to doctors and family members in the event of any unusual activities or emergencies.

Mobile Health Services

IoT-based m-Health uses smart devices and biosensors to deliver primary healthcare services straight to people's mobile phones, allowing for real-time tracking and monitoring of their health. With the use of their individual health records, individuals are able to take preventive action. Patients' real-time data are gathered by biosensors and other smart sensor-based devices, which are integrated into different smart devices or worn on the body. Furthermore, in times of emergency or difficulty, this service makes it easier for doctors and patients to communicate. Doctors have remote access to patient data and can write prescriptions based on the data gathered.

Adverse Medication Response

Medication is vital for patients and the correct dose and method to administer them is necessary as complications may arise from improper medication use. Some medication may have side effects and are not always appropriate for each person. The IoT-based system has emerged as a solution to these problems. Barcode and NFC-enabled devices are used by the patient's terminal to identify the medication. This information is then synchronized to determine whether the medication is compatible with the patient's allergy profile and electronic health record with the aid of a pharmaceutical intelligent information system.

Community-based Healthcare

The approach of creating a network that encompasses the region surrounding a local community is the foundation of community healthcare monitoring. This could be an IoT network encircling a rural community, a residential neighborhood, or a municipal hospital. The integration of hospitals and users into a single framework facilitates access to an array of healthcare services, such as family member monitoring, doctor consultations, and child care. In addition, the system allows for real-time tracking and monitoring, guaranteeing families and individuals receive individualized care.

Child Health Information

Child care services, focused on emotional, behavioral, and mental health support, are offered by the IoT-based child health informatics system. In this context, an IoT-based m-health service that can motivate kids to develop healthy eating habits with the support of their educators and parents is presented in Ref. [5].

Smart Wearables

Smart wearables powered by IoT are becoming more common and essential to daily life. With the use of sensors and other smart technologies, wearables are intended for personal care, allowing users to track and monitor their health. Fitness bands and smartwatches are two of the most widely used and embraced gadgets globally. They offer many useful features that can be tailored to meet individual preferences, such as blood pressure tracking, sleep analysis, calorie burn measurement, and heart rate monitoring. These wearables allow users to tailor their health improvement plans according to their conditions and track their health in real time.

Semantic Medical Access

Information about diseases and their consequences is made available to users through IoT-based semantic medical access. Users can learn about underlying conditions, medications, safety measures, and other pertinent information with this system. This information can help with diet plans, workout regimens and sleep schedules. Crucial health indicators like blood pressure, heart rate, oxygen levels, glucose levels, and more can also be monitored with its assistance.

Emergency Healthcare

Healthcare concerns play a major role in many emergency scenarios, such as bad weather, transportation accidents (aircraft, ship, train, and vehicle), to name a few. Solutions including information availability, alert notification, post-accident action, and record keeping can be provided by a dedicated service.

Embedded Gateway Configuration

The Internet, to which necessary servers and clients are directly connected, network nodes (to which patients are directly connected), and other medical equipment are all connected by the architectural embedded gateway configuration (EGC) service. From a service standpoint, even though a gateway may appear with distinct features, depending on the deployed gateway's particular purpose, this requires some common integration features.

Embedded Context

IoT-based embedded context is a security mechanism that entails sending encrypted data via third party service providers or less secure communication channels. By guaranteeing that the encrypted data cannot be decrypted without the proper security key, this method improves data security. Consequently, confidentiality and data integrity are upheld.

3.2 *IoHT Applications*

Applications are separated into two categories: single conditions and clustered conditions. A single condition application pertains to a single illness or condition, whereas a clustered condition application addresses several illnesses or conditions collectively. The many applications based on single and cluster conditions are presented and discussed.

3.2.1 Single Condition Applications

These applications are solution-specific and tailored since it is customized for personal care and well-being. To meet these objectives, a range of task-specific or single condition applications are in development.

Glucose Monitoring

Diabetes is a common metabolic illness characterized by prolonged increase in blood glucose (sugar) levels. Individuals generally don't have the time in their busy lifestyles to visit labs for routine blood glucose testing. This challenge pushes researchers and organizations to design intelligent IoHT systems that can track blood glucose levels in real time and allow users to customize food plans, manage medications, and modify their physical activity levels.

ECG Monitoring

Capturing the electrical activity of the heart, the electrocardiogram (ECG) is an essential diagnostic tool. It is helpful in diagnosing a number of heart-related disorders and offers insightful information on the heart functions. With the help of these cutting-edge technologies, it is possible to continuously monitor ECG signals and check heart health in real time without having to schedule frequent hospital appointments. Healthcare professionals can identify and diagnose a variety of cardiac conditions efficiently by using these monitoring devices. Prolonged QT intervals, for example, may be indicative of complicated arrhythmias, myocardial ischemia (a disease in which the heart's blood flow is limited), and other related conditions. By taking a proactive stance when it comes to heart health monitoring, patients can better control their health and receive improved patient care.

Blood Pressure Monitoring

IoHT solutions support blood pressure monitoring, which is essential for controlling high blood pressure, preventing hypertension, evaluating the risk of cardiovascular disease, encouraging healthier lifestyle choices, monitoring conditions related to pregnancy, making sure patients heal from surgery, and managing chronic illnesses like diabetes and kidney disease.

Body Temperature Monitoring

Monitoring body temperature is essential for assessing the severity of a fever, monitoring the effectiveness of treatment and ensuring post-surgery care. It also helps with the management of chronic illnesses and supports medical decisions.

Oxygen Levels Monitoring

An essential component of smart healthcare services is oxygen level monitoring. In order to track the oxygen levels of healthy and ill patients, sophisticated monitoring tools or software could be used. For continuous, non-invasive monitoring of blood oxygen saturation, pulse oximetry is the best option. Pulse oximetry and IoT together improve technology-driven medical healthcare applications.

Smart Insulin

Blood glucose or sugar levels can rise in diabetics over an extended period of time. As a result, insulin is needed to manage diabetes in patients. This procedure can be quite complicated and frequently calls for more nursing support, which raises the expense of healthcare and increases reliance on nurses. Patients with diabetes can better manage their insulin dosage and, consequently, their diabetes condition by utilizing IoHT solutions.

Smart Vision

Individuals who are visually impaired can use the smart vision application as an assistive system. It helps with a variety of tasks, including locating stores and navigating crossings. Furthermore, the goal of this technology is to improve the quality of life for those who are visually impaired by making their experiences more routine and manageable.

Smart Hearables

The smart Hearables software serves as a deaf or hard of hearing person's assistive technology. With the goal of improving and simplifying the daily experiences of individuals who have hearing impairments, this cutting edge technology provides sophisticated hearing aid programs that are easier to use and more manageable.

3.2.2 Cluster Condition Applications

With a focus on medical-specific capabilities and a multipurpose design, cluster view applications are specifically developed for public health and welfare. It facilitates easier communication between patients and medical professionals, such as physicians and nurses. The clustered view's numerous applications are covered.

Rehabilitation System

For those with physical disabilities, a rehabilitation system improves their functional capacities and general quality of life. IoT can improve rehabilitation systems by tackling issues related to the shortage of medical staff and ageing populations. Essentially, the real-time analytical capabilities of the smart rehabilitation system provide prompt and efficient patient assistance and treatment.

Medicine Management

Medication management is an essential component of IoHT applications since it has a direct impact on health; skipping a dose might have detrimental effects. Monitoring the impact of medication on patients' health is another benefit of this system. Patients and their families can efficiently manage medication schedules and dosages with the help of this program.

Wheelchair Management

The smart wheelchair is an IoHT solution that combines standard wheelchair features with a variety of sensors, making it ideal for those with physical disabilities. To track and handle specific medical conditions, it might establish a connection with local or international health databases. It can also track a person's whereabouts in an emergency by using a variety of sensors. Functionalities including behavior analysis, resource optimization, parameter optimization, strategy optimization, and subsystem optimization may also be included in the smart wheelchair.

Imminent Healthcare Solutions

The field of imminent healthcare is centered on medically specific applications that are intended to identify and track a variety of health-related conditions, such as abnormal cell growth, peak expiratory flow, cancer treatment, hemoglobin levels, skin infections, and eye diseases. Remote surgery is made possible by smart imminent healthcare applications that combine medical personnel and equipment into one system.

Healthcare Solutions using Smartphones

Electronic devices with smartphone-controlled sensors have increased significantly in the last few years, highlighting smartphones' pivotal role as IoT drivers. Numerous hardware and software solutions have been created to enable smartphones to function as multifunctional healthcare tools. Based on their functions, mobile health applications can be divided into six major categories: Diagnostic apps provide access to diagnosis and treatment information. Drug reference apps offer information on medications, such as their names, dosages, distinctive characteristics, and costs. Literature search apps assist users in locating pertinent medical information from biomedical literature databases. Medical education apps feature medical textbooks, training, tutorials, surgical demonstrations, and illustrations. Calculator apps include numerous medical equations and formulas to compute values such as body surface burn percentage. Clinical communication apps in a hospital setting aid communication between clinicians.

Disease Diagnosis

In IoHT-based systems, disease diagnostics are an essential application. Medical diagnostic applications use information obtained from patients' biosensors to identify a wide range of illnesses. A healthcare professional makes the final diagnosis, even though these apps can offer preliminary diagnoses based on accumulated knowledge and prior experiences. They can function well in systems with constrained resources and are helpful in addressing the physician shortage. Doctors and patients can both continuously monitor the progress of their health through the collection of real-time data.

4. Ongoing Trends of IoHT

4.1 Wearables

Wearables are cutting edge devices designed to be worn, allow individuals to track their fitness and health. The sensors in them let users track multiple aspects of their well-being. They are integrated into fashionable accessories like watches or clothing. Figure 2 adapted from Ref. [4] illustrates the different wearables in the market.

There are several advantages to using wearable technology for health monitoring, such as:

Continuous Monitoring: Enable continuous health tracking by providing real-time information on physical activity and vital signs.

Early Detection: Wearable technology makes it easier to spot possible health problems early on by detecting minute changes in health metrics.

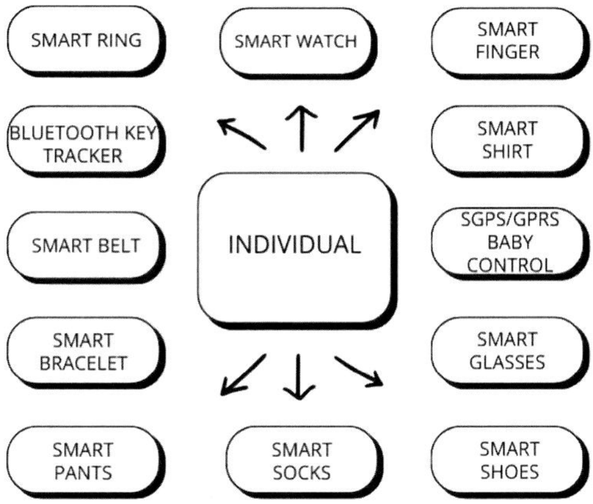

Figure 2: IoHT wearables.

Personalized Health Insights: They produce unique health information that can guide customized drug schedules and treatment strategies.

Medication Adherence: By tracking intake and sending reminders, some devices assist users in adhering to their medication schedules.

Lifestyle Decisions: By tracking sleep patterns, calories and physical activity, wearable technology promotes better lifestyle choices.

Safety Features: Some devices can identify risks to patients and notify emergency services or carers, improving safety, especially for senior citizens.

Cost Savings: By encouraging early intervention and preventative treatment, wearable technology can lower medical expenses associated with emergency visits and hospital stays.

Wearable technology is becoming increasingly popular due to factors like growing consumer spending on electronics, urbanization trends, improved lifestyles among the growing population, and increased health and safety awareness. Figure 3 adapted from Ref. [4] depicts the increase in market size.

The adaptability of wearable flexible sensors in fitness tracking, healthcare, and human-machine interactions has drawn a lot of interest. However, a number of obstacles prevent their efficient and broad application. Sensor adhesion and data accuracy may be impacted by differences in human body types, including skin thickness, elasticity, and texture. Sensor calibration is further complicated by different physical activities, since intensive exercise may make it more difficult for devices to record correct data than inactive tasks. Long-term success depends on user comfort and compliance, which calls for constant innovation in

Figure 3: Wearables market size.

sensor design to support a variety of body types and activities. In order to ensure durability, flexible sensors must also withstand mechanical stresses from bending and stretching, which calls for careful material selection. Soft, breathable materials and non-irritating attachment techniques are crucial for user comfort. It is difficult to maintain sensor accuracy over time, so calibration processes are required to address data drift. In medical applications, biocompatibility is essential for preventing allergic reactions, and efficient power management is required to prolong battery life and lower the frequency of recharging.

4.2 Healthcare 4.0

The integration of digital technologies, data analytics, and artificial intelligence into the healthcare industry is known as Healthcare 4.0. This includes personalized medicine, AI-based diagnostics, telehealth, and electronic health records. AI-driven diagnostics improve diagnosis timeliness and accuracy, which improves treatment results. Furthermore, telehealth services reduce the strain on physical healthcare institutions and enable broader access to healthcare [7]. However, some limitations include:

Discrimination: Digital technologies have the potential to treat certain communities unfairly, mostly because of incomplete or biased AI training data that can contribute to healthcare inequities by giving under-represented groups incorrect diagnoses and treatments. Disparities in access to healthcare technologies can be amplified by socioeconomic and geographic constraints.

Consent and Privacy: Considerable privacy concerns are brought up by the massive accumulation of personal health information. Obtaining appropriate patient consent for data usage is essential, as is putting in place efficient procedures for controlling privacy concerns and guaranteeing secure data management.

Health Insurance Discrimination: Individuals with certain medical conditions may face unfair premium changes if health data are exploited by insurance companies to generate risk profiles.

Misuse of Personal Health Data: As healthcare becomes more digitally connected, there is a greater chance of data misuse and cybercrime. As a result, strict rules are needed to secure patient data from breaches and make sure it is used legally and with express authorization.

Job Displacement: Healthcare staff may lose their jobs as a result of automation brought about by digital technologies. There has to be a balance between automation and the preservation of high-quality patient care while institutions should concentrate on workforce planning and reskilling initiatives.

4.3 *Nanotechnology*

Nanotechnology enables the creation of new smart technologies and devices as well as the development of better and more advanced materials for industrial and medical applications. Recent advances in nanotechnology have led to the emergence of nanodevices, which are made up of small components capable of performing basic functions like sensing and actuation. For efficient information exchange, these devices can also be connected to the internet through smooth nanoscale communication technology. The Internet of Nano Things (IoNT) is a concept that essentially scales the IoT down to the nanoscale by integrating IoT with nanotechnology. In IoNT, nanosensors, also known as "nano things," are linked together via a nanoscale network and exchange information with each other via nanocommunication technologies.

The Internet of Nano Things (IoNT) makes it easier for different nanobiosensors that can be attached to or implanted in the body to network with one another. Individual nanobiosensors function separately, but IoNT makes it possible for these devices to function effectively together, creating a more comprehensive information flow. Clinical decision-making is more accurate when data from many body parts are combined. Doctors, medical service providers, patients, and their families are among the important stakeholders who can receive health information collected by the biosensors thanks to IoNT. As a result, IoNT creates an all-encompassing healthcare system that makes it possible to continuously and instantly gauge a patient's health from anywhere at any time. This capacity promotes early disease detection and diagnosis in addition to facilitating timely medical intervention [8].

Scientists and medical professionals are concerned about the implantation of electronic devices that generate radiating signals, even though nanotechnology has enormous potential to address a number of healthcare issues, including cancer diagnosis and prompt medicine administration. The following are the main risks connected to nanodevice implants: Individual differences in the body's response to implanted nanodevices could cause organ and soft tissue damage. Long-term exposure to substances like silicon and silver can also interfere with the body's cells and organs regular processes. There is a possibility that nanodevices could build up inside organs and limit the supply of oxygen and blood. Additionally, the body might identify nanodevices as foreign substances, which could lead to an immune response that gradually weakens the immune system.

4.4 Edge Computing

According to Ref. [6], edge computing is a promising component of the IoT that aims to address challenging processing problems. By improving the speed of processing and transmission of IoT devices, edge computing may be able to supply data with lower latency. In IoT-enabled edge computing-based healthcare systems, load balancing and efficient resource use can be encouraged by using AI and creating optimized networks. However, these devices are not nearly as powerful, and their data are more vulnerable to security risks. Therefore, it is crucial to create a safe framework for software defined networks (SDN)-based healthcare systems that are enabled by the IoT and rely on edge computing. Edge servers use a lightweight authentication technique to verify IoT devices.

4.5 Blockchain

A block on a blockchain is made up of a group of data that have been categorized as a transaction. To form a blockchain, several blocks are connected together. The size of the blockchain increases in proportion to the number of transactions [2].

Despite being created originally for Bitcoin, the blockchain technology has started to show promise in a number of unexpected and new industries. The limitations of IoT devices, especially with regard to storing the complete blockchain, make the practical implementation of the blockchain of things (BCoT) difficult. There are two different ways to store data: full storage, which stores the complete blockchain, and partial storage, which holds a portion of the data blocks. Complete nodes, such cloud or edge servers, can store the whole blockchain and have the processing power required for mining and other functions. IoT devices with limited resources, on the other hand, function as lightweight nodes that validate transactions without storing the entire blockchain and frequently simply save partial data, such as hash values. Full nodes are necessary for lightweight nodes to function. According to a BCoT deployment scenario, IoT devices can only keep a portion of the blockchain data, but cloud and edge servers can store all or part of it. There are several ways that blockchain and IoT can interact: There are three types of interactions: (1) direct, in which IoT devices use edge servers to access blockchain data; (2) direct, in which IoT nodes exchange partial data through device-to-device links; and (3) hybrid, in which IoT devices use edge or cloud servers to interface with blockchain data [3]. Integrating blockchain technology into healthcare networks has the potential to address the challenges related to preserving privacy and ensuring the security of healthcare data. Healthcare data produced by medical sensors can be automatically gathered and sent to the system through the execution of smart contracts, thereby facilitating real-time patient monitoring. Throughout this process, privacy is maintained through the underlying blockchain technology.

5. Challenges with IoHT

The IoT is growing rapidly and the use of IoT applications and devices in the medical field has increased significantly. The promise of IoT to transform healthcare is driving this movement. However, because these devices may be connected to global networks and handle sensitive personal health information, the growing usage of IoT devices in healthcare presents security and privacy concerns. It is essential to identify and evaluate the various features of IoT security and privacy from a healthcare perspective in order to guarantee the effective and broad adoption of IoT in the healthcare sector. Every layer of IoHT systems has different functionalities, resulting in varying security and privacy protocols at each level. As a result, requirements for every level can be reviewed.

5.1 Requirements

5.1.1 Data Level

Confidentiality ensures the inaccessibility of medical information to unauthorized users. Legal and ethical privacy regulations, such as the General Data Protection Regulation (GDPR) and the Health Insurance Portability and Accountability Act (HIPAA), must be followed when collecting and storing patient health data. Only authorized individuals have the right to have access to personal health information according to these regulations. Healthcare companies need to put strong safeguards in place to protect patient data confidentiality in order to prevent data breaches. The significance of these precautions cannot be emphasized since stolen medical records may be sold on black markets, putting patients' privacy at risk as well as causing them to suffer financial loss and reputational harm. The GDPR's Article 5(e) mandates that personal data be erased after they is no longer required for processing, with certain exceptions listed in Article 89 for archiving, scientific, historical, and statistical purposes. This idea is fundamental to safeguarding individual's privacy and avoiding the collection of unnecessary information that could attract malicious parties.

The data integrity requirement in IoHT healthcare systems attempts to guarantee that information travels wirelessly to its intended location without alteration. Cybercriminals may take advantage of wireless networks' broadcast feature to access and alter patient data, which could have dangerous repercussions in urgent circumstances. Mechanisms that can identify any unauthorized changes or manipulations must be in place in order to guarantee the preservation of data integrity. This involves making sure that the data on medical servers are kept intact and not tampered with. Medical service providers are required by GDPR Article 5(d) to put in place procedures that maintain accurate and current patient data. Additionally, they have to quickly update or remove any inaccurate personal data. The GDPR highlights the significance of accurate data further by enabling data owners to request corrections for any inaccuracies. Service providers are obligated to respond to these requests within a month. Likewise, HIPAA requires healthcare providers to take all reasonable precautions against unauthorized modification of protected health information (PHI) that is stored on their databases.

Authorized users must always have easy access to services and data. These services and data offered by medical servers and devices could become unavailable in the event of denial-of-service (DoS) attacks. Life-threatening circumstances, like not being able to send out timely alerts during a heart attack, can result from such inaccessibility. Healthcare applications need to be constantly active to reduce the risk of availability loss and guarantee that data are available to users and emergency services. Medical service providers must be able to quickly restore access to personal data in accordance with GDPR Article 32. This includes putting preventive security measures and countermeasures against DoS attacks in place. Furthermore, patients in the EU have the "Right to Be Forgotten," or the ability to request that the data pertaining to them that is held by medical service providers be deleted, under Article 17 of the GDPR. However, HIPAA does not require this right.

In the healthcare industry, ensuring high-quality data is essential because they have a direct impact on treatment decisions. Inaccurate or inadequate data may result in misdiagnoses and harm to patients. Problems with data quality can occur when IoHT devices are used. Malfunctioning equipment, poor data transmission, and inaccurate patient input are examples of potential sources of error in the healthcare system. Using redundant data collection, data cleaning methods, and validation checks is crucial to overcoming these challenges. In order to preserve data integrity, healthcare providers ought to communicate to patients and device users the significance of accurate data input.

IoHT devices generate enormous amounts of data, which have benefits and drawbacks. Healthcare systems could be overloaded by these data, despite the fact that they have the potential to greatly improve healthcare delivery. Applying machine learning and advanced data analysis techniques is crucial to solving this. With the help of these tools, we can effectively handle vast amounts of data, derive insightful information, and share that information with medical professionals. Additionally, through establishing data governance frameworks, businesses can organize, prioritize, and archive data based on its value and regulations.

5.1.2 Sensor Level

The IoHT healthcare system's sensor level is responsible for gathering and sending health data from a variety of sensors and medical devices. Due to the limited computational capacity and power limitations of medical devices and sensors, it faces the most security and privacy challenges.

IoHT devices are susceptible to physical theft, which could give hackers access to sensitive data. These attackers can also reprogram stolen devices and reintroduce them into the system, which enables them to monitor communications undercover. It is therefore crucial that IoHT healthcare systems take action to mitigate the serious security risk posed by medical device theft. Medical devices should have tamper-resistant integrated circuits to reduce this risk by preventing outside parties from accessing the codes that are stored on the devices after they are deployed.

The two types of sensor localization that researchers are focusing on are on-body sensor positioning and location of sensors or patients inside of buildings. The primary goal of the first kind, on body sensor positioning, is to verify whether sensors are positioned correctly on the body, which is essential for activity recognition. The second kind, called Location of Things (LoT), aims to track the patient wearing the sensor around the facility or determine the sensor's location within a room. Medical devices frequently switch between networks. Therefore, in order to monitor and manage sensors that leave and rejoin the network irregularly, real-time intrusion detection measures are crucial.

Based on Autonomic Computing, self-healing refers to a system's capacity to automatically identify, assess, and recover from errors or attacks with the least amount of human intervention. For IoHT systems to continue working in the face of cyberattacks, this capability is essential. This includes: Identifying security breaches through monitoring network traffic and device behavior, examining the type and scope of attacks detected to choose the best course of action, taking action automatically to mitigate the effects of an attack and restore normal operations, reducing the need for manual responses to minimize human intervention and ensure patient safety in healthcare settings.

The technique known as over-the-air programming, or OTA, has become popular for updating IoT systems made up of multiple sensor nodes. This strategy, however, presents safety concerns such as the potential for malicious sensor nodes to eavesdrop on updates and impersonate identities within the network. The self-healing mechanism may include OTA, which enables rapid updating of security protocols throughout the network. It is essential to set up security measures that guard against potential exploitation by attackers during the update process in order to guarantee the successful implementation of OTA. System administrators will find this capability useful as it allows them to improve security features, deploy updates, and address bugs without requiring physical access to every device.

The prompt replacement of malfunctioning medical sensors with new ones is imperative in real-time healthcare applications. Forward compatibility ensures that messages sent after medical sensors have left the network cannot be deciphered by the sensors in the future. Conversely, backward compatibility demonstrates that a sensor that has recently joined the network is unable to understand messages that were sent in the past. These compatibility issues could be resolved by using OTA programming to distribute the newest software updates.

5.1.3 Personal Server Level

A personal server, such as a smartphone, must authenticate any data received from medical devices and sensors before accepting it. To protect the confidentiality and integrity of data, the device authentication scheme should provide encrypted and secure communication. Clinical diagnoses and treatment choices may be greatly impacted if malicious devices provide misleading information about patients' physical conditions. As a result, device authentication must be implemented in every IoMT healthcare system. The devices and personal servers engage in a mutual authentication process; however, since personal servers are usually more powerful and capable than medical devices and sensors, they would perform the majority of the computational tasks.

Effective user authentication schemes are necessary given that only patients and medical staff, including carers, should have access to the data that are temporarily or permanently stored on personal servers. IoHT healthcare systems' personal servers need to enable emergency data access for patients experiencing life-threatening conditions such as a stroke or seizure. Biometrics is a popular solution for user authentication at the personal server level. It is particularly useful as the majority of biometrics are easily obtained from medical and healthcare devices that are worn by or implanted in individuals.

5.1.4 Medical Server Level

Access to the data must be limited to authorized individuals and devices, and the data must always be encrypted while being stored in the databases. These are two essential requirements for guaranteeing the security and privacy of patient data at the medical server level. The conversion of paper-based medical records into Electronic Medical Records (EMRs) has led to a rise in concerns about the security and privacy of the medical servers used to store these EMRs. As a result, strong security measures must be implemented at the medical server level.

Adequate access control schemes must be put in place to ensure that only authorized personnel and devices can access the medical servers. Medical server service providers need to provide selective access control since it can be difficult to get patient permission or consent for each request for access to data. This gives patients control over what information can be shared with which third parties.

Key management protocols, which are intended to deploy and distribute cryptographic keys to sensor nodes, play a critical role in the development of secure systems. Key pre-distribution protocols and trusted server protocols are the two main categories of key management protocols used in IoHT. Trusted server protocols perform well in hierarchical networks as they allow key agreement between nodes in the network via a trusted base station. However, for essential applications, like healthcare, this might not be sufficient since in real-time scenarios, a total network failure could render the trusted server inoperable. Conversely, symmetric key cryptography is usually used by key pre-distribution protocols to distribute secret keys throughout the network prior to the network being fully functional. These protocols' simple implementation and low processing requirements make them especially well-suited for sensor networks with limited resources.

When two reliable nodes, such a network coordinator and a sensor node, communicate data with one another, that relationship is referred to as mutual trust. The degree to which a node is safe and dependable when interacting with another node is known as trust. The success of wireless healthcare applications depends on network nodes working together effectively across distances. In this situation, trust management systems are critical in determining a node's credibility, especially through analyzing its behavior and the quality and accuracy of the data it provides—a vital component for healthcare applications.

5.1.5 Resistance to DOS Attacks

Denial-of-service (DoS) attacks have the potential to seriously harm these apps' functionality by flooding the network or obstructing valid communications. Attackers frequently use a technique called jamming, which transmits high energy signals to disrupt wireless communication at the physical layer, hence preventing devices from communicating correctly [12]. Research is urgently needed to develop strong defenses against DoS assaults for IoHT systems, given the unique challenges presented by the mobile and dynamic nature of wireless networks.

5.1.6 Computational Limits

IoHT devices have low computational power and speed. This limitation restricts their processing capabilities, making complex operations computationally intensive and leading to slower performance and increased energy consumption. It is challenging to create efficient security solutions for these devices since they require extra processing power, which might deplete the low power processors' limited capacity. The goal is to develop security solutions that effectively maintain a balance between resource conservation and security, guaranteeing that the devices continue to be responsive and operational while protecting patient safety and sensitive healthcare data.

5.1.7 Scalability

The extensive use of IoHT devices in healthcare infrastructure presents significant scaling concerns. Healthcare organizations need to make investments in infrastructure and systems that can manage the increasing load as new devices, sensors, and data streams emerge. Scalability problems can appear in a number of contexts. To properly handle the steadily growing amounts of data, it is first necessary to improve data processing and storage capabilities. This improvement is essential to guarantee that these systems can handle the growing volume of data. Furthermore, the network design needs to be scalable and robust in order to provide uninterrupted, smooth data transfer.

5.1.8 *Multiplicity of Devices*

Devices of various sizes and capacities, both homogeneous and heterogeneous, make up the IoHT. The computing power, energy consumption, memory utilization, and embedded software of these devices vary. As a result, creating a thorough security mechanism or protocol that satisfies the sophisticated security needs for every kind of device presents a challenge.

5.1.9 *Multiprotocol Network*

Proprietary network protocols, which are customized by manufacturers to satisfy the particular requirements of their applications, are commonly used by smart devices in IoHT for communication. Furthermore, by connecting to IoHT service providers via conventional IP networks, these smart devices can transmit and receive data over the internet and utilize cloud services, data storage, and remote monitoring features. Creating a security solution that successfully supports the different dynamic systems while satisfying sophisticated security criteria can be difficult.

5.2 *Attacks*

As new technologies emerge, attacks against them are becoming more frequent. Smart devices and associated networks are now common targets for attackers in the context of the IoHT architecture. Threats may arise from both inside and outside the networks, and they can be a variety of types. Some are obvious and observable, while others are hard to predict. Attacks that originate from smart health devices on adjacent networks can have severe consequences. Attacks can be classified into three main categories within the IoHT system: attacks based on host properties, network properties, and information disruption [10].

5.2.1 *Information Disruption*

The attacker retrieves health data either while it is being transmitted or from stored records. The attacker then modifies these data by removing or changing information from the medical records. They consist of:

i. Interruptions: To turn lines of communication inoperable or unavailable, an attacker initiates denial-of-service (DoS) attacks. The availability of network or healthcare services, network functionality, and device responsibility are all at risk from this type of attack. ii. Interception: To compromise data privacy and confidentiality, an attacker intercepts messages containing medical information. iii. Modification: To confuse and mislead individuals in the IoT health network, an attacker obtains unauthorized access to health data and tampers with it. iv. Fabrication: To undermine the legitimacy of a message and confuse uninformed participants, an adversary inserts are misleading. v. Replay: To undermine the freshness of a transmission, an adversary plays back previous messages. Furthermore, this causes more confusion and misleads innocent parties.

5.2.2 Host Properties

There are three types of host properties-based attacks: software, hardware, and user attacks. In order to take advantage of vulnerabilities, attackers can target any of them.

i. User compromise: occurs when an adversary uses fraud or theft to get access to the user's networks and health equipment. Sensitive data, including user information, passwords, and cryptographic keys, are exposed. ii. Hardware compromise: occurs when an adversary tampers with physical devices in order to obtain data, keys, and program codes from them. Malicious programs could be used by an attacker to reprogram hacked devices. iii. Software compromise: occurs when an attacker exploits flaws and vulnerabilities in software (such as operating systems, system software, and apps) to cause IoT health devices to malfunction or enter dysfunctional states (such as buffer overflow and resource exhaustion).

5.2.3 Network Properties

Standard Protocol Compromise: Attackers target standard protocols by compromising or altering security policies pertaining to integrity, authenticity, service availability, and message privacy. Network Protocol Stack Attack: Attackers find various vulnerabilities in the networking protocol and use them to force the layers to carry out harmful operations.

5.3 Solution

It is difficult to identify and anticipate all potential vulnerabilities, threats, and attacks within the IoT healthcare domain since IoT medical paradigms are still developing. However, these security measures must also be able to handle unforeseen or unpredictable challenges that could arise in the future, as security specialists strive to develop initial security solutions for known and predictable risks. In order to achieve this security goal, security services should be built with dynamic features that enable them to make decisions on neglected concerns using their knowledge and expertise. If an attacker launches a new kind of attack and a security service is able to identify existing attacks, the security system should ideally be able to identify this new threat through the use of dynamic algorithms or artificial intelligence-based techniques. This study [10] suggests a security paradigm designed specifically for IoT-based healthcare services in order to address this. The resulting intelligent security model makes use of the most recent knowledge base, which comprises of:

i. Protection Services: These are intended to reduce the risk of attacks.

ii. Detection Services: These services gather activity information from networks, devices, and healthcare apps. They then examine the information to find any irregularities.

iii. Reaction Services: These services help healthcare organizations respond to and recover from attacks.

To protect against known, unknown, and possible threats, these security services collaborate closely and employ dynamic algorithms. In order to lessen the possibility of additional attacks, the detection services notify the protection services of any anomalies they identify and provide action directives to the reaction services upon detection of an attack. By reducing the likelihood of system failures and exchanging experiences with both detection and protection services, the reaction services in turn react to the instructions from detection services. This strategy encourages efficient inter-service cooperation.

6. Conclusion

Through the transformative power of the IoHT, researchers from all over the world are creating a range of technology solutions targeted at improving smart healthcare facilities and solving the complexity of current healthcare services. The main features of IoHT technologies are reviewed in this chapter, along with the IoT platforms and architectures that serve as the foundation of IoHT infrastructure and enable effective health data response and transmission.

The functionality of IoHT services and applications is being improved through extensive research and development. The article also looks at a number of ongoing research and trends, such as Healthcare 4.0, Nanotechnology, edge computing, and blockchain.

It seeks to motivate enterprises to develop user-centered, cost-effective healthcare devices and build a network of intelligent, sensor-based connected devices that provide a variety of services. Additionally, in order to comprehend the intricacies of IoHT security, the chapter explores the weaknesses and difficulties associated with privacy and security, addressing security requirements, challenges, and an attack on taxonomy from the standpoint of smart healthcare.

References

[1] Aghdam, Z. N., A. M. Rahmani and M. Hosseinzadeh. 2021. The role of the Internet of Things in Healthcare: Future trends and challenges. *Computer Methods and Programs in Biomedicine*, 199: 105903. [Online]. doi: https://doi.org/10.1016/j.cmpb.2020.105903.

[2] Bhuiyan, M. Z. A., A. Zaman, T. Wang, G. Wang, H. Tao and M. M. Hassan. 2018. Blockchain and big data to transform the healthcare. *Proceedings of the International Conference on Data Processing and Applications—ICDPA*. doi: https://doi.org/10.1145/3224207.3224220.

[3] Dai, H. -N., Z. Zheng and Y. Zhang. 2019. Blockchain for Internet of Things: A survey. *IEEE Internet of Things Journal*, 6(5): 1–1. [Online]. doi: https://doi.org/10.1109/jiot.2019.2920987.

[4] Kazanskiy, N. L., S. N. Khonina and M. A. Butt. 2024. A review on flexible wearables—Recent developments in non-invasive continuous health monitoring. *Sensors and Actuators A: Physical*, 366: 114993. [Online]. doi: https://doi.org/10.1016/j.sna.2023.114993.

[5] Ketu, S. and P. K. Mishra. 2021. Internet of Healthcare Things: A contemporary survey. *Journal of Network and Computer Applications*, 192: 103179. doi: https://doi.org/10.1016/j.jnca.2021.103179.

[6] Kumar, M., A. Kumar, S. Verma, P. Bhattacharya, D. Ghimire, S. Kim and A. S. M. S. Hosen. 2023. Healthcare Internet of Things (H-IoT): Current trends, future prospects, applications, challenges, and security issues. *Electronics*, 12(9): 2050. [Online]. doi: https://doi.org/10.3390/electronics12092050.

[7] Osama, M., A. A. Ateya, M. S. Sayed, M. Hammad, P. Pławiak, A. A. A. E. Latif and R. A. Elsayed. 2023. Internet of Medical Things and Healthcare 4.0: Trends, requirements, challenges, and research directions. *Sensors*, 23(17): 7435. [Online]. doi: https://doi.org/10.3390/s23177435.

[8] Pramanik, P. K. D., A. Solanki, A. Debnath, A. Nayyar, S. El-Sappagh and K. -S. Kwak. 2020. Advancing modern healthcare with nanotechnology, nanobiosensors, and internet of nano things: Taxonomies, applications, architecture, and challenges. *IEEE Access*, 8: 65230–65266. doi: https://doi.org/10.1109/access.2020.2984269.

[9] Rahul Priyadarshi and Mehdi Gheisari. 2024. Security and privacy in machine learning for IoHT and IoMT: A review. doi: https://doi.org/10.20944/preprints202403.0329.v1.

[10] Riazul Islam, S. M., Daehan Kwak, M. Humaun Kabir, M. Hossain and Kyung-Sup Kwak. 2015. The Internet of Things for Health Care: A comprehensive survey. *IEEE Access*, 3(2169-3536): 678–708. doi: https://doi.org/10.1109/access.2015.2437951.

[11] Naresh, S., V. S. Pericherla, P. Sita Rama Murty and S. Reddi. 2020. Internet of Things in Healthcare: Architecture, applications, challenges, and solutions. *Computer Systems Science and Engineering*, 35(6): 411–421. doi: https://doi.org/10.32604/csse.2020.35.411.

[12] Sun, Y., F. P. -W. Lo and B. Lo. 2019. Security and privacy for the internet of medical things enabled healthcare systems: A survey. *IEEE Access*, 7: 183339–183355. doi: https://doi.org/10.1109/access.2019.2960617.

Chapter 11

Responsible IoHT Ecosystem for Smart Healthcare

Md. Hasanul Ferdaus,[a,*] *Fares Alharbi,*[b] *Savitri Bevinakoppa,*[c] *Md. Sawkat Ali,*[a] *Mohammad Manzurul Islam,*[a] *Maheen Islam,*[a] *Taskeed Jabid,*[a] *Sadia Nur Amin*[a] and *Rajkumar Buyya*[d]

1. Introduction to the Internet of Health Things

1.1 Definition and Scope

The Internet of Health Things, simply IoHT, means the application of Internet of Things (IoT) technologies in the healthcare sector [1]. IoHT forms networks of interconnected medical devices, sensors, software applications, and health-monitoring systems that communicate with each other to collect, analyze, share, and store health-related data through internet connectivity. This reduces human intervention in the processes and aims at enhancing healthcare delivery and patient outcomes [2]. These

[a] Department of Computer Science and Engineering, East West University, Dhaka, Bangladesh.
[b] Department of Computer Science, College of Computing and IT, Shaqra University, Shaqra, Saudi Arabia.
[c] School of IT and Engineering, Melbourne Institute of Technology, Melbourne, Australia.
[d] School of Computing and Information Systems, The University of Melbourne, Melbourne, Australia.
Emails: faalhrbi@su.edu.sa, savitri@mit.edu.au, alim@ewubd.edu, mohammad.islam@ewubd.edu, maheen@ewubd.edu, taskeed@ewubd.edu, sadian.amin@ewubd.edu, rbuyya@unimelb.edu.au
* Corresponding author: hasanul.ferdaus@ewubd.edu

DOI: 10.1201/9781003483267-15

interconnected devices such as wearable health trackers, implantable sensors, and remote monitoring systems are designed to collect real-time information on a range of health indicators such as body temperature, blood pressure, heart rate, glucose levels, and oxygen saturation. The IoHT integrates patient data seamlessly which enables healthcare providers to monitor health conditions continuously, make data-driven decisions, and deliver personalized care in a timely manner. IoHT systems reduce the need for frequent in-person visits and enable proactive health management, primarily for chronic conditions, which contributes to enhanced healthcare efficiency.

The impact of IoHT extends beyond mere patient care. It facilitates advancements in healthcare research, predictive analytics, and clinical trials. IoHT facilitates the analysis of large-scale health data. This enables researchers to identify trends, assess the effectiveness of treatments, and detect potential outbreaks. This way IoHT supports evidence-based medical practices. Notwithstanding the immense benefits and potentials of IoHT technologies, this digital transformation brings forth significant challenges, such as cybersecurity, data privacy, and system interoperability. Such hurdles and issues must be addressed to ensure IoHT systems are safe, reliable, and compliant with healthcare standards.

1.1.1 The Architecture of IoHT

The IoHT has a multilayer architecture that integrates various components at different layers to support data collection, processing, transmission, and storage. This layered architecture ultimately facilitates secure and efficient healthcare delivery [3]. Typically, the IoHT architecture comprises four main layers at its core (Figure 1): the Sensing Layer, the Network Layer, the Processing and Storage Layer, and the Application layer [4–6]. Each of these layers serves distinct functions within the healthcare ecosystem.

- **Sensing Layer:** This is the foundational layer where various IoHT devices, such as wearable health trackers, implantable devices, smart medical devices, and environmental sensors, collect relevant data. These devices continuously collect healthcare data, such as heart rate, glucose levels, temperature, and patient activity, through monitoring of physiological and environmental parameters. Various edge devices that pre-process data to reduce latency and bandwidth requirements are also included in this layer.
- **Network Layer:** The network layer transmits data securely from IoHT devices to the cloud or healthcare information systems for further processing and storage. This layer contains wireless communication technologies such as Wi-Fi, Bluetooth, cellular networks, and emerging

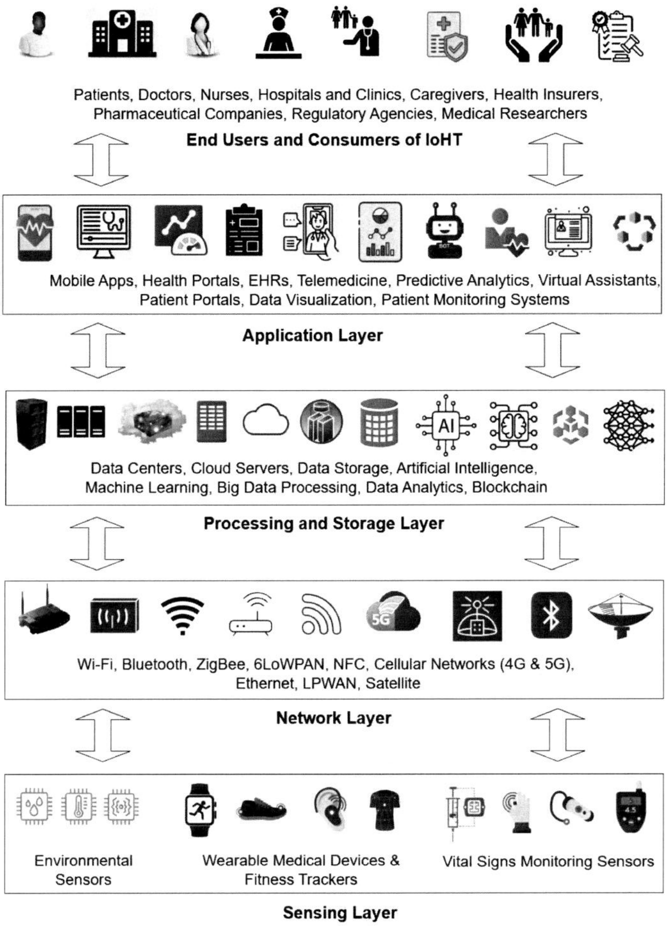

Figure 1: Layered architecture of IoHT.

5G technology. Such communication facilities enable seamless data transfer across devices and systems. This layer is responsible for ensuring appropriate security protocols are put in place to protect the data from unauthorized access and interception during transmission.

- **Processing and Storage Layer:** This layer includes data centers and cloud servers where large volumes of patient data are stored, processed, and analyzed. In some cases, this layer can be incorporated into the network layer. Analytical techniques leveraging Artificial Intelligence (AI), Machine Learning (ML), and Deep Learning (DL) algorithms can be utilized in this layer to extract actionable insights from raw data, such as identifying health trends or predicting potential health risks.

- **Application Layer:** This layer interacts directly with patients and healthcare providers by presenting analyzed data via user-friendly interfaces. Mobile health applications, electronic health records (EHRs), and healthcare management platforms are included in this layer. These facilities allow patients, doctors, and caregivers to access healthcare data and make informed decisions. Various health alerts and notifications can be generated in this layer so that immediate medical intervention can be carried out whenever necessary.

This multilayered architecture of IoHT supports seamless flows of healthcare data from sensors to relevant observation and practical recommendations. Moreover, the integration of security protocols at each layer addresses data privacy and integrity challenges which are extremely crucial for secure and effective functioning of digital health ecosystems.

1.1.2 The Scope of IoHT

The IoHT represents a significant evolution in healthcare technology that integrates advanced connectivity with health-related devices. This enhances patient care, streamlines operations, and promotes better health outcomes. The IoHT aims to create a holistic ecosystem by leveraging the power of cutting-edge IoT technologies within the healthcare sector. This connects patients, medical providers, and healthcare systems, bringing them under a single umbrella. The following key points outline the expansive scope of IoHT [3, 4, 6–8] (Figure 2):

- **Remote Patient Monitoring:** IoHT facilitates continuous and remote monitoring of health data through wearable devices, smart sensors, and medical implants. These devices sense and collect vital health data such as heart rate, blood pressure, blood oxygen levels, glucose levels, and body temperature. This assists in providing real-time health information to both patients and healthcare providers, which in turn facilitates timely interventions and personalized care.
- **Telehealth Services:** Integration of IoHT facilitates virtual consultations and telemedicine services, and improves access to care for patients in remote or underserved areas.
- **Personalized Medicine:** By analyzing data collected from health devices, IoHT supports tailored treatment plans that align with individual patient needs and preferences.
- **Enhanced Data Analytics:** IoHT devices collect and generate vast amounts of healthcare data that can be harnessed for predictive analytics. This can help in early disease diagnosis and prevention and facilitate in creating personalized care plans.

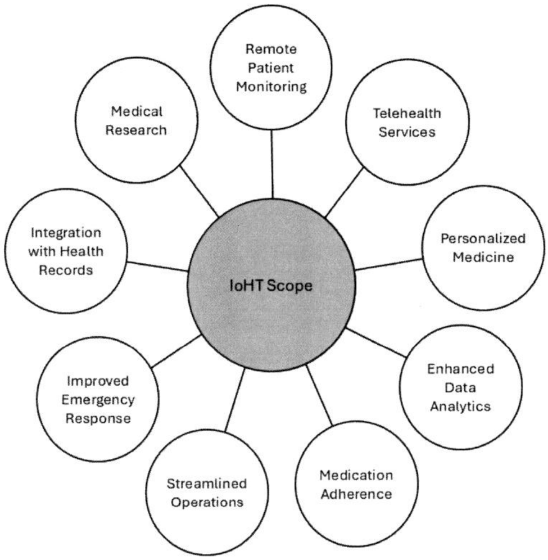

Figure 2: The scope of the IoHT.

- **Medication Adherence:** Digital tools and apps, such as smart pillboxes and reminders, connected to IoHT can improve medication adherence among patients, particularly the elderly and those with chronic conditions.
- **Streamlined Operations:** Healthcare provider organizations, such as hospitals and clinics, can utilize IoHT for efficient management of resources, such as staff allocation and inventory control. Moreover, they can optimize operations through automated workflows and real-time tracking of medical equipment. This can potentially lead to increased efficiency and cost-effective solutions.
- **Improved Emergency Response:** Smart sensors, medical gadgets, and other IoHT-enabled devices can alert healthcare providers in emergencies by tracking vital signs and detecting early signs of chronic diseases. This can ensure timely interventions and potentially save lives.
- **Integration with Health Records:** IoHT can seamlessly integrate with EHRs and enable comprehensive patient profiles, thus empowering healthcare providers in decision-making.
- **Medical Research:** IoHT has been accelerating medical research by enabling large-scale data collection and analysis for drug discovery and personalized treatment plans.

In summary, the scope of IoHT covers a broad spectrum of applications and services. These applications and services, through their enhanced efficiency and data-driven insights, collectively strive to revolutionize healthcare delivery, improve patient outcomes, and reduce operational costs.

1.2 The Rise of IoHT

The rise of the IoHT has been accelerated by progressive technological advancements, the integration of connectivity, and healthcare demands. The rapid evolution of IoHT has reshaped patient-centered care and health system efficiencies. The inception of digital health technologies has its roots back in 1947 when the initial steps into the digital revolution began with the emergence of transistors and integrated circuits [9]. Initially, IoHT appeared as a part of the broader IoT movement. As wearable devices and remote monitoring technologies become more prevalent, IoHT quickly gained traction among the stakeholders of the healthcare industry. IoHT can be traced back to the early 2000s when wireless communication technologies and the miniaturization of electronic devices fostered the development of wearable health devices such as fitness trackers, activity monitors, sleep trackers, and heart rate monitors.

Early applications primarily focused on fitness tracking and chronic disease management. Advancements in sensor technologies, AI, and data analytics have expanded the potential and efficiency of IoHT technologies. However, IoHT has seen its true proliferation with the improvements in cloud computing, big data analytics, and AI. Gradually the field has seen exponential growth over time through the development of various applications such as high-throughput genomic sequencing, robotic care assistants, and EHRs [10, 11]. Today, a wide range of medical applications and services function in the field of IoHT, including telemedicine, remote diagnostics, personalized treatment plans, and predictive healthcare. These technologies have improved operational efficiency, patient outcomes, and public health responses, enhancing global healthcare services significantly [12, 13]. For example, in the field of cardiovascular care, the application of digital technologies has shown promising results in reducing morbidity and mortality rates. To accommodate digital health technologies and tools, regulatory frameworks have also been adapted. This emphasizes the need for collaboration among stakeholders for successful implementation in IoHT development.

From the inception of IoHT, the development of the IoHT can be discussed as a five-stage process (Figure 3):

- **Initial Connectivity and Data Collection:** The early stages of IoHT started with basic health devices, such as fitness trackers and glucose monitors, that collect vital health data. These health devices had data communication services for basic data sharing. This laid the foundation for more advanced IoHT applications.

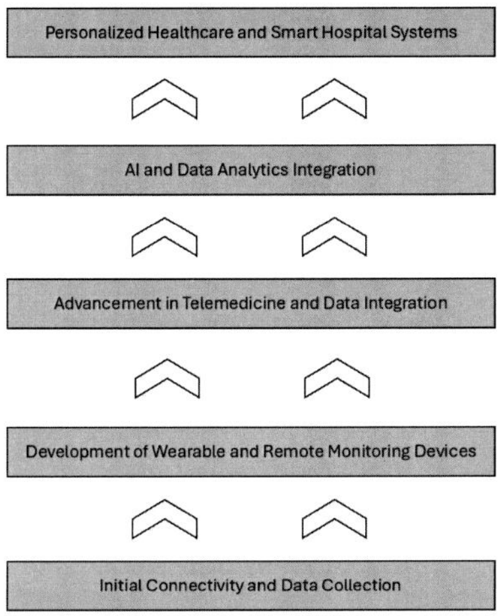

Figure 3: The rise of IoHT development.

- **Development of Wearable and Remote Monitoring Devices:** Later wearables and sensors were developed which were capable of continuously tracking health metrics, such as heart rate and blood oxygen levels. This facilitated remote patient monitoring services that were helpful for the early detection of health issues without hospital visits.
- **Advancement in Telemedicine and Data Integration:** The proliferation of wireless technologies and global internet connectivity paved the way for efficient real-time data transmission from devices to healthcare providers. Professional-grade telemedicine services were developed by leveraging this connectivity. Moreover, the health data were integrated with EHRs through efficient communication facilities for creating holistic patient profiles.
- **AI and Data Analytics Integration:** The various health devices collect and generate large volumes of health data by monitoring patients and their environments. This opened the opportunity to apply AI algorithms and tools for predictive analytics to identify trends and patterns that are leveraged for proactive healthcare measures.
- **Personalized Healthcare and Smart Hospital Systems:** Through the development of mobile applications and integration with cloud services, the IoHT capabilities now support personalized medicine and smart hospital systems. It enables patient-centered care with predictive insights, efficient use of resources, and better patient outcomes.

2. Understanding the Cybersecurity Landscape in Digital Health

2.1 Unique Risks Posed by IoHT Devices

The IoHT connects sensors, medical devices, and healthcare systems to facilitate real-time patient monitoring and health data exchange. This integration improves the efficiency and outcomes of healthcare services. However, it also introduces unique security risks due to the sensitive nature of health data and the high level of interconnectedness of medical devices [14]. The IoHT devices are often highly specialized, resource-constrained, and deployed in sensitive environments. This makes them vulnerable to cyberattacks and privacy breaches.

Usually, traditional medical systems operate within controlled environments. Unlike this, IoHT devices often function in less secure settings, such as patients' homes or wearable technologies. This can make them more vulnerable to exploitation. Moreover, the growing number of connected medical devices exacerbates these issues by expanding the attack surface and increasing the likelihood of security breaches. A compromised device could lead to the exposure of personal health information (PHI). This could have serious legal and ethical consequences for healthcare providers. The proliferation of IoHT devices has introduced new and complex security challenges. Understanding the specific risks posed by IoHT devices is essential. This knowledge helps in developing robust security measures to protect patient safety and ensure data privacy and integrity [15]. Figure 4 presents a taxonomy of the unique security risks posed by IoHT devices. These risks are further discussed below [16–18].

- **Limited Security Capabilities:** Many IoHT devices are designed with limited computational power and memory. This restricts their ability to implement strong security protocols such as encryption and authentication. As a result, such limitations make them easier targets for cyberattacks.
- **Unauthorized Access:** The IoHT devices can serve as entry points for malicious actors to gain unauthorized access to sensitive patient data due to their interconnected nature. This has the potential to disrupt healthcare operations and even compromise patient safety.
- **Data Breaches and Privacy Violations:** Wearable Internet of Medical Things (WIoMT) devices are particularly vulnerable to security risks. Examples include smartwatches, fitness bands, and other health-monitoring wearables. Such gadgets are frequently used for constant tracking of health metrics and transmitting real-time data to healthcare providers. This can make them vulnerable to data breaches if sufficient

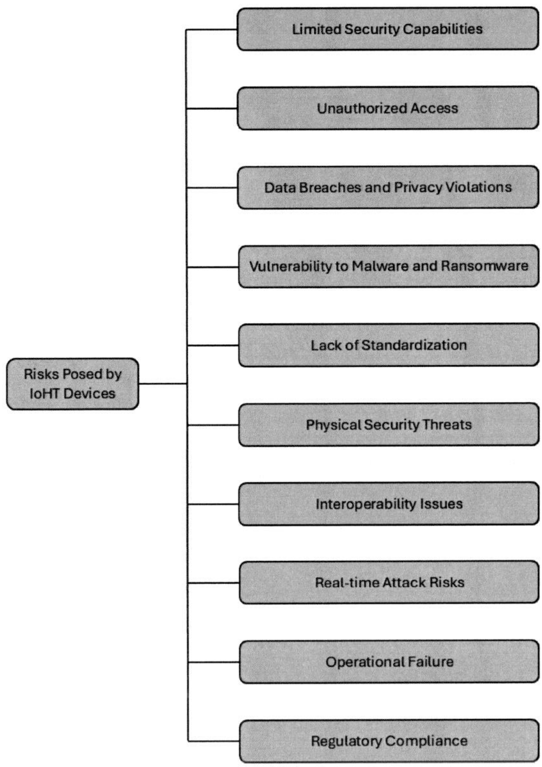

Figure 4: A taxonomy of the unique risks posed by IoHT devices.

protection mechanisms are not employed. As a consequence, this can expose patients to identity theft, discrimination, and privacy violations. Furthermore, the sharing of patient data between different healthcare providers and organizations can increase the risk of data breaches and unauthorized access. This raises security concerns requiring a focus on security and privacy measures to protect users' personal information.

- **Vulnerability to Malware and Ransomware:** IoHT devices often operate on outdated or unsupported software. This makes them vulnerable to malware and ransomware attacks. Such malware and ransomware have the potential to disable critical medical equipment and compromise patient safety.
- **Lack of Standardization:** The lack of uniform security standards across IoHT devices and manufacturers leads to inconsistent security practices. This effectively increases the overall risk of vulnerabilities in healthcare ecosystems.

- **Physical Security Threats:** IoHT devices can be physically accessed by unauthorized personnel as they are deployed in hospital environments. This increases the risk of device tampering or device theft.
- **Interoperability Issues:** Due to the inherent heterogeneity in the design and implementation, IoHT devices from different manufacturers often lack seamless interoperability. This can lead to communication gaps and vulnerabilities in data transmission between devices and healthcare systems. As a result, such interoperability issues make it easier for attackers to exploit the weak points.
- **Real-time Attack Risks:** Many IoHT devices are deployed for providing real-time monitoring of critical patient health data. Any successful attack on such devices can lead to immediate consequences, such as altering medical treatments and delaying life-saving interventions. Effectively this can put patients' lives at risk.
- **Operational Failure:** Another critical risk associated with IoHT devices is their potential for operational failures and device malfunctions. Many IoHT devices play a direct role in patient care, such as insulin pumps or heart monitors. Any malfunction or failure of such medical devices could have life-threatening consequences. These devices are dependent on stable connectivity and accurate data transmission. As a result, any disruption in network performance or incorrect data processing could result in delayed medical interventions or erroneous diagnoses. Moreover, regulatory standards for the development and security of IoHT devices are still evolving. This leads to inconsistencies in safety measures across manufacturers that increase the risks associated with their deployment in healthcare settings.
- **Regulatory Compliance:** Ensuring compliance with data privacy and security regulations can be challenging for healthcare organizations, especially as the regulatory landscape continues to evolve.

The world of IoHT devices is evolving rapidly. To address the unique risks associated with IoHT devices, dynamic risk assessment approaches are emerging to limit unauthorized intrusions, secure personal data, and ensure uninterrupted device usage [19]. Notwithstanding the advantages of IoHT for healthcare, patient-specific health information security is still a major issue that requires constant attention and creative solutions [20].

2.2 *Threat Actors Targeting Digital Health Systems*

Healthcare organizations are developing a growing dependence on the usage of digital health technologies for providing various health services. These digital health systems encompass EHRs, telemedicine platforms, and IoHT devices. This renders them one of the prime targets for cybercriminals [21]. The sensitive nature and high value of PHI and the critical reliance on these systems in healthcare delivery make them highly attractive to various threat actors. Threat actors targeting digital health systems have become increasingly sophisticated, exploiting vulnerabilities in the expanding landscape of interconnected healthcare technologies [22].

A variety of threat actors, including cybercriminals, nation-states, organized crime groups, individual hackers, and hacktivists, are targeting digital health systems for various malicious purposes. These attackers seek to exploit vulnerabilities in digital health infrastructure for financial gain, political motives, or disruption of healthcare services. The IoHT faces challenges such as network interruptions, denial of service attacks, and privacy threats, leading to compromised patient data and healthcare infrastructure [23]. The disruption of health services can also lead to severe operational consequences, incentivizing organizations to meet attackers' demands to minimize patient harm. These attackers may seek access to digital health systems for the purpose of obtaining sensitive research, intellectual property related to medical technologies, or population health data, which can be exploited for strategic advantages.

Figure 5 presents a taxonomic classification of the threat actors that target digital health systems. Each of these threat actors is further discussed below [24–26].

- **Cybercriminals:** Motivated primarily by financial gain, cybercriminals target digital health systems to steal patient data for identity theft, launch ransomware attacks, or sell health records on the black market. The high value of medical data makes healthcare systems particularly lucrative for these actors.

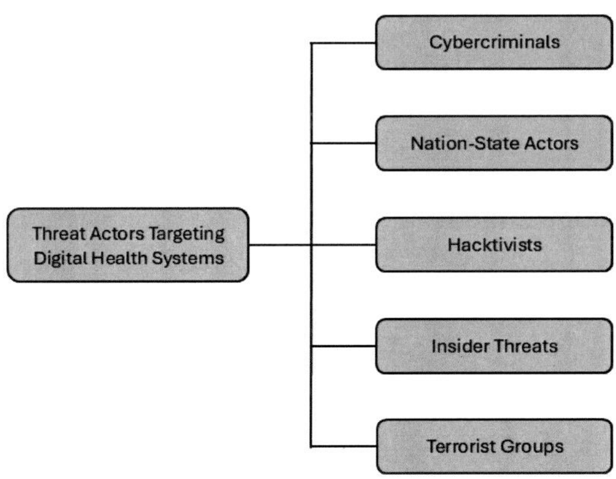

Figure 5: A taxonomy of threat actors targeting digital health systems.

- **Nation-State Actors:** State-sponsored attackers pose a different set of threats and may target healthcare systems for espionage or disruption, especially during geopolitical tensions. These actors are often highly sophisticated and launch cyberattacks to disrupt critical healthcare infrastructure, obtain sensitive medical research, and steal intellectual property to gain a strategic advantage.
- **Hacktivists:** Hacktivists are groups who are driven by certain ideologies or political motives. Such groups may target healthcare organizations to protest or raise awareness of specific causes. As part of their campaigns, they may deface websites, leak sensitive information, or disrupt services.
- **Insider Threats:** Employees or contractors, who have access to healthcare systems and sensitive data, can pose significant risks. Motivations or causes of insider threats may include personal gain, sabotage, or negligence. Insider threats expose significant risks as they can exploit their privileged access to compromise data or systems.
- **Terrorist Groups:** Terrorist organizations may target digital health systems to disrupt healthcare services or instill fear. Attacks on critical infrastructure, such as hospitals and clinics, can have far-reaching consequences on public safety.

The motivations of threat actors targeting digital health systems can vary widely. However, the potential consequences of their attacks are severe. Cyberattacks on healthcare organizations can result in data breaches, disruptions in patient care, financial losses, and reputational damage. Additionally, the theft of sensitive patient data can have far-reaching consequences, including identity theft, discrimination, and emotional distress for affected individuals. These threats are further amplified due to the growing connectivity of healthcare systems through the pervasive use of IoHT. Each of these connected devices presents a potential entry point for threat actors to exploit any vulnerabilities. Consequently, understanding the diverse range of threat actors is essential for healthcare organizations to implement effective security strategies and protect patient safety. Robust security measures, such as lightweight identity authentication protocols [27] and ML models for optimal security [28], are essential to mitigate the risks posed by the diverse array of threat actors. It is extremely crucial to understand the specific threat models and privacy policy gaps in the domain of IoHT to tackle the unique risks and ensure user confidence in these fast-evolving digital health systems.

2.3 Regulatory Scrutiny and Compliance

Regulatory scrutiny and compliance for cybersecurity in the digital health sector are essential due to the wide adoption of advanced healthcare technologies, such as IoHT. The growing vulnerability of healthcare systems to cyber threats underscores the need for strong cybersecurity measures. Regulations relating to digital health are critical to protect patient safety, ensure data privacy, and maintain the integrity of healthcare services [29]. With the increasing collection, transmission, and storage of sensitive health data, regulators are emphasizing that healthcare providers and technology companies maintain stringent safeguards to protect patient privacy and security. The evolution of digital technologies in healthcare necessitates adherence to industry standards, laws, and guidelines to mitigate risks effectively [29]. Compliance management includes activities such as risk identification, assessment, and treatment.

The global implementation of digital medication and treatment requires strict compliance with existing laws and regulations. This highlights the need for strong political will to protect confidential data and increase accountability among stakeholders [30]. A proper understanding of the common vulnerabilities and challenges faced in regulatory compliance is essential for safeguarding healthcare infrastructure and digital applications in the face of cybersecurity threats. As healthcare increasingly relies on digital technologies, governments worldwide have implemented various regulations to address the unique challenges posed by digital health solutions. The most important and relevant regulations in this context are the Health Insurance Portability and Accountability Act (HIPAA) in the United States, the General Data Protection Regulation (GDPR) and Medical Device Regulation (MDR) in the European Union, and the Cyber Security Act in Singapore. These regulations set stringent standards for handling sensitive health data. Compliance with these regulations helps ensure that healthcare providers and technology developers implement robust protections by mitigating the risks of data breaches, cyberattacks, and device malfunctions [31]. This can foster trust among patients and healthcare providers and promote the ethical and secure use of digital health innovations. Ultimately, regulatory scrutiny and compliance contribute to a more trustworthy and secure digital health ecosystem. This facilitates fostering public confidence and promoting innovation in healthcare delivery. Further details on legal compliance and governance challenges in IoHT are discussed in Section 4.

3. Vulnerabilities in the IoHT Ecosystem

3.1 Insecure Device Design and Configuration

The design and configuration of IoHT devices pose significant vulnerabilities [32–34]. One of the primary reasons is that the traditional encryption models may not be optimized for IoT devices. This leads to the development of lightweight encryption algorithms to ensure strong security while minimizing computational and power requirements [35]. Moreover, vulnerability scans have revealed alarming statistics showing outdated components in webcams, devices with expired SSL certificates, and insecure default settings in consumer devices [36]. Furthermore, the interconnected nature of IoHT devices, such as wearables, sensors, and implantable devices, and the lack of built-in security features in medical equipment open avenues for cyberattacks [37]. This can lead to data theft and manipulation, denial-of-service, facility disruptions, and even patient harm [38]. Additionally, the shift toward remote access and monitoring in medical implants introduces new risks that increase end-user vulnerability. As a consequence, such vulnerabilities due to insecure device design and configuration can have a wide range of adverse impacts.

Insecure device design and configuration in IoHT raise the following key concerns (Figure 6):

- **Increased Vulnerability to Cyberattacks:** Poorly designed and configured IoHT devices are easier targets for malware, ransomware, and unauthorized access, compromising the entire healthcare network.
- **Data Breaches and Privacy Violations:** Insecure devices can lead to the exposure of sensitive patient data, resulting in privacy violations and regulatory non-compliance.
- **Disruption of Critical Healthcare Services:** Compromised IoHT devices may malfunction or become unavailable, affecting the timely delivery of essential medical care.
- **Patient Safety Risks:** Insecure devices can be manipulated, leading to inaccurate diagnoses or inappropriate treatments that put patient lives at risk.
- **Compliance Challenges:** Inadequately secured devices fail to meet regulatory standards such as HIPAA, leading to potential legal and financial repercussions for healthcare providers.

Designers of medical devices must consider security from the beginning to completion of their designs, focusing on hardware security to address concerns about patient data privacy [39]. Implementing security checks throughout the design and development phases, along with incorporating advanced security measures such as DL and other AI models, is crucial to mitigating cyber threats in the medical IoT ecosystem. Furthermore, it is critical to implement robust cybersecurity measures, adhere to regulatory requirements, and continuously assess and update the security protocols of IoHT devices.

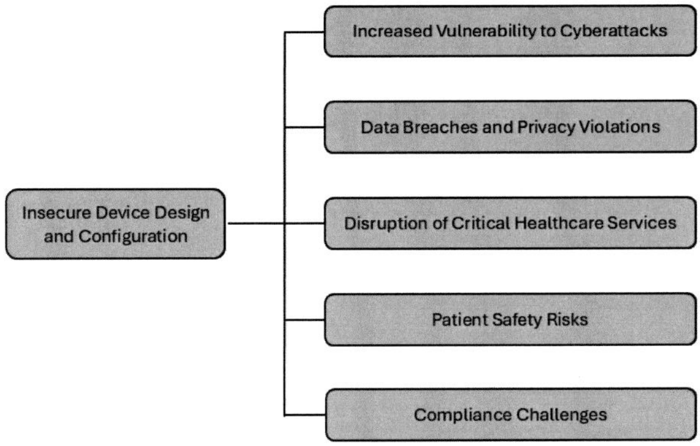

Figure 6: Key concerns due to insecure IoHT device design and configuration.

3.2 *Lack of Standardized Security Protocols*

The lack of standardized security protocols and consistent guidelines and requirements across IoHT devices and platforms poses significant risks. Without consistent and universally adopted security measures, the entire IoHT infrastructure remains vulnerable to cyberattacks, data breaches, and privacy violations. These concerns highlight the critical need for establishing robust and standardized security frameworks to ensure the safety, privacy, and reliability of IoHT systems. The lack of standardized security protocols in IoHT can potentially raise the following key concerns [40, 41, 43] (Figure 7):

- **Interoperability Challenges:** IoHT devices are often designed by different manufacturers with varying security practices. This can potentially create fragmented and inconsistent security frameworks. This fragmentation increases vulnerabilities and makes healthcare networks more susceptible to cyberattacks. Moreover, the absence of unified standards complicates the integration of devices into existing healthcare infrastructure. This could reduce operational efficiency and increase patient safety risks.
- **Vulnerability to Cyberattacks:** The lack of uniform security standards makes IoHT systems more vulnerable to cyberattacks such as ransomware, phishing, and unauthorized access. Attackers can exploit inconsistencies in security practices and infiltrate networks to commit further crimes.
- **Data Privacy Issues:** Without standardized encryption and data protection mechanisms, patient information is at greater risk of unauthorized access and breaches. This can compromise sensitive personal and medical data.

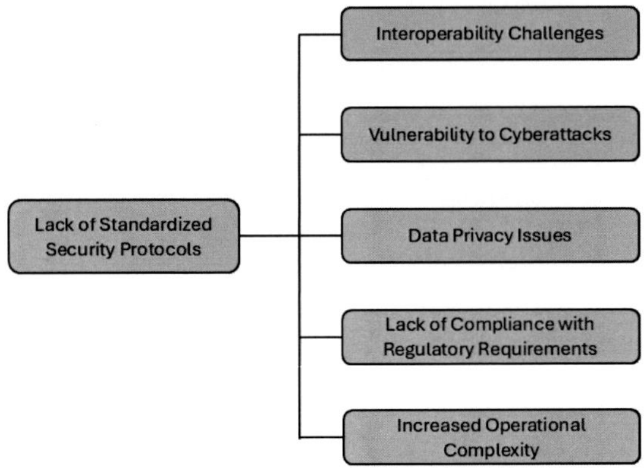

Figure 7: Key concerns due to the lack of standardized security protocols in IoHT.

- **Lack of Compliance with Regulatory Requirements:** The variations in security measures make it harder for healthcare providers to comply with healthcare regulations such as HIPAA and GDPR. This can potentially result in legal consequences for healthcare providers.
- **Increased Operational Complexity:** To ensure security for various IoHT devices manufactured by different vendors, healthcare organizations must implement multiple security solutions. This increases operational complexity and costs while possibly leaving gaps in security coverage.

As solution measures, various security protocols have been proposed. However, many of the protocols suffer from extensive communication, storage, and computation overheads due to negligence on crucial attack models [42, 43]. To address the lack of standardized security protocols in the IoHT, a unified and comprehensive approach is needed to mitigate risks and enhance the security of medical devices and healthcare systems. Implementation of standardized security measures can ensure interoperability, protect patient data, and safeguard healthcare networks from cyber threats. A list of potential solution approaches to address the lack of standardized security protocols in IoHT is discussed below [41, 44, 45] (Figure 8):

- **Development of Universal Security Standards:** Regulatory bodies and industry stakeholders should collaborate to establish universal security protocols. Such protocols must apply to all IoHT devices so that they ensure secure communication and data exchange across platforms and manufacturers.
- **Mandating End-to-End Encryption:** End-to-end encryption should be enforced for all IoHT devices to protect sensitive health data from

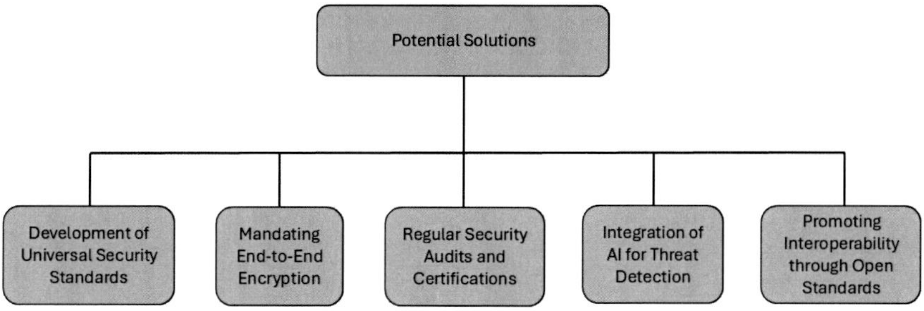

Figure 8: Potential solutions to the lack of standardized security protocols in IoHT.

security attacks, such as eavesdropping and man-in-the-middle attacks. This will prevent unauthorized access and data breaches during transmission and ensure confidentiality and integrity.

- **Regular Security Audits and Certifications:** IoHT devices should undergo compulsory security audits and obtain certifications to ensure regulatory compliance according to the established security standards. This would ensure that devices meet baseline security requirements before their deployments.
- **Integration of AI for Threat Detection:** AI-driven security systems can monitor IoHT devices in real time and help detect and respond to potential threats. This can effectively prevent and reduce the risk of cyberattacks.
- **Promoting Interoperability through Open Standards:** Open standards should be adopted to promote interoperability between different IoHT devices while maintaining security standards. This can effectively reduce compatibility issues and simplify the integration process for healthcare providers.

3.3 Vulnerabilities in Connected Medical Devices

Vulnerabilities in connected medical devices within the IoHT pose significant risks due to the potential exposure of patient-specific data. This can lead to wider attack surfaces and increase damage possibilities, including unauthorized data access, cyberattacks, and device tampering [16]. These devices, also known as Medical Internet-of-Things (MIoT), are crucial for remote patient care and require robust security measures to protect against cyberattacks in real time [19]. Connected medical devices offer advantages such as enhanced patient monitoring and improved healthcare delivery. Such MIoT devices are especially beneficial for remote or immobile patients; however, they also introduce risks to patient privacy and medical record integrity [46]. Furthermore, IoHT devices, such as wearables, implants, and remote monitoring systems, often lack robust security features that make them susceptible to threats such as malware, ransomware, and phishing attacks. These vulnerabilities are exacerbated by the increasing number of connected IoHT devices. This can effectively expand the attack surface within healthcare networks. For instance, a breach in one device can compromise an entire system and lead to the exposure of sensitive patient data or disruption of essential medical services.

The commonly identified vulnerabilities in connected medical devices are discussed below [47–49] (Figure 9):

- **Weak Authentication Mechanisms:** Many connected medical devices lack strong authentication, allowing unauthorized access to sensitive data or device control.
- **Unencrypted Data Transmission:** Data transmitted between devices and healthcare systems are often unencrypted, making them vulnerable to interception and theft.
- **Outdated Software and Firmware:** Many IoHT devices run on outdated software, leaving them susceptible to known vulnerabilities and exploits.
- **Lack of Secure Updates:** Insufficient mechanisms for securely updating device software can lead to exploitable weaknesses being left unpatched.
- **Insecure Default Configurations:** Many devices are deployed with default settings that have weak security, making them easy targets for attackers.

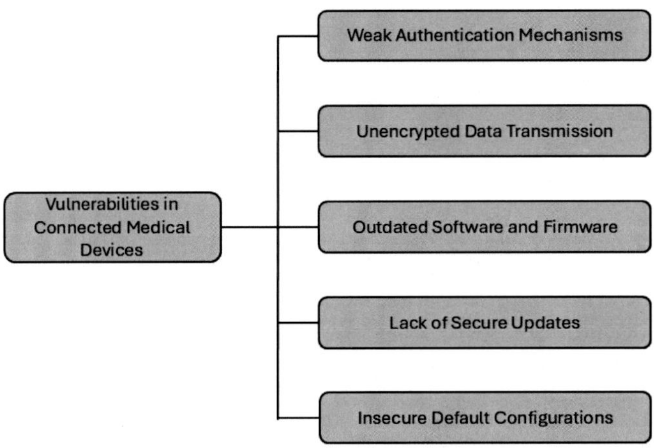

Figure 9: Common vulnerabilities in connected medical devices.

To ensure the security of these devices and their communications, it is critical to protect patient data and maintain system integrity. Vulnerabilities in device communication channels and network protocols can lead to data breaches, device malfunctions, or even patient harm. Figure 10 presents the strategies specifically designed to mitigate risks in connected devices and their communications discussed below [48–50].

- **Secure Communication Protocols:** Secure communication protocols, such as TLS (Transport Layer Security) and DTLS (Datagram TLS), can be implemented to encrypt data transmitted between connected devices and healthcare systems. This can prevent data interception and tampering during transit.
- **Device Authentication and Pairing:** It is crucial to ensure that devices are authenticated before being allowed to communicate with the network. For this purpose, techniques such as digital certificates or secure device pairing can be utilized to prevent unauthorized devices from accessing the system.
- **Network Segmentation:** Appropriate network segmentation should be implemented to isolate IoHT devices from other parts of the healthcare network. This can minimize the potential spread of attacks and contain security breaches to specific device groups.
- **Device Firmware Integrity Checks:** Integrity checks for device firmware must be implemented to verify that it has not been altered or compromised during updates or communication. This will guarantee that only trusted firmware is running on devices.
- **Encrypted Device-to-Device Communication:** It is critical to ensure that data exchanges between connected medical devices are encrypted to prevent eavesdropping and manipulation during real-time patient monitoring and treatment.
- **Wireless Security Enhancements:** Wireless communication security must be strengthened by using WPA3 (Wi-Fi Protected Access 3) or

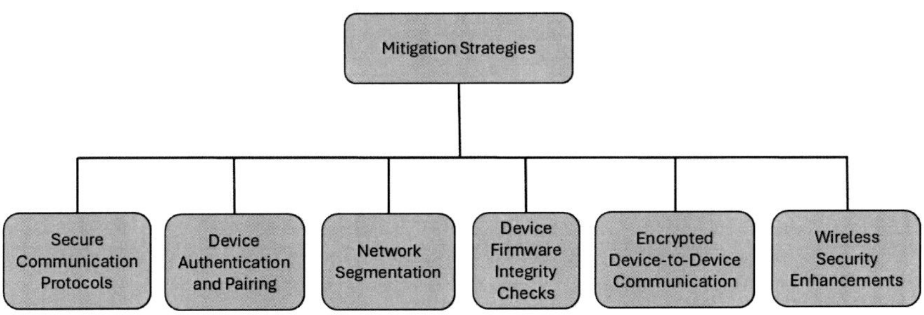

Figure 10: Mitigation strategies of risks in connected devices and their communications.

other advanced encryption standards for Wi-Fi networks that IoHT devices rely on. This is important to protect against unauthorized access to the network and devices.

3.4 Data Privacy and Confidentiality Concerns

Data privacy and confidentiality are critical concerns in the IoHT due to the continuous exchange of sensitive healthcare data across interconnected devices [51–55]. The rapid expansion and pervasive use of IoMT (Internet of Medical Things) devices increase the risk of data breaches, unauthorized access, and misuse of PHI [51–55]. These devices, such as wearables and implantable sensors, remote diagnostic tools, smart insulin pumps, and wearable health monitors, are vulnerable to cyberattacks such as keyloggers and spyware. This can compromise patient data and lead to identity theft. A breach in confidentiality can lead to a loss of trust in healthcare providers and legal repercussions under regulations such as HIPAA and GDPR.

Figure 11 presents the primary concerns relating to data privacy and confidentiality in IoHT that are discussed below [51–55]:

- **Data Breaches and Unauthorized Access:** The interconnected nature of IoMT devices can increase the risk of data breaches and unauthorized access to sensitive patient data.
- **Identity Theft and Discrimination:** The misuse of medical data can lead to identity theft, discrimination, or other harmful consequences.

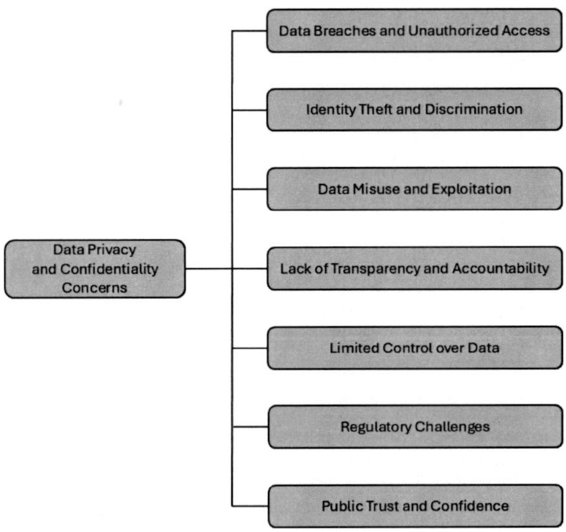

Figure 11: Primary concerns relating to data privacy and confidentiality in IoHT.

- **Data Misuse and Exploitation:** Unauthorized access to medical data can lead to its misuse and exploitation for various purposes.
- **Lack of Transparency and Accountability:** It can be very difficult to ensure transparency and accountability in the handling of patient data without clear guidelines and regulations.
- **Limited Control over Data:** Patients may have limited control over their medical data and lack of knowledge regarding how their data are utilized, stored, and shared.
- **Regulatory Challenges:** Ensuring compliance with data privacy and security regulations can be complex and costly for healthcare organizations.
- **Public Trust and Confidence:** Concerns about data privacy and confidentiality can erode public trust and confidence in IoMT technologies.

The growing field of smart healthcare highlights the urgent need for strong security measures to safeguard patient privacy. It is a critical concern to protect data in the interconnected IoMT environment. To address these concerns, several solution approaches are proposed as discussed below [56–60] (Figure 12):

- **Strong Encryption:** Implementation of robust and end-to-end encryption for data transmission, such as the Secret Sharing Algorithm (SSA) [61], is crucial. This can protect sensitive patient data from unauthorized access even though the devices are compromised.
- **Access Control:** Implementing multi-factor authentication and role-based access controls is essential to restrict access to IoMT systems and patient data to authorized individuals only.
- **Data Minimization:** Risks of data breaches and misuse can be reduced by collecting only the required data.
- **Secure Data Sharing:** Developing secure and standardized protocols for sharing patient data can ensure that data are transmitted and stored securely.
- **Blockchain Technology:** Adopting **blockchain technology** can enhance data security by providing a decentralized, tamper-proof system for managing medical records.
- **Security Audits and Vulnerability Assessments:** Regular **audits and vulnerability assessments** should be conducted to identify weaknesses and mitigate potential security gaps in IoMT systems.
- **Privacy-preserving Technologies:** Utilizing privacy-preserving technologies, such as differential privacy and homomorphic

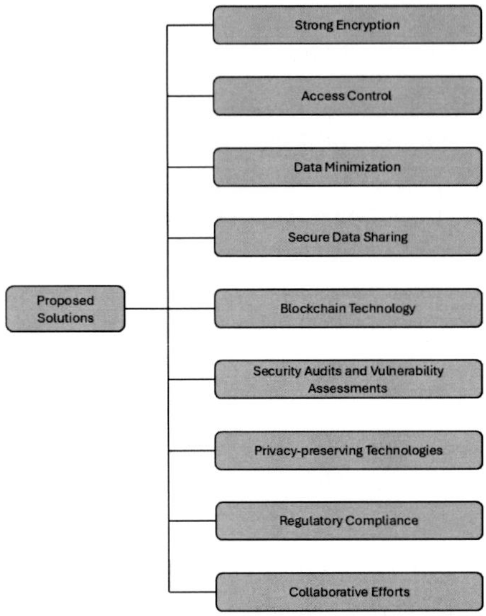

Figure 12: Solution approaches for data privacy and confidentiality concerns in IoHT.

encryption, can enable data analysis without compromising individual privacy.

- **Regulatory Compliance:** Adhering to relevant regulations, such as HIPAA and GDPR, can help ensure that IoMT devices and systems are compliant with data privacy and security standards.
- **Collaborative Efforts:** Effective collaboration between healthcare providers, regulatory bodies, and technology developers is necessary to establish comprehensive security frameworks. This is essential for safeguarding patient privacy and confidentiality in IoMT systems.

3.4.1 Patient Data Leakage Risks

Patient data leakage risks pose a significant threat to data privacy in the IoHT. The IoMT integrates medical devices with the IoT. Such medical devices contain sensitive patient health data [62]. Traditional ML and DL models face challenges as patient data must be transferred to central servers. This increases risks of security and privacy breaches [63]. To address these risks, dynamic risk assessment (DRA) approaches are emerging to combat sophisticated cyberattacks in real time. This can safeguard patient data and ensure uninterrupted device usage [64]. Specialized encryption algorithms, such as Rail Fence Data Encryption (RFDE), can be utilized to protect Personal Health Records (PHRs) in the cloud, enhancing data security and privacy [65]. Overall, mitigating patient data leakage risks is crucial to maintaining the confidentiality and integrity of healthcare information in the IoMT ecosystem.

3.4.2 Challenges of Securing Health Data in Transit and Storage

The sensitive nature of healthcare data collected by IoMT devices makes it vulnerable to malicious attacks such as tampering, eavesdropping, and forgery [66]. These security risks emphasize the need for data integrity, authenticity, and privacy [53]. Innovative approaches, such as utilizing distributed InterPlanetary File System (IPFS) storage, blockchain technology, redactable signature schemes, and specialized encryption algorithms such as Rail Fence Data Encryption (RFDE) are proposed to address these challenges. Implementing these security measures ensures that health data remain confidential, secure, and integral during transmission and storage. This can effectively safeguard patient privacy and the integrity of medical information in IoMT systems.

3.5 Targeted Attacks on IoHT Infrastructure

Targeted attacks on IoHT infrastructure pose significant security risks due to the sensitive nature of medical data [67]. Various attack scenarios, including Deauthentication (Deauth), Distributed Denial of Service (DDoS), brute force, and so on, target data transfer, storage, and access points within the IoHT ecosystem [68]. Additionally, the IoHT domain faces threats from malicious intruders conducting blackhole, rank, and DoDAG (Destination-Oriented Directed Acyclic Graph) attacks that impact the performance of patient-centric IoHT systems [69]. Understanding these attack methodologies and vulnerabilities is crucial to implementing robust security measures and safeguarding patient data and healthcare infrastructure in the IoHT environment.

Figure 13 presents the most common targeted attacks on IoHT infrastructures as discussed below [70–73].

- **Ransomware Attacks:** Cybercriminals often deploy ransomware to encrypt critical health data and demand payment for its release. Such attacks disrupt healthcare services, cause delays in treatments, and compromise patient safety.
- **Data Breaches:** Attackers target IoHT devices to steal sensitive patient information, such as medical records. These data can be sold on the dark web or used for identity theft. These breaches effectively erode patient trust, cause significant financial losses, and lead to legal consequences for healthcare providers.
- **Device Manipulation:** Malicious actors can compromise IoHT devices, such as insulin pumps or pacemakers. This can lead to potentially life-threatening situations. Device manipulation can result in altered dosages of medications or malfunction of critical health devices.
- **Distributed Denial-of-Service (DDoS) Attacks:** IoHT infrastructure can be overwhelmed by DDoS attacks that can render systems

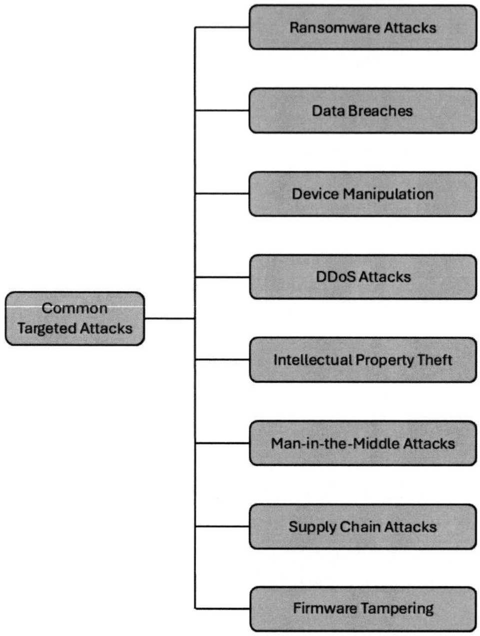

Figure 13: The most common targeted attacks on IoHT infrastructures.

inaccessible to legitimate users. This paralysis of healthcare operations can delay critical care, especially in emergency scenarios.

- **Intellectual Property Theft:** Attackers also target IoHT systems to steal proprietary medical technology and research data. This can result in the loss of competitive advantage and stifle innovation.
- **Man-in-the-Middle (MitM) Attacks:** In this attack, cybercriminals intercept and potentially alter the communication between IoHT devices and healthcare systems. This can lead to unauthorized data access, tampering with medical records, or even the manipulation of real-time medical data being transmitted by devices. Such attacks pose a severe threat to patient safety.
- **Supply Chain Attacks:** IoHT systems are often dependent on multiple third-party components. Attackers may exploit vulnerabilities in the supply chain, such as compromised software or hardware updates. This can open opportunities for attackers to infiltrate healthcare systems. These attacks can introduce malware or backdoors that facilitate attackers with prolonged access to IoHT networks.
- **Firmware Tampering:** Attackers also target the firmware of IoHT devices which controls the basic operations of these devices. By altering the firmware, attackers can disable the devices, modify

their functionality, or even take control of them. This can lead to malfunctions in critical devices, such as pacemakers or insulin pumps, and pose direct risks to patient health.

3.6 Exploitation of Weaknesses in IoHT Networks and Protocols

The IoHT relies on interconnected devices and networks to monitor, transmit, and analyze patient data in real time. This connectivity is crucial for enhancing healthcare efficiency. However, it also introduces significant security vulnerabilities [74]. The complexity and heterogeneity of IoHT networks, and the weaknesses in communication protocols make healthcare systems particularly susceptible to cyberattacks. These security gaps can lead to data breaches, compromised patient safety, and disruptions in medical services. Therefore, it is critical to understand the specific threats arising from weak networks and protocols to safeguarding IoHT infrastructure and ensuring the secure handling of sensitive health information [75].

The major security threats associated with the weaknesses of the IoHT network and protocol, and their consequences are discussed below [76–79] (Figure 14):

- **Unsecured Communication Channels:** IoHT devices often transmit data through unsecured or poorly encrypted channels. This exposes sensitive medical information to eavesdropping or interception. Consequently, this can lead to data breaches that violate privacy regulations (such as HIPAA and GDPR) and could cause identity theft.
- **Vulnerable Wireless Protocols:** Many IoHT devices rely on outdated or weak wireless protocols. This makes the devices easy targets for attacks such as MitM attacks. These attacks enable cybercriminals to intercept, alter, or inject malicious data and potentially compromise the integrity of medical treatments.
- **Insufficient Device Authentication:** Weak authentication protocols or their absence allow attackers to gain unauthorized access to IoHT devices. This can lead to device manipulation, such as altering the performance of life-critical systems (e.g., pacemakers) and endanger patient lives.
- **Inadequate Firmware Security:** Many IoHT devices run on outdated firmware with security flaws. Attackers can exploit these vulnerabilities to introduce malware or disable devices. This can lead to disruptions in healthcare services and delayed treatment for patients.
- **DDoS (Distributed Denial-of-Service) Attacks:** DDoS attacks target IoHT infrastructure by overwhelming it with a flood of traffic from multiple sources. This situation causes legitimate requests to be

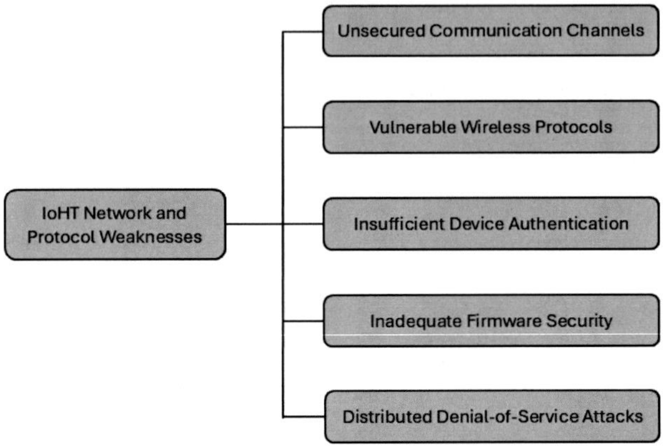

Figure 14: Major security threats associated with the weaknesses of the IoHT networks and protocols.

denied. This can render critical healthcare systems and services inaccessible which can lead to significant operational disruptions. In emergency situations, such downtime can delay critical medical treatments and potentially jeopardize patient health and safety. Furthermore, the inability to access patient data during such attacks can hinder healthcare providers' ability to make informed decisions. This effectively can lead to further complications in patient care and treatment outcomes. Additionally, prolonged service outages can result in financial losses for healthcare organizations and damage their reputation among patients and stakeholders.

To address these issues, researchers have proposed improved lightweight authentication schemes utilizing techniques such as hash functions, XOR operations, and Elliptic Curve Cryptography [80, 81]. Additionally, security experiments have been conducted to identify flaws in existing IoMT security protocols and recommend solutions to mitigate cyberattacks on smart medical devices in Healthcare systems. The focus remains on enhancing the security of IoMT networks to ensure the confidentiality and integrity of patient data.

3.7 Supply Chain Risks

Risks in IoMT-based supply chains include lack of knowledge, technical infrastructure maintenance, cybersecurity, and network dependability [82]. These risks can lead to disruptions, expiry of products, and compromised patient safety [83, 84]. Implementing smart systems in IoMT-based supply chains requires addressing these risks through comprehensive risk management strategies. Blockchain technology can enhance security, integrity, and data provenance in health E-supply chains. However, further research and integration with regulatory frameworks are needed to unlock its full potential. Healthcare supply chains can be made more reliable, traceable, and secure by leveraging IoMT and blockchain technologies. Ultimately, this can improve patient outcomes and operational efficiency [83].

4. Legal Compliance and Governance Challenges of IoHT

4.1 Regulatory Authorities for Digital Health

The most relevant and prominent regulations relating to IoHT and digital health are discussed below:

- **Health Insurance Portability and Accountability Act (HIPPA):**[1] One of the most important regulations in this space is the HIPAA in the United States, which establishes national standards for the protection of PHI. HIPAA mandates that healthcare organizations implement technical, administrative, and physical safeguards to ensure the confidentiality, integrity, and availability of PHI. Effectively, this makes HIPPA a cornerstone of digital health compliance. HIPAA was enacted in 1996 and it sets standards for the privacy and security of patient health information. It requires healthcare providers and their business associates to implement safeguards to protect EHRs from unauthorized access, disclosure, or use.
- **General Data Protection Regulations (GDPR):**[2] The GDPR is a comprehensive data protection law that applies to any organization processing personal data of EU residents. It grants individuals greater control over their personal data and imposes stringent requirements on data controllers and processors to ensure data security and privacy. It went into effect in 2018. In addition to HIPAA, the GDPR in the European Union (EU) plays a vital role in shaping data privacy practices in digital health. GDPR applies to any organization that processes the personal data of EU citizens. This includes healthcare providers, medical device manufacturers, and digital health platforms. GDPR sets a high bar for data protection and requires organizations to obtain explicit consent from patients. Consequently, this ensures data minimization and implements stringent security measures to protect patient information.
- **Medical Device Regulation (MDR):**[3] The MDR, also in the EU, imposes additional compliance requirements for digital health

[1] https://www.hhs.gov/hipaa/index.html.

[2] https://ec.europa.eu/info/law/law-topic/data-protection_en.

[3] https://health.ec.europa.eu/medical-devices-sector/overview_en.

products classified as medical devices. This regulation emphasizes the need for rigorous testing, clinical evaluation, and continuous monitoring of medical devices. This helps in ensuring the safety and efficacy of the medical devices, especially as they integrate with IoHT ecosystems.

- **Cyber Security Act:**[4] The Cyber Security Act in Singapore was passed in 2017. It aims to enhance the cybersecurity capabilities of critical information infrastructure, including healthcare organizations. It requires the implementation of cybersecurity measures and mandates organizations to report data breaches to the government.

4.2 Legal Compliance Issues and Solutions

Compliance with healthcare legal authorities and regulations in the IoMT is a critical challenge due to the complexities involved in managing vast amounts of sensitive health data across interconnected devices. Various challenges, such as data privacy protection, security risks, and compliance issues, have been identified [85, 86]. Regulations such as the Health Insurance Portability and Accountability Act (HIPAA) and the General Data Protection Regulation (GDPR) impose strict requirements for data privacy, security, and patient confidentiality. However, the integration of diverse IoHT devices often results in fragmented security measures. This makes compliance difficult and increases the risk of security breaches. Non-compliance can lead to severe financial penalties, operational disruptions, and reputational risks. Consequently, this can be damaging to the trust between patients and healthcare providers, and lead to potential legal consequences [86, 87].

The key concerns relating to compliance with healthcare regulations in IoHT are discussed below [87–90] (Figure 15):

- **Multiple Regulations:** Healthcare organizations must comply with a complex array of regulations, including HIPAA, GDPR, and local data protection laws.
- **Regulatory Complexity:** Understanding and interpreting regulations can be challenging, especially as regulations evolve.
- **Changing Regulatory Landscape:** Regulations can change frequently, making it difficult for organizations to keep up with the latest requirements.
- **Data Privacy and Security:** Ensuring compliance with data privacy and security regulations is essential to protect patient data and avoid penalties.

[4] https://www.csa.gov.sg/Legislation/cybersecurity-act.

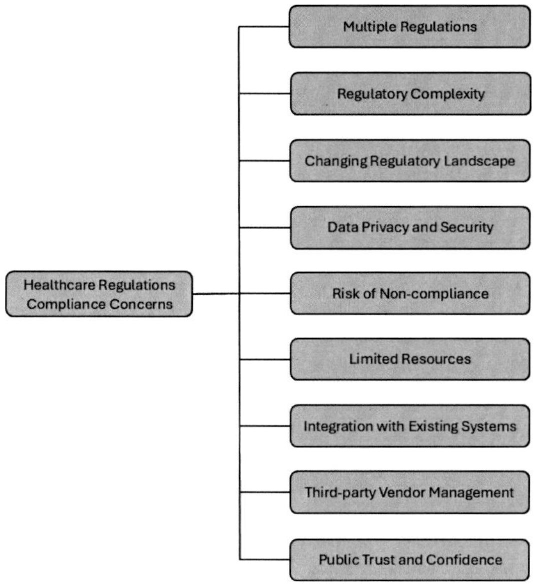

Figure 15: Concerns relating to compliance with healthcare regulations in IoHT.

- **Risk of Non-compliance:** Non-compliance with regulations can result in hefty fines, reputational damage, and legal consequences.
- **Limited Resources:** Healthcare organizations may have limited resources to allocate to compliance efforts.
- **Integration with Existing Systems:** Ensuring that IoHT devices and systems comply with existing regulatory frameworks can be complex.
- **Third-party Vendor Management:** Managing the compliance of third-party vendors can be challenging.
- **Public Trust and Confidence:** Non-compliance with regulations can erode public trust and confidence in healthcare organizations and IoHT technologies.

To mitigate the above-mentioned concerns, privacy-by-design frameworks are essential, embedding regulatory compliance and robust security protocols into the development and deployment of IoHT devices from the outset [91]. Furthermore, continuous monitoring and real-time auditing of IoHT systems are necessary to identify and address vulnerabilities that may arise over time, ensuring ongoing adherence to regulatory standards. The use of advanced encryption and data anonymization techniques can also help protect patient data while ensuring compliance with regulations such as HIPAA and GDPR.

To address these concerns, several solutions are proposed [86, 92–95] (Figure 16):

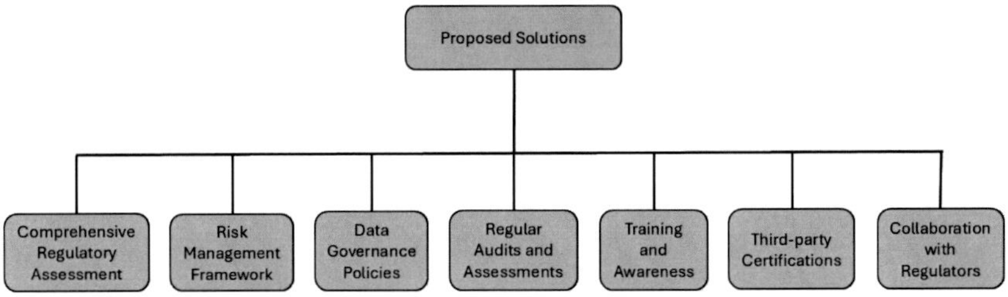

Figure 16: Proposed solutions to healthcare regulatory compliance concerns in IoHT.

- **Comprehensive Regulatory Assessment:** A thorough assessment of applicable regulations can help organizations identify and address potential compliance gaps.
- **Risk Management Framework:** Implementation of a risk management framework can help organizations prioritize compliance efforts and allocate resources effectively.
- **Data Governance Policies:** The design and development of robust data governance policies can establish clear guidelines for data collection, storage, use, and sharing.
- **Regular Audits and Assessments:** Regular audits and assessments can be conducted to help organizations identify and address compliance issues proactively.
- **Training and Awareness:** Training and awareness programs can be provided to employees to ensure that they understand and comply with relevant regulations.
- **Third-party Certifications:** Obtaining third-party certifications, such as ISO 27001[5] or HITRUST,[6] can demonstrate an organization's commitment to data security and compliance.
- **Collaboration with Regulators:** Collaboration with regulatory bodies can help organizations stay informed about regulatory changes and best practices.

Overall, robust regulatory frameworks based on standardized practices, security measures, and compliance standards are crucial for the successful implementation and adoption of IoHT technologies. By fostering collaboration among regulators, healthcare providers, and device

[5] https://www.iso.org/standard/27001.
[6] https://hitrustalliance.net.

manufacturers, such frameworks can help build a secure compliance ecosystem and protect sensitive health information.

4.3 Fragmentation of Regulatory Standards for IoHT and Solutions

The lack of uniform regulatory standards in the IoHT creates major obstacles to maintaining the security, privacy, and safety of healthcare devices. This fragmentation is caused by a diverse range of standards development organizations (SDOs) and the absence of a universally accepted vision [96]. The IoHT devices are developed and deployed across various jurisdictions. In such situations, the absence of harmonized regulations creates inconsistencies in data protection, security protocols, and device interoperability. This fragmentation increases vulnerabilities as health devices created under weaker regulations may fall short of essential cybersecurity and privacy standards. Consequently, healthcare networks become more susceptible to data breaches and cyberattacks. Moreover, the lack of standardized protocols hinders cross-border data sharing and collaboration, thus slowing down the advancements in global healthcare systems.

This issue mirrors the broader problem seen in the IoT security standards. In IoT, a fragmented environment led by various de facto standards makes it challenging to establish uniform security measures across different applications and domains. This lack of a consistent baseline for security increases risks and complicates the protection of connected systems [97]. The current surge in collaboration of distributed IoT devices exacerbates interoperability issues. This, in turn, limits data reuse and new service development due to diverse networking technologies and performance impairments with increasing device interactions [98].

The major issues relating to the fragmentation of regulatory standards for IoHT are discussed below [93, 99, 100] (Figure 17):

- **Inconsistent Security Protocols:** Different jurisdictions have varying security standards. This leads to IoHT devices with inconsistent cybersecurity measures that increases the risks of data breaches and cyberattacks.
- **Privacy Vulnerabilities:** Fragmented regulations create gaps in data privacy protection. This makes it difficult to ensure compliance with global privacy laws such as HIPAA and GDPR.
- **Device Interoperability Challenges:** Lack of standardized protocols across different regions impairs the interoperability of IoHT devices. As a consequence, this leads to inefficiencies in communication and data sharing between healthcare systems.
- **Regulatory Compliance Complexity:** Manufacturers of IoHT devices often face challenges in ensuring their devices meet the diverse and

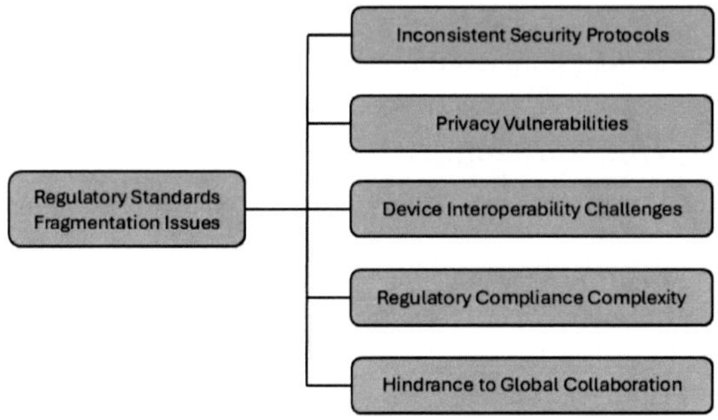

Figure 17: Major issues relating to the fragmentation of regulatory standards for IoHT.

sometimes conflicting regulatory requirements across multiple jurisdictions. This increases the costs and risks associated with regulatory compliances.

- **Hindrance to Global Collaboration:** Regulatory fragmentation limits the ability to share patient data and collaborate on healthcare innovations across borders. This potentially slows down advancements in global health solutions.

Addressing this issue requires strong leadership, collaboration, and a coherent approach to standard development. Such a holistic approach can ensure the successful establishment of foundational standards for a robust digital health ecosystem [87]. Collaborative efforts between international regulatory bodies, such as the U.S. Food and Drug Administration[7] (FDA) and the European Medicines Agency[8] (EMA), can promote the creation of unified standards for IoHT devices. Additionally, the implementation of seamless communication could facilitate smooth and secure information exchange between devices. This could potentially reduce operational inefficiencies and improve patient outcomes. Controlled environments for testing IoHT innovations could also enable developers to ensure compliance with diverse regulations before market release. As a result, this can effectively promote harmonization and security across the IoHT ecosystem.

Potential solutions to the fragmentation of regulatory standards in IoHT include the following [92, 101–104] (Figure 18):

- **Global Regulatory Frameworks:** Collaborative efforts between international regulatory bodies (e.g., FDA and EMA) can create unified standards for IoHT devices. This can ensure consistent security and privacy protection.

[7] https://www.fda.gov.

[8] https://www.ema.europa.eu.

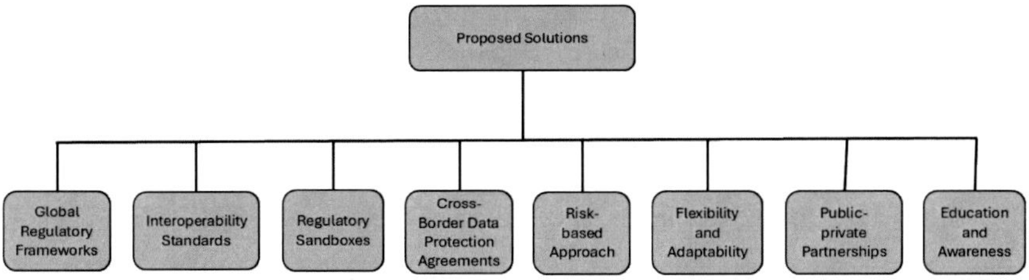

Figure 18: Potential solutions to the fragmentation of regulatory standards in IoHT.

- **Interoperability Standards:** The development and implementation of standardized interoperability frameworks can ensure seamless communication and data exchange between IoHT devices across different healthcare systems.
- **Regulatory Sandboxes:** Controlled environments for IoHT developers can be established to test devices for compliance with various regional regulations before releasing them to the market.
- **Cross-Border Data Protection Agreements:** International agreements can be formulated to standardize data privacy protections and allow safe cross-border data sharing within the IoHT ecosystem.
- **Risk-based Approach:** A risk-based approach can be adopted for regulation so that it can focus on addressing the most significant risks and avoid excessive burdens on healthcare organizations.
- **Flexibility and Adaptability:** Regulatory standards should be flexible and adaptable so that they can accommodate technological advancements and emerging trends.
- **Public–Private Partnerships:** Collaborating with industry stakeholders can help develop and implement effective regulatory frameworks.
- **Education and Awareness:** Raising knowledge and awareness among healthcare professionals and the public regarding the importance of regulatory compliance can help foster a more educated and harmonized environment.

4.4 Cross-Border Data Sharing and Jurisdictional Challenges in IoHT

Cross-border data sharing in the IoHT is essential for global healthcare collaboration. However, it introduces significant jurisdictional challenges [105]. Varying regulatory frameworks, differing privacy standards, and geopolitical complexities complicate the process of seamless data exchange and information sharing among the different stakeholders within the IoHT ecosystem. A holistic approach is required to ensure secure and compliant international health data sharing, including harmonization, innovative technological solutions, and robust governance.

The primary challenges and complexities associated with cross-border data sharing in IoHT are discussed below [86, 105–108] (Figure 19):

- **Regulatory Variations:** Conflicts in compliance arise due to different data protection laws such as GDPR in Europe and HIPAA in the USA.
- **Data Sovereignty:** Nation states have strict regulations on where and how health data can be stored, processed, and transmitted.
- **Lack of Standardization:** Due to the inconsistent data formats and exchange protocols interoperability across IoHT borders is hindered severely.
- **Geopolitical Tensions:** Political and economic conflicts and trade restrictions can sometimes obstruct data-sharing agreements.
- **Cybersecurity Risks:** The potential risks of cyberattacks and unauthorized access increases due to cross-border data exchanges.
- **Data Ownership Disputes:** In the context of multiple jurisdictions, unclear data ownership laws can lead to operational complexities and challenges.

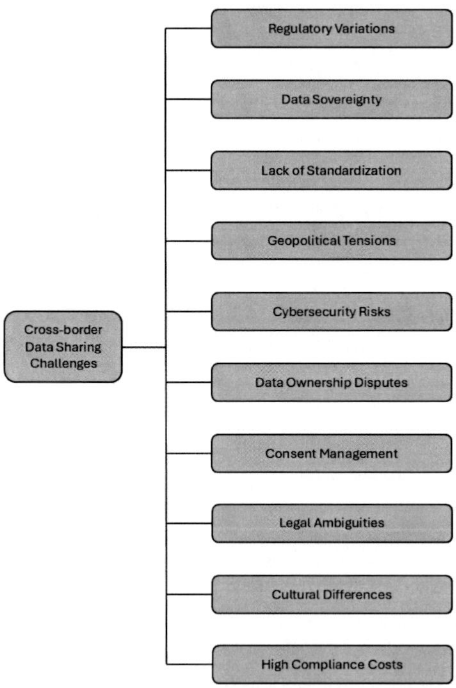

Figure 19: Primary challenges and complexities associated with cross-border data sharing in IoHT.

- **Consent Management:** Standards for obtaining and verifying patient consent for data use differ across jurisdictions which complicates the overall IoHT operations management.
- **Legal Ambiguities:** In the events of data breaches or misuse, unclear definitions of legal liabilities increase vagueness and nuances.
- **Cultural Differences:** Health data governance is further complicated by the varied perspectives on privacy and healthcare ethics across diverse cultures.
- **High Compliance Costs:** Adhering to multiple international regulations imposes financial burdens on IoHT stakeholders.

To address the above-mentioned issues and challenges, the following solution approaches are suggested to ensure secure and compliant data exchange, foster international healthcare cooperation, and improve patient outcomes [86, 105, 107, 109, 110] (Figure 20):

- **Global Regulatory Frameworks:** The development of unified international guidelines can harmonize data protection standards across regions for unified cross-border IoHT governance.

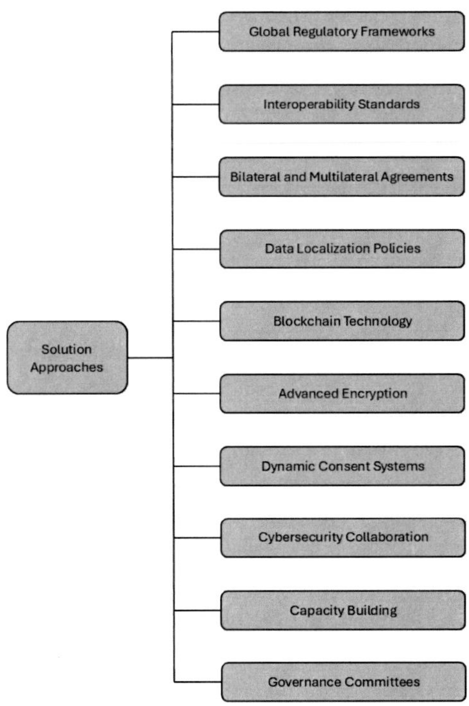

Figure 20: Solution approaches to address challenges associated with cross-border data sharing in IoHT.

- **Interoperability Standards:** Promotion of standardized data formats and exchange protocols globally can foster seamless data exchanges among IoHT stakeholders.
- **Bilateral and Multilateral Agreements:** The establishment of treaties and agreements among nations can foster consistent cross-border data exchange.
- **Data Localization Policies:** Implementation of hybrid models for data localization has the potential for balancing data sovereignty with diverse sharing needs.
- **Blockchain Technology:** The adoption of blockchain-based solutions, such as smart contracts and decentralized ledgers, can be leveraged for secure and auditable cross-border health data transactions and traceability in the IoHT ecosystem.
- **Advanced Encryption:** The application of advanced, robust data encryption methods can improve overall security during data transfer and storage.
- **Dynamic Consent Systems:** Digital solutions can be employed for secure and efficient management of patient consent activities, including obtaining, tracking, and managing patient consent.
- **Cybersecurity Collaboration:** Global partnerships for sharing threat intelligence and best practices can be fostered to improve cybersecurity measures across the IoHT landscape.
- **Capacity Building:** Global workshops on legal and regulatory requirements for IoHT can be conducted regularly to educate and train IoHT stakeholders on international compliance requirements.
- **Governance Committees:** Cross-national and global governance bodies can be developed to oversee cross-border IoHT data sharing and compliance frameworks to address disputes and enforce standards.

5. Strategies for Securing the Internet of Health Things

5.1 Implementing Strong Authentication and Access Controls

As the IoHT continues to expand, ensuring robust authentication and access control mechanisms becomes increasingly critical for the protection of sensitive health information and maintaining patient safety [111]. Strong authentication methods verify the identity of users and devices. On the other hand, access control measures restrict unauthorized access to medical data and IoHT systems. Implementing effective authentication and access control techniques helps mitigate security risks and enhances overall system integrity. Consequently, these techniques ensure that only authorized personnel can access sensitive information.

For implementing strong authentication and access controls in IoHT, the following methods and techniques are proposed [112–115] (Figure 21):

- **Multi-Factor Authentication (MFA):** MFA requires multiple forms of verification, such as passwords, biometrics (fingerprints or facial recognition), and security tokens. This way MFA enhances user identity verification and can reduce the risk of unauthorized access.
- **Multimodal Biometrics:** Methods that utilize multimodal biometrics, such as fingerprint and iris recognition, can develop robust identification and access control systems.
- **Role-Based Access Control (RBAC):** Implementation of RBAC allows organizations to grant permissions based on user roles. This can affirm that healthcare professionals have access only to the information that is necessary for their specific job functions and, thus, minimizes the risk of data exposure.
- **Public Key Infrastructure (PKI):** Utilization of PKI for encryption, digital signatures, and digital certificates helps verify device identities and secure communications. This can guarantee that data transmitted between IoHT devices and healthcare systems remains confidential and intact.

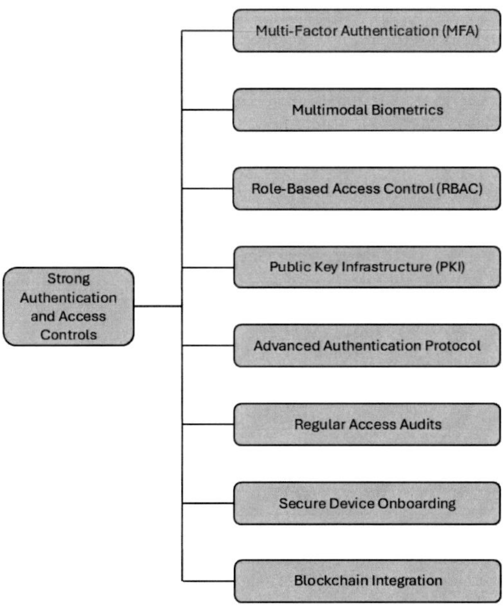

Figure 21: Methods and techniques for implementing strong authentication and access controls in IoHT.

- **Advanced Authentication Protocol:** Advanced secure authentication protocols, such as the Q-Net-based secret key generation approach [116], can be effective in assuring accurate authentication and improving system security.
- **Regular Access Audits:** Conducting periodic audits of user access rights helps identify and revoke unnecessary permissions. This can ensure that only authorized individuals retain access to sensitive medical data.
- **Secure Device Onboarding:** Secure onboarding processes can be established for new IoHT devices including authentication checks and firmware verification. This could help ensure that only trusted devices connect to the healthcare network.
- **Blockchain Integration:** Integration of blockchain technology into access control systems for the IoHT demonstrates effectiveness in improving security by blocking data tampering and minimizing trust-related expenses. Such incorporation has the potential to enhance the overall reliability of the system.

5.2 *Encryption Techniques for Data Protection*

In the context of the IoHT, protecting sensitive patient data is paramount due to the increasing prevalence of cyber threats. Encryption techniques play a vital role in safeguarding data during transmission and storage, ensuring that only authorized parties can access and interpret sensitive health information [117]. By converting plaintext into ciphertext, encryption helps maintain the confidentiality and integrity of medical data, thereby fostering patient trust and compliance with regulations such as HIPAA and GDPR. Employing effective encryption methods is essential for mitigating risks associated with data breaches and unauthorized access in IoHT environments.

The following encryption techniques for data protection in IoHT are proposed [35, 60, 76, 118, 119] (Figure 22):

- **Symmetric Encryption:** Utilizing a single shared key for both encryption and decryption, symmetric encryption algorithms such as Advanced Encryption Standard (AES) offer fast processing speeds, making them suitable for encrypting large volumes of data transmitted between IoHT devices and healthcare systems.
- **Asymmetric Encryption:** Asymmetric algorithms, such as RSA or Elliptic Curve Cryptography (ECC), use a pair of keys (public and private) for secure data exchange. This method enhances security for communications between devices, allowing for secure key exchanges without transmitting sensitive information.

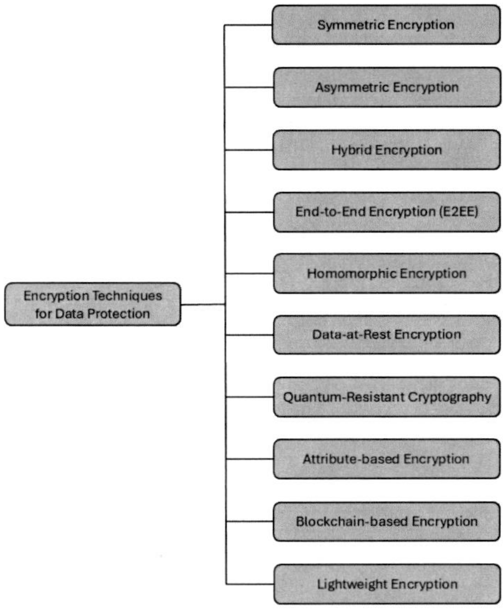

Figure 22: Proposed encryption techniques for data protection in IoHT.

- **Hybrid Encryption:** Combines symmetric and asymmetric encryption for optimal security and performance. A symmetric key is used to encrypt the data, and the symmetric key itself is encrypted using a public key.
- **End-to-End Encryption (E2EE):** Implementing E2EE ensures that data are encrypted on the sender's device and only decrypted on the recipient's device. This approach protects data throughout its entire journey, preventing interception during transmission.
- **Homomorphic Encryption:** This advanced technique allows computations to be performed on encrypted data without decrypting it, preserving data privacy while enabling data analysis in healthcare applications, even in cloud environments.
- **Data-at-Rest Encryption:** Encrypting stored data on IoHT devices and databases protect sensitive health information from unauthorized access in the event of physical device theft or compromise.
- **Quantum-Resistant Cryptography:** Exploits quantum mechanics to provide security against potential quantum computing attacks. Examples: Lattice-based cryptography, code-based cryptography, and multivariate cryptography.
- **Attribute-based Encryption:** Implements access control policies based on user attributes, ensuring fine-grained data access management.

- **Blockchain-based Encryption:** Leverages distributed ledger technology to create tamper-resistant and transparent data storage systems.
- **Lightweight Encryption:** Lightweight Cryptography (LWC) is commonly used for securing IoHT data due to its efficiency in low-power environments. Additionally, Lightweight Medical Image Cryptography (LW-MIC) systems, utilizing ensemble lightweight cryptographic protocols, enhance security for sensitive medical data transmitted through IoMT devices.

These encryption techniques not only secure health data but also optimize performance in resource-constrained IoHT environments, emphasizing the importance of tailored cryptographic solutions for data protection in healthcare IoT applications.

5.2.1 End-to-End Encryption

End-to-end encryption plays a crucial role in safeguarding sensitive health data in the IoHT. Various encryption techniques have been proposed to address security challenges in IoHT devices [120, 121]. Lightweight encryption systems, such as the Photon-Beetle AEAD algorithm and ensemble lightweight cryptographic protocols, have been designed to ensure robust security while minimizing resource consumption in resource-constrained IoHT devices [122, 123]. These encryption methods utilize techniques such as the Secret Sharing Algorithm (SSA) and Cha-Cha-based encryption to protect medical data during transmission and storage. Implementing end-to-end encryption through these lightweight cryptographic solutions enhances data privacy, security, and integrity in IoHT environments, addressing the critical need for secure communication and storage of sensitive health information.

5.2.2 Data Masking and Tokenization

Tokenization is a technique that replaces sensitive data with non-sensitive tokens, reducing the risk of data breaches. Data masking and tokenization play crucial roles in safeguarding data in the IoHT systems. In the realm of IoMT, where security and privacy are paramount [124], techniques such as masking-enabled data protection and Physically Unclonable Functions (PUFs) are employed to ensure data privacy [59]. The use of masking techniques, such as the Secret Sharing Algorithm (SSA) and the Octopus, helps in splitting and encrypting health data, preventing unauthorized access, and maintaining data integrity [125]. These methods not only secure sensitive health information but also leverage ML for data retrieval with high accuracy, showcasing their effectiveness in enhancing data protection in IoHT environments.

5.3 Secure Software Development Practices for IoHT Applications

Given that IoHT is a rapidly evolving domain, for ensuring the protection of sensitive health data and the integrity of connected medical devices, it is essential to secure the software development practices [126, 127]. Various applications run on IoHT devices and infrastructures providing different healthcare services. Day by day an increasing number of cyber threats are being directed to these healthcare applications. Consequently, the integration of security into every phase of the software development lifecycle (SDLC) is extremely critical. Moreover, the incorporation of frameworks that can enable secure and scalable IoHT platforms is essential for further strengthening application security [128]. Such proactive approaches mitigate vulnerabilities and foster a culture of security awareness among developers. This can guarantee that IoHT applications are resilient against potential attacks. Furthermore, establishing data security during data flow and storage is a prerequisite for ensuring privacy and confidentiality in medical IoT environments [129]. To mitigate risks and build resilient IoHT applications, system and software developers need to follow standards and recommendations and leverage advanced security protocols. Through the adoption of secure software development practices, the overall reliability and safety of healthcare systems be protected which will facilitate safeguarding patient information and maintaining trust in IoHT technologies.

For robust protection of IoHT applications, the following secure software development practices are proposed [126, 130–134] (Figure 23):

- **Threat Analysis and Modeling:** For creating a secure IoHT system, it is essential to analyze threats that are specific to healthcare IoT applications so that the security measures can be tailored accordingly. Threat modeling should be conducted starting from the design phase as it can identify potential security risks and vulnerabilities from the beginning of SDLC. This empowers developers to implement appropriate countermeasures early in the development process.
- **Secure Coding Practices:** Software developers should follow established secure coding guidelines such as OWASP Top Ten. Adhering to the standards and best coding practices, developers can avoid common vulnerabilities such as SQL injection and cross-site scripting (XSS) that would reduce the risk of exploitation.
- **Input Validation:** Input validation and sanitization process can prevent malicious code injection and other attacks.
- **Output Encoding:** The application of appropriate encoding for outputs can prevent vulnerabilities such as cross-site scripting and other vulnerabilities.

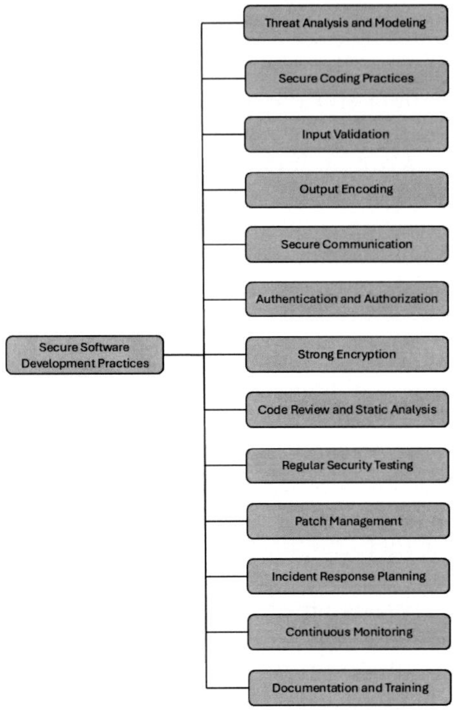

Figure 23: Secure software development practices for IoHT applications.

- **Secure Communication:** Secure Communication: Data in transit must be secured using secure communication protocols such as TLS/SSL and HTTPS.
- **Robust Authentication and Authorization:** Strong privacy-preserving authentication and authorization mechanisms must be implemented to control access to IoHT applications and data, including Zero-Knowledge Proof Authentication [135] and Anonymous Credential Systems [136].
- **Strong Encryption:** Encryption mechanisms must be applied to sensitive data at rest and in transit to protect it from unauthorized access.
- **Code Review and Static Analysis:** Ahead of software deployment, regular code review exercises and static analysis tools should be applied so that any security flaws and vulnerabilities can be detected early enough. This can guarantee higher levels of code quality and security.
- **Regular Security Testing:** To identify and fix security weaknesses in IoHT applications, periodic security testing, such as penetration

testing and vulnerability assessments, must be conducted throughout the SDLC before rolling out the software applications.

- **Patch Management:** A robust patch management process must be ensured so that software can be updated in a timely fashion and any security vulnerabilities can be corrected before security attacks can be successful. This can reduce the risk of exploitation in IoHT applications active in operations.
- **Incident Response Planning:** An incident response plan must be developed and implemented so that any unforeseen security breaches can be responded quickly and effectively to minimize the adverse effects.
- **Continuous Monitoring:** IoHT applications and services need to be monitored closely to identify any signs of security attacks and take necessary actions promptly to contain the security risks and reduce the impact.
- **Documentation and Training:** Software developers should be provided with proper documentation of security practices and facilitated with regular training for their continuous and sustained professional development. Such measures and activities foster a culture of security awareness and promote adherence to secure software development practices.

6. Risk Management in Digital Health

6.1 Conducting Threat Modeling Exercises

Threat modeling plays a crucial role in risk management within digital health systems [130, 137]. The interconnected nature of healthcare IT infrastructures makes them susceptible to cyber threats due to the heterogeneity of systems and the varied stakeholders involved [31]. The adoption of IoT in healthcare brings about numerous benefits but also introduces new vulnerabilities and risks that need to be addressed through effective threat and risk management strategies [138, 139]. By utilizing ML models and customized threat modeling techniques, organizations can identify and analyze potential security threats, ultimately enhancing the security posture of digital health systems. Implementing qualitative risk approaches and tailored threat modeling frameworks can help mitigate risks and ensure the confidentiality and integrity of sensitive health data in the evolving digital health landscape.

Threat modeling is a proactive approach to identifying, assessing, and mitigating potential threats to systems and networks. In the context of the IoHT and digital health, where patient data, critical devices, and healthcare services are involved, threat modeling is essential to ensure

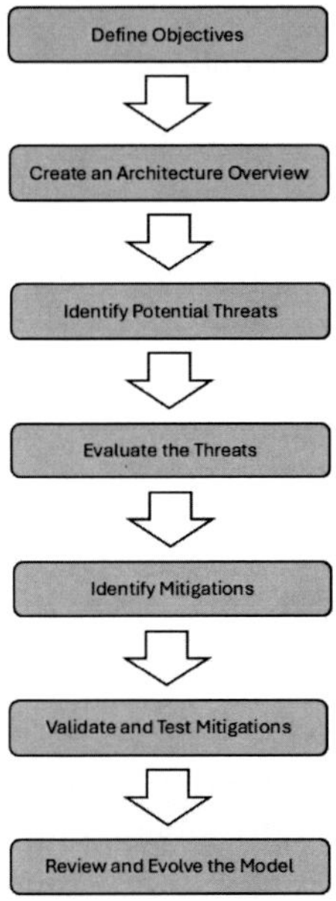

Figure 24: Standard procedure for conducting threat modeling exercises in IoHT.

security, privacy, and reliability [140]. The following outlines a standard procedure for conducting threat modeling exercises tailored to IoHT and digital health systems [141–144] (Figure 24).

A. Define Objectives

- **Identify Key Assets:** In IoHT and Digital Health systems, critical assets typically include patient data (e.g., medical records, diagnostic information), connected medical devices (e.g., pacemakers, insulin pumps), and digital platforms (e.g., telemedicine services).
- **Understand the Context:** Define the scope of the system (e.g., hospital networks, remote patient monitoring systems) and its regulatory environment (e.g., HIPAA in the U.S., GDPR in the EU).
- **Security Goals:** Determine core security requirements such as confidentiality, integrity, availability, and data privacy.

B. Create an Architecture Overview

- **Identify Components:** List all devices, sensors, applications, and networks in the IoHT ecosystem. This may include wearable health monitors, patient data gateways, hospital information systems, cloud services, and mobile health apps.

- **Draw Data Flows:** Map out how data flow between IoHT devices, cloud platforms, and healthcare providers. Include how patient data are collected, transmitted, stored, and accessed.
- **Determine Trust Boundaries:** Identify areas where data move from one system to another, such as between a patient's wearable device and the cloud, or a healthcare provider's app and a medical database.

C. Identify Potential Threats

- **Use Threat Modeling Frameworks:** Apply frameworks such as STRIDE (Spoofing, Tampering, Repudiation, Information Disclosure, Denial of Service, and Elevation of Privilege) or PASTA (Process for Attack Simulation and Threat Analysis).
- **Understand Common IoHT Vulnerabilities:** Focus on known vulnerabilities in medical devices and health data systems, such as weak encryption, default credentials, and unpatched software.
- **Consider Insider and Outsider Threats:** Both external cybercriminals and internal personnel (such as healthcare workers or IT staff) can pose security risks.
- **Evaluate Supply Chain Risks:** Medical devices and health platforms often rely on third-party vendors, so assess risks in the supply chain, including hardware backdoors and software vulnerabilities.

D. Evaluate the Threats

- **Assess Threat Likelihood and Impact:** The probability of each of the identified threats to occur should be evaluated. Then, the potential impact of each threat on patient safety, data security, or healthcare operations should be assessed.
- **Prioritize Risks:** The threats should be ranked according to their severity on the IoHT ecosystem. Risks that could have impacts on patient safety, such as tampering with medical device data, must be given the highest priority.

E. Identify Mitigations

- **Implement Security Controls:** Based on the prioritized threats, propose mitigations such as encryption for data transmission, access control mechanisms (e.g., multi-factor authentication), and device integrity checks.
- **Address Privacy Concerns:** For the threats that can compromise sensitive data, implement security measures that preserve privacy such as data anonymization and secure cloud storage.

- **Mitigate Supply Chain Risks:** Ensure that third-party vendors comply with security standards. Regularly audit their devices and software for vulnerabilities.

F. Validate and Test Mitigations

- **Penetration Testing:** Conduct penetration tests on the IoHT ecosystem to evaluate the effectiveness of the implemented mitigation techniques.
- **Vulnerability Assessments:** Vulnerability assessments must be conducted on a regular basis, in particular after deployment of new devices or updates.
- **Monitor Security Events:** Use real-time monitoring and logging tools to detect potential security incidents early.

G. Review and Evolve the Model

- **Continuous Improvement:** Threat modeling should not be considered as a one-time exercise. The model should be revisited and reviewed periodically to check for new threats, technologies, and system updates.
- **Collaborate with Stakeholders:** Involve healthcare providers, IT professionals, and medical device manufacturers in periodic threat assessments to ensure the model remains relevant.
- **Stay Updated on Regulations:** Continuously adapt the threat model to evolving healthcare regulations and compliance requirements, such as FDA cybersecurity guidelines for medical devices.

Securing IoHT and Digital Health systems requires ongoing attention to potential threats, vulnerabilities, and mitigations. By following a systematic threat modeling process, healthcare providers can identify and address risks before they lead to significant data breaches, service disruptions, or patient harm.

6.2 *Continuous Monitoring and Incident Response*

Continuous monitoring and incident response play crucial roles in risk management within digital health settings [145, 146]. Continuous data monitoring through digital devices enables the collection of real-time high-quality data, aiding in feedback-led optimization and ensuring the safety and performance of digital health applications [147]. This monitoring allows for the identification of patterns and relationships in data, supporting healthcare decision-making and improving patient outcomes [148]. Additionally, incident monitoring and response systems can limit functionality during incidents, enhancing security and response capabilities. To manage risks effectively, a proactive approach is essential, involving the adaptation of traditional risk management standards to work continuously, incorporating incident and event management tools, misbehavior detection, and threat intelligence. Continuous monitoring and incident response are vital components in maintaining the security and effectiveness of digital health technologies.

7. Collaborative Approaches to IoHT Security

7.1 Industry Partnerships for Threat Intelligence Sharing

Industry partnerships play a crucial role in enhancing threat intelligence sharing for IoHT security [149]. Collaborative efforts, such as the SECANT[9] project, aims to strengthen cybersecurity risk assessment in complex ICT infrastructures such as healthcare, emphasizing the importance of sharing threat intelligence for improved digital security and privacy [150]. Additionally, the development of new threat intelligence frameworks, such as the one focusing on CoAP protocol attacks, highlights the need for industry partnerships to model and mitigate advanced cyber threats effectively [151]. There is a high potential that industry collaborations and partnerships can significantly improve the security of IoHT ecosystems by leveraging centralized and federated transfer learning modes and innovative algorithms for threat detection and classification [35]. These partnerships facilitate the implementation of comprehensive security measures, ensuring the protection of sensitive healthcare data and systems.

7.1.1 Challenges Associated with Threat Intelligence Sharing

Although the benefits are evident, industry partnerships for threat intelligence sharing in the IoHT face numerous challenges, ranging from privacy concerns to interoperability issues. These obstacles hinder collaboration and the timely exchange of critical information [152]. As a consequence, addressing these complexities is essential for enhancing IoHT security and safeguarding sensitive healthcare data from emerging threats.

Figure 25 presents a taxonomy of the challenges associated with industry partnerships for threat intelligence sharing in the field of IoHT [153–156]:

- **Data Privacy Concerns**: Sensitive patient or healthcare data may need to be shared among organizations for threat intelligence. This can raise concerns about violating privacy laws such as HIPAA or GDPR.

[9] https://secant-project.eu.

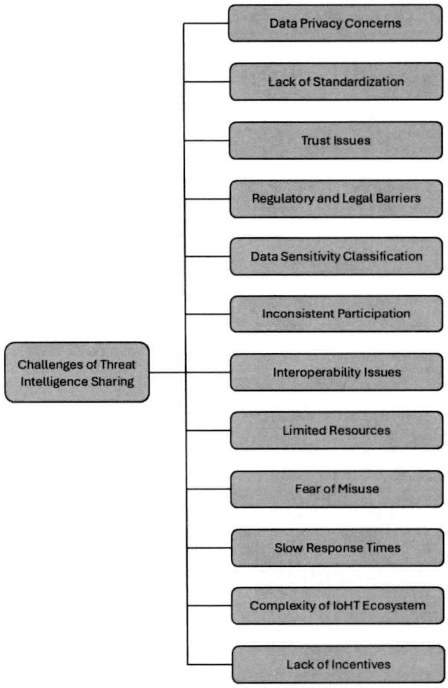

Figure 25: A taxonomy of the challenges associated with threat intelligence sharing in the IoHT.

- **Lack of Standardization:** Different organizations may use varying formats and frameworks for threat intelligence, making it difficult to share and interpret data efficiently.
- **Trust Issues:** Industry partners may not be interested in exchanging threat data considering concerns about reputational damage, legal liability, or exposing their vulnerabilities to competitors.
- **Regulatory and Legal Barriers:** Threat intelligence may be hindered due to the strict healthcare regulations. This can complicate the process of sharing threat intelligence data. Such complications can be even harder to manage when working across borders or in jurisdictions with different legal requirements.
- **Data Sensitivity Classification:** Difficulty in distinguishing between sensitive and non-sensitive threat intelligence can slow down or prevent sharing due to concerns over inadvertently disclosing critical data.
- **Inconsistent Participation:** There may be some stakeholders within the IoHT ecosystem who are not equally interested or committed to or

capable of contributing to threat intelligence sharing. This can create gaps in intelligence coverage.

- **Interoperability Issues:** In the process of sharing threat intelligence across different platforms, compatibility challenges may arise in situations where healthcare systems and IoHT devices use proprietary technology with incompatible interfaces for information exchange.
- **Limited Resources:** Smaller healthcare providers or IoHT device manufacturers may lack the technical and financial resources to participate effectively in threat intelligence networks.
- **Fear of Misuse:** There may be worries among organizations that the shared threat intelligence could be misused by competitors or malicious actors within the network.
- **Slow Response Times:** Industry partnerships may result in bureaucratic delays, making it difficult to share threat intelligence quickly enough to respond to emerging threats in real time.
- **Complexity of IoHT Ecosystem:** The complexity of identifying and sharing relevant threat intelligence can be exacerbated due to the diverse range of connected devices and systems in IoHT increases.
- **Lack of Incentives:** Without clear incentives or benefits, organizations may be reluctant to invest time and resources into threat intelligence sharing partnerships.

7.1.2 Potential Solution Approaches

To overcome the challenges associated with threat intelligence sharing in the IoHT ecosystem, coordinated efforts among IoHT organizations and innovative strategies are essential. The following potential solution approaches aim to address issues related to privacy, interoperability, trust, and other barriers to promote a more secure and collaborative environment for safeguarding IoHT systems [15, 86, 94, 153, 157] (Figure 26):

- **Develop Standardized Frameworks:** To facilitate smooth sharing of threat intelligence across industry partners, common formats and protocols can be established, such as utilizing STIX/TAXII[10] (Structured Threat Information Expression/Trusted Automated Exchange of Indicator Information).
- **Enhance Privacy-Preserving Techniques:** Implement data anonymization and encryption methods to ensure sensitive healthcare data are protected while still allowing for effective threat intelligence sharing.

[10] https://oasis-open.org.

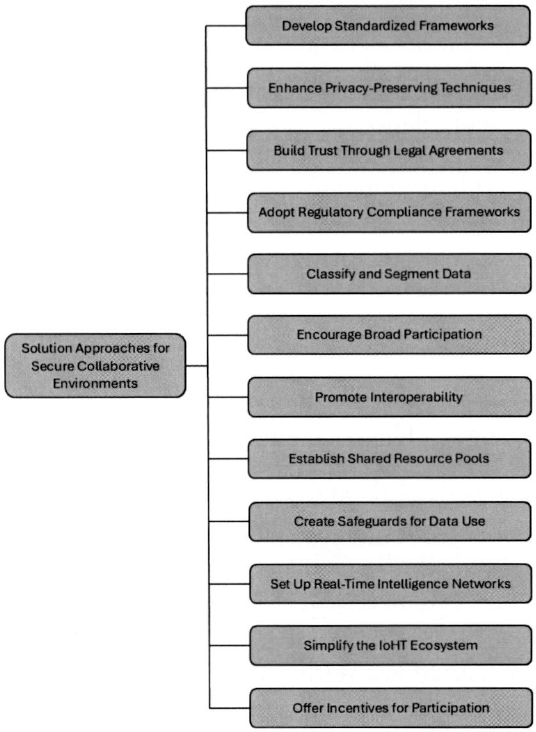

Figure 26: Potential solution approaches for secure and collaborative IoHT environments.

- **Build Trust Through Legal Agreements:** Formal legal agreements can be made among IoHT collaborators, such as Memorandums of Understanding (MoUs) or Non-Disclosure Agreements (NDAs) that can foster trust and ensure the proper handling of shared threat intelligence.
- **Adopt Regulatory Compliance Frameworks:** Develop threat intelligence-sharing frameworks that align with healthcare regulations such as HIPAA and GDPR to ensure legal compliance and streamline cross-border data exchange.
- **Classify and Segment Data:** Establish clear guidelines for distinguishing between sensitive and non-sensitive information to facilitate more efficient and safer sharing of threat intelligence.
- **Encourage Broad Participation:** Smaller organizations and stakeholders can be motivated by incentivizing them to contribute by providing financial or technical assistance. This can effectively foster a more inclusive threat intelligence network.

- **Promote Interoperability:** Advocate for the adoption of open standards and APIs that enable seamless communication and integration between different IoHT devices and platforms.
- **Establish Shared Resource Pools:** Pool resources such as shared threat intelligence platforms, cybersecurity training, and tools to support smaller players in the IoHT ecosystem who may lack the capacity to participate fully.
- **Create Safeguards for Data Use:** To prevent the misuse of shared threat intelligence, policies and governance structures can be developed. This can guarantee that information is used only for cybersecurity purposes.
- **Set Up Real-Time Intelligence Networks:** Implement automated, real-time threat intelligence-sharing platforms that minimize delays and allow for quick responses to emerging threats across the IoHT ecosystem.
- **Simplify the IoHT Ecosystem:** Promotion of the development of interoperable, modular systems that reduce complexity and make it easier for organizations to share relevant threat intelligence.
- **Offer Incentives for Participation:** Provide tangible incentives, such as cybersecurity certifications, risk reduction benefits, or financial rewards, to motivate organizations to actively engage in threat intelligence sharing.

7.2 *Cross-Sector Collaboration with Technology and Security Experts*

Cross-sector collaborations involving technology and security experts are crucial for enhancing the security of the IoHT. Security risks in IoMT devices, such as vulnerabilities due to limited processing power and memory [35], underscore the need for collaborative efforts. Research highlights the security challenges faced by medical IoT devices and emphasizes the importance of focusing on security issues throughout the device life cycle [158]. Additionally, integrating multi-ledger blockchain architecture in IoMT can enhance security by providing decentralized data storage. This can effectively eliminate single points of failure and improve trust and reliability [159]. By leveraging ML techniques for anomaly detection and risk assessment in IoMT environments, a holistic evaluation of security risks in Connected Medical Devices (CMD) can be achieved [160]. Collaborative initiatives between experts from different sectors can lead to effective processes for securing IoMT devices and safeguarding patient data.

8. Responsible Practices in Digital Health Security

8.1 *Protecting Patient Anonymity in Data Analytics*

In data analytics, maintaining patient anonymity within IoHT is an important criterion for upholding privacy standards and fostering trust. By anonymizing and de-identifying health data, healthcare providers can perform insightful analyses without exposing individuals' identities [161]. Valuable medical insights can be extracted using this approach. It also helps protect patient confidentiality and create an ethical framework. Both patient rights and regulatory requirements can be ensured by respecting patient anonymity.

8.2 *Minimizing Data Collection and Retention*

Minimizing data collection and retention in digital health systems reduces exposure to cyber threats and respects patient privacy [162]. Regulatory frameworks, such as HIPAA and GDPR, also emphasize only essential information collection and require IoHT organizations to retain it for the shortest possible time. This practice helps limit the potential for unauthorized access and signals respect for patients' digital privacy. Consequently, it can ensure maintaining data protection is a priority within IoHT security practices.

8.3 *Preventing Unauthorized Surveillance and Data Misuse*

In digital health, unauthorized surveillance and data misuse are critical ethical violations [163]. To protect sensitive health data from both internal and external threats, security and regulatory mechanisms, such as strong access controls, standard surveillance protocols, and regular audits, can be effective in guaranteeing data protection. Ethical practices that guard against unauthorized data usage and monitoring preserve patient trust, prevent exploitation, and help healthcare organizations maintain the integrity of their digital health infrastructures.

8.4 *Ensuring Accountability in Data Breaches*

Accountability in data breaches is essential for maintaining patient trust in IoHT systems [164]. Ethical standards require that organizations disclose breaches promptly, take corrective actions, and learn from incidents to bolster future security. This transparency helps mitigate harm to affected patients and reinforces public trust. Holding organizations accountable ensures that patient interests remain central in digital health, even when cybersecurity failures occur.

8.5 Empowering Patients with Data Access and Control

Empowering patients with control over their data reinforces trust and transparency in digital health systems [165]. Providing patients with options to view, manage, and consent to the use of their personal data promotes a patient-centric approach to IoHT security. This practice acknowledges patient autonomy, allows for informed decision-making, and aligns with ethical principles that place the individual's rights at the forefront of digital health security.

8.6 Ethical Implications of AI and Automation in IoHT Security

AI and automation in IoHT security present significant ethical considerations, particularly regarding transparency and bias [166]. Ethical practices call for algorithms that are explainable, fair, and aligned with patient interests. Responsible AI use ensures that automated security measures support rather than undermine patient trust, enabling healthcare providers to maintain transparency while leveraging technological advancements to protect sensitive health information securely and fairly.

8.7 Equitable Access to Secure Digital Health Services

Equitable and fair access to secure digital health services must be ensured regardless of socioeconomic status so that security protections can be made available to all patients. Addressing access disparities helps eliminate health inequities, providing secure, reliable care for everyone [167]. This ethical approach to IoHT security fosters inclusivity and ensures marginalized populations are not left vulnerable to digital threats due to a lack of resources or technological infrastructure.

8.8 Transparency in Security Measures and Data Usage

Transparency in data security and usage practices is an ethical necessity within IoHT. This is essential for building patient trust and supporting informed consent [168]. Accessible and clear information regarding data collection, storage, and protection helps patients understand their roles in the overall security landscape. Healthcare providers can create partnerships with patients by fostering data transparency. This can effectively empower patients to make informed decisions and knowledgeable choices about their digital health interactions.

8.9 Ensuring Ethical Use of Health Data in Cybersecurity Practices

Ethical leadership plays a crucial role in ensuring the ethical use of health data in cybersecurity practices in digital health. Healthcare organizations face significant risks from cyber data thefts, often leading to breaches that compromise patient care [169]. The healthcare industry's adoption of digital technology, including AI tools, has increased the need to address ethical issues in data security. Researchers have proposed novel ethical hacking methods tailored for Health Information Systems (HISs) to enhance cybersecurity protection [170]. Privacy concerns regarding the use of aggregated personal information in health practices highlight the importance of ethical decisions in data analytics technologies [171]. By integrating ethical leadership, cybersecurity measures, AI tools, and privacy considerations, healthcare organizations can navigate the complexities of maintaining ethical standards in digital health data security.

9. Future Directions and Conclusion

9.1 Anticipating the Evolution of IoHT Threat Landscape

Future threats and attacks on the IoHT encompass a range of vulnerabilities that need to be addressed to ensure the security and privacy of healthcare data. Various studies highlight the critical importance of implementing robust security measures [47, 68, 172–174]. Potential attacks include Deauth, DDOS, brute force, hashcat, MitM, Injection, Short Address Attack, and Smart Contract Overflow. These attacks target different stages such as home internet connection resources, data transfer, data storage, and access, emphasizing the need for comprehensive security protocols. Additionally, the use of blockchain and smart contracts is emerging as a preferred method for enhancing data security within the IoHT ecosystem. Addressing these future threats requires a multi-faceted approach that includes encryption, authentication, access control, and continuous monitoring to safeguard sensitive healthcare information.

9.2 Investing in Research and Innovation for Sustainable IoHT Security Solutions

Future directions in investing in research and innovation for sustainable IoHT security solutions involve leveraging technologies such as Blockchain-Assisted Cybersecurity (BCCS) [175], Computational Intelligence (CI), and AI for secure data transmission, collection, and storage [176]. Additionally, the integration of smart technologies with conventional medical procedures using AI techniques can enhance the quality of services while reducing environmental impact [177]. Emphasizing lightweight cryptography techniques for secure and eco-friendly IoT deployment is crucial for sustainable and secure IoMT systems [178]. Furthermore, exploring state-of-the-art techniques such as gated recurrent units (GRUs) combined with recurrent neural networks (RNNs) for disease detection, such as breast cancer, can pave the way for more efficient and secure IoMT models [179]. These approaches can guide future research toward developing robust, secure, and sustainable IoMT systems.

9.3 The Role of Stakeholders in Promoting a Secure and Trustworthy Digital Health Environment

Stakeholders play a crucial role in securing the digital health environment by addressing ethical, regulatory, and trust-related challenges [180]. Engaging stakeholders, including health professionals, IT practitioners, patients, and researchers, is essential for responsible digital health innovation [181, 182]. Understanding stakeholders' perspectives on big data and digital health is key to restoring trust and ensuring data governance [183]. Stakeholder collaboration, ethical awareness, and relevant regulations are identified as core impediments to responsible digital health. Involving users early in the innovation process, understanding their behavior changes, and ensuring true inclusion in the design space are critical for sustainable digital health solutions. Identifying and engaging relevant stakeholders using appropriate methods can enhance the efficacy and sustainability of digital health applications and services in the long run.

References

[1] Kaur, M., M. Sugadev, H. Kaur, M. R. Mahmood and V. Maheshwari. 2022. Healthcare Internet of Things. pp. 301–337. *In*: R. R. H. K. S. K. K. K. N. Md Rashid Mahmood (ed.). *Ambient Intelligence and Internet of Things*, Wiley. doi: 10.1002/9781119821847.ch10.

[2] Zakaria, R., A. H. Choudhury, M. Razin, M. S. Hossain, N. Hasan and M. I. Tahmid. 2022. Internet of Things (IoT) based Health Monitor Device. *4th International Conference on Electrical, Computer and Telecommunication Engineering, ICECTE 2022*, doi: 10.1109/ICECTE57896.2022.10114509.

[3] Wei, K., L. Zhang, Y. Guo and X. Jiang. 2020. Health monitoring based on internet of medical things: Architecture, enabling technologies, and applications. *IEEE Access*, 8: 27468–27478, doi: 10.1109/ACCESS.2020.2971654.

[4] Naresh, V. S., S. S. Pericherla, P. Sita Rama Murty and S. Reddi. 2020. Internet of Things in Healthcare: Architecture, applications, challenges, and solutions. *Computer Systems Science and Engineering*, 35(6): 411–421, doi: 10.32604/csse.2020.35.411.

[5] Askar, N. A., A. Habbal, A. H. Mohammed, M. S. Sajat, Z. Y. Ziyodulla Yusupov and D. Kodirov. 2022. Architecture, protocols, and applications of the Internet of Medical Things (IoMT). *Journal of Communications*, pp. 900–918, doi: 10.12720/jcm.17.11.900-918.

[6] Pramanik, P. K. D., A. Solanki, A. Debnath, A. Nayyar, S. El-Sappagh and K. -S. Kwak. 2020. Advancing modern healthcare with nanotechnology, nanobiosensors, and internet of nano things: Taxonomies, applications, architecture, and challenges. *IEEE Access*, 8: 65230–65266, doi: 10.1109/ACCESS.2020.2984269.

[7] Abrar, I., Z. Ayub and F. Masoodi. 2021. Current trends and future scope for the Internet of Things. In *Internet of Things in Business Transformation*, Wiley, pp. 185–209. doi: 10.1002/9781119711148.ch11.

[8] Khatoon, N., S. Roy and P. Pranav. 2020. A survey on applications of Internet of Things in Healthcare, pp. 89–106. doi: 10.1007/978-3-030-39119-5_6.

[9] Johnston, C. 2022. *Digital Health Technologies*. First Edition. London: Routledge. doi: 10.4324/9781003220190.

[10] Imuede, J. and K. Imuede. 2023. Digital technologies on health services: A systemic review. In *Handbook of Research on AI and Knowledge Engineering for Real-Time Business Intelligence*, IGI Global, pp. 168–182. doi: 10.4018/978-1-6684-6519-6.ch011.

[11] Desai, A. and G. Karous. 2023. Digital health. In *Medical Innovation*, 1st Edition., Boca Raton: CRC Press, pp. 121–129. doi: 10.1201/9781003164609-15.

[12] Zwack, C. C., M. Haghani, M. Hollings, L. Zhang, S. Gauci, R. Gallagher and J. Redfern. Jan. 2023. The evolution of digital health technologies in cardiovascular disease research. *NPJ Digit. Med.*, 6(1), doi: 10.1038/s41746-022-00734-2.

[13] Colloud, S., T. Metcalfe, S. Askin, S. Belachew, J. Ammann, E. Bos, T. Kilchenmann, P. Strijbos, D. Eggenspieler, L. Servais, C. Garay, A. Konstantakopoulos, A. Ritzhaupt, T. Vetter, C. Vincenzi and F. Cerreta. Mar. 2023. Evolving regulatory perspectives on digital health technologies for medicinal product development. *NPJ Digit. Med.*, 6(1): 56, doi: 10.1038/s41746-023-00790-2.

[14] Adil, M., M. K. Khan, N. Kumar, M. Attique, A. Farouk, M. Guizani and Z. Jin. Jun. 2024. Healthcare Internet of Things: Security threats, challenges, and future research directions. *IEEE Internet Things J.*, 11(11): 19046–19069, doi: 10.1109/JIOT.2024.3360289.

[15] Yaacoub, J. P. A., M. Noura, H. N. Noura, O. Salman, E. Yaacoub, R. Couturier and A. Chehab. 2020. Securing internet of medical things systems: Limitations, issues and recommendations. *Future Generation Computer Systems*, 105: 581–606, doi: 10.1016/j.future.2019.12.028.

[16] Affia, A. O., H. Finch, W. Jung, I. A. Samori, L. Potter and X. -L. Palmer. May 2023. IoT health devices: Exploring security risks in the connected landscape. *IoT*, 4(2): 150–182, doi: 10.3390/iot4020009.

[17] Kiran, R., A. Kumbhare, P. K. Thakur and S. Mane. 2023. Security and privacy in the Internet of Medical Things (IoMT). In *Revolutionizing Healthcare Through Artificial Intelligence and Internet of Things Applications*, IGI Global, pp. 1–27. doi: 10.4018/978-1-6684-5422-0.ch001.

[18] Thapa, S., A. Bello, A. Maurushat and F. Farid. Apr. 2023. Security risks and user perception towards adopting wearable Internet of Medical Things. *Int. J. Environ. Res. Public Health*, 20(8): 5519, doi: 10.3390/ijerph20085519.

[19] Czekster, R. M., P. Grace, C. Marcon, F. Hessel and S. C. Cazella. Jun. 2023. Challenges and opportunities for conducting dynamic risk assessments in medical IoT. *Applied Sciences*, 13(13): 7406, doi: 10.3390/app13137406.

[20] Sharma, M. and Dr. A. Kumar Bindal. Nov. 2022. Security issues in IoT: A review. In *2022 Seventh International Conference on Parallel, Distributed and Grid Computing (PDGC)*, Solan, Himachal Pradesh, India: IEEE, pp. 119–124. doi: 10.1109/PDGC56933.2022.10053255.

[21] Roobini, S., M. Kavitha, M. Sujaritha and D. Rajesh Kumar. 2022. Cyber-security threats to IoMT-enabled healthcare systems. In *Cognitive Computing for Internet of Medical Things*, Boca Raton: Chapman and Hall/CRC, pp. 105–130. doi: 10.1201/9781003256243-6.

[22] Abdi, A., H. Bennouri and A. Keane. Jun. 2024. Emerging cyber risks & threats in healthcare systems: A case study in resilient cybersecurity solutions. In *2024 13th Mediterranean Conference on Embedded Computing (MECO)*, IEEE, pp. 1–8. doi: 10.1109/MECO62516.2024.10577790.

[23] Wang, Z., J. Zhao, P. Sun, J. Yang, R. Wang and X. Zhang. Feb. 2023. A lightweight three-party mutual authentication protocol for Internet of Health Things Systems. *J. Healthc Eng.*, 2023: 1–15, doi: 10.1155/2023/1044282.

[24] Ahmed, M. M., L. Maglaras and M. A. Ferrag. 2022. Cyber threats in the healthcare sector and countermeasures. In *Research Anthology on Securing Medical Systems and Records*, IGI Global, pp. 1–16. doi: 10.4018/978-1-6684-6311-6.ch001.

[25] Kovács, A. M. and J. Besenyő. Apr. 2023. Healthcare cybersecurity threat context and mitigation opportunities. *Security Science Journal*, 4(1): 83–101, doi: 10.37458/ssj.4.1.6.

[26] Rai, S., R. Sharma, D. Mishra and N. Pathak. 2024. Cyber Terrorism in Health Information Systems, pp. 220–247. doi: 10.4018/979-8-3693-5976-1.ch011.

[27] Gupta, D. S., S. H. Islam, M. S. Obaidat, A. Karati and B. Sadoun. Sep. 2021. LAAC: Lightweight lattice-based authentication and access control protocol for E-Health systems in IoT environments. *IEEE Syst. J.*, 15(3): 3620–3627, doi: 10.1109/JSYST.2020.3016065.

[28] Hameed, S. S., W. H. Hassan, L. Abdul Latiff and F. Ghabban. Mar. 2021. A systematic review of security and privacy issues in the internet of medical things; The role of machine learning approaches. *Peer J. Comput. Sci.*, 7: e414, doi: 10.7717/peerj-cs.414.

[29] Yamcharoen, P., O. S. Folorunsho, A. Bayewu and T. P. Ojo. Dec. 2022. Impact of digitalizing healthcare business operations on cybersecurity landscape. *Advances in Multidisciplinary and Scientific Research Journal Publication*, 8(4): 27–34, doi: 10.22624/AIMS/BHI/V8N4P3.

[30] Osadchuk, M. A., A. M. Osadchuk, N. V. Kireeva and M. V. Trushin. Mar. 2020. Legal regulation in digital medicine. *Journal of Advanced Research in Law and Economics*, 11(1): 148, doi: 10.14505//jarle.v11.1(47).18.

[31] Surridge, M., K. Meacham, J. Papay, S. C. Phillips, J. B. Pickering, A. Shafiee and T. Wilkinson. 2019. Modelling compliance threats and security analysis of cross border health data exchange. In *International Conference on Model and Data Engineering* (pp. 180–189). Cham: Springer International Publishing.

[32] Liagkou, V., S. Sakka and C. Stylios. Sep. 2022. Security and privacy vulnerabilities in human activity recognition systems. In *2022 7th South-East Europe Design Automation, Computer Engineering, Computer Networks and Social Media Conference (SEEDA-CECNSM)*, IEEE, pp. 1–6. doi: 10.1109/SEEDA-CECNSM57760.2022.9932957.

[33] Debar, H., R. Beuran and Y. Tan. 2020. A quantitative study of vulnerabilities in the Internet of Medical Things. In *Proceedings of the 6th International Conference on Information Systems Security and Privacy*, SCITEPRESS—Science and Technology Publications, pp. 164–175. doi: 10.5220/0009105801640175.

[34] Badrouchi, F., A. Aymond, M. Haerinia, S. Badrouchi, D. F. Selvaraj, K. Tavakolian, P. Ranganathan and S. Eswaran. 2020. Cybersecurity vulnerabilities in biomedical devices: A hierarchical layered framework. *Internet of Things Use Cases for the Healthcare Industry*, 157–184.

[35] Jammula, M., V. M. Vakamulla and S. K. Kondoju. Jun. 2023. Secure and scalable internet of medical things using ensemble lightweight cryptographic model. In *2023 International Conference on Sustainable Computing and Smart Systems (ICSCSS)*, IEEE, pp. 982–987. doi: 10.1109/ICSCSS57650.2023.10169857.

[36] Robertson, L. and A. Munoz. Mar. 2017. System configuration contributions to vulnerability: Applications to connected personal devices. *IEEE Technology and Society Magazine*, 36(1): 52–57, doi: 10.1109/MTS.2017.2654289.

[37] Rajasekar, V. R. and S. Rajkumar. Jul. 2023. A study on Internet of Things devices vulnerabilities using Shodan. *International Journal of Computing*, pp. 149–158, doi: 10.47839/ijc.22.2.3084.

[38] Nomikos, K., A. Papadimitriou, G. Stergiopoulos, D. Koutras, M. Psarakis and P. Kotzanikolaou. Aug. 2020. On a security-oriented design framework for medical IoT devices: The hardware security perspective. In *2020 23rd Euromicro Conference on Digital System Design (DSD)*, IEEE, pp. 301–308. doi: 10.1109/DSD51259.2020.00056.

[39] Somasundaram, R. and M. Thirugnanam. Nov. 2021. Review of security challenges in healthcare internet of things. *Wireless Networks*, 27(8): 5503–5509, doi: 10.1007/s11276-020-02340-0.

[40] Nissar, G., R. A. Khan, S. Mushtaq, S. A. Lone and A. H. Moon. 2023. A lightweight authentication scheme and security key establishment for internet of medical things, pp. 797–809. doi: 10.1007/978-981-99-1479-1_59.

[41] Rubí, J. N. S. and P. R. de L. Gondim. Jan. 2020. Interoperable internet of medical things platform for E-health applications. *Int. J. Distrib. Sens. Netw.*, 16(1): 155014771988959, doi: 10.1177/1550147719889591.

[42] Mwansa, G. and N. Mabanza. Feb. 2023. Review of Internet of Things security protocols—A bibliometric analysis. In *2023 25th International Conference on Advanced Communication Technology (ICACT)*, IEEE, pp. 394–400. doi: 10.23919/ICACT56868.2023.10079641.

[43] Nyangaresi, V. O. and J. Ma. Jun. 2022. A formally verified message validation protocol for intelligent IoT E-health systems. In *2022 IEEE World Conference on Applied Intelligence and Computing (AIC)*, IEEE, pp. 416–422. doi: 10.1109/AIC55036.2022.9848874.

[44] Md. M. Islam, S. Nooruddin, F. Karray and G. Muhammad. Feb. 2023. Internet of Things: Device capabilities, architectures, protocols, and smart applications in healthcare domain. *IEEE Internet Things J.*, 10(4): 3611–3641, doi: 10.1109/JIOT.2022.3228795.

[45] Cirne, A., P. R. Sousa, J. S. Resende and L. Antunes. May 2022. IoT security certifications: Challenges and potential approaches. *Comput. Secur.*, 116: 102669, doi: 10.1016/j.cose.2022.102669.

[46] Machal, M. L. 2023. An Overview About Connected Medical Devices and their Risks. doi: 10.3233/SHTI230438.

[47] Al-Abadi, A. A. J., M. B. Mohamed and A. Fakhfakh. Jun. 2023. Impact of availability attacks on enabling IoT based healthcare applications. In *2023 International Wireless Communications and Mobile Computing (IWCMC)*, IEEE, pp. 1666–1671. doi: 10.1109/IWCMC58020.2023.10183010.

[48] Jeyavel, J., T. Parameswaran, J. M. Mannan and U. Hariharan. 2021. Security vulnerabilities and intelligent solutions for IoMT systems, pp. 175–194. doi: 10.1007/978-3-030-63937-2_10.

[49] Jegatheswaran, R. A., I. J. Sakira and N. A. A. Rahman. Dec. 2020. A review on IoMT device vulnerabilities and countermeasures. *J. Phys. Conf. Ser.*, 1712(1): 012020, doi: 10.1088/1742-6596/1712/1/012020.

[50] Koutras, D., G. Stergiopoulos, T. Dasaklis, P. Kotzanikolaou, D. Glynos and C. Douligeris. Aug. 2020. Security in IoMT communications: A survey. *Sensors*, 20(17): 4828, doi: 10.3390/s20174828.

[51] Kumar, A. and I. Sharma. May 2023. Enhancing data privacy of IoT healthcare with Keylogger attack mitigation. In *2023 4th International Conference for Emerging Technology (INCET)*, IEEE, pp. 1–6. doi: 10.1109/INCET57972.2023.10170531.

[52] Shree, S., C. Zhou and M. Barati. 2024. Data protection in internet of medical things using blockchain and secret sharing method. *J. Supercomput.*, 80(4): 5108–5135.

[53] Wani, R. U. Z., F. Thabit and O. Can. 2023. Security and Privacy Challenges, Issues, and Enhancing techniques for Internet of Medical Things: A systematic review.

[54] AbdulRaheem, M., J. B. Awotunde, C. Chakraborty, E. A. Adeniyi, I. D. Oladipo and A. K. Bhoi. 2023. Security and privacy concerns in smart healthcare system. In *Implementation of Smart Healthcare Systems using AI, IoT, and Blockchain*, Elsevier, pp. 243–273. doi: 10.1016/B978-0-323-91916-6.00002-3.

[55] Krishnan, D. and S. Singh. 2022. Medical IoT: Opportunities, issues in security and privacy—A comprehensive review. In *Smart and Secure Internet of Healthcare Things*, Boca Raton: CRC Press, pp. 91–112. doi: 10.1201/9781003239895-6.

[56] Hasan, M. K. et al 2021. Lightweight encryption technique to enhance medical image security on Internet of Medical things applications. *IEEE Access*, 9: 47731–47742, doi: 10.1109/ACCESS.2021.3061710.

[57] Kamalov, F., B. Pourghebleh, M. Gheisari, Y. Liu and S. Moussa. Feb. 2023. Internet of Medical Things privacy and security: Challenges, solutions, and future trends from a new perspective. *Sustainability*, 15(4): 3317, doi: 10.3390/su15043317.

[58] Ghubaish, A., T. Salman, M. Zolanvari, D. Unal, A. Al-Ali and R. Jain. Jun. 2021. Recent advances in the Internet-of-Medical-Things (IoMT) systems security. *IEEE Internet Things J.*, 8(11): 8707–8718, doi: 10.1109/JIOT.2020.3045653.

[59] Shree, S., C. Zhou and M. Barati. 2024. Data protection in internet of medical things using blockchain and secret sharing method. *J. Supercomput.*, 80(4): 5108–5135.

[60] Munjal, K. and R. Bhatia. Aug. 2023. A systematic review of homomorphic encryption and its contributions in healthcare industry. *Complex & Intelligent Systems*, 9(4): 3759–3786, doi: 10.1007/s40747-022-00756-z.

[61] Hineman, A. and M. Blaum. Apr. 2022. A modified shamir secret sharing scheme with efficient encoding. *IEEE Communications Letters*, 26(4): 758–762, doi: 10.1109/LCOMM.2022.3144375.

[62] Mohan, P. Feb. 2023. IoT preserving patient-centric models for privacy preserving based personal health records sharing in cloud. In *2023 IEEE International Conference on Integrated Circuits and Communication Systems (ICICACS)*, IEEE, pp. 1–6. doi: 10.1109/ICICACS57338.2023.10100155.

[63] Khatiwada, P. and B. Yang. 2022. An overview on security and privacy of data in IoMT devices: Performance Metrics, Merits, Demerits, and Challenges. doi: 10.3233/SHTI220970.

[64] Gadekallu, T. R., M. Alazab, J. Hemanth and W. Wang. Feb. 2023. Guest editorial federated learning for privacy preservation of healthcare data in internet of medical things and patient monitoring. *IEEE J. Biomed. Health Inform.*, 27(2): 648–651, doi: 10.1109/JBHI.2023.3234604.

[65] Mittal, A. and F. Sidney. Feb. 2023. Privacy preserving based personal health records sharing using Rail Fence Data Encryption (RFDE) for secure cloud environment. In *2023 IEEE International Conference on Integrated Circuits and Communication Systems (ICICACS)*, IEEE, pp. 1–5. doi: 10.1109/ICICACS57338.2023.10099585.

[66] Liu, J., J. Yang, W. Wu, X. Huang and Y. Xiang. May 2023. Lightweight authentication scheme for data dissemination in cloud-assisted healthcare IoT. *IEEE Transactions on Computers*, 72(5): 1384–1395, doi: 10.1109/TC.2022.3207138.

[67] Diop, I. M., C. Cherifi, C. Diallo and H. Cherifi. 2023. Targeted Attacks Based on Networks Component Structure, pp. 62–73. doi: 10.1007/978-3-031-28276-8_6.

[68] Süzen, A. A. Apr. 2023. Cyber attacks for data breach and possible defense strategies in Internet of Healthcare Things ecosystem. *International Journal of 3D Printing Technologies and Digital Industry*, 7(1): 55–63, doi: 10.46519/ij3dptdi.1240743.

[69] Kumar, A. and I. Sharma. May 2023. Augmenting IoT healthcare security and reliability with early detection of IoT botnet attacks. In *2023 4th International Conference for Emerging Technology (INCET)*, IEEE, pp. 1–6. doi: 10.1109/INCET57972.2023.10170738.

[70] Nusairat, T., M. M. Saudi and A. Bin Ahmad. Aug. 2023. A recent assessment for the ransomware attacks against the Internet of Medical Things (IoMT): A review. In *2023 IEEE 13th International Conference on Control System, Computing and Engineering (ICCSCE)*, IEEE, pp. 238–242. doi: 10.1109/ICCSCE58721.2023.10237161.

[71] Garcia-Perez, A., J. G. Cegarra-Navarro, M. P. Sallos, E. Martinez-Caro and A. Chinnaswamy. Mar. 2023. Resilience in healthcare systems: Cyber security and digital transformation. *Technovation*, 121: 102583, doi: 10.1016/j.technovation.2022.102583.

[72] Al-Abadi, A. A. J., M. B. Mohamed and A. Fakhfakh. Dec. 2023. Enhanced Random Forest Classifier with K-Means Clustering (ERF-KMC) for detecting and preventing distributed-denial-of-service and man-in-the-middle attacks in internet-of-medical-things networks. *Computers*, 12(12): 262, doi: 10.3390/computers12120262.

[73] Peddle, B., W. Lu and Q. Yu. 2024. Detecting DDoS Attacks in the Internet of Medical Things Through Machine Learning-Based Classification, pp. 191–203. doi: 10.1007/978-3-031-47126-1_13.

[74] Kim, K., J. Ryu, Y. Lee and D. Won. Jan. 2023. An improved lightweight user authentication scheme for the internet of medical things. *Sensors*, 23(3): 1122, doi: 10.3390/s23031122.

[75] Zubair, M., D. Unal, A. Al-Ali and A. Shikfa. Jul. 2019. Exploiting bluetooth vulnerabilities in e-Health IoT devices. In *Proceedings of the 3rd International Conference on Future Networks and Distributed Systems*, New York, NY, USA: ACM, pp. 1–7. doi: 10.1145/3341325.3342000.

[76] Sowjanya, K., M. Dasgupta and S. Ray. May 2021. Elliptic Curve Cryptography based authentication scheme for Internet of Medical Things. *Journal of Information Security and Applications*, 58: 102761, doi: 10.1016/j.jisa.2021.102761.

[77] Rahman, M. and H. Jahankhani. 2021. Security vulnerabilities in existing security mechanisms for IoMT and potential solutions for mitigating cyber-attacks, pp. 307–334. doi: 10.1007/978-3-030-72120-6_12.

[78] Li, N., M. Xu, Q. Li, J. Liu, S. Bao, Y. Li, J. Li and H. Zheng. 2023. A review of security issues and solutions for precision health in Internet-of-Medical-Things systems. *Security and Safety*, 2: 2022010, doi: 10.1051/sands/2022010.

[79] Verma, H., N. Chauhan and L. K. Awasthi. Nov. 2023. A comprehensive review of 'Internet of Healthcare Things': Networking aspects, technologies, services, applications, challenges, and security concerns. *Comput. Sci. Rev.*, 50: 100591, doi: 10.1016/j.cosrev.2023.100591.

[80] Gaikwad, V. P., J. V. Tembhurne, C. Meshram and C. -C. Lee. Aug. 2021. Provably secure lightweight client authentication scheme with anonymity for TMIS using chaotic hash function. *J. Supercomput.*, 77(8): 8281–8304, doi: 10.1007/s11227-020-03553-y.

[81] Xie, Y., H. Luo, L. Liang and J. Gan. Nov. 2024. A lightweight dual-link accelerated authentication protocol based on NLFSR-XOR APUF. *Microelectronics J.*, 153: 106446, doi: 10.1016/j.mejo.2024.106446.

[82] Ghazal, T. M., N. A. Al-Dmour, T. Mohamed, Z. Chabani, S. Harguem, S. Noamas and N. ALMaazmi. Nov. 2022. E-supply chain issues in internet of medical things. In *2022 14th International Conference on Mathematics, Actuarial Science, Computer Science and Statistics (MACS)* (pp. 1–5). IEEE.

[83] Rawat, R. Nov. 2022. A systematic review of blockchain technology use in E-Supply chain in Internet of Medical Things (IoMT). *International Journal of Computations, Information and Manufacturing (IJCIM)*, 2(2), doi: 10.54489/ijcim.v2i2.119.

[84] Guergov, S. Nov. 2022. Investigating E-Supply chain issues in Internet of Medical Things (IoMT): Evidence from the healthcare. *International Journal of Computations, Information and Manufacturing (IJCIM)*, 2(2), doi: 10.54489/ijcim.v2i2.110.

[85] Qadri, Y. A., Zulqarnain, A. Nauman, A. Musaddiq, E. Garcia-Villegas and S. W. Kim. Aug. 2022. Preparing Wi-Fi 7 for healthcare Internet-of-Things. *Sensors*, 22(16): 6209, doi: 10.3390/s22166209.

[86] Shahid, J., R. Ahmad, A. K. Kiani, T. Ahmad, S. Saeed and A. M. Almuhaideb. Feb. 2022. Data protection and privacy of the Internet of Healthcare Things (IoHTs). *Applied Sciences*, 12(4): 1927, doi: 10.3390/app12041927.

[87] Iqbal, J. D. and N. Biller-Andorno. Sep. 2022. The regulatory gap in digital health and alternative pathways to bridge it. *Health Policy Technol.*, 11(3): 100663, doi: 10.1016/j.hlpt.2022.100663.

[88] Elhoseny, M., N. N. Thilakarathne, M. I. Alghamdi, R. K. Mahendran, A. A. Gardezi, H. Weerasinghe and A. Welhenge. 2021. Security and privacy issues in medical internet of things: Overview, countermeasures, challenges and future directions. *Sustainability*, 13(21): 11645.

[89] Guo, C., H. Ashrafian, S. Ghafur, G. Fontana, C. Gardner and M. Prime. Aug. 2020. Challenges for the evaluation of digital health solutions—A call for innovative evidence generation approaches. *NPJ Digit. Med.*, 3(1): 110, doi: 10.1038/s41746-020-00314-2.

[90] Oliva, A., S. Grassi, G. Vetrugno, R. Rossi, G. Della Morte, V. Pinchi and M. Caputo. 2022. Management of medico-legal risks in digital health era: A scoping review. *Frontiers in Medicine*, 8: 821756.

[91] Amankona, V., A. Asante, M. Opoku, P. Ohemeng-Gyaase, C. Srekumah, A. K. Peprah and P. Amankwa-Danquah. Dec. 2021. Integrating privacy-by-design in e-Health. In *2021 International Conference on Electrical, Computer and Energy Technologies (ICECET)* (pp. 1–7). IEEE.

[92] Winter, J. S. and E. Davidson. Jun. 2022. Harmonizing regulatory regimes for the governance of patient-generated health data. *Telecomm Policy*, 46(5): 102285, doi: 10.1016/j.telpol.2021.102285.

[93] Bhuiyan, M. N., M. M. Rahman, M. M. Billah and D. Saha. Jul. 2021. Internet of Things (IoT): A review of its enabling technologies in healthcare applications, standards protocols, security, and market opportunities. *IEEE Internet Things J.*, 8(13): 10474–10498, doi: 10.1109/JIOT.2021.3062630.

[94] Butpheng, C., K. -H. Yeh and H. Xiong. Jul. 2020. Security and privacy in IoT-cloud-based E-health systems—A comprehensive review. *Symmetry (Basel)*, 12(7): 1191, doi: 10.3390/sym12071191.

[95] Manteghinejad, A. and S. H. Javanmard. Jan. 2021. Challenges and opportunities of digital health in a post-COVID19 world. *Journal of Research in Medical Sciences*, 26(1): 11, doi: 10.4103/jrms.JRMS_1255_20.

[96] Hovenga, E., H. Grain and T. Beale. 2022. Fragmented global standards development organisations. In *Roadmap to Successful Digital Health Ecosystems*, Elsevier, pp. 65–96. doi: 10.1016/B978-0-12-823413-6.00025-2.

[97] Brass, I., L. Tanczer, M. Carr, M. Elsden and J. Blackstock. 2018. Standardising a moving target: The development and evolution of IoT security standards. In *Living in the Internet of Things: Cybersecurity of the IoT—2018*, Institution of Engineering and Technology, pp. 24 (9 pp.)–24 (9 pp.). doi: 10.1049/cp.2018.0024.

[98] Aly, M., F. Khomh, Y. -G. Guéhéneuc, H. Washizaki and S. Yacout. 2018. Is fragmentation a threat to the success of the Internet of Things? *IEEE Internet Things J.*, 6(1): 472–487.

[99] Karunarathne, S. M., N. Saxena and M. K. Khan. Jul. 2021. Security and privacy in IoT smart healthcare. *IEEE Internet Comput.*, 25(4): 37–48, doi: 10.1109/MIC.2021.3051675.

[100] Thilakarathne, N. N., M. K. Kagita and T. R. Gadekallu. 2020. The role of the Internet of Things in health care: A systematic and comprehensive study. *SSRN Electronic Journal*, doi: 10.2139/ssrn.3690815.

[101] Brewer, L. C., K. L. Fortuna, C. Jones, R. Walker, S. N. Hayes, C. A. Patten and L. A. Cooper. 2020. Back to the future: Achieving health equity through health informatics and digital health. *JMIR mHealth and uHealth*, 8(1): e14512.

[102] Sheikh, A., M. Anderson, S. Albala, B. Casadei, B. D. Franklin, M. Richards, D. Taylor, H. Tibble and E. Mossialos. 2021. Health information technology and digital innovation for national learning health and care systems. *The Lancet Digital Health*, 3(6): e383–e396.

[103] Wang, Q., M. Su, M. Zhang and R. Li. Jun. 2021. Integrating digital technologies and public health to fight Covid-19 pandemic: Key technologies, applications, challenges and outlook of digital healthcare. *Int. J. Environ. Res. Public Health*, 18(11): 6053, doi: 10.3390/ijerph18116053.

[104] Trocin, C., P. Mikalef, Z. Papamitsiou and K. Conboy. Dec. 2023. Responsible AI for digital health: A synthesis and a research agenda. *Information Systems Frontiers*, 25(6): 2139–2157, doi: 10.1007/s10796-021-10146-4.

[105] Salim Omambia Matagi and Satoshi Kaneko. Jan. 2023. Challenges and opportunities on data protection and privacy in healthcare. *International Journal of Scientific Research Updates*, 5(1): 023–041, doi: 10.53430/ijsru.2023.5.1.0001.

[106] Surridge, M., K. Meacham, J. Papay, S. C. Phillips, J. B. Pickering, A. Shafiee and T. Wilkinson. Oct. 2019. Modelling compliance threats and security analysis of cross border health data exchange. In *International Conference on Model and Data Engineering* (pp. 180–189). Cham: Springer International Publishing.
[107] Sommer, A., C. Rehbock, C. Vos, C. Borgs, S. Chevalier, S. Doreleijers, M. Gontariuk, S. Hennau, E. Pilot, H. Schröder, L. d. A. Auwermeulen, A. Ghuysen, S. K. Beckers and T. Krafft. 2022. Impacts and lessons learned of the first three COVID-19 waves on cross-border collaboration in the field of emergency medical services and Interhospital transports in the Euregio-Meuse-Rhine: A qualitative review of expert opinions. *Frontiers in Public Health,* 10: 841013.
[108] van der Molen, I. N. and M. J. Commers. Nov. 2013. Unresolved legal questions in cross-border health care in Europe: Liability and data protection. *Public Health,* 127(11): 987–993, doi: 10.1016/j.puhe.2013.08.020.
[109] Andanda, P. and L. Mlotshwa. Oct. 2024. Streamlining the ethical-legal governance of cross-border health data sharing during global health emergencies. *Res Ethics,* 20(4): 812–834, doi: 10.1177/17470161241261907.
[110] Gavrilov, G., E. Vlahu-Gjorgievska and V. Trajkovik. Jun. 2020. Healthcare data warehouse system supporting cross-border interoperability. *Health Informatics J.,* 26(2): 1321–1332, doi: 10.1177/1460458219876793.
[111] Gupta, D. S., N. Mazumdar, A. Nag and J. P. Singh. May, 2023. Secure data authentication and access control protocol for industrial healthcare system. *J. Ambient Intell. Humaniz. Comput.,* 14(5): 4853–4864, doi: 10.1007/s12652-022-04370-2.
[112] Ami, O., Y. Elovici and D. Hendler. Apr. 2018. Ransomware prevention using application authentication-based file access control. *Proceedings of the ACM Symposium on Applied Computing,* pp. 1610–1619, doi: 10.1145/3167132.3167304.
[113] Liu, Y., F. Ju, Q. Zhang, M. Zhang, Z. Ma, M. Li, A. Yang and F. Liu. 2023. Overview of internet of medical things security based on blockchain access control. *Journal of Database Management (JDM),* 34(3): 1–20.
[114] Mahajan, R., S. Chavan, D. A. Ajalkar, B. S. V. and P. A. Khadkikar. Nov. 2023. A secure authentication protocol for healthcare service in IoT with Q-net based secret key generation. *Web Intelligence,* 21(4): 407–433, doi: 10.3233/WEB-220104.
[115] Ahmed, T., S. Samima, M. Zuhair, H. Ghayvat, M. A. Khan and N. Kumar. Apr. 2023. FIMBISAE: A multimodal biometric secured data access framework for Internet of Medical Things ecosystem. *IEEE Internet Things J.,* 10(7): 6259–6270, doi: 10.1109/JIOT.2022.3225518.
[116] Mahajan, R., S. Chavan, D. A. Ajalkar, B. S. V. and P. A. Khadkikar. Nov. 2023. A secure authentication protocol for healthcare service in IoT with Q-net based secret key generation. *Web Intelligence,* 21(4): 407–433, doi: 10.3233/WEB-220104.
[117] Riya, K. S., R. Surendran, C. Andr Tavera Romero and M. Sadish Sendil. 2023. Encryption with user authentication model for Internet of Medical Things environment. *Intelligent Automation & Soft Computing,* 35(1): 507–520, doi: 10.32604/iasc.2023.027779.
[118] Kok, S., A. Abdullah, N. Jhanjhi and M. Supramaniam. Nov. 2019. Prevention of crypto-ransomware using a pre-encryption detection algorithm. *Computers,* 8(4): 79, doi: 10.3390/computers8040079.
[119] K P, B. M., K. S. K and N. Patwari. Apr. 2023. Embedded light-weight cryptography technique to preserve privacy of healthcare wearable IoT device data. In *2023 International Conference on Distributed Computing and Electrical Circuits and Electronics (ICDCECE),* IEEE, pp. 1–6. doi: 10.1109/ICDCECE57866.2023.10151002.
[120] Tsantikidou, K. and N. Sklavos. Jun. 2023. Minimal resource required E-health system with end-to-end authenticated encryption mechanism. In *2023 12th International Conference on Modern Circuits and Systems Technologies (MOCAST),* IEEE, pp. 1–4. doi: 10.1109/MOCAST57943.2023.10176534.

[121] Dhivya, R., M. Kumar S, M. J, V. Thanikaiselvan, H. Mahalingam and R. Amirtharajan. 2023. Secure health data transmission on IOT. In *2023 2nd International Conference on Vision Towards Emerging Trends in Communication and Networking Technologies (ViTECoN)*, IEEE, pp. 1–4. doi: 10.1109/ViTECoN58111.2023.10156896.

[122] Jana, A. and G. Paul. Nov. 2022. Differential fault attack on PHOTON-Beetle. In *Proceedings of the 2022 Workshop on Attacks and Solutions in Hardware Security*, New York, NY, USA: ACM, pp. 25–34. doi: 10.1145/3560834.3563824.

[123] Buchanan, W. J. and L. Maglaras. Jun. 2023. Review of the NIST light-weight cryptography finalists. In *2023 19th International Conference on Distributed Computing in Smart Systems and the Internet of Things (DCOSS-IoT)*, IEEE, pp. 469–474. doi: 10.1109/DCOSS-IoT58021.2023.00079.

[124] Liu, S., L. Xin, X. Lyu and C. Ren. Mar. 2023. Masking-enabled data protection approach for accurate split learning. In *2023 IEEE Wireless Communications and Networking Conference (WCNC)*, IEEE, pp. 1–6. doi: 10.1109/WCNC55385.2023.10118971.

[125] Satra, S., P. K. Sadhu, V. P. Yanambaka and A. Abdelgawad. Apr. 2023. Octopus: A novel approach for health data masking and retrieving using physical unclonable functions and machine learning. *Sensors*, 23(8): 4082, doi: 10.3390/s23084082.

[126] Shirgur, P. and S. Chaurasia. Jan. 2023. Development of secure IoT ecosystems for healthcare. In *2023 3rd International Conference on Intelligent Communication and Computational Techniques (ICCT)*, IEEE, pp. 1–6. doi: 10.1109/ICCT56969.2023.10076119.

[127] Krishna, T. B. M., S. P. Praveen, S. Ahmed and P. N. Srinivasu. May 2023. Software-driven secure framework for mobile healthcare applications in IoMT. *Intelligent Decision Technologies*, 17(2): 377–393, doi: 10.3233/IDT-220132.

[128] Potorochina, K. L. and E. Yu. Nikitina. 2022. Security of IoT applications in health care. *Вестник Пермского университета. Математика. Механика. Информатика*, 4(59): 68–81, doi: 10.17072/1993-0550-2022-4-68-81.

[129] Barapatre, P., Y. Ingolikar, P. Desai, P. Jajoo and P. Thakre. Dec. 2022. A secured architecture for IoT-based healthcare system. *3C Empresa. Investigación y pensamiento crítico*, 11(02): 222–230, doi: 10.17993/3cemp.2022.110250.222-230.

[130] Silvestri, S., S. Islam, S. Papastergiou, C. Tzagkarakis and M. Ciampi. Jan. 2023. A machine learning approach for the NLP-based analysis of cyber threats and vulnerabilities of the healthcare ecosystem. *Sensors*, 23(2): 651, doi: 10.3390/s23020651.

[131] Alzahrani, F. A., M. Ahmad and M. T. J. Ansari. Aug. 2022. Towards design and development of security assessment framework for Internet of Medical Things. *Applied Sciences*, 12(16): 8148, doi: 10.3390/app12168148.

[132] Al Ali, A., O. Al-Blooshi, R. Al Ali and H. Al Hamadi. Jun. 2024. Securing the Internet of Things (IoT) application: Best practices and challenges in IoT software. In *2024 Advances in Science and Engineering Technology International Conferences (ASET)*, IEEE, pp. 1–7. doi: 10.1109/ASET60340.2024.10708648.

[133] Natarajan, R., G. H. Lokesh, F. Flammini, A. Premkumar, V. K. Venkatesan and S. K. Gupta. Feb. 2023. A novel framework on security and energy enhancement based on Internet of Medical Things for healthcare 5.0. *Infrastructures (Basel)*, 8(2): 22, doi: 10.3390/infrastructures8020022.

[134] Balasamy, K., N. Krishnaraj, J. Ramprasath and P. Ramprakash. 2022. A secure framework for protecting clinical data in medical IoT environment. In *Smart Healthcare System Design*, Wiley, pp. 203–234. doi: 10.1002/9781119792253.ch9.

[135] Gaba, G. S., M. Hedabou, P. Kumar, A. Braeken, M. Liyanage and M. Alazab. May 2022. Zero knowledge proofs based authenticated key agreement protocol for sustainable healthcare. *Sustain Cities Soc.*, 80: 103766, doi: 10.1016/j.scs.2022.103766.

[136] Kakvi, S. A., K. M. Martin, C. Putman and E. A. Quaglia. 2023. SoK: Anonymous Credentials, pp. 129–151. doi: 10.1007/978-3-031-30731-7_6.

[137] Junior, A. S. C. and C. H. Arima. Jan. 2023. Threat modeling: A study on its application in digital transformation from the perspective of risk. *Revista de Gestão e Secretariado*, 14(1): 1158–1169, doi: 10.7769/gesec.v14i1.1581.

[138] Tomashchuk, O. Oct. 2020. Threat and risk management framework for eHealth IoT applications. In *Proceedings of the 24th ACM International Systems and Software Product Line Conference - Volume B*, New York, NY, USA: ACM, pp. 120–126. doi: 10.1145/3382026.3431250.

[139] Salih, F. I., N. A. Abu Bakar, N. H. Hassan, F. Yahya, N. Kama and J. Shah. Dec. 2019. IoT security risk management model for healthcare industry. *Malaysian Journal of Computer Science*, pp. 131–144, doi: 10.22452/mjcs.sp2019no3.9.

[140] Yeng, P. K. S. D. and B. Yang. 2020. Comparative analysis of threat modeling methods for cloud computing towards healthcare security practice. *International Journal of Advanced Computer Science and Applications*, 11(11), doi: 10.14569/IJACSA.2020.0111194.

[141] Kwarteng, E. and M. Cebe. Jun. 2024. MEDICALHARM: A threat modeling designed for modern medical devices and a comprehensive study on effectiveness, user satisfaction, and security perspectives. *Int. J. Inf. Secur.*, 23(3): 2225–2268, doi: 10.1007/s10207-024-00826-y.

[142] Kandasamy, K., S. Srinivas, K. Achuthan and V. P. Rangan. Dec. 2020. IoT cyber risk: A holistic analysis of cyber risk assessment frameworks, risk vectors, and risk ranking process. *EURASIP J. Inf. Secur.*, 2020(1): 8, doi: 10.1186/s13635-020-00111-0.

[143] Salami, A. A., U. T. I. Igwenagu, C. E. Mesode, O. O. Olaniyi and O. B. Oladoyinbo. Apr. 2024. Beyond conventional threat defense: Implementing advanced threat modeling techniques, risk modeling frameworks and contingency planning in the healthcare sector for enhanced data security. *Journal of Engineering Research and Reports*, 26(5): 304–323, doi: 10.9734/jerr/2024/v26i51156.

[144] Saurabh, K., D. Gajjala, K. Kaipa, R. Vyas, O. P. Vyas and R. Khondoker. Sep. 2024. TMAP: A Threat Modeling and Attack Path analysis framework for industrial IoT systems (A case study of IoM and IoP. *Arab. J. Sci. Eng.*, 49(9): 13163–13183, doi: 10.1007/s13369-023-08600-3.

[145] Christogianni, A. 2024. The Benefits of Continuous Health Data Monitoring in Cardiovascular Diseases and Dementia, pp. 1–22. doi: 10.4018/978-1-6684-7366-5.ch014.

[146] Gilbert, S., A. Pimenta, A. Stratton-Powell, C. Welzel and T. Melvin. Sep. 2023. Continuous improvement of digital health applications linked to real-world performance monitoring: Safe moving targets? *Mayo Clinic Proceedings: Digital Health*, 1(3): 276–287, doi: 10.1016/j.mcpdig.2023.05.010.

[147] Adaros-Boye, C., P. Kearney and M. Josephs. 2020. Continuous Risk Management for Industrial IoT: A Methodological View, pp. 34–49. doi: 10.1007/978-3-030-41568-6_3.

[148] Kott, A. and C. Arnold. Jan. 2013. The promises and challenges of continuous monitoring and risk scoring. *IEEE Secur. Priv.*, 11(1): 90–93, doi: 10.1109/MSP.2013.19.

[149] Caballero, M., D. Kavallieros, A. Spyros, A. Tavernarakisv, A. Tziouvaras, S. Bonacina, K. Chandrarmouli, M. Coroiu, L. Chen, T. Dounia, I. Giannoulakis, N. Gligoric, E. Kafetzakis, T. Kasig, V. Koumaras, T. Krousarlis, K. Lapidaki, A. Markakis, S. Marin, M. Manulis, S. Menesidou, S. Nifakos, L. Meng, S. Mhiri, M. Nati, K. Ntafloukas, D. Oniga, D. Papamartzivanos, S. Papastergiou, K. Sanchez, C. Sakkas, K. Stelliou, L. Trujillo, T. Tsikrika, E. Venegas, S. Vrochidis and D. Xydias. 2022. ICT in Healthcare: The role of IoT and the SECANT solution. In *2022 IEEE International Conference on Cyber Security and Resilience (CSR), IEEE*, pp. 104–111.

[150] Chakraborty, C., S. M. Nagarajan, G. G. Devarajan, T. V. Ramana and R. Mohanty. May 2023. Intelligent AI-based healthcare cyber security system using multi-source transfer learning method. *ACM Trans. Sens. Netw.*, doi: 10.1145/3597210.

[151] Al-Hawawreh, M., N. Moustafa and J. Slay. Jan. 2024. A threat intelligence framework for protecting smart satellite-based healthcare networks. *Neural Comput. Appl.*, 36(1): 15–35, doi: 10.1007/s00521-021-06441-5.

[152] Wagner, T. D., K. Mahbub, E. Palomar and A. E. Abdallah. Nov. 2019. Cyber threat intelligence sharing: Survey and research directions. *Comput. Secur.*, 87: 101589, doi: 10.1016/j.cose.2019.101589.

[153] Sarker, I. H., A. I. Khan, Y. B. Abushark and F. Alsolami. Feb. 2023. Internet of Things (IoT) security intelligence: A comprehensive overview, machine learning solutions and research directions. *Mobile Networks and Applications*, 28(1): 296–312, doi: 10.1007/s11036-022-01937-3.

[154] Jesus, V., B. Bains and V. Chang. 2024. Sharing is caring: Hurdles and prospects of open, crowd-sourced cyber threat intelligence. *IEEE Trans. Eng. Manag.*, 71: 6854–6873, doi: 10.1109/TEM.2023.3279274.

[155] Jin, B., E. Kim, H. Lee, E. Bertino, D. Kim and H. Kim. 2024. Sharing cyber threat intelligence: Does it really help? In *Proceedings 2024 Network and Distributed System Security Symposium*, Reston, VA: Internet Society. doi: 10.14722/ndss.2024.24228.

[156] Mabodi, K., M. Yusefi, S. Zandiyan, L. Irankhah and R. Fotohi. Sep. 2020. Multi-level trust-based intelligence schema for securing of internet of things (IoT) against security threats using cryptographic authentication. *J. Supercomput.*, 76(9): 7081–7106, doi: 10.1007/s11227-019-03137-5.

[157] Hasan, M. K., T. M. Ghazal, R. A. Saeed, B. Pandey, H. Gohel, A. A. Eshmawi, S. Abdel-Khalek and H. M. Alkhassawneh. 2022. A review on security threats, vulnerabilities, and counter measures of 5G enabled Internet-of-Medical-Things. *IET Communications*, 16(5): 421–432.

[158] Gutfleisch, M., M. Schöps, J. Hielscher, M. Cheney, S. Sayin, N. Schuhmacher, M. Ali and M. A. Sasse. Sep. 2022. Caring about iot-security–An interview study in the healthcare sector. In *Proceedings of the 2022 European Symposium on Usable Security*, pp. 202–215.

[159] Ksibi, S., F. Jaidi and A. Bouhoula. Jun. 2023. IoMT security model based on machine learning and risk assessment techniques. In *2023 International Wireless Communications and Mobile Computing (IWCMC)*, IEEE, pp. 614–619. doi: 10.1109/IWCMC58020.2023.10182654.

[160] Ramzan, T. and S. Zafar. Dec. 2022. Blockchain-based security for Internet of Medical Things Application. In *2022 International Conference on Cyber Warfare and Security (ICCWS)*, IEEE, pp. 69–74. doi: 10.1109/ICCWS56285.2022.9998443.

[161] Zuo, Z., M. Watson, D. Budgen, R. Hall, C. Kennelly and N. Al Moubayed. Oct. 2021. Data anonymization for pervasive health care: Systematic literature mapping study. *JMIR Med. Inform.*, 9(10): e29871, doi: 10.2196/29871.

[162] Kwok, C. S., E. -A. Muntean, C. D. Mallen and J. A. Borovac. Oct. 2022. Data collection theory in healthcare research: The minimum dataset in quantitative studies. *Clin. Pract.*, 12(6): 832–844, doi: 10.3390/clinpract12060088.

[163] Akkaya, F. D. 2023. HES: A case study on cybersecurity and privacy risks in health surveillance systems. *In*: Adedoyin, F. F. and B. Christiansen (eds.). *Effective Cybersecurity Operations for Enterprise-Wide Systems*, IGI Global, pp. 123–146. doi: 10.4018/978-1-6684-9018-1.ch006.

[164] Kayes, A. S. M., M. Hammoudeh, S. Badsha, P. A. Watters, A. Ng, F. Mohammed and M. Islam. Feb. 2020. Responsibility attribution against data breaches. In *2020 IEEE International Conference on Informatics, IoT, and Enabling Technologies (ICIoT)* (pp. 498–503). IEEE.

[165] Kan, E. May 2024. Empowering patients through transparent access to personal health data. *International Journal of Law and Policy*, 2(5): 37–41, doi: 10.59022/ijlp.188.

[166] Goel, P. K. 2024. Ethical Considerations in Implementing Artificial Intelligence in Cybersecurity, pp. 72–91. doi: 10.4018/979-8-3693-6517-5.ch005.

[167] Wambua, R. N. Jul. 2024. A systematic literature review of digital health strategies for equitable access to universal health coverage in developing countries. *Journal of Science, Innovation and Creativity*, 3(1): 11–21, doi: 10.58721/jsic.v3i1.647.

[168] Idoko, B., J. A. Alakwe, O. J. Ugwu, J. E. Idoko, F. O. Idoko, V. B. Ayoola, E. V. Ejembi and T. Adeyinka. 2024. Enhancing healthcare data privacy and security: A comparative study of regulations and best practices in the US and Nigeria. *Magna Scientia Advanced Research and Reviews*, 11(02): 151–167.

[169] Lorenzini, G., D. M. Shaw and B. S. Elger. Dec. 2022. It takes a pirate to know one: Ethical hackers for healthcare cybersecurity. *BMC Med Ethics*, 23(1): 131, doi: 10.1186/s12910-022-00872-y.

[170] He, Y., E. Zamani, I. Yevseyeva and C. Luo. Apr. 2023. Artificial intelligence–based ethical hacking for health information systems: Simulation study. *J. Med. Internet Res.*, 25: e41748, doi: 10.2196/41748.

[171] Pyrrho, M., L. Cambraia and V. F. de Vasconcelos. Jul. 2022. Privacy and health practices in the digital age. *The American Journal of Bioethics*, 22(7): 50–59, doi: 10.1080/15265161.2022.2040648.

[172] Smys, S. and J. S. Raj. Feb. 2022. Future challenges of the Internet of Things in the health care domain—An overview. *Journal of Trends in Computer Science and Smart Technology*, 3(4): 274–286, doi: 10.36548/jtcsst.2021.4.003.

[173] Shafi, M. and R. Kumar Jha. 2022. Recent security issues and countermeasures on IoHT. In *Smart and Secure Internet of Healthcare Things*, Boca Raton: CRC Press, pp. 127–136. doi: 10.1201/9781003239895-8.

[174] Bahalul Haque, A. K. M., B. Bhushan, A. Nawar, K. R. Talha and S. J. Ayesha. 2022. Attacks and Countermeasures in IoT Based Smart Healthcare Applications, pp. 67–90. doi: 10.1007/978-3-030-90119-6_6.

[175] Bhushan, B., A. Kumar, A. K. Agarwal, A. Kumar, P. Bhattacharya and A. Kumar. Apr. 2023. Towards a secure and sustainable Internet of Medical Things (IoMT): Requirements, design challenges, security techniques, and future trends. *Sustainability*, 15(7): 6177, doi: 10.3390/su15076177.

[176] Alkatheiri, M. S. and A. S. Alghamdi. Apr. 2023. Blockchain-assisted cybersecurity for the Internet of Medical Things in the healthcare industry. *Electronics (Basel)*, 12(8): 1801, doi: 10.3390/electronics12081801.

[177] Villegas-Ch, W., J. García-Ortiz and I. Urbina-Camacho. May 2023. Framework for a secure and sustainable internet of medical things, requirements, design challenges, and future trends. *Applied Sciences*, 13(11): 6634, doi: 10.3390/app13116634.

[178] Aldhyani, T. H. H., M. A. Khan, M. A. Almaiah, N. Alnazzawi, A. K. A. Hwaitat, A. Elhag, R. T. Shehab and A. S. Alshebami. 2023. A secure internet of medical things framework for breast cancer detection in sustainable smart cities. *Electronics*, 12(4): 858.

[179] Badawy, M. Jan. 2023. Sustainable secure Internet of Things (SS-IoT). In *2023 1st International Conference on Advanced Innovations in Smart Cities (ICAISC)*, IEEE, pp. 1–6. doi: 10.1109/ICAISC56366.2023.10085280.

[180] Maina,A. M. and U. G. Singh. Sep. 2022. Rebuilding stakeholder confidence in health-relevant big data applications: A social representations perspective. *Information*, 13(9): 441, doi: 10.3390/info13090441.

[181] Landers, C., E. Vayena, J. Amann and A. Blasimme. Feb. 2023. Stuck in translation: Stakeholder perspectives on impediments to responsible digital health. *Front. Digit. Health*, 5, doi: 10.3389/fdgth.2023.1069410.

[182] Iakovleva, T., E. Oftedal and J. Bessant. 2021. Changing role of users—innovating responsibly in digital health. *Sustainability*, 13(4): 1616.

[183] Nipa, N. S., M. Alam and M. S. Haque. 2021. Identifying Relevant Stakeholders in Digital Healthcare, pp. 349–357. doi: 10.1007/978-3-030-82269-9_27.

Chapter 12

Artificial Intelligence, Privacy, Governance, and Ethics for the Internet of Healthcare Things

Md. Hasanul Ferdaus,[1,*] *Fares Alharbi,*[2] *Mohammad Rifat Ahmmad Rashid,*[1] *Md. Mostofa Kamal Rasel,*[1] *Taskeed Jabid,*[1] *Md. Sawkat Ali,*[1] *Mohammad Manzurul Islam,*[1] *Maheen Islam*[1] and *Rajkumar Buyya*[3]

1. Introduction

The Internet of Health Things (IoHT) is a subset of the broader technological revolution termed the Internet of Things (IoT). It has brought forth a crucial evolution in healthcare technology. The IoHT technologies are transforming the landscape of medical services, including patient care, healthcare operations, and medical data management, by combining physical and digital components within medical environments [1]. Advanced technologies such as smart sensors, complex data analytics,

[1] Department of Computer Science and Engineering, East West University, Dhaka, Bangladesh.
[2] Department of Computer Science, College of Computing and IT, Shaqra University, Shaqra, Saudi Arabia.
[3] School of Computing and Information Systems, The University of Melbourne, Melbourne, Australia.
Emails: faalhrbi@su.edu.sa, rifat.rashid@ewubd.edu, mostofa.kamal@ewubd.edu, taskeed@ewubd.edu, alim@ewubd.edu, mohammad.islam@ewubd.edu, maheen@ewubd.edu, rbuyya@unimelb.edu.au
* Corresponding author: hasanul.ferdaus@ewubd.edu

DOI: 10.1201/9781003483267-16

efficient machine learning and deep learning algorithms, cloud computing, and networking infrastructures have been integrated to form the IoHT ecosystem that fosters remote and real-time health monitoring, enhances medical outcomes, and improves the efficiency of healthcare services significantly.

1.1 Evolution of IoHT Technologies

IoHT technologies have undergone rapid development within the last two decades. While at the initial stage, IoHT focused primarily on simple health data collection and patient condition monitoring technologies, recent improvements of IoHT expanded the scope profoundly including online patient diagnostics, advanced predictive analytics, and advice on personalized medicine. Modern sophisticated developments such as wearable medical devices and smart hospital beds have enabled healthcare professionals to access critical health information in real time, as well as increased patient engagement and comfort. Innovations in smart sensor developments, wireless communications, artificial intelligence (AI), and cloud technologies continue to drive further the evolution of IoHT technologies as delineated in research studies [2] and [3].

1.2 Importance of Cybersecurity

Cybersecurity has appeared as a great concern for IoHT given the rapid and comprehensive expansion of the IoHT technologies. The various components and devices of the IoHT ecosystem are highly interconnected which can expose them to a wide range of cyber threats, from data breaches and malware to phishing attacks and ransomware attacks [4]. As a consequence, protecting sensitive health information holds paramount significance and calls for the implementation of robust security measures. Confidential patient information can be effectively safeguarded by employing robust encryption techniques, secure device authentication, and regular software updates. Confidentiality and integrity of sensitive health information can be ensured through ongoing vigilance and effective response to emerging security threats, as duly emphasized by the researchers in [5].

1.3 Regulatory Frameworks

Regulatory bodies and frameworks play a crucial role in shaping the development, implementation, application, and scope of the IoHT technologies. Safety and confidentiality of healthcare devices are primarily guaranteed by the guidelines from the regulatory frameworks, which ultimately protect individuals and their information in the IoHT ecosystem. Examples of such frameworks include the General Data Protection Regulation (GDPR) effective within the territories of the European Union and the Health Insurance Portability and Accountability Act (HIPAA) within the United States which offer regulations for data confidentiality and protection within the healthcare sector [2]. Such authoritative bodies continue to evolve in response to the transformations and associated challenges posed by the IoHT ecosystem balancing the overall patient welfare and confidentiality and privacy of health data [3].

2. The Convergence of AI and IoHT

The convergence of AI and the Internet of Healthcare Things (IoHT) has made a revolutionary transformation in the healthcare services area as they help achieve extraordinary innovations and improve both the efficiency and quality of the healthcare sector. Healthcare providers can now provide higher levels of tailored and proactive treatments by leveraging AI's sophisticated data-processing capabilities in parallel with the connectivity of smart IoHT devices. Such integration of technologies expedites clinical operations and boosts patient care with the help of continuous monitoring facilities and predictive intelligence. With the continuous development of AI and IoHT, they have emerged as extremely effective tools to address critical healthcare challenges collectively, such as controlling chronic diseases and maximizing resource allocation [6]. Notwithstanding the obvious benefits, such technological convergence also introduces potential challenges in interoperability, security, and ethical issues that must be addressed appropriately to leverage the utmost potential of these technologies in improving patient experience and operational performance. Figure 1 illustrates the integration of AI with the IoHT.

2.1 AI-driven Healthcare Transformation

In the field of healthcare, the integration of AI and IoHT devices transforms patient care by improving accuracy in medical diagnosis, personalizing treatment, and enhancing patient outcomes. This AI-driven transformation is extremely crucial for the transformation from traditional reactive medical practices to proactive healthcare management.

2.1.1 Securing AI Models and Data

Implementing robust cybersecurity measures is paramount to securing the AI models and the vast amounts of data they process so that data breaches can be prevented effectively and patient privacy can be guaranteed [7]. This can be achieved through the utilization of encryption of data

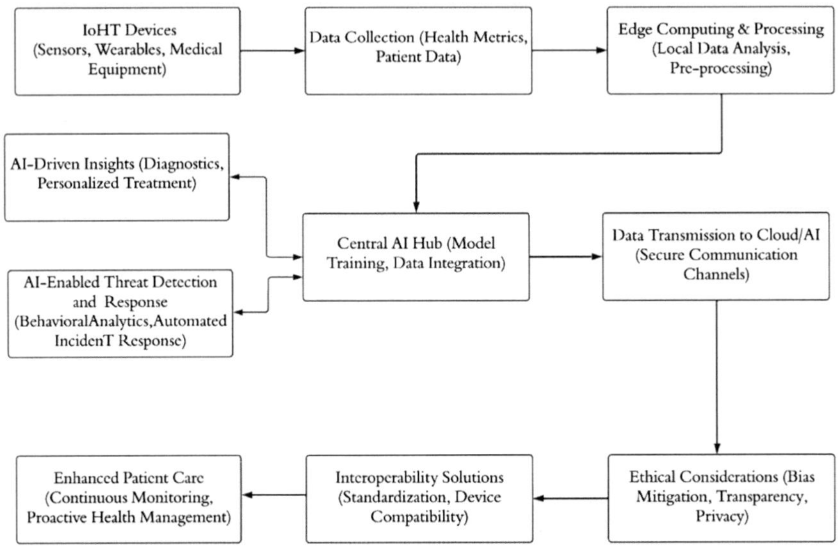

Figure 1: The convergence of AI and IoHT.

transfers, secure storage practices, and regular security audits that would help identify and mitigate potential vulnerabilities.

2.1.2 Ethical Considerations

The ethical repercussions of the use of AI in patient care are extremely crucial including concerns such as bias in AI algorithms, the transparency of decisions generated by AI tools, and the possibility of patient privacy violations [8]. In this context, appropriate guidelines and standards for the ethical use of AI must be formulated to ensure integrity and maintain trust in the overall healthcare system.

2.1.3 Interoperability Issues

Due to the use of different types of sensors and components and their applications, as well as different sources for data and data formats, interoperability issues among the various IoHT devices and healthcare systems continue to pose significant challenges that hamper the seamless integration of AI applications. Standardization of data formats, improved device compatibility, and enhanced collaborations among technology providers can play significant roles in alleviating interoperability and portability issues and ensuring cohesive healthcare ecosystems [9].

2.2 *AI-enabled Threat Detection and Response*

AI enhances the capabilities of IoHT by providing advanced tools for real-time threat detection and response, thus safeguarding healthcare networks from various cyber threats and ensuring continuous patient care.

2.2.1 Behavioral Analytics

Anomalous behaviors that may indicate potential security threats can be detected by AI-driven behavioral analytics that effectively utilize pattern recognition and machine learning. AI-enabled tools can be used for analyzing typical user interactions with IoHT devices and can effectively identify deviations suggesting unauthorized access or malicious activities [10].

2.2.2 Automated Incident Response

With the help of AI tools, the present-day automated incident response systems can rapidly respond to any identified cyber threats reduce the overall damage, and contain security breaches more effectively. Such response systems are capable of initiating appropriate protocols spontaneously, such as isolating affected devices and notifying security personnel of the incidents. This helps the management by reducing the reliance on manual intervention and accelerating response times [11].

3. Privacy-Preserving Data Analytics

The advancement of privacy-preserving data analytics is now a requirement due to the proliferation of data-driven decision-making. This domain ensures the protection and security of confidential data and the extraction of valuable insights from the dataset at the same time. Table 1 provides a summary of the privacy-preserving techniques in Privacy-Preserving Data Analytics and highlights the key methods.

3.1 *Anonymization Approaches*

Anonymization is a technique that is used to safeguard from personal identification as individuals, while simultaneously maintaining integrity of data for analytical purposes. Several methods can be applied to achieve this goal:

3.1.1 Data Masking

Data masking is the process that obscures particular data elements within a database to guarantee that personal data items are incomprehensible. With this approach, data masking minimizes the possibility of data breaches [11]. Sensitive data, such as personal health information, credit

Table 1: Summary of privacy-preserving data analytics techniques.

Areas	Method	Description	Reference
Anonymization Approaches	Data Masking	Obscures specific data elements within a database to make personal data incomprehensible.	[11]
	Pseudonymization	Replaces identifying fields with artificial identifiers, making reversal possible under certain conditions.	[11]
	Generalization	Reduces precision of data (e.g., replacing exact age with age range) to protect identities.	[12]
	Differential Privacy	Adds randomness to data so that the inclusion/exclusion of a single item does not significantly affect query outcomes.	[13]
Multi-Party Computation Security	Secure Protocols	Uses cryptographic techniques like secret sharing and zero-knowledge proofs to protect data during computation.	[14]
	Garbled Circuits	A secure two-party computation method where one party creates a "garbled" circuit and the other evaluates it with encrypted inputs.	[15]
	Oblivious Transfer	Ensures a sender transfers one piece of information to a receiver without knowing which piece was transferred.	[16]

card information, and social security numbers, are usually protected using data masking techniques.

3.1.2 Pseudonymization

Pseudonymization is another technique that substitutes identifying fields within a data record having one or more artificial identifiers or pseudonyms, thus minimizing the probability of the dataset with the original identity of individuals [11]. However, within certain conditions, the pseudonymization process can be reversed which is unlike anonymization.

3.1.3 Generalization

Generalization is an approach that reduces the precision for a range of data that facilitates individuals' identity protection while enabling data analysis on broader trends. Examples of such generalization techniques could be replacing precise attributes such as zip code or exact age with larger categories such as age groups or the first few digits of zip codes [12].

3.1.4 Differential Privacy

Differential privacy injects randomness into the data in such a way that the results of queries do not affect significantly if a single database item in included or excluded [13]. This approach ensures strong privacy and it is extremely effective in statistical databases in particular where aggregate data are shared.

3.2 Multi-Party Computation Security

Multi-party computation (MPC) is a process where several entities can compute a function using their inputs in a collaborative fashion where it is guaranteed that the inputs remain confidential. In scenarios where sharing raw data is not practical due to concerns over data privacy or business competition, MPC has proved to be an effective solution for privacy-preserving data analytics.

3.2.1 Secure Protocols

These protocols utilize cryptographic methods such as secret sharing, zero-knowledge proofs, and homomorphic encryption to verify the correctness of computation outputs without revealing any additional information. Such protocols make use of cryptographic techniques and algorithms such as zero-knowledge proofs, secret sharing, and homomorphic encryption so that the computation outputs are correct without revealing any further information [14].

3.2.2 Garbled Circuits

Another technique used to secure two-party computation is the Garbled circuit. In this approach, one party creates a "garbled" version of a circuit, and the other party assesses the circuit using encrypted inputs. It guarantees that the assessor learns nothing except the outcome [15].

3.2.3 Oblivious Transfer

One of the fundamental protocols in MPC is the Oblivious Transfer. It allows a sender to transfer one of potentially many pieces of information to a receiver; however, the sender stays unaware of the exact piece that was transferred. For many different MPC protocols, the Oblivious Transfer is a crucial component, particularly in the execution of garbled circuits [16].

3.2.4 Implementation Challenges

There are several hurdles in the effective implementation of MPC in the context of practical scenarios such as computational overheads, intricacies of protocol design, and network latency. Authors in [15] have presented several recent advancements in this field that aim at optimizing these aspects to make MPC viable for real-world use cases.

4. Threat Landscape and Vulnerability Assessment

4.1 Understanding IoHT Cyber Threats

The IoHT utilizes a diverse array of medical devices and applications that connect to healthcare networks and offer critical data and functionalities. As a consequence, IoHT-enabled healthcare systems are exposed to various cyber threats. To understand these potential threats, it is very important to identify and analyze potential vulnerabilities in IoHT devices such as medical wearables, implanted medical devices, and even hospital infrastructure systems, that cybercriminals may exploit [17]. The most common types of threats in healthcare are data breaches that compromise patient confidentiality, ransomware attacks that block access to critical systems, and DoS and DDoS attacks that disrupt service availability [18]. The heterogeneity and complexity of IoHT devices, as well as their integration with legacy systems extend the cyberattack surface making it crucial to identify and understand these threats thoroughly.

4.2 Vulnerability Assessment Techniques

For the purpose of vulnerability assessment in IoHT, security weaknesses are identified in systematic methods across the network of connected medical devices. Such techniques include the following:

- **Automated Scanning Tools:** These tools are used to scan systems and networks in an automated way to identify common and known security vulnerabilities. Such automated scanning tools are quite helpful in providing insights into potential security gaps within the infrastructure [19].
- **Penetration Testing:** Simulated cyberattacks are carried out to understand how an intruder could gain unauthorized access to the IoHT systems and networks [20].
- **Risk Analysis:** In this approach, the potential impacts and likelihood of threats are evaluated. Through such analysis, security experts can prioritize the vulnerabilities based on their impact and potential to cause harm [20].
- **Compliance Audits:** Regular audits are conducted to ensure that IoHT practices align with industry standards and regulations, such as the HIPAA in the U.S. These audits are helpful in detecting non-compliance issues and the associated vulnerabilities [21].

4.3 Continuous Monitoring and Incident Response

Continuous monitoring of IoHT systems is an extremely effective technique for early detection of unusual activities that could signal a potential cyberattack. Sophisticated monitoring tools can be implemented and rolled out to capture and analyze data relating to application activity and network traffic with the objective of detecting anomalies and potential threats. Moreover, incident response mechanisms are equally important and must incorporate a planned approach for managing and recovering the services after any security incidents take place [22]. The following are the steps needed for proper incident response:

- **Incident Detection:** Modern and advanced threat detection systems must be utilized for comprehensive security.
- **Response Procedures:** Appropriate and standard response protocols must be established within the organization to contain and mitigate the impacts of cyberattacks.
- **Recovery Plans:** Proper recovery strategies must be devised well ahead for restoring information systems after any incident happens. This involves the elimination of any malicious threats, such as malware and ransomware, and strengthening the network against potential future attacks [23].
- **Post-Incident Analysis:** This involves reviewing and learning from any incident that took place within the infrastructure so that future security measures of the systems and networks can be improved.

4.4 User Awareness and Training

Human users are one of the most critical vulnerabilities in any security system. Regular training sessions and boosting user awareness of cybersecurity are essential parts of a comprehensive IoHT security strategy [24]. Such training sessions must cover the following aspects [25]:

- **Recognizing Phishing Attacks:** Users must be educated and trained regularly so that they can identify and avoid any potential phishing attempts, such as via phishing emails or phone calls, that could cause any unauthorized access to sensitive data and systems.
- **Secure Usage Practices:** Users must be trained on the appropriate use of IoHT devices. They should be educated on the significance of effective password management and maintaining regular updates.
- **Response to Suspected Security Breaches:** Proper measures should be taken to educate users on the instructions that they must follow in case they suspect a security breach.

5. Ethical Considerations in Cybersecurity for IoHT

Complex ethical challenges are arising due to the integration of the IoHT into medical practices. These ethical considerations must be addressed to safeguard patient rights and maintain trust in healthcare technologies [26]. In this section, key ethical issues concerning patient consent and data ownership, and the delicate balance between securing health information and ensuring its accessibility are delineated.

5.1 *Patient Consent and Data Ownership*

In the realm of healthcare and data privacy legislation, a fundamental principle is patient consent. In the specific domain of the IoHT, this consent involves providing informed consent by the patients. Healthcare service providers are supposed to provide their patients with clear and comprehensive information in regard to the acquisition, dissemination, utilization, and retention of their health-related data. Often patients face challenges in understanding the complex technical details and the potential extent of data utilization, in many cases due to the opaque nature of certain IoHT systems, which creates ethical dilemmas [27]. Therefore, it is imperative for the IoHT ecosystems to have provisions for upholding patient autonomy such that they ensure that patients' consent is fully informed and revocable under specific conditions.

The data ownership issues in the IoHT raise several concerns relating to the patient's rights. In particular, this raises questions about who has the right to access, control, and benefit from health data. Data custodians or controllers are defined as the appropriate data owners on the basis of the legal frameworks. However, when ethical considerations indicate that patients should have at least partial ownership of their data [28], such a shared ownership model helps patients to benefit from the use of their data. Furthermore, it also empowers patients to have opinions on its secondary uses, for example, in research or the development of new medical technologies [29, 30].

5.2 *Balancing Security and Accessibility*

In the domain of IoHT, there are significant ethical challenges in balancing the dual requirements of strong security and broad accessibility of health-related data [31]. On one hand, robust cybersecurity mechanisms must be enforced to protect sensitive health information from breaches so that privacy violations and potential harm can be minimized. On the other hand, it should be maintained that implementation of these security measures must not excessively limit access to health data, particularly in cases where access is vital for emergency services and standard patient care [32].

6. Regulatory Landscape and Compliance

The incorporation of the IoHT into the healthcare sector has brought forth numerous technological innovations. However, there are significant regulatory implications that arise with the use of technologies within the healthcare sector [33]. The remaining parts of this section explore key aspects of compliance with existing regulations such as HIPAA and GDPR, the need for international standards and harmonization, as well as the emerging regulatory trends.

6.1 HIPAA and GDPR Compliance

The Health Insurance Portability and Accountability Act, commonly known as HIPAA, is a regulation primarily applicable within the United States. It sets a standard for protecting sensitive patient information. According to HIPAA, every organization that handles protected health information (PHI) is obligated to ensure that all necessary physical, network, and procedural security measures are established and followed. As IoHT technologies are being integrated into the healthcare sector, this obligation is extending to the devices that collect, store, or transmit PHI [34]. Unlike HIPAA, the General Data Protection Regulation, commonly known as GDPR, addresses every organization that manages any personal information of individuals within the European Union. Its primary focus areas are on the consent and rights of the data subjects, as well as the regulation of cross-border data transfers. Moreover, factors that can affect the deployment and management of IoHT devices, such as data minimization and restriction of data usage for specific purposes, are also covered within GDPR [35]. To comply with these regulations, organizations handling PHI need to conduct periodic risk assessments, employ necessary technological protections, and establish transparent communication with patients about their data rights and their use.

6.2 Emerging Regulatory Trends

The regulatory landscape is continuously evolving with the advancement of technologies. Increasing data privacy, improvement of security measures, and expansion of the definition of health data are among the principal emerging trends in regulation transformation. For instance, if some non-traditional data are collected from wearable devices and used for making health-related decisions, it may be put under regulatory scrutiny [36]. Moreover, regulators are paying more attention to the security of interconnected systems where IoHT devices interact with other medical and non-medical systems, potentially leading to the introduction of new guidelines addressing such scenarios. Furthermore, many autonomous systems in IoHT environments leverage the strengths of machine learning and AI to make decisions. This is prompting regulators to devise mechanisms and procedures for auditing the process of making algorithmic decisions and formulate accountability mechanisms that are needed for such autonomous systems [37].

6.3 International Standards and Harmonization

Considering the global nature of technology and data transmission, it is highly important to formulate international standards and bring harmony within the IoHT regulations. Global organizations, such as the International Organization for Standardization (ISO) and the International Electrotechnical Commission (IEC), are exercising ongoing efforts with the objective of establishing regulations that ensure the safety, reliability, and interoperability of IoHT devices worldwide [38]. Ethical use of IoHT is also addressed by such harmonization endeavors so that devices adhere to both local legislations as well as comply with global human rights principles [35]. This aspect is especially important in scenarios where the operation of IoHT devices spans various regions and countries, each governed by its own regulatory framework.

7. Challenges and Future Directions

The IoHT is a continuously evolving sector in the healthcare landscape. As it is advancing, it is also encountering new challenges and opportunities while integrating more deeply into the healthcare ecosystem. Table 2 provides an overview of future directions and challenges in IoHT. The part of this section explores the future trajectory of IoHT in further detail focusing on integration with emerging technologies, the future of IoHT security, collaborative approaches to cybersecurity, the significance of regulatory compliance, and the role of research and innovation.

7.1 Integration with Emerging Technologies

As IoHT grows and matures over time, its integration with other emerging technologies, such as machine learning, AI, cloud computing, and blockchain, will be highly crucial. AI and machine learning can be leveraged further so that various IoHT devices can process and analyze health data more efficiently in real time. This can facilitate to enhance the accuracy of medical diagnostics and enable personalized treatment options. Moreover, cloud computing can be utilized to provide scalable and flexible storage and processing capabilities that enable real-time analysis and sharing of vast amounts of health data from various IoHT

Table 2: Future directions and challenges in IoHT.

Areas	Direction/Challenge	Focus
Integration with Emerging Technologies	AI and Machine Learning	Real-time data processing for enhanced diagnostics and treatment.
	Blockchain	Secure, decentralized data storage and sharing.
	Advanced Wireless Technologies (5G)	Improved communication speed and reliability between devices.
IoHT Security	Robust Encryption Methods	Stronger encryption to counter sophisticated cyber threats.
	Advanced Anomaly Detection Systems	AI-driven prediction and mitigation of security breaches.
	Unified Security Framework	Standardized security across various platforms and devices.
Collaborative Approaches to Cybersecurity	Common Security Standards	Effective cooperation through unified security standards.
	Industry-Wide Collaborations	Sharing best practices and threat intelligence among stakeholders.
Regulatory Compliance and Standards	Evolving Regulatory Frameworks	Continuous updates to regulations addressing IoHT challenges.
	Harmonization and International Standards	Global standards for international technology providers and healthcare services.
Research and Innovation	Technological Advancements	Innovations in battery life, miniaturization, and sensor accuracy.
	Impact Studies	Research on IoHT's effects on patient outcomes, privacy, and healthcare delivery.
	Social, Ethical, and Economic Research	Investigating the broader impacts of IoHT to address integration challenges.

devices. This can also improve remote access to healthcare services and patient data, thus enhancing telemedicine and supporting advanced data-driven decision-making in healthcare. Furthermore, the decentralized nature of blockchain architecture offers a promising solution to the privacy and security concerns in IoHT. This technology can be leveraged to provide a secure, decentralized platform for storing and sharing medical data. Additionally, the adoption and utilization of advanced wireless technologies, such as 5G (Fifth Generation Wireless Technology), Wi-Fi 6 (802.11ax), and LoRaWAN (Long Range Wide Area Network), can facilitate faster and more reliable communications between IoHT devices, thus enhance the capabilities and efficiency of IoHT applications.

7.2 Charting the Future of IoHT Security

With the expansion of the IoHT domain and its integration with other technologies, security concerns are also growing at a higher rate. As new devices and networks are being incorporated into the IoHT infrastructures, new threat actors and sophisticated cyber-attacks are emerging. As a result, future security strategies must be adjusted appropriately to address evolving security threats. Approaches such as developing stronger encryption methods, improved detection techniques for system anomalies, and security protocols powered by AI and machine learning can be effective in predicting and preventing potential security breaches before they occur. Moreover, with the growing interconnectivity of IoHT devices, a standardized unified security framework needs to be formulated so that different platforms and devices can operate seamlessly.

7.3 Collaborative Approaches to Cybersecurity

Collaborative efforts by the relevant stakeholders, including technology developers, healthcare providers, patients and advocacy groups, policymakers, and ethics committees, can effectively address IoHT security challenges. Furthermore, higher levels of effective cooperation and unified response to cyber threats can be ensured by developing common security standards and practices across the IoHT landscape. In addition, industry-wide collaborations can be leveraged for sharing best practices, threat intelligence, and resources that can be effective in strengthening the overall security of the IoHT ecosystem.

7.4 Regulatory Compliance and Standards

Regulatory frameworks for IoHT technologies need continuous updates to maintain the maximum utility of these technologies. Unique challenges associated with the utilization of IoHT, such as data protection, interconnectivity, and patient safety, must be addressed by future regulations. This can be ensured via constant monitoring and adaptation of the practices of IoHT. Additionally, harmonization and the establishment of international standards are required so that the global scope of technology providers and healthcare services can be managed seamlessly and efficiently.

7.5 Research and Innovation

The challenges and difficulties encountered by the wide adoption and application of IoHT can be overcome by ongoing research and innovation. The potential research and innovation facets include both technological advancements and investigations into the effects of IoHT on patient outcomes, privacy, and healthcare delivery. Directions for technological innovations include the miniaturization of IoHT devices, extending their battery life, and increasing the accuracy of sensors utilized in the healthcare sector. Such advancements will greatly enhance the utility and functionality of IoHT devices. Moreover, extended research and analysis of the economic, social, and ethical impacts of IoHT must be carried out for the successful incorporation of IoHT into regular healthcare practices.

8. Conclusions

The IoHT is playing significant and pivotal roles in modernizing the healthcare sector by facilitating real-time patient monitoring, efficient diagnostics, personalized treatment, and improved patient management. With its immense benefits to both healthcare providers and the patient community, investigation of cybersecurity challenges and their solutions within the IoHT domain reveals not only the profound potential but also significant risks of this rapidly advancing field that warrants immediate and comprehensive attention. The healthcare infrastructure is integrating widely and rapidly with advanced digital technologies which is raising demands for robust, dynamic, and ethical cybersecurity measures. IoHT technologies incorporate AI, machine learning, and blockchain to improve healthcare services' accuracy and efficiency. This powers the healthcare providers and improves patient experiences. However, this integration of modern devices and technologies brings forth complex cybersecurity challenges for protecting sensitive health data and maintaining the integrity of healthcare systems.

For successful deployment and integration of IoHT devices into the healthcare sector, the security assurance of these devices is of the highest importance as these devices are vulnerable to a range of cyber threats including unauthorized access, data breaches, ransomware, DoS attacks, malware infection, device hijacking, and insider threats. To protect the IoHT ecosystem from these threats, the implementation of cutting age and reliable security mechanisms such as strong encryption methods, data anonymization and minimization, multi-factor authentication (MFA), AI-driven threat detection, network segmentation, intrusion detection and prevention systems (IDPS), and ongoing vulnerability assessments are crucial. Moreover, besides technological improvements that aspire to protect the devices and networks, regulatory standards, access control policies, incident response planning, third-party risk management, user training and awareness programs, security culture development, as well as ethical considerations must be addressed appropriately to minimize risks and challenges associated with human errors and natural disasters. Regulatory frameworks such as GDPR, HIPAA, Medical

Device Regulation (MDR), and the National Institute of Standards and Technology (NIST) Cybersecurity Framework set specific standards and structured guidelines that shape the development and deployment of IoHT technologies and enforce security and privacy IoHT devices and health data. As cybersecurity challenges evolve and technological advancements move rapidly, the relevant regulatory frameworks must be upgraded to safeguard patient data effectively and foster trust among the stakeholders.

IoHT, being a quickly progressing field, is rapidly evolving and opening new directions for further research and development. Directions for future research include the implementation of effective integration strategies with emerging technologies, improving interoperability and portability among diverse IoHT devices and healthcare systems, and reinforcing collaborative approaches to strengthen cybersecurity. To establish an efficient, secure, and trustworthy IoHT ecosystem, comprehensive and cooperative approaches are essential that incorporate relevant stakeholders across various sectors including technology developers, healthcare providers, policymakers, and most importantly the patient communities. In summary, with the immense potential of IoHT technologies to transform the healthcare sector, significant cybersecurity challenges must be overcome to realize the vision. Through continuous research and development with a priority on enhancing privacy, security, compliance, and ethical considerations, the field has tremendous prospects and promises to progress toward a future where healthcare will be more efficient, accessible, secure, and beneficial to all stakeholders involved.

References

[1] Dhanvijay, M. M. and S. C. Patil. 2019. Internet of Things: A survey of enabling technologies in healthcare and its applications. *Computer Networks*, 153: 113–131.

[2] Bhuiyan, M. N., M. M. Rahman, M. M. Billah and D. Saha. 2021. Internet of things (IoT): A review of its enabling technologies in healthcare applications, standards protocols, security, and market opportunities. *IEEE Internet of Things Journal*, 8(13): 10474–10498.

[3] Wang, J., M. K. Lim and M. -L. Tseng. 2021. The evolution of the IoT over the past 20 years. *Computers & Industrial Engineering*, 155: 107174.

[4] Qadri, Y. A., A. Nauman, Y. B. Zikria, A. V. Vasilakos and S.W. Kim. 2020. The future of healthcare internet of things: a survey of emerging technologies. *IEEE Communications Surveys & Tutorials*, 22(2): 1121–1167.

[5] Razdan, S. and S. Sharma. 2022. Internet of medical things (IoMT): Overview, emerging technologies, and case studies. *IETE Technical Review*, 39(4): 775–788.

[6] Sahu, A. K., S. Sharma, M. Tanveer and R. Raja. 2021. Internet of things attack detection using hybrid deep learning model. *Computer Communications*, 176: 146–154.

[7] Thamilarasu, G., A. Odesile and A. Hoang. 2020. An intrusion detection system for internet of medical things. *IEEE Access*, 8: 181560–181576.

[8] Ge, M., N. F. Syed, X. Fu, Z. Baig and A. Robles-Kelly. 2021. Towards a deep learning-driven intrusion detection approach for Internet of Things. *Computer Networks*, 186: 107784.

[9] Judith, A., G. J. W. Kathrine, S. Silas and A. J. 2023. Efficient deep learning-based cyber-attack detection for Internet of Medical Things devices. *Engineering Proceedings*, 59: 139.
[10] Kishor, A. and C. Chakraborty. 2022. Artificial Intelligence and Internet of Things based Healthcare 4.0 monitoring system. *Wireless Personal Communications*, 127: 1615–1631. DOI: 10.1007/s11277-021-08708-5.
[11] Sun, Y., J. Liu, K. Yu, M. Alazab and K. Lin. 2021. PMRSS: Privacy-preserving Medical Record Searching Scheme for intelligent diagnosis in IoT healthcare. *IEEE Transactions on Industrial Informatics*. DOI: 10.1109/TII.2021.3070544.
[12] Zeadally, S., F. Siddiqui, Z. Baig and A. Ibrahim. 2020. Smart healthcare: Challenges and potential solutions using internet of things (IoT) and big data analytics. *PSU Research Review*, 4(2): 149–168.
[13] Cano, M. D. and A. Cañavate-Sanchez. 2020. Preserving data privacy in the Internet of Medical Things using dual signature ECDSA. *Security and Communication Networks*. DOI: 10.1155/2020/4960964.
[14] Li, Q., J. Ma, X. Liu and J. Xiong. 2021. A survey on machine learning-based big data analytics for IoT-enabled smart healthcare system. *ACM Computing Surveys (CSUR)*. DOI: 10.1145/3436756.
[15] Zhao, Z., C. Hsu, L. Harn, Q. Yang and L. Ke. 2021. Lightweight privacy-preserving data sharing scheme for internet of medical things. *Wireless Communications and Mobile Computing*, 2021(1): 8402138.
[16] Ahammed, S., N. Hassan, S. H. Cheragee and A. Z. M. T. Islam. 2021. An IoT-based real-time remote health monitoring system. *International Journal of Research Engineering Science*, 8(3): 23–29.
[17] Kim, D., J. Choi and K. Han. 2020. Risk management-based security evaluation model for telemedicine systems. *BMC Medical Informatics and Decision Making*, 20: 1–14.
[18] Nurgalieva, L., D. O'Callaghan and G. Doherty. 2020. Security and privacy of mHealth applications: A scoping review. *IEEE Access*, 8: 104247–104268.
[19] Papaioannou, M., M. Karageorgou, G. Mantas, V. Sucasas, I. Essop, J. Rodriguez and D. Lymberopoulos. 2022. A survey on security threats and countermeasures in internet of medical things (IoMT). *Transactions on Emerging Telecommunications Technologies*, 33(6): e4049.
[20] Zarour, M., M. Alenezi, M. T. J., Ansari, A. K. Pandey, M. Ahmad, A. Agrawal, ... and R. A. Khan. 2021. Ensuring data integrity of healthcare information in the era of digital health. *Healthcare Technology Letters*, 8(3): 66–77.
[21] Elhoseny, M., N. N. Thilakarathne, M. I. Alghamdi, R. K. Mahendran, A. A. Gardezi, H. Weerasinghe and A. Welhenge. 2021. Security and privacy issues in medical internet of things: Overview, countermeasures, challenges and future directions. *Sustainability*, 13(21): 11645.
[22] Malamas, V., F. Chantzis, T. K. Dasaklis, G. Stergiopoulos, P. Kotzanikolaou and C. Douligeris. 2021. Risk assessment methodologies for the Internet of Medical Things: A survey and comparative appraisal. *IEEE Access*, 9: 40049–40075. DOI: 10.1109/ACCESS.2021.3064682.
[23] Negro-Calduch, E., N. Azzopardi-Muscat, R. S. Krishnamurthy and D. Novillo-Ortiz. 2021. Technological progress in electronic health record system optimization: Systematic review of systematic literature reviews. *International Journal of Medical Informatics*, 152: 104507.
[24] Thomasian, N. M. and E. Y. Adashi. 2021. Cybersecurity in the internet of medical things. *Health Policy and Technology*, 10(3): 100549.
[25] Shahid, J., R. Ahmad, A. K. Kiani, T. Ahmad, S. Saeed and A. M. Almuhaideb. 2022. Data protection and privacy of the internet of healthcare things (IoHTs). *Applied Sciences*, 12(4): 1927.

[26] Ballantyne, A. 2020. How should we think about clinical data ownership. *Journal of Medical Ethics*, 46: 289–294. DOI: 10.1136/medethics-2018-105340.

[27] Deebak, B. D. and F. Al-Turjman. 2020. Smart mutual authentication protocol for cloud based medical healthcare systems using internet of medical things. *IEEE Journal on Selected Areas in Communications*, 39(2): 346–360.

[28] Egala, B. S., A. K. Pradhan, V. Badarla and S. P. Mohanty. 2021. Fortified-chain: A blockchain-based framework for security and privacy-assured internet of medical things with effective access control. *IEEE Internet of Things Journal*, 8(14): 11717–11731.

[29] Galvin, H. K. and P. R. DeMuro. 2020. Developments in privacy and data ownership in mobile health technologies, 2016–2019. *Yearbook of Medical Informatics*, 29(1): 32–43.

[30] Abbas, A., R. Alroobaea, S. Krichen, S. Rubaiee, S. Vimal and F. M. Almansour. 2024. Blockchain-assisted secured data management framework for health information analysis based on Internet of Medical Things. *Personal and Ubiquitous Computing*, 28(1): 59–72.

[31] Kumar, R. and R. Tripathi. 2021. Towards design and implementation of security and privacy framework for Internet of Medical Things (IoMT) by leveraging blockchain and IPFS technology. *Journal of Supercomputing*, 77(8): 7916–7955.

[32] Liddell, K., D. A. Simon and A. Lucassen. 2021. Patient data ownership: Who owns your health? *Journal of Law and the Biosciences*, 8(2).

[33] Ballantyne, A. 2020. How should we think about clinical data ownership? *Journal of Medical Ethics*, 46(5): 289–294.

[34] Calvillo-Arbizu, J., I. Román-Martínez and J. Reina-Tosina. 2021. Internet of Things in health: Requirements, issues, and gaps. *Computer Methods and Programs in Biomedicine*, 208: 106231.

[35] Lee, T. -F., I. -P. Chang and G. -J. Su. 2023. Compliance with HIPAA and GDPR in certificateless-based authenticated key agreement using extended chaotic maps. *Electronics*, 12(5): 1108.

[36] Galvin, H. K. and P. R. DeMuro. 2020. Developments in privacy and data ownership in mobile health technologies, 2016–2019. *Yearbook of Medical Informatics*, 29(1): 32–43.

[37] Liddell, K., D. A. Simon and A. Lucassen. 2021. Patient data ownership: Who owns your health? *Journal of Law and the Biosciences*, 8(2): 1–50.

[38] Nurgalieva, L., D. O'Callaghan and G. Doherty. 2020. Security and privacy of mHealth applications: A scoping review. *IEEE Access*, 8: 104247–104268.

Chapter 13

Securing Healthcare IoT in the Quantum Age

Challenges and Mitigation Strategies

Asif Alif,[1] *Khondokar Fida Hasan*,[2,*] *Jesse Laeuchli*[2] and *Mohammad Jabed Morshed Chowdhury*[3]

1. Introduction

The healthcare sector has been significantly influenced by the digital revolution, leading to the emergence of the Digital Health era. One of the primary catalysts behind this paradigm shift is the Internet of Things (IoT), which facilitates the interconnection of medical equipment, sensors, and wearables to gather patient data in real time. The interconnectivity facilitates the ability to remotely monitor patients, manage chronic diseases, and enhance drug adherence [1]. Nevertheless, the advantages of the IoT give rise to security concerns, which could undermine the security of sensitive health data [2].

The emergence of quantum computing poses a significant and imminent threat. Quantum machines utilize the principles of quantum mechanics to achieve significantly faster calculations compared to

[1] Islamic University, Kushtia, Bangladesh.
[2] University of New South Wales (UNSW), Canberra, Australia.
[3] La Trobe University, Melbourne, Australia.
* Corresponding author: fida.hasan@unsw.edu.au

DOI: 10.1201/9781003483267-17

conventional computers [3]. The potential exists for the breach of existing encryption standards, which serve as the fundamental basis for ensuring data security in the healthcare IoT [4]. Although the general implementation of large-scale quantum computers may be delayed by a few years, it is essential to take early steps to guarantee the enduring security of critical patient data.

The cryptographic algorithms employed in healthcare IoT systems offer the CIA triad, which encompasses Confidentiality (ensuring the privacy of data), Integrity (ensuring that data remains unaltered), and Availability (ensuring authorized access to data) [3]. Nevertheless, the advent of quantum computing poses a potential threat to these protective measures. Quantum computers have the capacity to decrypt existing encrypted data, which could result in the exposure of patient health information, disruption of medical device operations, and the ability to manipulate healthcare records.

This chapter focuses on the crucial matter of ensuring the security of healthcare IoT devices in the quantum age. This study examines the risks presented by quantum computing and investigates the potential solutions of post-quantum cryptography (PQC) and other quantum-resistant approaches. This study examines the limits associated with conventional healthcare IoT devices, such as pacemakers, monitoring tools, and telemedicine equipment. Additionally, it investigates the potential adaptations of PQC primitives to address the unique resource limitations of these devices. We will go deeper into the current mitigation initiatives and present a strategic plan for ensuring the security of healthcare IoT in the era of quantum technology.

The chapter is organized in the following manner: In Section 2, an overview of the quantum threat to cryptography is presented. In Section 3, a comprehensive examination of the quantum threat and PQC approaches is presented. Section 4 examines the cryptographic requirements of the healthcare IoT and investigates appropriate PQC primitives for various scenarios. Section 5 delves into the difficulties associated with implementing these strategies and investigates current mitigation initiatives on a global scale. Section 6 is concluded prior to the presentation of the reference.

2. An Overview of Quantum Threat to Cryptography

This section briefly introduces quantum computing and its threat to popular cryptographic systems that are the cornerstone of today's digital world.

2.1 *A Brief Introduction to Quantum Computers*

Quantum computing represents a revolutionary approach to processing information, leveraging the principle of quantum mechanics to solve problems that are intractable for classical computers. It employs the laws of quantum mechanics to perform complex computations in seconds that are too complex for classical computers. At the heart of this technology are qubits (as shown in the Figure 1), which, unlike the binary bits of classical computing that are either "on" (1) or "off" (0), can exist in both states simultaneously through a property called superposition.

In addition, qubits exhibit entanglement, a unique quantum condition where the state of one qubit is intrinsically linked to another, irrespective of distance. The combined capabilities of superposition and entanglement grant quantum computers their extraordinary potential, far surpassing the limits of classical computational power [5].

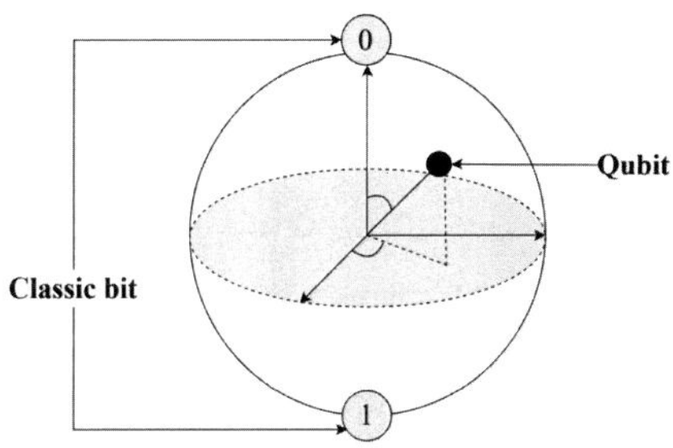

Figure 1: A simplified presentation of Qubit.

2.2 *Quantum Threat*

Quantum computing heralds a new frontier in technological advancement, promising unprecedented progress in fields ranging from medicine and chemistry to automated systems and artificial intelligence. Yet, this cutting-edge innovation brings with it a formidable challenge to cybersecurity: the quantum threat. Traditional encryption methods, which safeguard our most sensitive data, rely on the computational difficulty of tasks like factoring large numbers or calculating discrete logarithms—tasks that quantum computers could solve with alarming speed and efficiency.

Encryption, the cornerstone of secure communication, employs complex codes—keys and algorithms—to ensure that only authorized recipients can access and interpret the information. This protective measure is vital for maintaining the confidentiality and integrity of digital communications, including emails, passwords, and financial transactions. The advent of quantum computing, however, could render these encryption systems obsolete, potentially laying bare the very secrets they were designed to protect. This could be used by hackers or state actors to cause great disruption or for illegal means, such as stealing personal information, spying on communications, or sabotaging critical infrastructure. This is what we call the quantum threat, and it is one of the most urgent and important challenges for cryptography nowadays [6].

Cryptography, the science of secure communication, is built primarily on two foundational algorithm types. The Symmetric Key Algorithm, or single-key encryption, requires both sender and receiver to use identical keys for encrypting and decrypting messages. In contrast, the Asymmetric Key Algorithm employs a public key for encryption and a private key for decryption, with RSA being a prominent example in contemporary digital security [7].

Addressing the quantum threat is thus one of the most pressing and complex challenges facing cryptography today. It necessitates re-evaluating our current security paradigms and developing quantum-resistant cryptographic techniques to protect against the vulnerabilities exposed by quantum computing's rise.

2.3 *Quantum Threats to Asymmetric Cryptography*

Asymmetric cryptography, also known as public-key cryptography, is a type of encryption that uses two different keys: a public key and a private key. The public key is used to encrypt messages and can be shared with anyone, while the private key is used to decrypt messages and must be kept secret. A widely used asymmetric cryptography algorithm in today's digital world is RSA, which stands for Rivest-Shamir-Adleman, the names of its inventors. RSA relies on the difficulty of factoring large semi-primes, which are numbers that are the product of two prime numbers, such as 15 = 3 x 5 [8]. The security of RSA depends on the size of the key, which is measured in bits. For example, RSA 1024 uses a 1024-bit key, which is equivalent to a 309-digit number. The larger the key, the harder it is to factor in and compromise the encryption [9, 10].

The security of the RSA algorithm solely depends on the computational cost of factoring two large numbers. A quantum computer with appropriate algorithms can compromise RSA encryption with ease. For example, a quantum computer can use Shor's algorithm, discovered by Peter Shor in 1994, to factor large numbers much faster than classical computers. This poses a threat to RSA and other public-key encryption schemes. Shor's algorithm operates in polynomial time, meaning its computational time grows slowly with input size. In contrast, the best classical factoring algorithms work in exponential time. For instance, Shor's algorithm can factor a 1024-bit number in about 10 hours, while classical methods would take around 10 billion years [11].

To break RSA 1024, a quantum computer would need approximately 2,050 logical qubits. Logical qubits, which are error-corrected, enable reliable computations by encoding multiple physical qubits to protect against errors [12].

Currently, quantum computers are not yet capable of achieving this level of performance. However, advancements are ongoing. For example, IBM's 1,121-qubit processor, IBM Condor, introduced in December 2023, demonstrates significant progress toward achieving quantum supremacy [13–15].

Table 1 presents different kinds of today's cryptosystems with their category, key size, and security parameters. Quantum algorithm, logical Qubits, physical qubits, and time required to break specific key size of each cryptosystem are also presented in Table 1 [15].

More generally, quantum computers are capable of attacking any cryptosystem that is based on the hidden abelian subgroup problem [16, 17]. While RSA is one popular cryptosystem that reduces to this problem, other popular methods, such as those based on the elliptic curve discrete logarithm problem, are also vulnerable.

2.4 *Quantum Threat to Symmetric Cryptography*

Symmetric cryptography, or secret-key cryptography, uses the same key for both encryption and decryption. The key must be securely shared between the sender and receiver and kept secret from others. AES (Advanced Encryption Standard) is a popular symmetric algorithm, with its security depending on key size. For example, AES 128 uses a 128-bit key. The larger the key, the harder it is to find and break the encryption [18].

While symmetric cryptography is more resistant to quantum threats than asymmetric cryptography, quantum computers can still pose a risk. They offer a quadratic speedup in brute force attacks, reducing the effective security of keys. For instance, a quantum computer would need roughly 2^64 attempts to break a 128-bit key, halving its security. To maintain security against quantum attacks, larger keys, such as AES 256, are recommended [19].

This threat to symmetric key cryptography arises from Grover's algorithm. This algorithm, discovered by Lov Grover in 1996, is a quantum algorithm that can search unsorted databases much faster than classical computers. It can find an item in a database of N items in about $\sqrt{N}$ steps, compared to the classical average of N/2 steps. For example, Grover's algorithm can search a billion-item database in about 31,623 steps, while a classical algorithm would need about 500 million steps [20]. By treating a symmetric key encryption function, as such an unsorted search problem, the attacker can obtain a similar quadratic speedup.

Table 1: Quantum resources and estimated time required to break current common cryptosystems [15].

Cryptosystem	Category	Key Size	Security Parameter	Quantum Algorithm	Requirement		
					Logical Qubits	Physical Qubits	Time
RSA	Asymmetric Encryption	1024	80	Shor's algorithm	2,050	8.05 × 10^6	3.58 hours
		2048	112		4,098	8.56 × 10^6	28.63 hours
		4096	128		8,194	1.12 × 10^7	229 hours
ECC Discrete log problem	Asymmetric Encryption	256	128	Shor's algorithm	2,330	8.56 × 10^6	10.5 hours
		384	192		3,484	9.05 × 10^6	37.67 hours
		521	256		4,719	1.13 × 10^6	55 hours
AES-GCM	Symmetric Encryption	128	128	Grover's algorithm	2,953	4.61 × 10^6	2.61 × 10^12 yrs
		192	192		4,449	1.68 × 10^7	1.97× 10^22 yrs
		256	256		6,681	3.36 × 10^7	2.29 × 10^32 yrs
SHA256	Bitcoin mining	N/A	72	Grover's algorithm	2,403	2.23 × 10^6	1.8 × 10^4 yrs
PBKDF2 with 1000 iterations	Password hashing	N/A	66	Grover's algorithm	2,403	2.23 × 10^6	2.3 × 10^7 yrs

The quantum threat to cryptography is not only a future concern but also a current one. Quantum computers could retroactively break encryption by storing encrypted data today and decrypting it later when sufficiently powerful quantum computers are available. This means that data protected by current encryption methods could be vulnerable to future quantum attacks [20].

To estimate the time required to break symmetric cryptographic algorithms using Grover's algorithm, we'll need to consider the number of operations Grover's algorithm performs and the speed of quantum computers.

For simplicity, let's assume a hypothetical quantum computer can perform 10^9 (1 billion) quantum operations per second, then the time required to break a symmetric cryptographic algorithm is: Time (seconds) = Grover's Algorithm Complexity/Operations per Second and Time (years) = Time (seconds)/60×60×24×365.

Table 2 provides a comprehensive analysis of the time required to break various cryptosystems using Grover's algorithm under the assumption of performing 10^9 operations per second. The table includes symmetric encryption algorithms such as AES, DES, 3DES, Blowfish, and RC4, detailing their key sizes and the corresponding computational complexity with Grover's algorithm. This research emphasizes the critical necessity for the development and implementation of quantum-resistant encryption solutions to strengthen cybersecurity in the age of quantum computing achievements.

2.5 *Quantum Threat to Hash Cryptography*

Hash cryptography serves as a cornerstone in contemporary security frameworks, facilitating crucial functionalities such as data integrity verification, digital signatures, and password hashing. Its operation revolves around converting input data, regardless of its size, into fixed-length hash values. This process guarantees that even minor alterations in the input yield markedly distinct hash outputs. Hash functions stand as pivotal constructs in cryptography, facilitating validation while preserving confidentiality. Consequently, they play a pivotal role in bolstering mechanisms for data authentication and integrity, exemplified by hash-based message authentication codes (HMAC) and digital signatures. Cryptographic hash functions (CHFs) provide efficient and secure methods for authentication and integrity verification without compromising confidentiality. They are crucial for tasks like software verification and user authentication in web applications. A useful CHF should satisfy several key properties like uniformity, determinism, irreversibility, approximate injectivity to validate a piece of data against

Table 2: Quantum attack time estimates for various symmetric cryptosystems.

Cryptosystem	Category	Key Size	Quantum Algorithm	Complexity with Grover's Algorithm (Operations)	Operations per Second	Time (Approximately)
AES	Symmetric Encryption	128	Grover's algorithm	O(2^64)	10^9	585 yrs
		192		O(2^96)		2.51 × 10^11 yrs
		256		O(2^128)		1.08 × 10^21 yrs
DES	Symmetric Encryption	56	Grover's algorithm	O(2^28)	10^9	Instant
3DES	Symmetric Encryption	112	Grover's algorithm	O(2^56)	10^9	2.28 yrs
		168		O(2^84)		6.12 × 10^8 yrs
Blowfish	Symmetric Encryption	32	Grover's algorithm	O(2^16)	10^9	Instant
		448		O(2^224)		1.18 × 10^51 yrs
RC4	Symmetric Encryption	40	Grover's algorithm	O(2^20)	10^9	Instant
		2048		O(2^1024)		1.69 × 10^300 yrs

the original instance by comparing a digest of the data to a digest of the original [21].

CHFs are evaluated according to how well they withstand collision and pre-image attacks as pre-image resistance makes it difficult to locate the original input given a hash, whereas collision resistance makes it difficult to locate two inputs that produce the same hash [21]. Both are essential for applications such as digital signatures to maintain security.

Brute force attacks are the principal quantum threat to cryptographic hashing. In order to find an input that yields the same digest, an attacker would experiment with different ones until they find one that works. 2^n possible values may be obtained using n bits in the input. To have a greater than 50% probability of success, the attacker must thus try out around 2^(n-1) inputs. Grover's approach applies quantum amplitude amplification to provide a quadratic speedup for such an unstructured search environment as this method increases the likelihood (amplitude) of the right answer when searching through a wide collection of options/definitions by utilizing certain phenomena at the quantum interface. When this happens, a pre-image attack's time-based complexity drops to 2^n/2 [21]. In practical terms, this means that a 256-bit CHF, which is currently considered secure against pre-image attacks by classical computers, would provide the same level of security as a 128-bit CHF when faced with a quantum attacker utilizing Grover's algorithm.

BHT algorithm, a quantum algorithm proposed by Bassard, Høyer, and Tapp (BHT) in 1997, combines elements of the birthday attack with Grover search, offering a theoretical scaling of O(2^n/3) for finding hash collisions [22]. However, this improved scaling relies on the existence of quantum random access memory (QRAM) technology, which is not currently available. With ongoing research and advancements in quantum computing, there's a possibility that in the future, sufficient quantum random access memory (QRAM) may become available to effectively run the BHT algorithm. If realized, this scenario could pose a significant threat to Hash cryptographic security.

3. Introduction to PQC and other Quantum-Resistant Techniques

In anticipation of the quantum computing era, the development of quantum-resistant cryptographic methods has become eminent. These methods, also known as quantum-secure, post-quantum, or quantum-safe cryptography, are designed to thwart the advanced capabilities of quantum computers that could otherwise compromise traditional encryption techniques. Among these, PQC stands out as a pivotal innovation. PQC encompasses algorithms that, while operational on conventional computers, are engineered to protect data against the formidable computational force of quantum attacks [23]. Such methods are based on problems that are known to be hard for quantum computers to solve. For example, while quantum computers can attack the abelian subgroup problem, they cannot solve such problems when the group is non-abelian, so crypto systems based on this problem should be secure. The National Institute of Standards and Technology (NIST) has been proactive in this domain, initiating a call for post-quantum algorithm proposals in 2016 to identify solutions resilient to quantum computing's prowess, with the standardization process currently in its fourth round.

Figure 2 provides a concise visual representation of the NIST PQC standardization process, delineating the four pivotal rounds undertaken by the NIST. This figure serves as an illustrative guide, offering a comprehensive overview of the progressive stages through which cryptographic algorithms are rigorously evaluated and ultimately standardized to ensure resilience against emerging quantum computing threats.

Another significant advancement in quantum-resistant technology is quantum key distribution (QKD). Rooted in quantum physics, QKD is a method for generating and sharing encryption keys that are impervious to decryption efforts, even by quantum computers. QKD protects data from being attacked by quantum computers and other powerful computational resources. It offers defense against existing attack techniques and, critically, against upcoming advancements in mathematics and quantum computing [25].

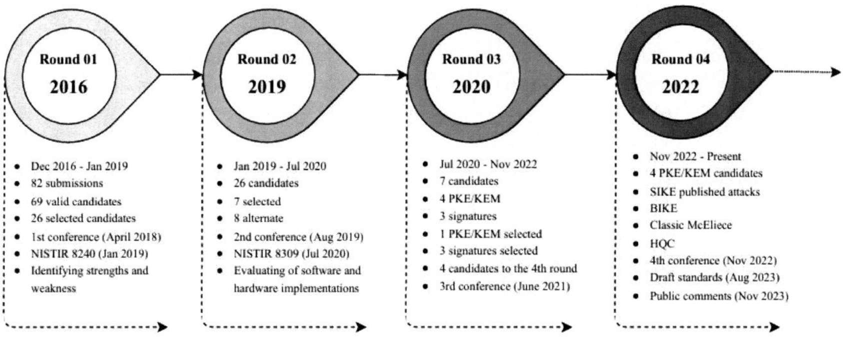

Figure 2: PQC standardization process of NIST [24].

3.1 PQC Primitives

PQC primitives are the essential building blocks utilized to create cryptographic algorithms that are resistant to threats from quantum computers. These primitives are essential to many cryptographic operations, guaranteeing the confidentiality, integrity, and authenticity of the data. Key Exchange and Key Encapsulation Mechanisms, Digital Signatures, and Encryption are the 3 PQC primitives. Hardware post-quantum cryptographic primitives consist of four frequently used security components, i.e., Public Key Cryptosystem, Key Exchange, Oblivious transfer, and Zero-Knowledge Proof [26].

3.2 PQC General Implementation Requirements

As quantum computing capabilities advance, the security of traditional cryptographic algorithms becomes increasingly precarious. PQC offers a solution by developing algorithms resistant to quantum computer attacks. However, successful implementation requires adherence to general requirements, ensuring security, efficiency, and practicality. Figure 3

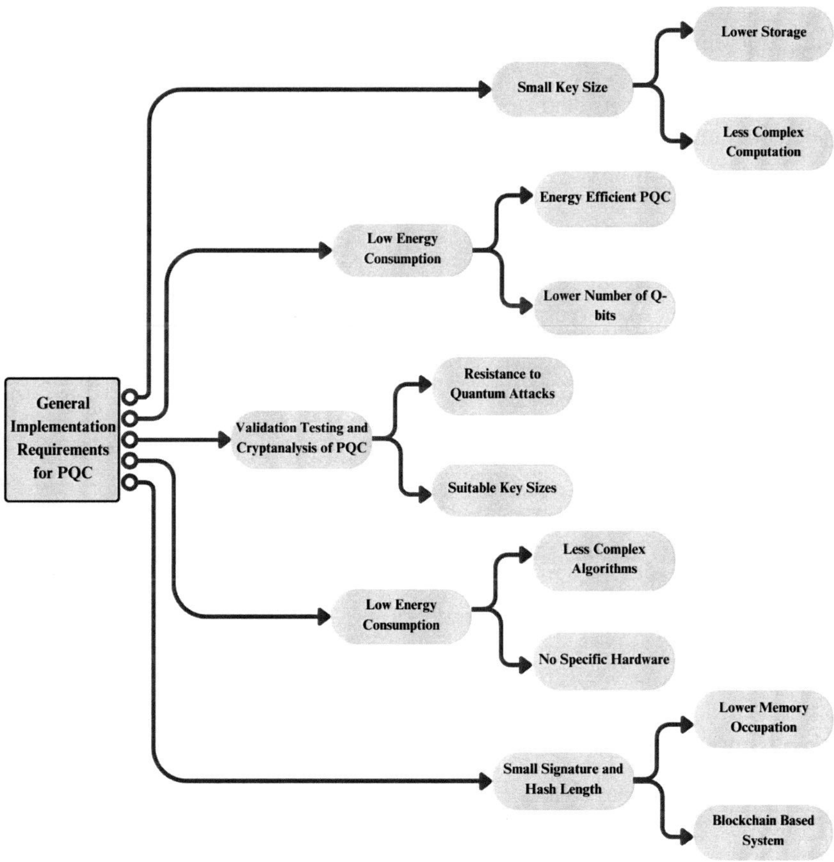

Figure 3: PQC general implementation requirements [27].

explores visual representation of the requirements for deploying effective post-quantum cryptographic systems in real-world settings.

3.3 IoT Perspective

In today's digital landscape, a vast number of interconnected IoT devices are seamlessly integrated across various sectors. The number of connected IoT devices is expected to be 29.42 billion by 2030. These interconnected IoT devices communicate with each other and use existing cryptographic algorithms like RSA, ECC, and AES for encryption. As quantum computers will break the existing cryptographic algorithms in the near future, massive amounts of data generated by interconnected IoT devices will be in danger. Fundamental building blocks of cryptography, key exchange, and encryption will be compromised. IoT networks are vulnerable to various attacks, including Sybil, eclipse, replay, side-channel, and false data injection. As a result, quantum-resistant PQC needs to be integrated into IoT.

Major IoT applications such as smart homes, smart cities, healthcare, agriculture, smart grids, smart traffic light systems, and smart transportation systems usually make use of small and resource-constrained devices (belonging to Class 0, Class 1, or Class 2 devices with less than 10 KB of RAM or storage space and can have less than 100 KB of code in their flash memory) [28]. As a result, it is really hard to integrate PQC into resource-constrained IoT devices. ARM Cortex M3 or even M0 processors that are used in many IoT devices have a clock speed (execution performance) often as low as 8–24 MHz and rising to 100–300 MHz [29]. The PQM4 project suggests integrating performance metrics, such as code size, RAM consumption, and cycle counts, into NIST's PQC decision-making [29]. The assumption is that code and RAM utilization won't rise much when moving from M4 to smaller devices (M3 or M0) [29]. A comparison of Falcon and Dilithium, which are NIST PQC digital signature schemes, reveals that while the Falcon code is 160 KB and only needs 500 B of RAM (with an 80 KB code-size trade-off for 4–8K RAM), the Dilithium code is 12–20 KB but uses 40–70 KB of RAM [29]. As a result, Dilithium does not fit on these low-end resource-constrained IoT devices, even if it is 100 times better than Falcon. On the other hand, Kyber (NIST PQC KEMs) takes precedence due to its lower resource requirements.

4. Overview of Healthcare IoT

The integration of the IoT into healthcare systems has changed the landscape of patient care, data management, and medical infrastructure.

IoT offers real-time monitoring, remote care, and data-driven insights by combining sensors, devices, and software, revolutionizing healthcare delivery and patient outcomes. Various IoT sensors and devices serve different purposes, and each has a distinct role to play in contributing to diverse healthcare IoT applications.

Figure 4 showcases the popular sensors commonly employed in healthcare IoT. These sensors play a vital role in collecting patient data, providing real-time health updates in the healthcare IoT industry, and securely transmitting the data to the cloud through an IoT gateway. These acquired data points are crucial inputs for doctors, allowing them to conduct thorough studies and provide detailed reports. Based on the report generated by the cloud, doctors or healthcare professionals can remotely adjust the IoT wearable device settings and send alerts to emergency services if the patient's condition is critical. The integration of an interconnected network of sensors, IoT devices, medical professionals, the IoT cloud, and emergency systems forms an IoT-based smart healthcare system. In Figure 5, an IoT-based smart healthcare system is given.

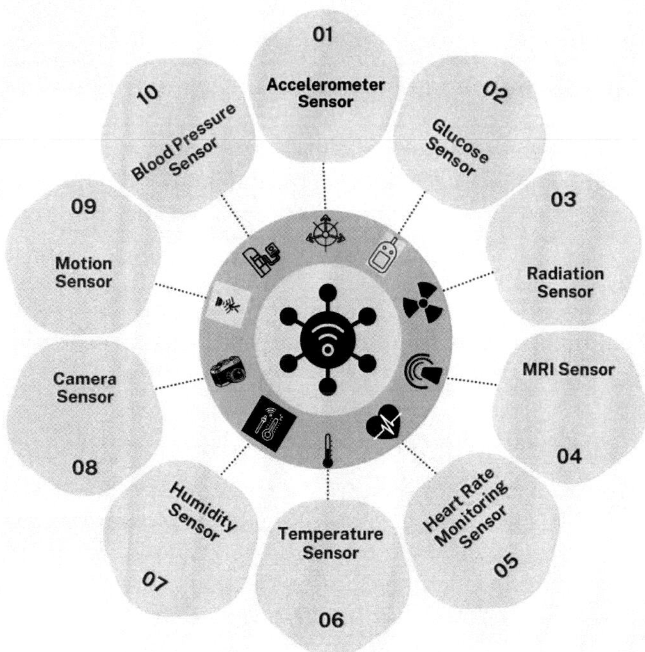

Figure 4: Popular healthcare IOT sensors.

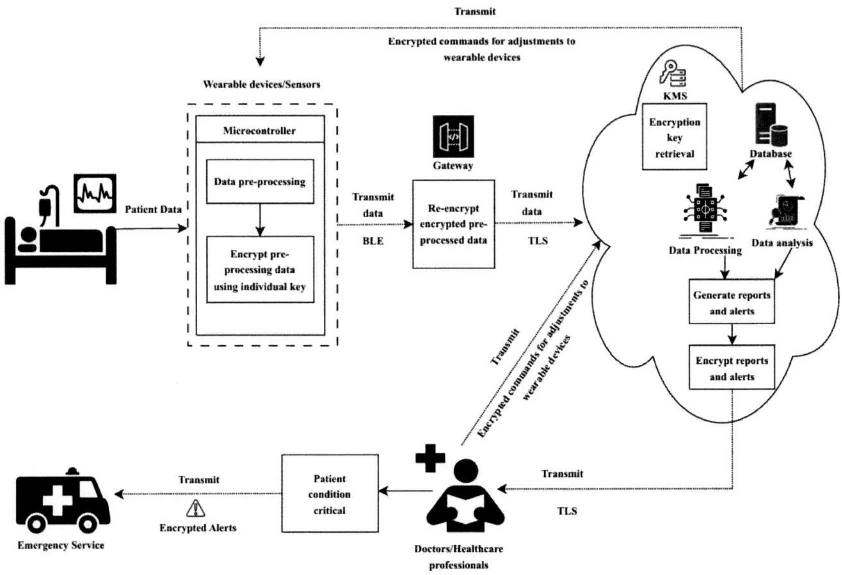

Figure 5: IOT-based smart healthcare system.

4.1 *Cryptographic Applications in Healthcare IoT*

Cryptographic techniques are crucial in safeguarding the confidentiality and integrity of sensitive medical data in the quickly changing healthcare IoT sector. This section explores how cryptography ensures confidentiality, integrity, and availability (CIA) of medical data. Cryptographic solutions safeguard against unwanted access and preserve the reliability of healthcare services by encrypting data transmissions, confirming data integrity, and establishing secure communication channels. Table 3 provides an overview of cryptographic applications mapped to the CIA triad in healthcare IoT highlighting their roles, examples, and associated security benefits.

4.2 *Implications of Quantum Threat to Healthcare IoT*

To protect sensitive patient data transferred across networks, healthcare IoT devices frequently use traditional cryptographic encryption. Encryption algorithms, including RSA, AES, and ECC, are commonly used by healthcare IoT devices to provide secure data transmission and storage [31]. With the extraordinary computational power of quantum computers, traditional cryptographic algorithms that are widely being used in today's healthcare IoT devices will be vulnerable in the near future. In the future, with the quantum computer attack, hackers could hack healthcare IoT devices and access, read, and change private healthcare

Table 3: Cryptographic applications associated with the CIA triad for securing healthcare IoT Environments.

CIA	Application	Examples	Benefits
Confidentiality	Ensures encryption of medical data during transmission and storage to safeguard patient privacy [30].	TLS, AES, ECC	Prevents unauthorized access, mitigates data breaches, ensures compliance with privacy regulations (e.g., HIPAA, GDPR).
Integrity	Utilizes cryptographic hash algorithms to verify authenticity and integrity of transactions and medical information [30].	SHA-256, HMAC	Detects unauthorized alterations, maintains data accuracy, enhances trust in medical records.
Availability	Ensures continuous availability and accessibility of medical records and equipment to authorized users [30].	TLS, PKI	Facilitates prompt access to critical information, improves patient outcomes, enhances operational efficiency.

information, including medical records like patients' names, diagnoses, allergies, treatment histories, and others, which would compromise the confidentiality and integrity of healthcare data. Real-time health data like heart rate, blood sugar levels, and even brain activity will also become vulnerable due to the quantum computer attack. Hackers could take device control, such as pacemakers, insulin pumps, smart inhalers, and other critical IoT devices, which could lead to life-threatening consequences. There is also another threat known as "Harvest Now, Decrypt Later," in which cybercriminals seize encrypted copies of vital medical data that have a lengthy shelf life in order to launch an assault when quantum computing becomes accessible [32]. The implication of quantum threats goes beyond privacy in the healthcare IoT sector, potentially endangering human life. Figure 6 visually represents the quantum threats to IoT-based smart healthcare systems, identifying threats across different sections.

Three use cases of IoT applications used in healthcare and impact of quantum threat on each of those use cases are given below:

4.2.1 Use Case-1: Remote Glucose Monitoring for Diabetics

Diabetic individuals may now regularly check their blood glucose levels without having to prick their fingers often thanks to remote glucose monitoring. This innovative approach is made possible through the use of Continuous Glucose Monitors (CGMs), compact wearable devices inserted beneath the skin that help to manage Type 1 or Type 2 diabetes with fewer finger-stick tests [33]. Every few minutes, these CGMs take a reading of the interstitial fluid's glucose data, which they then wirelessly send to a receiver or smartphone [33]. Unlike traditional blood glucose

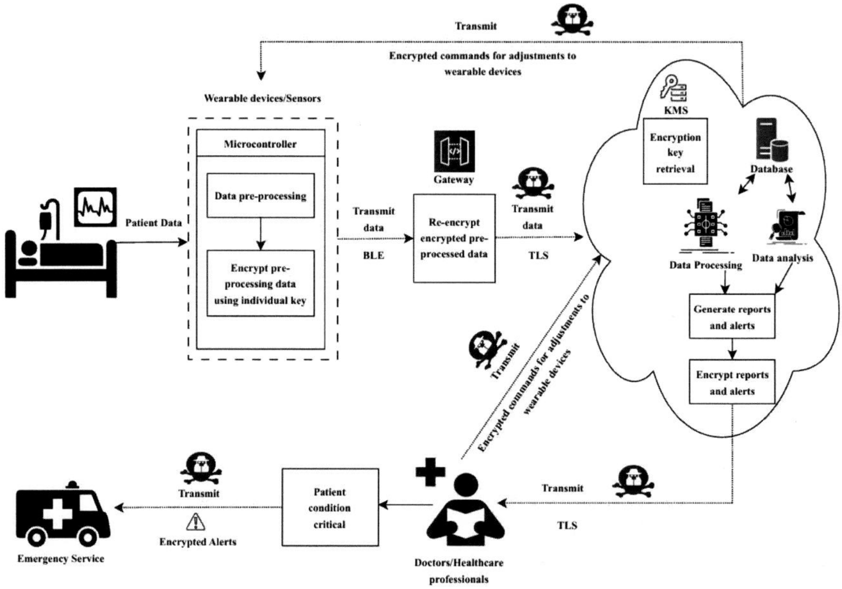

Figure 6: Quantum threat to IOT-based smart healthcare system.

meters (BGMs), which offer a single measurement at a specific moment in time, CGMs provide real-time glucose readings, typically updated every five minutes. This translates to approximately 288 readings per day, offering users a comprehensive and continuous view of their glucose levels throughout the day and night [34]. While offering invaluable insights, CGMs operate with limited resources where RAM is 32–64 KB, ROM is 1–2 MB, and clock speed is 16–32 MHz.

Quantum Threats to Remote Glucose Monitoring for Diabetics IoT Devices

Continuous glucose monitors (CGMs) provide remote glucose monitoring, which is a revolutionary development in diabetes care as it provides real-time information on blood glucose levels without requiring regular finger-stick testing. The security and integrity of patient data, however, are at danger due to the integration of this cutting-edge technology, which also creates vulnerabilities to quantum assaults. Weaknesses in the encryption algorithms used for the wireless transfer of glucose data from CGMs to receivers or smartphones might be exploited by quantum attackers. Adversaries might jeopardize patient privacy and security by intercepting these data and compromising the confidentiality of critical medical information, including real-time glucose levels.

Furthermore, strong quantum algorithms may be able to break the encryption techniques now used in CGMs. This flaw would make it possible for quantum attackers to crack encryption keys and have unauthorized access to patient data that CGMs store or communicate. Consequently, attackers may take part in illicit glucose reading tampering or manipulation, which might affect the precision of diabetes treatment and jeopardize patient care. In addition, CGMs are vulnerable to firmware flaws since they have limited resources, including RAM, ROM, and clock speed. Quantum attackers may take advantage of these flaws to compromise the usefulness and dependability of remote glucose monitoring for diabetics by gaining unauthorized access, inserting malware, or manipulating data within the CGMs.

With the advent of quantum computing, attackers possess the capability to intercept and decrypt CGM data, manipulate it, and subsequently transmit it back to the smartphone or cloud. Such manipulation of data could lead to healthcare providers administering incorrect treatments, thereby posing serious risks to patient safety and potentially endangering lives.

Mitigating Quantum Threats Remote Glucose Monitoring for Diabetics IoT devices

Implementing PQC algorithms and hardware-based security measures within Continuous Glucose Monitors (CGMs) significantly enhances their resilience against emerging quantum threats. PQC techniques, such as lattice-based or hash-based encryption, preserve patient privacy by ensuring that glucose data are securely sent wirelessly. Additionally, tamper-proof modules and quantum-resistant key storage techniques protect CGMs against unwanted access or data tampering [35]. Regular firmware upgrades, including security patches, are critical for fixing vulnerabilities and keeping CGMs resilient to possible quantum assaults. These procedures together assure the dependability and security of remote glucose monitoring systems, protecting patient data in the digital era.

4.2.2 Use Case-2: Smart Inhaler for Asthma Management in Healthcare IoT

Smart inhalers, when connected to smartphones, provide real-world data on patients' adherence patterns and inhaler technique during regular usage. While they can detect when a dosage is ready or activated, they cannot directly verify inhalation of the dose [36]. However, clinical research has demonstrated their ability to improve adherence and health outcomes, and they can send reminders for missed doses [36]. Several smart inhaler models are available or in development, including HeroTracker®, Doser™, INCA, RS01, and i-Neb [36]. Within smart inhalers, microcontrollers such as the QN9090 and K32W061 play critical roles in controlling device operations, analyzing sensor data, and protecting patient information [37]. These microcontrollers also enable secure data transmission to the cloud, allowing healthcare professionals to remotely adjust inhaler settings based on patient requirements [37]. The K32W061, an ARM Cortex-M4 microcontroller, boasts a maximum computational power of 48MHz, along with 512 KB of RAM, 128 KB of ROM, and 640 KB of flash memory [38]. Similarly, the QN9090, also an ARM Cortex-M4 microcontroller, offers up to 48MHz computational power, 640 kB flash memory, up to 152 kB RAM, and 128 kB ROM [39]. These microcontrollers are integral to the functionality and security of smart inhalers, bridging the gap between patient care and technology.

Quantum Threats to Smart Inhaler for Asthma Management IoT Devices

The ARM Cortex-M4 microcontrollers found in smart inhalers for asthma management are vulnerable not only to quantum computing threats but also to side-channel attacks like Differential Power Analysis (DPA) and Fault Injection attacks [40]. DPA involves analyzing power consumption patterns to extract cryptographic keys processed on the Cortex-M4, while Fault Injection attacks manipulate the device's hardware to induce errors and potentially extract information or alter its behavior [40]. These microcontrollers are vital for regulating device operations, analyzing sensor data, and securely transmitting patient information to cloud-based platforms. During data transmission to cloud-based platforms, there's a risk of Man-in-the-Middle (MitM) attacks, where communication between the Cortex-M4 and other devices may be intercepted, allowing eavesdropping or data modification. Additionally, traditional cryptographic algorithms implemented in ARM Cortex-M4 microcontrollers are susceptible to quantum computing advancements. The emergence of quantum computers makes conventional encryption algorithms vulnerable, potentially leading to the decryption of encrypted patient data from smart inhalers. Consequently, patient data confidentiality and integrity are at risk.

These quantum threats extend beyond data security concerns, potentially impacting patient health, well-being, and trust in healthcare technologies. If the embedded microcontrollers are successfully attacked, patients may face incorrect treatment adjustments, compromised confidentiality, and psychological distress. Manipulated data could lead to misdiagnosis or delays in medical interventions, posing risks to patient safety. Addressing these threats requires robust security measures to safeguard patient data and ensure the integrity of asthma management processes.

Mitigating Quantum Threats in Smart Inhaler Asthma Management IoT Devices

Mitigating quantum threats in smart inhalers for asthma management within IoT systems demands proactive measures to fortify patient data security and device integrity. This involves adopting PQC algorithms such as Kyber and Dilithium, providing robust encryption capabilities resilient to quantum attacks [24]. Furthermore, enhancing ARM Cortex-M4 microcontroller security against side-channel attacks and implementing secure communication protocols like TLS, secure coding practices, and using well-tested libraries, regular security updates, and promptly patching vulnerabilities are imperative. Exploring quantum-resistant cryptography and ensuring continuous monitoring with timely security updates further fortify smart inhalers against evolving quantum threats, safeguarding patient health, well-being, and fostering trust in healthcare technologies.

4.2.3 Use Case-3: Heart Rate Monitoring

A heart rate monitoring system within the realm of healthcare IoT comprises a network of interconnected devices and sensors dedicated to continuously monitoring and tracking a patient's heart rate in real time. Standard components of such systems include wearables equipped with heart rate sensors alongside ancillary hardware like tablets, smartphones, or cloud-based platforms for data processing and analysis. Notably, Photoplethysmography (PPG) and Electrocardiogram (ECG or EKG) serve as the primary sensors utilized for heart rate monitoring [41, 42]. In terms of processing capabilities, heart rate monitoring systems commonly integrate microcontrollers from the STM32 and MSP430 series [43, 44]. For instance, STM32H5 microcontrollers feature Arm Cortex-M33 cores capable of operating at frequencies up to 250 MHz, accompanied by flash memory ranging from 128 Kbytes to 2 MB and up to 640 Kbytes of RAM [45]. On the other hand, MSP430 series microcontrollers typically offer 512 KB of flash memory and RAM capacities ranging from 125 bytes to 66 KB [46]. These microcontrollers play a pivotal role in managing data acquisition, processing, and transmission tasks within the heart rate monitoring system, ensuring real-time monitoring accuracy and efficiency.

Quantum Threats to Heart Rate Monitoring IoT Devices

The quantum threats confronting heart rate monitoring devices within healthcare IoT systems carry significant implications for patient well-being and overall healthcare outcomes. The vulnerability of conventional encryption protocols to decryption by advanced quantum algorithms, such as Shor's algorithm, jeopardizes patient data security. This risk extends to raw PPG and ECG data, exposing sensitive details about heart function, sleep patterns, and emotional states. Breaches in confidentiality not only compromise patient privacy but also undermine trust in healthcare systems. Furthermore, the exploitation of vulnerabilities in widely used microcontrollers like the STM32 and MSP430 series by quantum adversaries amplifies the threat to patient health. Manipulated heart rate data, resulting from unauthorized access, could lead to erroneous diagnoses and ineffective treatment plans, potentially aggravating existing medical conditions or delaying necessary interventions. Inaccurate monitoring due to data manipulation may also result in missed opportunities for early detection of cardiac abnormalities or other health concerns, further compromising patient outcomes. Heart rate monitoring devices in healthcare IoT systems remain vulnerable to side-channel attacks, leveraging weaknesses in commonly used microcontrollers like STM32 and MSP430 [47]. These attacks exploit unintended information leakage through physical characteristics such as power consumption or electromagnetic radiation [48]. By analyzing these patterns, attackers can infer sensitive data regarding patient health and device operations, potentially compromising the integrity of heart rate monitoring systems. The potential for large-scale Denial-of-Service (DoS) attacks adds another layer of risk, disrupting access to critical patient data precisely when it is needed most, such as during medical emergencies. Such disruptions could hinder healthcare professionals' ability to make timely and informed decisions, potentially compromising patient safety and exacerbating medical emergencies. Furthermore, the prospect of impersonation attacks enabled by quantum capabilities poses a significant threat to patient information integrity across the healthcare ecosystem. Unauthorized access to heart rate monitoring devices could lead to falsification of medical records or tampering with treatment protocols, undermining the trustworthiness of patient data and potentially endangering patient lives. In essence, the quantum threats to heart rate monitoring devices in healthcare IoT systems not only compromise data security but also directly impact patient health and safety.

Mitigating Quantum Threats in Heart Rate Monitoring IoT Devices

In light of the quantum threats faced by heart rate monitoring devices within healthcare IoT systems, it is crucial to implement tailored mitigation strategies. These strategies not only safeguard patient data but also ensure the integrity of healthcare outcomes. Specifically, for heart rate monitoring, proactive measures involve adopting PQC algorithms like Kyber, Dilithium, and NTRUEncrypt, as recommended by the NIST [49]. These robust algorithms provide long-term encryption resilience against quantum attacks, thereby maintaining the confidentiality of patient data transmitted by heart rate monitoring devices.

Furthermore, the utilization of QKD technology establishes secure communication channels exclusively for heart rate monitoring devices [50]. This approach guarantees both the confidentiality and integrity of data transmission. To enhance security at the device level, hardware-based solutions such as tamper-proof modules and quantum-resistant key storage mechanisms offer additional layers of protection [35]. Additionally, continuous monitoring and threat detection mechanisms enable proactive identification and mitigation of potential quantum threats. By adhering to these practices, we uphold patient privacy and safeguard the integrity of healthcare outcomes in an increasingly quantum-enabled environment.

5. Mitigation Prospect and Challenges

Fast-evolving quantum computing approaches continuously challenge traditional cryptography-enabled IoT applications in the healthcare industry. With its massive computational power, quantum computers will be able to break traditional cryptographic encryption algorithms used in healthcare IoT. However, with the advancement of quantum computers, the attackers are targeting the hardware part of the IoT devices that can affect the entire system. These attacks exploit physical vulnerabilities in the IoT hardware implementation rather than flaws in the mathematical structure of the cryptographic algorithms [51].

Figure 7 presents a hierarchical representation illustrating hardware attacks on IoT devices enabled by advancements in quantum computing. To withstand the quantum computer attacks against healthcare IoT, Post-Quantum Cryptographic schemes integration would be a valuable strategy. Code-based cryptography, Lattice-Based cryptography, Multivariate cryptography, and Hash-Based signatures are the four basic types of PQC [52]. Many organizations are trying to integrate these PQC algorithms on IoT networks to withstand quantum computer attacks in future. Furthermore, many IoT implementations, such as NB-IoT and LTE technologies, are currently undergoing standardization processes to enhance their security. This process poses limitations on the integration of secure quantum alternatives into current IoT models [52]. PQC schemes provide a feasible option for integration into current IoT/IT infrastructures, unlike quantum cryptography and QKD schemes, which demand specific and expensive equipment and primarily focus on key establishment; however, PQC schemes generally require greater memory and computational resources compared to traditional cryptographic solutions, presenting implementation hurdles for constrained IoT end nodes, such as low-performance microcontrollers with limited memory,

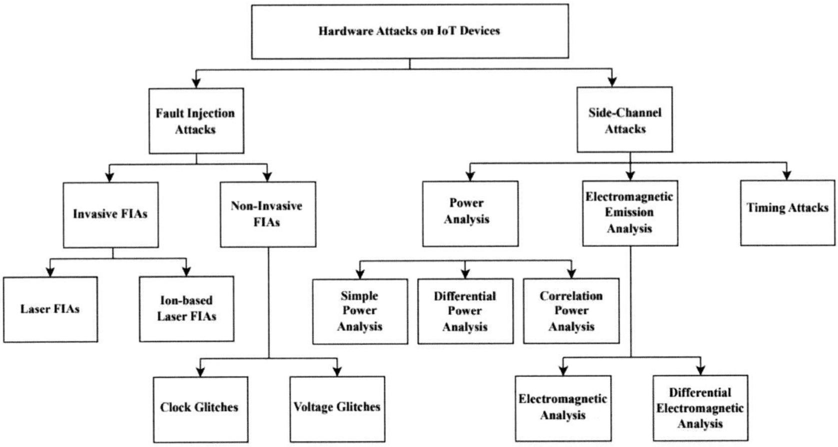

Figure 7: Hardware attacks on IoT devices [51].

even with traditional asymmetric cryptography such as RSA using 2K-bit keys [53]. Within the realm of PQC, lattice-based cryptosystems stand out as prime candidates for IoT devices, necessitating efficient polynomial-based multiplication calculations to minimize energy consumption and execution time, while similar optimization challenges arise in other PQC mechanisms operating within finite fields specifically tailored for IoT devices [28].

5.1 *Post-Quantum Cryptographic Projects and Initiatives*

A number of research efforts and standardization initiatives aiming at developing cryptographic solutions that can resist quantum challenges are being driven by post-quantum computing, which has emerged as a major field of study. Together with the development of standardized protocols, these efforts also include PQC projects.

PQCrypto Project: The PQCrypto project, funded by the European Union (EU), focused on investigating PQC for Internet communications, cloud computing, and low-power embedded devices. The pqm4 library, a result of the H2020 PQCRYPTO project, provides a practical solution customized for ARM Cortex-M4 microcontrollers, including various implementations of post-quantum key-encapsulation mechanisms and signature schemes, serving as a valuable benchmarking and testing framework specifically tailored for these microcontrollers [53].

Open Quantum Safe (OQS) Project: The OQS project, operating under the Linux Foundation's Post-Quantum Cryptography Alliance, is an open-source initiative dedicated to advancing quantum-resistant cryptography, providing quantum-resistant cryptographic algorithms through the liboqs C library and integrating these algorithms into various protocols and applications, including a provider for the widely used OpenSSL library, thus supporting both its own research efforts and the broader scientific community in addressing the challenges posed by quantum computing [54]. The OQS algorithm performance visualizations, derived from the OQS profiling project, offer crucial insights into the runtime, memory usage, and performance comparisons of Key Encapsulation Mechanism (KEM) and Signature (SIG) algorithms, vital for evaluating PQC's efficacy against quantum threats [55].

PQClean Project: PQClean collaboratively develops refined implementations of post-quantum cryptographic schemes identified by the NIST post-quantum project, aiming for seamless integration with libraries like liboqs, support in higher-level protocols such as Open Quantum Safe, and inclusion in benchmarking frameworks like SUPERCOP, while serving as optimal starting points for architecture-specific optimizations, security evaluations, and formal verification processes [56].

SAFECrypto Project: The SAFEcrypto project, funded by the EU and led by Queen's University of Belfast (United Kingdom), collaborated with partners from Switzerland, France, Germany, and Ireland to develop new post-quantum cryptosystems, focusing on lattice problems as a source of computational hardness [57].

NIST Initiatives: In December 2016, the NIST initiated a call for papers to standardize PQC algorithms. Among the 82 submission packages received, 69 met the requirements and were accepted. Following public review and feedback, seven finalists and eight alternative algorithms advanced to the third round in 2020. In 2022, NIST finalized the selection process, endorsing three digital signature algorithms, one Key Encapsulation Mechanism (KEM) algorithm for standardization and four KEM algorithms proceeded to the fourth round [58]. After rigorous evaluation during the third round, NIST identified four candidate algorithms among them for most use cases, NIST recommended implementing two primary algorithms: CRYSTALS-KYBER for key establishment and CRYSTALS-Dilithium for digital signatures [58].

IETF Initiatives: The Internet Engineering Task Force (IETF), in collaboration with the Crypto Forum Research Group (CFRG), is working on Internet-Drafts related to quantum cryptography. These drafts cover topics such as post-quantum cryptosystems for TLS and extending protocols like IKEv2 to be post-quantum resistant [59]. IETF is actively involved in updating security protocols for PQC to address quantum threats. Key initiatives include the formation of working groups like PQUIP, focused on integrating PQC algorithms into existing protocols [60]. These efforts aim to ensure interoperability, security, and resilience in internet communication protocols such as TLS, SSH, and HTTPS. Through collaboration across academia and industry, the IETF seeks to architect a smooth transition to PQC, safeguarding internet infrastructure against emerging quantum vulnerabilities.

5.2 *PQC Implementation Challenges in Healthcare IoT*

The rapid progress of quantum computing poses a significant risk to the security of traditional cryptographic methods used in today's healthcare IoT devices. While PQC presents a solution to this impending threat, its implementation in healthcare IoT environments introduces distinctive challenges. Adapting post-quantum cryptographic solutions to the specific needs of the healthcare sector and mitigating the vulnerabilities posed by quantum computing demand careful consideration and specialized approaches. Therefore, implementing PQC in healthcare IoT settings requires addressing these unique challenges effectively. Figure 8

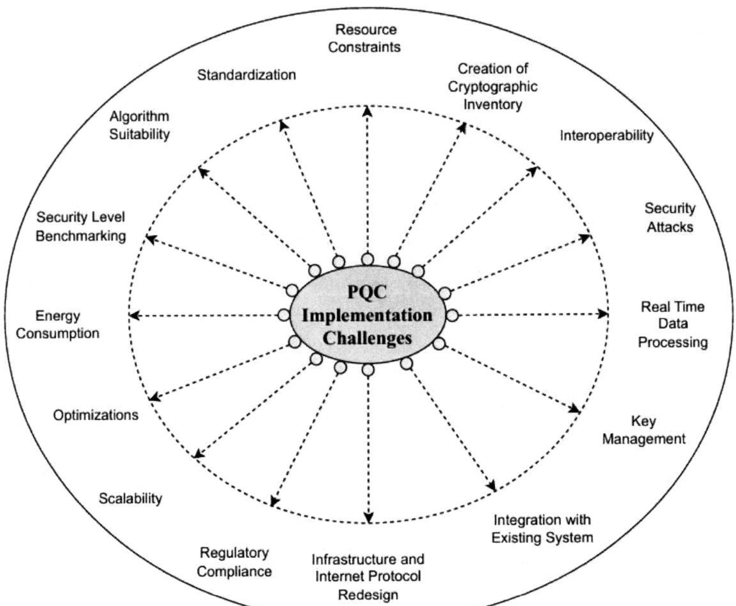

Figure 8: PQC implementation challenges in healthcare IoT.

illustrates the key challenges in implementing PQC within Healthcare IoT environments.

6. Conclusion

The quantum threat poses a significant risk to the healthcare IoT, jeopardizing the security of patient data and devices. We investigated PQC in this chapter as a possible means of protection, evaluating its appropriateness for medical devices with limited resources. Despite the presence of obstacles in implementation, the ongoing mitigation projects show potential. Collaboration among healthcare providers, manufacturers, and regulators is essential for ensuring the security of healthcare IoT. Ongoing PQC research and global collaboration are crucial. To ensure the protection of patient privacy, device functionality, and trust in the future of digital healthcare, it is crucial to take proactive measures at present.

References

[1] Farahani, B., F. Firouzi and K. Chakrabarty. 2020. Healthcare IoT. *Intelligent Internet of Things: From Device to Fog and Cloud*, 515–545.

[2] Chacko, A. and T. Hayajneh. 2018. Security and privacy issues with IoT in healthcare. *EAI Endorsed Transactions on Pervasive Health and Technology*, 4(14).

[3] Hasan, K. M., L. Simpson, M. A. R. Baee, C. Islam, Z. Rahman, W. Armstrong, P. Gauravaram and M. McKague. 2024. A framework for migrating to post-quantum cryptography: Security dependency analysis and case studies. *IEEE Access*, 12: 23427–23450.

[4] Fernández-Caramés, T. M. 2019. From pre-quantum to post-quantum IoT security: A survey on quantum-resistant cryptosystems for the Internet of Things. *IEEE Internet of Things Journal*, 7(7): 6457–6480.

[5] Niraula, T., A. Pokharel, A. Phuyal, P. Palikhel and M. Pokharel. 2022. Quantum computers' threat on current cryptographic measures and possible solutions, 12: 10–20.

[6] Denker, K. and A. Y. Javaid. (2019). Quantum computing as a threat to modern cryptography techniques. In *Proceedings of the International Conference on Foundations of Computer Science (FCS)*. The Steering Committee of The World Congress in Computer Science, Computer Engineering and Applied Computing (WorldComp).

[7] Castelluccio, M. 2021. The quantum threat to cryptography. *Strategic Finance*, 102(12): 55–56.

[8] Singh, S. and E. Sakk. 2024. Implementation and Analysis of Shor's Algorithm to Break RSA Cryptosystem Security.

[9] Davis, R. 2022. It's been 20 years since "15" was factored on quantum hardware.

[10] Madhav. 2024. ESG Research Unearths Critical Insights for Future-Proofing Encryption and Key Management.

[11] Houston-Edwards, K. 2024. Tomorrow's Quantum Computers Threaten Today's Secrets. Here's How to Protect Them.

[12] Quera. Logical Qubit. Available from: https://www.quera.com/glossary/logical-qubit#:~:text=The%20ratio%20that%20is%20commonly,will%20require%20 1%2C000%20physical%20qubits.

[13] Gambetta, J. 2023. Breaking the 1,000-qubit barrier with Condor, in The hardware and software for the era of quantum utility is here. *IBM*.

[14] Sharma, S. 2023. Navigating The Quantum Era: The Shift To Quantum-Safe Cryptography. Available from: https://www.forbes.com/sites/forbestechcouncil/2023/12/07/navigating-the-quantum-era-the-shift-to-quantum-safe-cryptography/?sh=485694085601.

[15] National Academies of Sciences, E. 2019. *Medicine, Quantum Computing: Progress and Prospects*, Grumbling, E. and M. Horowitz. (eds.). Washington, DC: The National Academies Press, 272.

[16] Buchanan, W. and A. J. J. o. C. S. T. Woodward. 2017. Will quantum computers be the end of public key encryption?, 1(1): 1–22.

[17] Jozsa, R. J. C. i. s. and Engineering. 2001. Quantum factoring, discrete logarithms, and the hidden subgroup problem, 3(2): 34–43.

[18] Rijmen, V. and J. Daemen. 2001. Advanced encryption standard. *Proceedings of Federal Information Processing Standards Publications, National Institute of Standards and Technology,* 19: 22.

[19] Bernstein, D. J. and T. Lange. 2017. Post-quantum cryptography. *Nature,* 549(7671): 188–194.

[20] Grover, L. K. 1996. A fast quantum mechanical algorithm for database search. In *Proceedings of the Twenty-eighth Annual ACM Symposium on Theory of Computing.*

[21] IBM. Practical Introduction to Quantum-safe Cryptography. Available from: https://learning.quantum.ibm.com/course/practical-introduction-to-quantum-safe-cryptography/cryptographic-hash-functions.

[22] Shi, T., W. Wu, L. Ding, M. Zhang, B. Hu, J. Guan and S. Wang. (Multi-Key) Quantum Analysis of Masked Even—Mansour with Applications to Offset Public Permutation and Elephant.

[23] Hekkala, J., M. Muurman, K. Halunen and V. Vallivaara. 2023. Implementing post-quantum cryptography for developers. 4(4): 365.

[24] Dam, D. -T., T. -H. Tran, V. -P. Hoang, C. -K. Pham and T. -T. Hoang. 2023. A survey of post-quantum cryptography: Start of a new race. 7(3): 40.

[25] Bennett, C. H. and G. J. T. c. s. Brassard. 2014. Quantum cryptography: Public key distribution and coin tossing, 560: 7–11.

[26] Bu, L., R. Agrawal, H. Cheng and M. A. Kinsy. 2019. Post-quantum cryptographic hardware primitives.

[27] Khan, W. Z., M. Raza and M. J. A. P. Imran. 2023. Quantum Cryptography a Real Threat to Classical Blockchain: Requirements and Challenges.

[28] Kumar, A., C. Ottaviani, S. S. Gill and R. Buyya. 2022. Securing the future internet of things with post-quantum cryptography. 5(2): e200.

[29] Derek, A. 2021. Requirements for post-quantum cryptography on embedded devices in the IoT. In *Conference Name: Third PQC Standardization Conference.*

[30] Nasiri, S., F. Sadoughi, M. H. Tadayon and A. Dehnad. 2019. Security requirements of internet of things-based healthcare system: A survey study 27(4): 253.

[31] Silva, C., V. A. Cunha, J. P. Barraca and R. L. Aguiar. 2024. Analysis of the cryptographic algorithms in IoT communications. 26(4): 1243–1260.

[32] Ott, D. and C. J. a. p. a. Peikert. 2019. Identifying research challenges in post quantum cryptography migration and cryptographic agility.

[33] Continuous Glucose Monitoring. Available from: https://my.clevelandclinic.org/health/treatments/11444-glucose-continuous-glucose-monitoring.

[34] Continuous Glucose Monitors (CGM). Available from: https://diatribe.org/continuous-glucose-monitors-cgm.

[35] Bajrić, S. J. I. A. 2023. Enabling secure and trustworthy quantum networks: Current state-of-the-art, key challenges, and potential solutions, 11: 128801–128809.

[36] Chrystyn, H., R. Audibert, M. Keller, B. Quaglia, L. Vecellio and N. Roche. 2019. Real-life inhaler adherence and technique: Time to get smarter! 158: 24–32.

[37] Smart Inhaler. Available from: https://www.nxp.com/design/design-center/designs/smart-inhaler:SMART-INHALER.

[38] K32W061/41: High-Performance, Secure and Ultra-Low-Power MCU for Zigbee®,Thread™, and Bluetooth® LE 5.0 with Built-In NFC Option. Available from: https://www.nxp.com/products/wireless-connectivity/multiprotocol-mcus/k32w061-41-high-performance-secure-and-ultra-low-power-mcu-for-zigbeethread-and-bluetooth-le-5-0-with-built-in-nfc-option:K32W061_41.

[39] QN9090/30: Bluetooth Low-Energy MCU with Arm®Cortex®-M4 CPU, Energy Efficiency, Analog and Digital Peripherals and NFC Tag Option. Available from: https://www.nxp.com/products/wireless-connectivity/bluetooth-low-energy/qn9090-30-bluetooth-low-energy-mcu-with-armcortex-m4-cpu-energy-efficiency-analog-and-digital-peripherals-and-nfc-tag-option:QN9090-30.

[40] Shepherd, C., K. Markantonakis, N. Van Heijningen, D. Aboulkassimi, C. Gaine, T. Heckmann and D. Naccache. 2021. Physical fault injection and side-channel attacks on mobile devices: A comprehensive analysis. 111: 102471.

[41] Kim, K. B. and H. J. J. E. Baek. 2023. Photoplethysmography in wearable devices: A comprehensive review of technological advances, current challenges, and future directions, 12(13): 2923.

[42] Saha, A., S. Saha, P. Mandal, P. Bawaly and M. Roy. 2022. Microcontroller-based heart rate monitor. In *Computational Advancement in Communication, Circuits and Systems: Proceedings of 3rd ICCACCS 2020*. Springer.

[43] Ai, Z., Z. Wang and W. Cui. 2019. Low-power wireless wearable ECG monitoring chestbelt based on ferroelectric microprocessor. In *2019 Chinese Control Conference (CCC)*. IEEE.

[44] Su, Y. -p. 2022. Design of ECG acquisition and display system based on ADS1292R and STM32 microcontroller. In *2022 15th International Congress on Image and Signal Processing, BioMedical Engineering and Informatics (CISP-BMEI)*. IEEE.

[45] STM32 High Performance MCUs. Available from: https://www.st.com/en/microcontrollers-microprocessors/stm32-high-performance-mcus.html.

[46] LaMeres, B. J. 2023. *The MSP430, in Embedded Systems Design using the MSP430FR2355 LaunchPad™*. Springer, 135–152.

[47] Dey, M., B. B. Yilmaz, M. Prvulovic and A. Zajić. 2021. PRIMER: Profiling interrupts using electromagnetic side-channel for embedded devices. 71(8): 1824–1838.

[48] Lavaud, C., R. Gerzaguet, M. Gautier, O. Berder, E. Nogues and S. Molton. 2021. Whispering devices: A survey on how side-channels lead to compromised information. 5: 143–168.

[49] Alagic, G., G. Alagic, D. Apon, D. Cooper, Q. Dang, T. Dang, J. Kelsey, J. Lichtinger, Y. -K. Liu and C. Miller. 2022. Status report on the third round of the NIST post-quantum cryptography standardization process.

[50] Kalaivani, V. J. P. and u. computing. 2023. Enhanced BB84 quantum cryptography protocol for secure communication in wireless body sensor networks for medical applications, 27(3): 875.

[51] Dione, D., B. Seck, I. Diop, P. -L. Cayrel, D. Faye and I. Gueye. 2023. Hardware security for IoT in the quantum era: Survey and challenges. 14(4): 227–249.

[52] Althobaiti, O. S. and M. J. I. A. Dohler. 2020. Cybersecurity challenges associated with the internet of things in a post-quantum world, 8: 157356–157381.

[53] Malina, L., P. Dzurenda, S. Ricci, J. Hajny, G. Srivastava, R. Matulevičius, A. -A. O. Affia, M. Laurent, N. H. Sultan and Q. Tang. 2021. Post-quantum era privacy protection for intelligent infrastructures. 9: 36038–36077.

[54] Safe, O. Q. Available from: https://openquantumsafe.org/.

[55] Open Quantum safe/liboqs. Available from: https://github.com/open-quantum-safe/liboqs.

[56] Kannwischer, M. J., P. Schwabe, D. Stebila and T. Wiggers. 2022. Improving software quality in cryptography standardization projects. In *2022 IEEE European Symposium on Security and Privacy Workshops (EuroS&PW)*. IEEE.
[57] Fernández-Caramés, T. M. J. I. I. o. T. J. 2019. From pre-quantum to post-quantum IoT security: A survey on quantum-resistant cryptosystems for the Internet of Things, 7(7): 6457–6480.
[58] Team, T. N. P. 2022. PQC Standardization Process: Announcing Four Candidates to be Standardized, Plus Fourth Round Candidates. Available from: https://csrc.nist.gov/news/2022/pqc-candidates-to-be-standardized-and-round-4.
[59] Tjhai, C., M. T., A. Cheng and G. Bartlett. 2017. Hybrid quantum-safe key exchange for Internet Key Exchange Protocol Version 2 (IKEv2) draft-tjhai-ipsecme-hybrid-qske-ikev2-00. 2017; Available from: https://datatracker.ietf.org/doc/html/draft-tjhai-ipsecme-hybrid-qske-ikev2-00.
[60] Gross, G. 2023. IETF news. In *IETF Launches Post-quantum Encryption Working Group*. IETF.

Chapter 14

Exploring Exoskeletons in Lower Limb Rehabilitation

A Review to Identify Critical Challenges for Enhanced Functional Outcomes

Md. Enamul Haque,[1,*] *Md. Rasedul Islam,*[2] *Md. Assad-Uz-Zaman,*[2] *Inga Wang*[3] and *Mohammad Habibur Rahman*[1]

1. Introduction

Human legs are essential for socializing, family, and independence [1]. Immobility owing to leg function impairment affects several facets of life [2]. Additionally, compromised leg mobility can hinder fulfilling family responsibilities and activities, increasing dependence on others [3, 4]. Regrettably, there exist various factors contributing to the loss of mobility in the lower extremities (LE) of individuals, stemming from conditions such as stroke, more than 15 million people are affected by

[1] BioRobotics Lab, Mechanical Engineering Department, University of Wisconsin Milwaukee, Wisconsin, USA.
[2] Mechanical Engineering Department, University of Wisconsin-Green Bay, WI 54311, USA.
[3] Department of Rehabilitation Sciences & Technology, University of Wisconsin Milwaukee, WI 53211, USA.
Emails: islamm@uwgb.edu, uzm@uwgb.edu, wang52@uwm.edu, rahmanmh@uwm.edu
* Corresponding author: mdenamul@uwm.edu

DOI: 10.1201/9781003483267-18

stroke annually, making it the third greatest cause of disability (as indicated by disability-adjusted life-years lost - DALYs) globally, according to the World Health Organization (WHO) and the World Stroke Organization (WSO) [5], among which two-thirds survive [6]. Approximately 65% of stroke survivors experience LE dysfunctions in the early stage [7] and 35% in the chronic stage [8]. The majority of these individuals live with long-term disabilities, leading to serious social and economic impacts. Indeed, study shows that average cost for rehabilitation purpose for stroke patient is $11,689 per individual/year [9] and in the USA annual stroke-related costs increasing from US$71.55 billion in 2012 to $183.13 billion by 2030 [10]. An individual who suffers from neurologic-related gait impairment can obtain rehabilitation and recovery of lower limb function with the assistance of appropriate physical therapy [11]. Increasing therapy dosage, intensity, number of repetitions, execution of task-oriented exercises, and combining top-down and bottom-up approaches can promote plasticity and functional recovery [12].

A person who has had a stroke usually experiences the most significant improvements in their condition within the first 3–6 months. The authors of [13] in their study found that people could see improvements even beyond 12 months. On this basis, they recommend the revision of clinical guidelines for stroke rehabilitation. Factors that can affect a person's recovery include: the part of the brain the stroke affected, how much of the brain the stroke affected, the person's motivation, the level of support a person has, the quantity and quality of their rehabilitation, the person's health before the stroke [14–16]. Staging the stroke is as: the first 2 weeks are defined as the acute stage, 3–11 weeks post-stroke is termed the subacute stage in which most changes occur, 12–24 weeks post-stroke is the early chronic stage, more than 24 weeks post-stroke is termed as chronic stage. On the other hand, in [17] the timeline is defined as follows: Hyper-acute: 0–24 hours, Acute: 1–7 days, Early sub-acute: 7 days–3 months, Late sub-acute: 3–6 months, Chronic: > 6 months.

According to the Swedish physical therapist Signe Brunnstrom, in 1960 the stroke stages and recovery can be divided in seven faces (Flaccidity, Spasticity, Increase-spasticity, Decrease-spasticity, Complex-movement-return, Spasticity-disappear, and Normal-function-return) and the recommended exercise for each stages are described in [18].

However, in the journey to recovery for patients who have suffered a stroke or a spinal cord injury (SCI), the rehabilitation process is typically phased into passive, active-assistive, and resistive therapies. In this three phases of exercise, according to [19] the therapist should cover 10 principles, and according to [20] the therapist should cover 15 principles (see the Islam M.R. (2020)) [21].

Throughout the rehabilitation period for the lower limb of a stroke patient, a therapist or clinician administered various exercises and

Table 1: Kleim's Principles (KP) & Maier's Principle (MP) for neuroplasticity.

Kleim and Jones' ten neuroplasticity principles for rehabilitation	
KP1-Use It or Lose It: "Neural circuits not actively engaged in task performance for an extended period of time begin to degrade." **KP2-Use It and Improve It:** "Training that drives a specific brain function can lead to enhancement of that function." **KP3-Specificity:** "The nature of the training experience dictates the nature of the plasticity." **KP4-Repetition Matters:** "Induction of plasticity requires sufficient repetition." **KP5-Intensity Matters:** "Induction of plasticity requires sufficient intensity." **KP6-Time Matters:** "Different forms of plasticity occur at different times during recovery." **KP7-Salience Matters:** "The training experience must be sufficiently salient to induce plasticity." **KP8-Age Matters:** "Training-induced plasticity occurs more readily in younger brains." **KP9-Transference or Generalization:** "Plasticity in response to one training experience can enhance the acquisition of similar behaviors." **KP10-Interference:** "Plasticity in response to one training experience can impede the acquisition of similar behaviors."	
Maier's 15 p neuroplasticity principles for rehabilitation	
MP1- Massed Practice/repeated practice **MP2-** Spaced Practice **MP3-** Dosage **MP4-** Task-Specific Practice **MP5-** Goal-oriented practice **MP6-** Variable Practice **MP7-** Increasing difficulty **MP8-** Multisensory Stimulation	**MP9-** Rhythmic Cueing **MP10-** Explicit feedback **MP11-** Implicit feedback **MP12-** Modulate Effector Selection **PM13-** Action Observation/Embodied Practice **MP14-** Motor Imagery/Mental Practice **MP15-** Social Interaction

movement, and utilized the ideas of neuroplasticity proposed by Kleim and Maier to address each stage of the stroke. However, conventional rehabilitation therapies require a long commitment by a therapist/ clinician, and the challenges for transportation of patients to Rehabilitation Centre and high cost of rehabilitation by physical therapist led to early withdrawal of the patients from rehabilitation services. Prolonged immobility not only leads to physical deterioration but also undermines the psychological well-being of individuals confined to their beds [22, 23]. These all signify to develop a lower limb rehabilitation device/robot to restore the function of the LE with all requirements. This article provides a comprehensive review of the hardware design and control aspects of existing upper limb rehabilitation exoskeletons, aiming to identify and address current challenges for enhanced functionality. The scope of this review is confined, excluding end-effector-type robotic devices and not covering exoskeletons designed for toe rehabilitation. The focus is primarily on lower limb exoskeletons supporting hip, knee, and/or ankle rehabilitation. It is important to note that the authors do not claim to include all available lower limb exoskeletons in this review.

2. Robot-Aided Rehabilitation

According to the principles of neuroplasticity and motor learning, robotic devices have been introduced in the rehabilitation process because they can maximize afferent input from peripheral joints and provide task-specific stimulation to the central nervous system to promote functional recovery [24]. The field of rehabilitation robotics has witnessed remarkable advancements in recent years. The technological innovations for lower limb rehabilitation can be categorized in two ways, based on the mapping of a device's joint onto human anatomical joints (e.g., end-effector type and exoskeleton type). The end-effector-type devices (e.g., Life Science Robotics (LSR) in Aalborg, Denmark developed an end-effector type rehab robot as ROBERT® as shown in Figure 1(a) [25], BTS ANYMOV as shown in Figure 1(b) [26], Hocoma Erigo in Figure 1(c) [27], and LLRTS in Figure 1(d) [28], LokoHelp [29]) are suitable for end-point exercises as they are unable to provide individual joint movement, meaning they cannot map onto human anatomical joints.

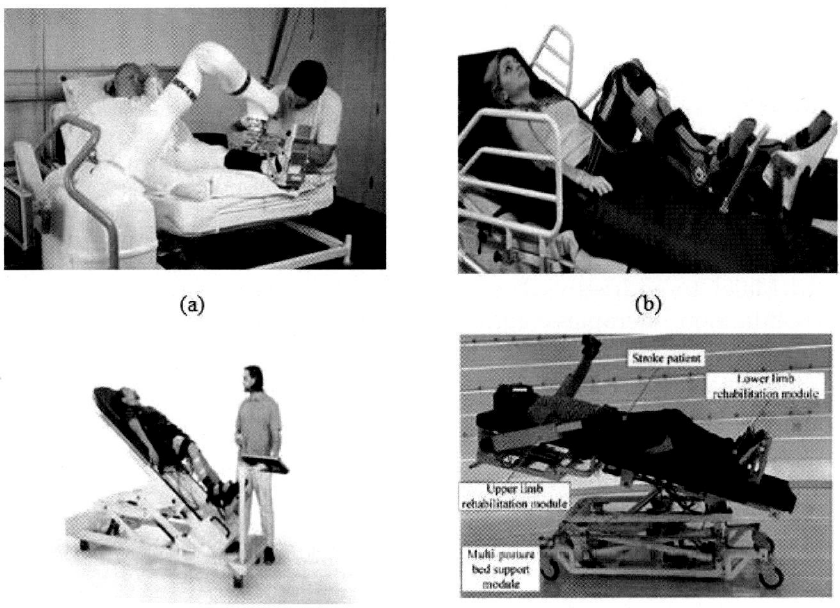

Figure 1: End-effector type rehab devices (a) ROBERT(Courtesy to Kuka), (b) BTS ANYMOV Courtesy to btsbioengineering), (c) Hocoma Erigo (Courtesy to Hocoma), (d) LLRTS.

An exoskeleton robot is a wearable mechanical device which has advantages over end-effector-type devices, as they have complete control over a patient's individual joint movement and applied torque, better guidance of motion, relatively larger range of motion (ROM), and better quantitative feedback (This covers all Kleim & Jones principle except KP8 as well as Maier's principles except MP14 & MP15). To date numerous research prototypes of exoskeletons have been developed for human lower limb rehabilitation (e.g., Physiotherabot, MotionMaker, LeHab, LLR-Ro, Lokomat, LOPES, HAL (Rehabilitation), Wearable walking Helper, Honda: SMA, Vanderbilt Lower limb Exo and so on; see Figures 2, 3, and 4 and also see their review in Tables 2 and 3). The implementation of exoskeletons in clinical environments such as hospitals and outpatient centers remains circumscribed, with a scant number of commercially available models (refer to Figure 3).

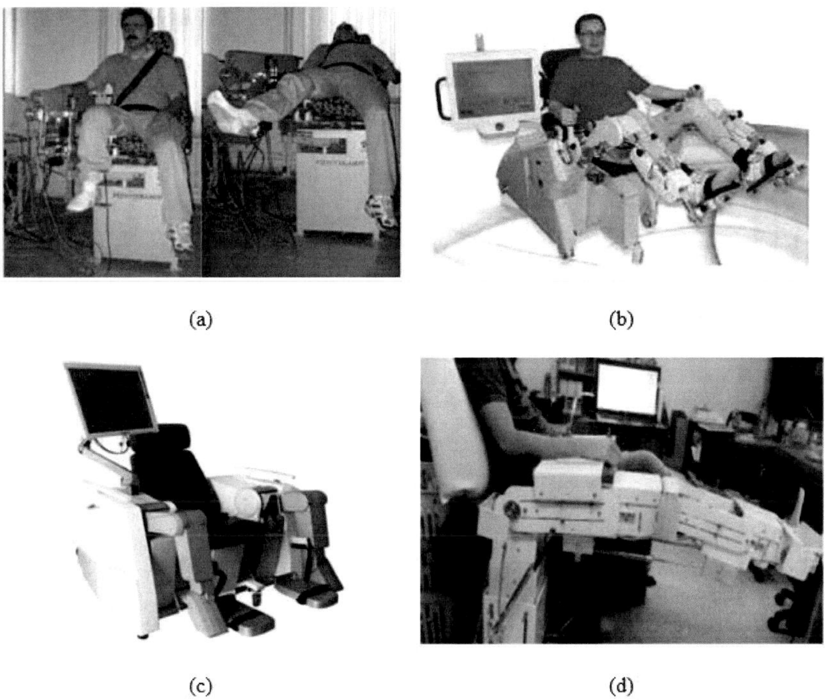

Figure 2: Leg rehab exoskeleton for bedridden patients, (a) Physiotherabot, (b) MotionMaker (Courtesy to Huanxiyl), (c) LLR-Ro, and (d) LeHab.

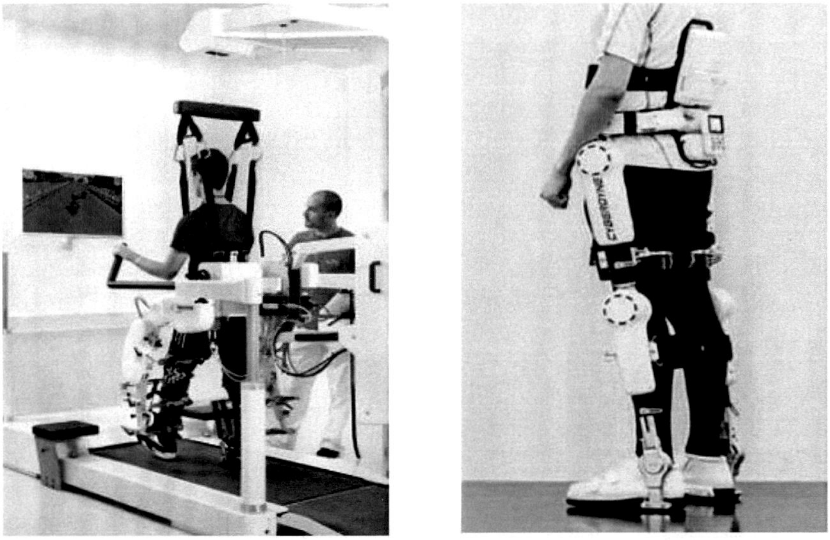

(a) (b)

Figure 3: Commercially available exoskeleton robot for rehabilitation: (a) Lokomat (Courtesy to Hocoma), and (b) HAL (Courtesy to Exoskeletonreport).

3. Design Requirements and Challenges

Lower limb exoskeleton type robots, unlike industrial or other robotic systems, have an inherently complex structure that requires high levels of ingenuity in their design. While researchers have implemented various measures to enhance functionality, some limitations persist and need to be addressed.

3.1 Safety

The interaction between humans and leg rehabilitation robots introduces unique safety challenges not encountered in other robotic applications. These can be categorized into mechanical, electronic, and control design safety.

Mechanical safety is critical due to the direct interface between the robot and human limbs. Features like stoppers are integrated into the mechanical design to ensure that the exoskeleton does not move beyond the natural human range of motion (ROM). For instance, if the robot assists in knee extension, stoppers can prevent hyperextension, protecting the joint. Some designs incorporate adjacent links that act as physical stoppers during extreme movements, ensuring safety even in cases of control system failure.

Table 2: Summary table of existing lower limb rehabilitation exoskeletons.

Device and Authors	Device or Robot Feature	Remarks
Physiotherabot [30]	**Total DOF:** 3 DOFs **Types of therapy:** Passive, Active, Resistive **Clinical test:** No **Actuation and Power transmission:** BLDC Motor with strain wave gear reduction **Control:** Position Control	**Strength:** No body support needed and suitable for bedridden patients. **Weakness:** No hip: R-R , and ankle: F-E, & Ab-Ad motion
MotionMaker [31]	**Total DOF:** 8 DOFs **Types of therapy:** Passive, Active, Resistive **Clinical test:** Yes Actuation and Power transmission: BLDC Motor with strain wave gear reduction **Control:** Force and Torque control	**Strength:** No body support needed and suitable for bedridden patients. It also used FES (Functional Electrical Stimulation) for active training. **Weakness:** No hip: Ab-Ad, R-R, and ankle: Ab-Ad motion
LLR-Ro [28, 32]	**Total DOF:** 3 DOFs **Types of therapy:** Passive, Active and Resistive **Clinical test:** No **Actuation and Power transmission:** DC Motor with mechanical gear **Control:** Force and Torque Control	**Strength:** No body support need and suitable for bedridden patients. **Weakness:** No hip: Ab-Ad, R-R , and ankle: F-E, & Ab-Ad motion
LeHab [33]	**Total DOF:** 3 DOFs **Types of therapy:** Passive and Active **Clinical test:** No **Actuation and Power transmission:** DC motor with harmonic drive **Control approach:** Position Control	**Strength:** No body support needed and suitable for bedridden patients. **Weakness:** No hip: Ab-Ad, R-R , and ankle: Ab-Ad motion
Lokomat [34, 35]	**Total DOF:** 14 DOFs **Types of therapy:** Passive, Active, Resistive **Clinical test:** Yes **Actuation and Power transmission:** Custom-designed drives with a precision ball screw and DC motor. **Control:** Impedance control, adaptive control	**Strength:** A parallelogram design that maintains the robotic pelvis segment's alignment while enabling passive vertical orthosis translations. **Weakness:** No hip Ab-Ad & R-R motion There is no ankle actuator
LOPES & LOPES II [36, 37]	**Total DOF:** 8 DOFs **Types of therapy:** Passive, Active, Resistive **Clinical test:** Yes **Actuation and Power transmission:** Cable-driven SEA (Pneumatic Actuators) **Control:** 1. Predefined joint trajectory control 2. Admittance controller	**Strength:** There is pelvis' Superior/inferior & Lateral motion exists. **Weakness:** No hip: R-R & ankle: F-E & Ab-Ad motion exists.

Table 2 contd. ...

...Table 2 contd.

Device and Authors	Device or Robot Feature	Remarks
ALEX II & ALEX III [38, 39]	**Total DOF:** 12 DOFs **Types of therapy:** Passive, Active, Resistive **Clinical test:** Yes **Actuation and Power transmission:** DC motors with cables and timing belts **Control:** Torque calculated by impedance controller	**Strength:** Variable damping force tunnel for gait training **Weakness:** There is no hip R-R motion and also there is no ankle Ab-Ad motion.
MIRAD [40, 41]	**Total DOF:** 6 DOFs **Types of therapy:** Passive & active **Clinical test:** No **Actuation and Power transmission:** Motor-driven Joints with manual preloaded tension springs **Control:** Predefined joint torque	**Strength:** Modular Variable Stiffness Actuators **Weakness:** No pelvis motion, and no hip & ankle Ab-Ad motion exists.
XoR & XoR2 [42, 43]	**Total DOF:** 14 DOFs **Types of therapy:** Active, Passive and resistive **Clinical test:** Yes **Actuation and Power transmission:** Pneumatic Actuated Muscle (PAMs) and DC servo motors. **Control:** Position and torque control	**Strength:** Pneumatic artificial muscles were combined with small high-response servo motors for the hip and knee joints. **Weakness:** There is no motion for pelvis motion.
HAL (Rehabilitation) [44, 45]	**Total DOF:** 6 DOFs **Therapy Type:** Passive, Active & resistive **Clinical test:** Yes **Actuation and Power transmission:** Electric motor- harmonic driven (Full lower body exoskeleton). **Control:** Estimate user's moving intention via GRF or pelvis tilt angles, and gait trajectories by defining initial and endpoints	**Strength:** This system provides motion support based on the EMG signals of the wearer. **Weakness:** No pelvis motion and no hip & ankle Ab-Ad motion
Wearable Walking Helper [46]	**Total DOF:** 6 DOFs **Types of therapy:** Not to mention. **Clinical test:** No **Actuation and Power transmission:** Electric motor with mechanical gear mechanism. **Control:** Trajectories based on spring-mass model and used in impedance control	**Strength:** Ground Reaction Force (GRF) sensor is used to measure the GRF applied to the user's foot. **Weakness:** No hip & ankle Ab-Ad motion

Table 2 contd. ...

...Table 2 contd.

Device and Authors	Device or Robot Feature	Remarks
Honda: SMA [47]	**Total DOF:** 6 DOFs **Types of therapy:** Not to mention. **Clinical test:** Yes **Actuation and Power transmission:** DC motors actuated exoskeleton **Control:** Generate symmetric hip joint trajectory with angle measurements feed into CPG.	**Strength:** Suitable for the individual with hip joint weakness. **Weakness:** No pelvis motion, even on in knee or ankle only hip joint actuated
Vanderbilt lower limb Exo. [48]	**Total DOF:** 4 DOFs **Type of therapy:** Passive, active and resistive **Clinical test:** Yes **Actuation and Power transmission:** DC motors with FES **Control:** Predefined joint trajectories, **FES:** Stimulation will stop if muscle fatigue is detected.	**Strength:** FES is used to reduce the torque and power output required from the hip and knee motors of the exoskeleton. **Weakness:** No pelvis or ankle joint motion.
Human Lower Extremity Rehabilitation Robot [49]	**Total DOF:** 8 DOFs **Type of therapy:** Not specified. **Clinical test:** No **Actuation and Power transmission:** DC motor with harmonic drive. **Control:** Sliding mode controller with super twisting algorithm	**Strength:** Knee- linear displacement and Shank- Internal/external ration **Weakness:** No pelvis motions.
RLLE [50]	**Total DOF:** 3 DOFs **Types of therapy:** Passive **Clinical test:** No **Actuation and Power transmission:** DC Motor with harmonic drive **Control:** Fuzzy control	**Strength:** swarm optimization based initialization of model reference adaptive for fuzzy logic proportional derivative controller (Adaptive-FLC-PD) **Weakness:** Only their F-E motion in the hip, knee, and ankle joint

F-E➡Flexion-Extension, Ab-Ad ➡Abduction-Adduction, R-R➡Internal – External Rotation

Electronic safety ensures the motors and actuators operate within safe parameters by placing limits on the current and voltage supplied. Overcurrent situations, which may indicate a jam or obstruction, trigger immediate system halts to prevent accidents. This ensures that movements remain within predefined safety thresholds.

Table 3: Overview of the exoskeleton robot for rehabilitation based on Pelvis, Hip, Knee, and Ankle Joint Motion.

Device Name	**Pelvis Joint**						**Hip Joint**			**Knee Joint**		**Ankle Joint**		
	Superior/inferior (Up/Down)	Lateral (Mediolateral)	Anterior/posterior	Obliquity (frontal rotation)	Tilt (Sagittal rotation)	Vertical/Transversal rotation	Flexion/extension	Adduction/abduction	Internal/external rotation	Flexion/extension	Linear displacement	Dorsiflexion/plantarflexion	Adduction/abduction	Inversion/ Eversion
Physitherabot [30]							X	X		X				
MotionMaker [31]							X	X		X		X		
LLR-Ro [28, 32]							X			X		X		
LeHab [33]							X			X		X		
Lokomat [34, 35]	X	X	X			X	X			X		X		
LOPES & LOPES II [36, 37]	X	X					X	X		X				
ALEX II &ALEX III [38, 39]	X	X	X			X	X	X		X		X		
MIRAD [40, 41]							X			X		X		
XoR & XoR2[42, 43]							X	X	X	X		X	X	X
HAL(Rehabilitation) [44, 45]							X			X		X		
Wearable Walking Helper [46]							X			X		X		
Honda [47]							X	X	X					
Vanderbilt Lower limb Exo [48]							X			X				
HLERR [49]							X	X	X	X	X	X		X
RLLE [50]							X			X		X		

Control design safety is equally essential, acting as the robot's brain. Control systems use sensors to monitor parameters such as torque, force, and velocity. These parameters are capped through saturation controls, which adjust or cut motor power if necessary. Real-time feedback mechanisms further enhance safety by allowing corrective actions. An emergency stop mechanism, easily accessible to the patient or therapist, provides an additional safety layer.

Together, these mechanical, electronic, and control systems ensure holistic safety, safeguarding the user throughout the rehabilitation process.

3.2 *Comfortability*

Comfort is a vital consideration during rehabilitation sessions, which may last anywhere from 30 minutes to several hours. During this time, the exoskeleton must not only be clinically effective but also comfortable for the user. Discomfort often arises from the reactive forces and torques generated between the exoskeleton and the user's joints, particularly due to the exoskeleton's weight.

Lightweight designs help reduce the reactive forces and strain exerted on the user's joints, making the device less intrusive and more comfortable to wear. Open-type designs [28, 32, 49] are increasingly preferred as they facilitate better air circulation, minimize sweating, and allow patients to don and doff the exoskeleton with minimal assistance. These designs foster independence and enhance the overall rehabilitation experience.

The attachment mechanisms also play a pivotal role in comfort. Flexible straps or connectors [33, 51] provide a snug fit and adapt to subtle changes in the user's posture, ensuring greater ease and compliance during therapy sessions.

3.3 *Alignment of Robot Joints to Human Joints*

For effective robotic-assisted rehabilitation, the alignment between the exoskeleton's joints and the user's joints is crucial. Misalignment can hinder force transmission, lead to discomfort, and negatively affect the rehabilitation process.

The human hip joint is a prime example of biomechanical complexity. It supports motions like flexion/extension, abduction/adduction, and internal/external rotation, with a dynamic center of rotation that shifts during movement. While many exoskeletons simplify the hip joint to a three-degree-of-freedom (DOF) ball-and-socket model, such simplifications can restrict range of motion and affect user comfort [28,49,52]. Some advanced designs include additional DOFs to better replicate the hip's natural movement.

Similarly, the ankle joint also presents challenges due to its three rotational motions: dorsiflexion/plantar flexion, inversion/eversion, and abduction/adduction. Most designs prioritize dorsiflexion/plantar flexion, with few addressing the other motions [39, 49, 53].

3.4 *Actuation*

Actuators play a defining role in the performance and weight of exoskeletons. Electric actuators, including DC brushed, DC brushless, and servomotors, are widely used due to their high power output, reliability, and ease of integration [30, 38, 44, 49]. Pneumatic actuators, while lightweight and offering low impedance, are limited by their need for onboard compressors, maintenance requirements, and constrained operational bandwidth [36]. Hydraulic actuators generate significant power but are bulky, noisy, and unsuitable for clinical environments due to their high impedance and leakage risks [54].

Pneumatic muscle actuators mimic the functionality of natural muscles by generating tension, but they often exhibit slow and nonlinear responses [43]. Series elastic actuators enhance shock tolerance through the integration of passive springs between the motor and load, but they compromise operational bandwidth [37]. Selecting the right actuator requires balancing factors like weight, power-to-weight ratio, safety, and durability [55].

3.5 Mechanical Power Transmission Mechanism

The transmission of mechanical power is critical in exoskeleton design to ensure smooth and uninterrupted therapy. Various mechanisms, including cable drives, gear systems, and harmonic drives, are used for this purpose.

Cable drives are commonly employed due to their simplicity, reduced inertia, and flexibility in installation. However, they are prone to stretching and slipping, which can lead to inadequate tension and unintended joint movements [56]. Gear drives, such as spur and bevel gears, provide robust power transmission but require maintenance and face challenges like backlash and friction, which can hinder precision [57]. Harmonic drives, increasingly favored in exoskeleton designs, offer smooth, backlash-free operation and minimal maintenance, although their weight can be a limiting factor [33,47,49,58]. An optimal transmission mechanism must be lightweight, compact, and capable of smooth and precise power delivery.

3.6 Sensors

Sensors are indispensable in ensuring the precision, safety, and efficacy of rehabilitation robots [59, 60]. They measure critical parameters such as joint positions, torque, and force. Position determination relies on technologies like inertial measurement units (IMUs), potentiometers, and Hall sensors, while six-axis and three-axis force sensors are commonly used to measure forces exerted by users [34, 61, 62].

Advanced technologies like electromyography (EMG) and electroencephalography (EEG) are being explored to enhance user interaction by interpreting muscle and brain activity. Non-invasive surface EMG electrodes capture muscle activity patterns, while EEG enables intent detection through brain signals [44, 63]. While unidirectional sensors dominate current designs, bidirectional sensors promise improved adaptability and maneuverability, paving the way for more intuitive rehabilitation robots.

4. Control Approaches

Rehabilitation robotics has become a transformative tool in medical rehabilitation, significantly enhancing patients' quality of life. These robots enable functional movements and support daily exercise regimens, offering promising therapeutic outcomes. However, achieving intelligent and agile human–machine collaborative movement remains a significant challenge [64, 65]. Current control strategies face three key hurdles: detecting human intent accurately, translating this intent into precise motion control, and adapting control parameters to individual patient needs [66]. To address these challenges, researchers have developed various control methodologies tailored to different exercise modes, including passive, active-assistive, active, and resistive.

4.1 Trajectory-Tracking Control

Trajectory-tracking control is fundamental in lower limb exoskeleton robots designed for individuals with mobility impairments. This control strategy enables precise tracking of predefined trajectories, such as gait patterns, to provide the necessary assistance for natural and coordinated movement [67, 68]. For instance, during walking rehabilitation, the exoskeleton's control system can follow a healthy gait cycle, continuously monitored and adjusted using sensors and feedback mechanisms. These adjustments ensure that the exoskeleton aligns with the user's movements, supporting proper leg motion and posture. Additionally, trajectory-tracking control enhances safety and stability, allowing for gradual trajectory adjustments as the user's abilities improve. By closely mimicking natural gait patterns, this control method helps achieve critical rehabilitation goals [69, 70].

4.2 Force-Feedback-Based Control

Force-feedback-based control enhances user interaction with the exoskeleton, creating a more natural and responsive experience [71, 72]. This method utilizes force sensors and actuators to detect and respond to user movements. For example, during the stance phase of walking, sensors in the exoskeleton's footplates detect weight shifts and apply appropriate forces to support the user's body, ensuring balance and stability. During the swing phase, the system assists in leg swings by applying forward forces, enabling smoother and more efficient steps [73]. By improving the physiological naturalness of walking patterns, force-feedback control reduces user effort and fatigue while contributing to effective gait rehabilitation [28, 74].

4.3 *Physiological-Signal-Based Control*

Physiological-signal-based control represents an innovative approach that leverages user-generated physiological signals, such as muscle activity or brain signals, to enhance exoskeleton functionality [65]. This method uses electromyography (EMG) sensors to detect muscle activity patterns and electroencephalography (EEG) sensors to interpret brain signals [63, 75]. For example, when a user attempts to initiate a movement, the control system detects the corresponding signals and synchronizes the exoskeleton's assistance. This intuitive operation creates a seamless user experience, enabling personalized rehabilitation. By aligning with the user's physiological cues, this approach promotes responsive and adaptive mobility, enhancing the recovery of lower limb function [75].

4.4 *Data-Driven Control*

Data-driven control relies on the collection and analysis of real-time sensor data to optimize the exoskeleton's assistance dynamically. Sensors continuously monitor the user's gait, balance, and movement patterns, feeding this information to the control system [76]. In real-world scenarios, such as encountering an obstacle, the exoskeleton adjusts joint angles or forces to help the user navigate safely. This approach ensures the system responds to environmental changes and user needs in real time, offering an adaptable and efficient rehabilitation experience [77]. By tailoring support to the user's unique requirements, data-driven control fosters safety and effectiveness in daily activities and therapy sessions [78, 79].

4.5 *Learning-Based Control*

Learning-based control incorporates machine learning algorithms to optimize the exoskeleton's performance based on user-specific data [80]. For example, reinforcement learning enables the exoskeleton to continuously refine its strategies by observing the user's movements and responses. Over time, this allows the system to fine-tune parameters like joint angles, force application, and timing, creating a more natural and personalized walking experience [81]. By adapting to the user's unique needs and preferences, learning-based control enhances mobility, comfort, and rehabilitation outcomes [82]. This approach exemplifies the potential of artificial intelligence to improve human–machine synergy, making exoskeletons more user-centric and effective.

4.6 Control Approaches for Passive Exercises

Control approaches for passive exercises focus on providing assisted movements to users with limited or no voluntary muscle function [83, 84]. In these scenarios, the exoskeleton guides the user's limbs through predefined ranges of motion. For example, in knee rehabilitation, the system gently flexes and extends the knee while monitoring resistance and range of motion to ensure smooth and safe movements. These passive exercises are vital for maintaining joint flexibility, preventing contractures, and improving circulation. By prioritizing safety and comfort, passive control approaches support early-stage rehabilitation and preserve overall lower limb health [50, 85].

4.7 Control Approaches for Active and Active-Assisted Exercises

Active-assisted control approaches combine voluntary user movements with exoskeleton support to achieve specific rehabilitation goals [86]. For instance, during gait training, the exoskeleton assists with leg lifting while allowing the user to initiate and control stepping motions. Techniques such as trajectory-tracking and force-feedback control are employed to guide users in following predefined patterns and ensure optimized movement. This balance of user engagement and exoskeleton assistance encourages active participation, promoting recovery while maintaining safety and proper biomechanics. Active-assisted control methods are essential for building strength, coordination, and confidence in users as they progress in their rehabilitation journey [49].

5. Virtual Reality and Augmented Reality in Lower Limb Rehabilitation

Virtual Reality (VR) and Augmented Reality (AR) are revolutionizing lower limb rehabilitation by making therapy engaging and effective [87–89] see Figure 5. VR immerses patients in computer-generated environments using headsets or screens, enhancing adherence to therapy [90]. It aligns with neuroplasticity principles like Maier's MP4, MP5, MP7, MP10, MP11, and Kleim's KP8, KP9, particularly appealing to younger patients. For example, VR allows patients recovering from injuries to virtually walk along a scenic beach, making the process enjoyable and effective [91]. It also provides data like step counts and gait analysis, helping therapists tailor rehabilitation to individual needs. AR complements this by overlaying digital cues onto real-world environments [92]. For instance, AR can guide balance exercises by projecting visual markers and offering real-time feedback on posture [93]. It creates interactive rehabilitation spaces, even

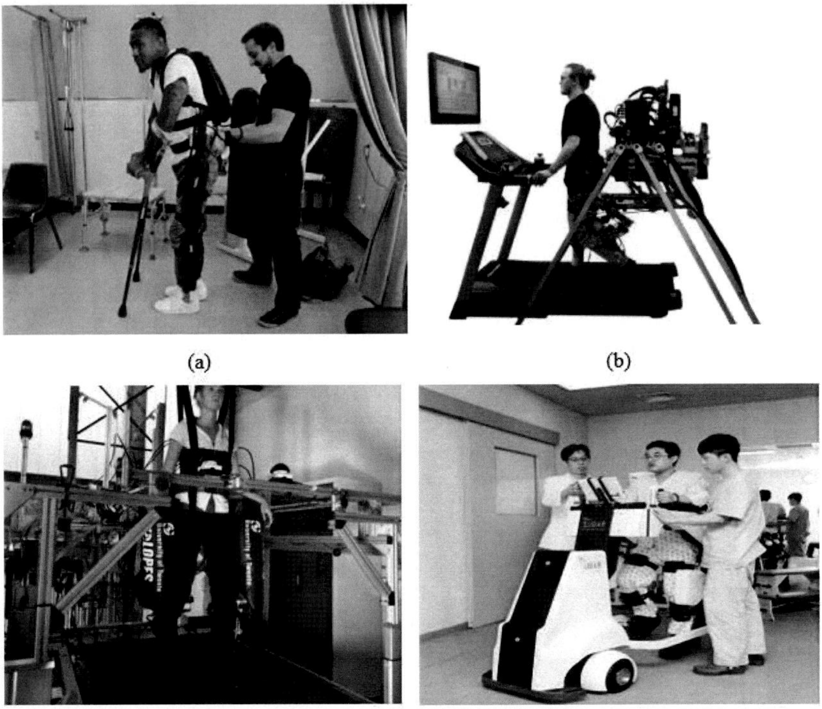

(a) (b) (c) (d)

Figure 4: Lower limb exoskeleton robot for rehabilitation: (a) Vanderbilt Exoskeleton, (b) ALEX-III, (c) LOPES, and (d) SUBAR.

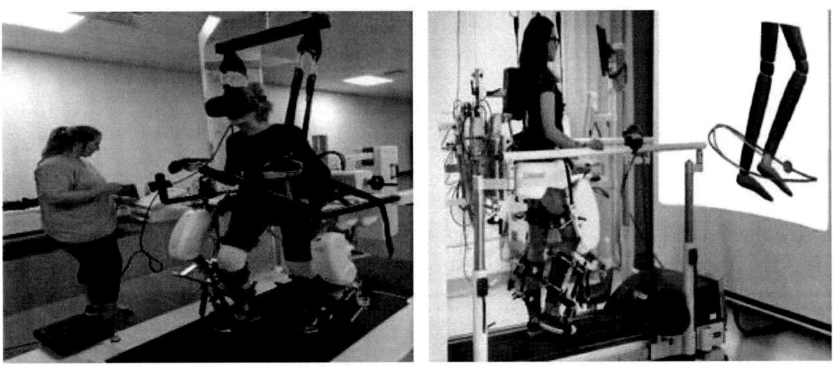

(a) (b)

Figure 5: (a) Virtual Reality, and (b) Augmented Reality in Lokomat (Courtesy to Hocoma) for lower limb rehabilitation.

enabling remote therapy where therapists monitor and guide patients virtually. Together, VR and AR enhance accessibility, personalization, and patient outcomes.

6. Telerehabilitation

Telerehabilitation integrates technology to deliver remote care, addressing accessibility and personalization challenges in lower limb rehabilitation. It enables patients in underserved areas to receive therapy at home, supported by real-time monitoring and adaptive plans tailored to their progress [94–96]. Tools like the Lokomat, a robotic-assisted treadmill, combine remote control of exercise parameters with video conferencing for motivation and support [97]. This approach ensures continuity of care and precise adjustments based on performance data, optimizing therapy outcomes. Telerehabilitation bridges geographic barriers, providing personalized, effective rehabilitation for diverse patient needs.

7. Discussion

Over the past two decades, rehabilitation robotics has advanced significantly, particularly in addressing lower limb disabilities. Research has concentrated on both hardware design and sophisticated control strategies to enhance therapeutic outcomes. This article outlines the evolving requirements of rehabilitative robotic devices, balancing patient needs with clinician and therapist expectations. It highlights advancements in hardware for optimizing human–robot interaction (HRI) and control strategies that ensure safety and therapeutic efficacy. Comparative evaluations of exoskeletons have focused on safety, wearability, structural alignment, actuation, and power transmission.

A key challenge in exoskeleton design is simulating comprehensive lower limb motion while maintaining anatomical alignment and accommodating diverse patient anatomies. Many existing exoskeletons fail to fully replicate the mobility of pelvis, hip, knee, and ankle joints, as illustrated in Table 3. Addressing this requires novel designs that preserve natural ranges of motion. Advanced actuators are essential, emphasizing lightweight construction, compactness, operational bandwidth, and reliability. Modular designs, enabling reconfiguration to suit patient-specific needs, offer promising solutions.

Virtual Reality (VR) and Augmented Reality (AR) have transformed lower limb rehabilitation, fostering patient engagement through immersive and interactive environments. By simulating real-world scenarios, VR and AR personalize therapy and encourage consistent participation, accelerating recovery. Telerehabilitation further enhances accessibility by facilitating remote monitoring and personalized guidance, ensuring continuous care for patients in remote areas. Integrating VR, AR, and telerehabilitation can create tailored, inclusive rehabilitation experiences, broadening access and efficacy.

Control strategies remain a dynamic area of development. Defining safe ranges of motion (ROM) and autonomously adapting interventions based on patient feedback are crucial. While conventional methods rely on manual assessments, robots should independently adjust protocols for optimal patient safety and performance. Additionally, mobile robotic rehabilitation systems could address logistical challenges by providing integrated, adaptive solutions for bedridden patients, offsetting torque demands and enhancing usability.

8. Conclusion

This study undertakes a comprehensive review of exoskeleton type robot-assisted therapy in comparison to the requirements of clinical practitioners and therapists for stroke patients. It critically examines the hardware architecture, safety measures, design compactness, control strategies, actuation methods, power transmission mechanism, and sensor integrations of prevailing lower limb rehabilitative in exoskeletons. A noteworthy observation from our investigation is that a significant proportion of research prototypes concerning exoskeletons have not successfully transitioned into commercial applications. A potential rationale for this discrepancy might be the limited emphasis on rigorous clinical evaluations. Consequently, this review delineates the key challenges that, when addressed, can enhance the efficacy and applicability of such robotic systems in therapeutic settings. Furthermore, based on the findings, pertinent recommendations have been proposed to augment the functional capabilities of rehabilitation robots in future developments.

References

[1] Gabriel, Z. and A. Bowling. 2004. Quality of life from the perspectives of older people. *Ageing Soc.*, 24(5): 675–691.

[2] Michaud, M., G. Lavigne, A. Desautels. et al. 2002. Effects of immobility on sensory and motor symptoms of restless legs syndrome. *Mov Disord.*, 17(1): 112–115.

[3] Bartenieff, I. and D. Lewis. 2002. *Body Movement: Coping with the Environment*. New York: Routledge.

[4] Pressman, S. D., T. Kraft and S. Bowlin. 2017. Well-being: Physical, psychological, and social. pp. 1–6. *In*: Gellman, M. and J. R. Turner. (eds.). *Encycl Behav. Med.* [Internet]. New York, NY: Springer New York; [cited 2023 Oct 25]. Available from: http://link.springer.com/10.1007/978-1-4614-6439-6_75-2.

[5] Feigin, V. L., M. Brainin, B. Norrving. et al. 2022. World Stroke Organization (WSO): Global Stroke Fact Sheet 2022. *Int. J. Stroke*, 17(1): 18–29.
[6] Statistics, Stroke, 2024. Statistics, Stroke, 2023. http://www.strokecenter.org/patients/about-stroke/ stroke-statistics/.
[7] Hendricks, H. T., J. Van Limbeek, A. C. Geurts. et al. 2002. Motor recovery after stroke: A systematic review of the literature. *Arch. Phys. Med. Rehabil.*, 83(11): 1629–1637.
[8] Dobkin, B. H. 2005. Rehabilitation after Stroke. *N. Engl. J. Med.*, 352(16): 1677–1684.
[9] Godwin, K. M., J. Wasserman and S. K. Ostwald. 2011. Cost associated with stroke: outpatient rehabilitative services and medication. *Top Stroke Rehabil.*, 18(sup1): 676–684.
[10] Ovbiagele, B., L. B. Goldstein, R. T. Higashida. et al. 2013. Forecasting the future of stroke in the united states: A policy statement from the american heart association and american stroke association. *Stroke*, 44(8): 2361–2375.
[11] Patton, J., D. A. Brown, M. Peshkin. et al. 2008. KineAssist: design and development of a robotic overground gait and balance therapy device. *Top Stroke Rehabil.*, 15(2): 131–139.
[12] Esquenazi, A. and M. Talaty. 2019. Robotics for lower limb rehabilitation. *Phys. Med. Rehabil. Clin. N. Am.*, 30(2): 385–397.
[13] Ballester, B. R., M. Maier, A. Duff. et al. 2019. A critical time window for recovery extends beyond one-year post-stroke. *J. Neurophysiol.*, 122(1): 350–357.
[14] O'Sullivan, S. B., T. J. Schmitz and G. D. Fulk. (eds.). 2019. Physical rehabilitation. Seventh edition. Philadelphia: F.A. Davis Company.
[15] Cramer, S. C. 2008. Repairing the human brain after stroke: I. Mechanisms of spontaneous recovery. *Ann. Neurol.*, 63(3): 272–287.
[16] Rehme, A. K., S. B. Eickhoff, C. Rottschy. et al. 2012. Activation likelihood estimation meta-analysis of motor-related neural activity after stroke. *NeuroImage*, 59(3): 2771–2782.
[17] Bernhardt, J., K. S. Hayward, G. Kwakkel. et al. 2017. Agreed definitions and a shared vision for new standards in stroke recovery research: The Stroke Recovery and Rehabilitation Roundtable taskforce. *Int. J. Stroke*, 12(5): 444–450.
[18] Elizabeth. 2022. The Brunnstrom Stages of Stroke Recovery: What Each Milestone Means [Internet]. Flint Rehab. Available from: https://www.flintrehab.com/brunnstrom-stages-of-stroke-recovery/#stage1.
[19] Kleim, J. A. and T. A. Jones. 2008. Principles of experience-dependent neural plasticity: implications for rehabilitation after brain damage. *J. Speech Lang Hear Res.* [Internet]. [cited 2023 Nov 6]; 51(1).
[20] Maier, M., B. R. Ballester and P. F. M. J. Verschure. 2019. Principles of neurorehabilitation after stroke based on motor learning and brain plasticity mechanisms. *Front. Syst. Neurosci.*, 13: 74.
[21] Islam, M. R. 2020. Design and development of a 7 dof robot with ergonomic shoulder for upper limb rehabilitation. *Univ Wis - Milwaukee ProQuest Diss. Publ.* [Internet].
[22] Charmaz, K. 1997. Good days, bad days: the self in chronic illness and time. 2. paperback print. New Brunswick, NJ: Rutgers.
[23] Smith, J. P. 1986. Nursing and health care in the twentieth century: myth, reality and dichotomy. *J. Adv. Nurs.*, 11(2): 127–132.
[24] Bourret, E. M., L. G. Bernick, C. A. Cott. et al. 2002. The meaning of mobility for residents and staff in long-term care facilities. *J. Adv. Nurs.*, 37(4): 338–345.
[25] Chan, A. 2022. A technical report on a novel robotic lower limb rehabilitation device—Is ROBERT® a cost-effective solution for rehabilitation in Hong Kong? *Hong Kong Physiother J. Off Publ. Hong Kong Physiother Assoc. Ltd. Wu Li Chih Liao.*, 42(2): 75–80.
[26] BTS Bioengineering Corp. BTS ANYMOV [Internet]. Available from: https://industry.hospitals-management.com/suppliers/bts/productspec/1490939217-bts-anymov.pdf.

[27] Hocoma, Erigo. Hocoma, A. G. 2024. [Internet]. Available from: http://www.hocoma.com/fileadmin/user/ Dokumente/Erigo/bro_ER_140702_en.pdf.
[28] Wang, X., Y. Feng, J. Zhang. et al. 2021. Design and analysis of a lower limb rehabilitation training component for bedridden stroke patients. *Machines*, 9(10): 224.
[29] Freivogel, S., J. Mehrholz, T. Husak-Sotomayor. et al. 2008. Gait training with the newly developed 'LokoHelp'-system is feasible for non-ambulatory patients after stroke, spinal cord and brain injury. A feasibility study. *Brain Inj.*, 22(7–8): 625–632.
[30] Akdoğan, E. and M. A. Adli. 2011. The design and control of a therapeutic exercise robot for lower limb rehabilitation: Physiotherabot. *Mechatronics*, 21(3): 509–522.
[31] Metrailler, P., V. Blanchard, I. Perrin. et al. 2006. Improvement of rehabilitation possibilities with the MotionMaker TM. *First IEEERAS-EMBS Int. Conf. Biomed Robot Biomechatronics* 2006 BioRob 2006 [Internet]. Pisa, Italy: IEEE [cited 2023 Oct 25]. pp. 359–364. Available from: http://ieeexplore.ieee.org/document/1639113/.
[32] Feng, Y., H. Wang, Y. Du. et al. 2017. Trajectory planning of a novel lower limb rehabilitation robot for stroke patient passive training. *Adv. Mech. Eng.*, 9(12): 168781401773766.
[33] Rachakorakit, M. and W. Charoensuk. 2017. Development of LeHab robot for human lower limb movement rehabilitation. *2017 10th Biomed. Eng. Int. Conf. BMEiCON* [Internet]. Hokkaido: IEEE; [cited 2023 Oct 25]. pp. 1–5. Available from: http://ieeexplore.ieee.org/document/8229148/.
[34] Marchal-Crespo, L. and R. Riener. 2022. Technology of the robotic gait orthosis lokomat. pp. 665–681. *In*: Reinkensmeyer, D. J., L. Marchal-Crespo and V. Dietz. (eds.). *Neurorehabilitation Technol.* [Internet]. Cham: Springer International Publishing; [cited 2023 Dec 13]. Available from: https://link.springer.com/10.1007/978-3-031-08995-4_29.
[35] Riener, R. 2016. Technology of the robotic gait orthosis lokomat. pp. 395–407. *In*: Reinkensmeyer, D. J. and V. Dietz. (eds.). *Neurorehabilitation Technol.* [Internet]. Cham: Springer International Publishing; [cited 2023 Dec 6]. Available from: http://link.springer.com/10.1007/978-3-319-28603-7_19.
[36] Meuleman, J., E. Van Asseldonk, G. Van Oort. et al. 2016. LOPES II—Design and evaluation of an admittance controlled gait training robot with shadow-leg approach. *IEEE Trans. Neural. Syst. Rehabil. Eng.*, 24(3): 352–363.
[37] Veneman, J. F., R. Kruidhof, E. E. G. Hekman. et al. 2007. Design and evaluation of the LOPES exoskeleton robot for interactive gait rehabilitation. *IEEE Trans. Neural. Syst. Rehabil. Eng.*, 15(3): 379–386.
[38] Stegall, P., D. Zanotto and S. K. Agrawal. 2017. Variable damping force tunnel for gait training using ALEX III. *IEEE Robot. Autom. Lett.*, 2(3): 1495–1501.
[39] Zanotto, D., P. Stegall and S. K. Agrawal. 2013. ALEX III: A novel robotic platform with 12 DOFs for human gait training. *2013 IEEE Int. Conf. Robot Autom.* [Internet]. Karlsruhe, Germany: IEEE; [cited 2023 Oct 25]. pp. 3914–3919. Available from: http://ieeexplore.ieee.org/document/6631128/.
[40] Grosu, V., C. Rodriguez-Guerrero, S. Grosu. et al. 2017. Design of smart modular variable stiffness actuators for robotic-assistive devices. *IEEEASME Trans. Mechatron.*, 22(4): 1777–1785.
[41] Junius, K., B. Brackx, V. Grosu. et al. 2014. Mechatronic design of a sit-to-stance exoskeleton. *5th IEEE RASEMBS Int. Conf. Biomed. Robot Biomechatronics* [Internet]. Sao Paulo, Brazil: IEEE; [cited 2023 Dec 6]. pp. 945–950. Available from: http://ieeexplore.ieee.org/document/6913902/.
[42] Hyon, S. -H., J. Morimoto, T. Matsubara. et al. 2011. XoR: Hybrid drive exoskeleton robot that can balance. *2011 IEEERSJ Int. Conf. Intell. Robots Syst.* [Internet]. San Francisco, CA: IEEE; [cited 2023 Oct 25]. p. 3975–3981. Available from: http://ieeexplore.ieee.org/document/6095079/.

[43] Sang-Ho Hyon, T. Hayashi, A. Yagi. et al. 2013. Design of hybrid drive exoskeleton robot XoR2. *2013 IEEERSJ Int. Conf. Intell. Robots Syst.* [Internet]. Tokyo: IEEE; [cited 2023 Oct 25]. pp. 4642–4648. Available from: http://ieeexplore.ieee.org/document/6697024/.

[44] Jansen, O., D. Grasmuecke, R. C. Meindl. et al. 2018. Hybrid assistive limb exoskeleton HAL in the rehabilitation of chronic spinal cord injury: Proof of Concept; the Results in 21 Patients. *World Neurosurg.*, 110: e73–e78.

[45] Tsukahara, A., Y. Hasegawa, K. Eguchi. et al. 2015. Restoration of gait for spinal cord injury patients using HAL with intention estimator for preferable swing speed. *IEEE Trans. Neural Syst. Rehabil. Eng.*, 23(2): 308–318.

[46] Suzuki, S., Y. Hirata and K. Kosuge. 2014. Walking support by wearable system based on the spring-mass model. *2014 IEEEASME Int. Conf. Adv. Intell Mechatron* [Internet]. Besacon: IEEE; [cited 2023 Oct 25]. pp. 285–290. Available from: http://ieeexplore.ieee.org/document/6878093/.

[47] Buesing, C., G. Fisch, M. O'Donnell. et al. 2015. Effects of a wearable exoskeleton stride management assist system (SMA®) on spatiotemporal gait characteristics in individuals after stroke: a randomized controlled trial. *J. NeuroEngineering Rehabil.*, 12(1): 69.

[48] Ha, K. H., S. A. Murray and M. Goldfarb. 2016. An approach for the cooperative control of FES with a powered exoskeleton during level walking for persons with paraplegia. *IEEE Trans. Neural Syst. Rehabil. Eng.*, 24(4): 455–466.

[49] Hasan, S. K. and A. K. Dhingra. 2022. Biomechanical design and control of an eight DOF human lower extremity rehabilitation exoskeleton robot. *Results Control Optim.*, 7: 100107.

[50] Aliman, N., R. Ramli, S. Mohamed Haris. et al. 2022. A robust adaptive-fuzzy-proportional-derivative controller for a rehabilitation lower limb exoskeleton. *Eng. Sci. Technol. Int. J.*, 35: 101097.

[51] Bortole, M., A. Venkatakrishnan, F. Zhu. et al. 2015. The H2 robotic exoskeleton for gait rehabilitation after stroke: early findings from a clinical study. *J. NeuroEngineering Rehabil.*, 12(1): 54.

[52] Menez, C., M. L'Hermette and J. Coquart. 2020. Orthotic insoles improve gait symmetry and reduce immediate pain in subjects with mild leg length discrepancy. *Front. Sports Act Living*, 2: 579152.

[53] Kyoungchul Kong and Doyoung Jeon. 2006. Design and control of an exoskeleton for the elderly and patients. *IEEEASME Trans. Mechatron.*, 11(4): 428–432.

[54] Dinh, V. -V., M. -C. Trinh, T. -D. Bui et al. 2023. Neural network based patient recovery estimation of a PAM-based rehabilitation robot. *Acta Polytech* [Internet]. [cited 2023 Dec 6]; 63(3).

[55] Manna, S. K. and V. N. Dubey. 2018. Comparative study of actuation systems for portable upper limb exoskeletons. *Med. Eng. Phys.*, 60: 1–13.

[56] Kong, K., M. Tomizuka, H. Moon et al. 2008. Mechanical design and impedance compensation of SUBAR (Sogang University’s Biomedical Assist Robot). 2008 *IEEEASME Int. Conf. Adv. Intell. Mechatron* [Internet]. Xian, China: IEEE; [cited 2023 Dec 13]. pp. 377–382. Available from: http://ieeexplore.ieee.org/document/4601690/.

[57] Gunasekara, M., R. Gopura and S. Jayawardena. 2015. 6-REXOS: Upper Limb Exoskeleton Robot with Improved pHRI. *Int. J. Adv. Robot Syst.*, 12(4): 47.

[58] Sankai, Y. 2010. HAL: Hybrid assistive limb based on cybernics. pp. 25–34. *In*: Kaneko, M. and Y. Nakamura. (eds.). *Robot Res.* [Internet]. Berlin, Heidelberg: Springer Berlin Heidelberg; [cited 2023 Oct 25]. Available from: http://link.springer.com/10.1007/978-3-642-14743-2_3.

[59] Sarker, A., D. -R. Emenonye, A. Kelliher. et al. 2022. Capturing upper body kinematics and localization with low-cost sensors for rehabilitation applications. *Sensors*, 22(6): 2300.

[60] Patel, S., H. Park, P. Bonato. et al. 2012. A review of wearable sensors and systems with application in rehabilitation. *J. NeuroEngineering Rehabil.*, 9(1): 21.

[61] Jezernik, S., G. Colombo, T. Keller. et al. 2003. Robotic orthosis lokomat: a rehabilitation and research tool. *Neuromodulation Technol. Neural Interface*, 6(2): 108–115.

[62] Ting, W. K. -C., F. A.-R. Fadul, S. Fecteau. et al. 2021. Neurostimulation for stroke rehabilitation. *Front Neurosci.*, 15: 649459.

[63] Wang, G., Y. Liu, Y. Shen. et al. 2022. sEMG-based multi-joints motion estimation of lower limb utilizing deep convolutional neural network. *2022 IEEE Int. Conf. Real-Time Comput Robot RCAR* [Internet]. Guiyang, China: IEEE; [cited 2023 Dec 7]. pp. 13–18. Available from: https://ieeexplore.ieee.org/document/9872282/.

[64] Cao, J., S. Q. Xie, R. Das. et al. 2014. Control strategies for effective robot assisted gait rehabilitation: The state of art and future prospects. *Med. Eng. Phys.*, 36(12): 1555–1566.

[65] Su, D., Z. Hu, J. Wu. et al. 2023. Review of adaptive control for stroke lower limb exoskeleton rehabilitation robot based on motion intention recognition. *Front. Neurorobotics*, 17: 1186175.

[66] Cesarini, D., P. Buonocunto, M. Marinoni. et al. 2014. A telerehabilitation framework for lower-limb functional recovery. *Proc. 9th Int. Conf. Body Area Netw.* [Internet]. London, Great Britain: ICST; [cited 2023 Nov 1]. Available from: http://eudl.eu/doi/10.4108/icst.bodynets.2014.256995.

[67] Yan, Y., M. Tang, W. Wang. et al. 2024. Trajectory tracking control of wearable upper limb rehabilitation robot based on Laguerre model predictive control. *Robot Auton. Syst.*, 179: 104745.

[68] Andrade, R. M., S. Sapienza, E. E. Fabara. et al. 2021. Trajectory tracking impedance controller in 6-DoF lower-limb exoskeleton for over-ground walking training: preliminary results. *2021 Int. Symp. Med. Robot ISMR* [Internet]. Atlanta, GA, USA: IEEE; [cited 2023 Dec 7]. p. 1–6. Available from: https://ieeexplore.ieee.org/document/9661558/.

[69] Li, J., W. Xia, C. Zhan. et al. 2021. Effectiveness of a telerehabilitation program for COVID-19 survivors (TERECO) on exercise capacity, pulmonary function, lower limb muscle strength, and quality of life: A randomized controlled trial [Internet]. *Respiratory Medicine*; [cited 2023 Nov 1]. Available from: http://medrxiv.org/lookup/doi/10.1101/2021.03.08.21253007.

[70] Zhang, F., Z. -G. Hou, L. Cheng et al. 2016. iLeg—A lower limb rehabilitation robot: A proof of concept. *IEEE Trans. Hum.-Mach. Syst.*, 46(5): 761–768.

[71] Xu, Q., C. Li, Y. Pan. et al. 2020. Impact of smart force feedback rehabilitation robot training on upper limb motor function in the subacute stage of stroke. *NeuroRehabilitation*, 47(2): 209–215.

[72] Divekar, N. V., J. Lin, C. Nesler. et al. 2020. A potential energy shaping controller with ground reaction force feedback for a multi-activity knee-ankle exoskeleton. *2020 8th IEEE RASEMBS Int. Conf. Biomed. Robot Biomechatronics BioRob* [Internet]. New York City, NY, USA: IEEE; [cited 2023 Dec 7]. pp. 997–1003. Available from: https://ieeexplore.ieee.org/document/9224341/.

[73] Peters, S., M. Botero, A. Evers. et al. 2021. Development and feasibility of a modified Fugl-Meyer lower extremity assessment for telerehabilitation: a pilot study. *Pilot Feasibility Stud.*, 7(1): 121.

[74] Yang, C., Y. Xie, S. Liu. et al. 2018. Force modeling, identification, and feedback control of robot-assisted needle insertion: a survey of the literature. *Sensors*, 18(2): 561.

[75] AL-Quraishi, M., I. Elamvazuthi, S. Daud. et al. 2018. EEG-based control for upper and lower limb exoskeletons and prostheses: A systematic review. *Sensors*, 18(10): 3342.

[76] Song, W., P. Zhao, X. Li. et al. 2023. Data-driven design of a six-bar lower-limb rehabilitation mechanism based on gait trajectory prediction. *IEEE Trans. Neural Syst. Rehabil. Eng.*, 31: 109–118.

[77] Peng, Z., R. Luo, R. Huang. et al. 2020. Data-driven optimal assistance control of a lower limb exoskeleton for hemiplegic patients. *Front. Neurorobotics*, 14: 37.
[78] Kaplanoglu, E. and G. Akgun. 2022. Data-driven predictive control of exoskeleton for hand rehabilitation with subspace identification. *Sensors*, 22(19): 7645.
[79] Sharifi, M., J. K. Mehr, V. K. Mushahwar. et al. 2022. Autonomous locomotion trajectory shaping and nonlinear control for lower limb exoskeletons. *IEEEASME Trans. Mechatron.*, 27(2): 645–655.
[80] Jiang, Z. -P., T. Bian and W. Gao. 2020. Learning-based control: A tutorial and some recent results. *Found Trends® Syst. Control*, 8(3): 176–284.
[81] Ai, Q., Z. Liu, W. Meng. et al. 2023. Machine learning in robot-assisted upper limb rehabilitation: a focused review. *IEEE Trans Cogn. Dev. Syst.*, 15(4): 2053–2063.
[82] Lydakis, A., Y. Meng, C. Munroe. et al. 2017. A learning-based agent for home neurorehabilitation. *2017 Int. Conf. Rehabil Robot ICORR* [Internet]. London: IEEE; [cited 2025 Jan 6]. pp. 1233–1238. Available from: https://ieeexplore.ieee.org/document/8009418/.
[83] Abu-Dakka, F. J., A. Valera, J. A. Escalera. et al. 2020. Passive exercise adaptation for ankle rehabilitation based on learning control framework. *Sensors*, 20(21): 6215.
[84] Jamwal, P. K., S. Hussain and S. Q. Xie. 2015. Review on design and control aspects of ankle rehabilitation robots. *Disabil. Rehabil. Assist. Technol.*, 10(2): 93–101.
[85] Gil-Agudo, A., A. J. Del Ama-Espinosa, V. Lozano-Berrio. et al. 2020. Terapia robótica con el exoesqueleto H2 en la rehabilitación de la marcha en pacientes con lesión medular incompleta. Una experiencia clínica. *Rehabilitación*, 54(2): 87–95.
[86] Teke Budaklı, M., C. Yılmaz and F. Bagcı. 2023. The design and control of a new lower limb rehabilitation robot for active and active-assisted exercises. [cited 2025 Jan 6]; doi: 10.5281/ZENODO.10445926.
[87] Chang, H., Y. Song and X. Cen. 2022. Effectiveness of augmented reality for lower limb rehabilitation: A systematic review. Chen, W. -M., editor. *Appl. Bionics. Biomech.*, 2022: 1–10.
[88] Patil, V., J. Narayan, K. Sandhu. et al. 2022. Integration of virtual reality and augmented reality in physical rehabilitation: a state-of-the-art review. *In*: Subburaj, K., K. Sandhu and S. Ćuković. (eds.). *Revolut. Prod. Des. Healthc.* [Internet]. Singapore: Springer Singapore; [cited 2023 Dec 18]. pp. 177–205. Available from: https://link.springer.com/10.1007/978-981-16-9455-4_10.
[89] Mubin, O., F. Alnajjar, N. Jishtu. et al. 2019. Exoskeletons with virtual reality, augmented reality, and gamification for stroke patients' rehabilitation: systematic review. *JMIR Rehabil. Assist. Technol.*, 6(2): e12010.
[90] Ferreira Dos Santos, L., O. Christ, K. Mate. et al. 2016. Movement visualisation in virtual reality rehabilitation of the lower limb: A systematic review. *Biomed. Eng. OnLine.*, 15(S3): 144.
[91] Luque-Moreno, C., A. Ferragut-Garcías, C. Rodríguez-Blanco. et al. 2015. A decade of progress using virtual reality for poststroke lower extremity rehabilitation: Systematic review of the intervention methods. *BioMed. Res. Int.*, 2015: 1–7.
[92] Toledo-Peral, C. L., G. Vega-Martínez, J. A. Mercado-Gutiérrez. et al. 2022. Virtual/augmented reality for rehabilitation applications using electromyography as control/biofeedback: systematic literature review. *Electronics*, 11(14): 2271.
[93] Marchal-Crespo, L., P. Tsangaridis, D. Obwegeser. et al. 2019. Haptic error modulation outperforms visual error amplification when learning a modified gait pattern. *Front. Neurosci.*, 13: 61.
[94] Suso-Martí, L., R. La Touche, A. Herranz-Gómez. et al. 2021. Effectiveness of telerehabilitation in physical therapist practice: An umbrella and mapping review with meta–meta-analysis. *Phys. Ther.*, 101(5): pzab075.

[95] Seron, P., M. -J. Oliveros, R. Gutierrez-Arias. et al. 2021. Effectiveness of telerehabilitation in physical therapy: A rapid overview. *Phys. Ther.*, 101(6): pzab053.

[96] Laver, K. E., Z. Adey-Wakeling, M. Crotty. et al. 2020. Telerehabilitation services for stroke. Cochrane Stroke Group, editor. *Cochrane Database Syst. Rev.* [Internet]. [cited 2023 Nov 1]; 2020(1).

[97] Celesti, A., A. Lay-Ekuakille, J. Wan. et al. 2020. Information management in IoT cloud-based tele-rehabilitation as a service for smart cities: Comparison of NoSQL approaches. *Measurement*, 151: 107218.

Index

I

L

M

N

O

P

Q

R

S

T

V

W

Z

For Product Safety Concerns and Information please contact our EU representative GPSR@taylorandfrancis.com Taylor & Francis Verlag GmbH, Kaufingerstraße 24, 80331 München, Germany